PRISON VIOLENCE IN AMERICA

SECOND EDITION

Michael C. Braswell, *East Tennessee State University*
Reid H. Montgomery, Jr., *University of South Carolina*
Lucien X. Lombardo, *Old Dominion University*

anderson publishing co.
p.o. box 1576
cincinnati, oh 45201-1576
513-421-4142

Gail Eccleston *Project Editor*   *Managing Editor* Kelly Humble

Cover design by Ross Heck

Dedication

This edition is dedicated to Bo and Sita Lozoff of the Human Kindness Foundation, to the memory of Professor Reid H. Montgomery, Sr., and to all those who have died or been injured as a result of violence in prison.

A portion of royalties from sales of this book will be donated to the Foundation.

Introduction

Recently the problem of violence in American communities has been receiving increased attention. Guns in schools, rape, and child abuse are prominent examples of the varieties of violence. Violence associated with the drug trade has also been the subject of much media and academic attention. More recently, the Rodney King incident and its aftermath have revisited concerns with police brutality and urban collective violence similar to those discussed during the 1960s and 1970s. Powerlessness, racism, injustice, oppression, abuse of authority, lack of accountability, and lack of communication between the authorities and the community are themes that are once again emerging in the 1990s.

If these themes are finding their expression in increased levels of violent conflict in the free community, can it be long before we once again find them expressed in the prison environment, the most purposefully repressive of American social institutions? If we are to be spared the sight of these overcrowded and understaffed monuments to American society's "best intentions" and "worst practices" exploding into new Attica and New Mexico State Prison riots, we must begin to face more directly and explore creatively the nature and meaning of violence in prison.

Although collective violence is perhaps the most visible and newsworthy form of prison violence, we should not divert our attention from the everyday violence that faces both prisoners and correctional personnel in the closed world of prisons. In an atmosphere where power is the currency of control, where exploitation and self-interest are the goals of control, violence takes many forms. Prisoners victimize each other economically, sexually, and psychologically. In addition, prisoners victimize staff and staff victimize prisoners with threats and the use of violence.

In order to understand prison violence, we believe it is necessary to understand the complex interrelationships that link individual personalities, social attitudes and beliefs, organizational conditions, structural patterns and cultures, legal doctrines, political processes, and broader perceptions about public opinion. Within these various contexts, beliefs about the occupational culture of staff and the inmate culture blend with historical images of prisoners, guards, and wardens. Mixed with moral and personal evaluations based on race, ethnicity, sexual orientation, low economic status, drug addiction, and crime, those who engage in violence and those who permit violent behavior to occur (or fail to take steps to prevent it), have available to them many means and supports on which to hinge "other and self-directed dehumanization processes" that support and promote violence.

Although the prison world is generally closed to the public, the lives and behaviors of the people who inhabit and work in these institutions are clearly affected by forces external to the institutions. For the past 200 years, prisons have been part of the political, administrative, and cultural landscape of the broader society. Prisons, prisoners, and prison staff are the answers to and the source of many broader social problems. They influence, are a often part of, political campaigns and intra-governmental political maneuvering. When prison problems become public, they draw the attention of "blue-ribbon" commissions that explore conditions and make recommendations for change. Too often, however, such activities only add to the sense of powerlessness and exploitation experienced by those who live and work in prisons. As Murton observes, they fail to address the most basic principles upon which the edifice of the prison is built: power and social stereotyping.

Prison violence also takes place in a legal and policy context. Constitutional principles of "due process of law" and "nor cruel and unusual punishments inflicted" theoretically place limits on the legitimacy of violence inflicted by authorities. However, the implementation of these principles is often limited by the good will and managerial acumen of correctional administrators and personnel as well as the ability of inmates to bring grievances to the attention of authorities both inside and outside the prison. In a contemporary judicial climate that increasingly relies on the "expertise" of prison officials and limits inmates access to the courts, isolation of prisons produced by a "hands-off" doctrine is likely to produce similar abuses of authority that led to the judicial activism of the 1960s and 1970s.

Although these various contexts may promote or reduce the amount and type of violence existing in our prisons, we must not lose sight of the human and existential character of prison violence. We know that people who experience violence, both as victims and as perpetrators, must cope with these experiences and are connected to each other in a myriad of ways. Some do so successfully, others do not. Some correctional personnel act to prevent violence, others abuse authority or fail to act when others (inmates and staff) inflict harm within the prison walls. People are hurt by violence in prison. While the visible expression of such hurt is not always forthcoming in the "macho" world of male institutions, long-term studies of reactions to violence point out that denial and repression are common coping mechanisms that are linked to destructive behavioral and psychological changes which usually surface long after the exposure to violence.

The readings collected for this volume provide the student and the scholar concerned with prison violence both historical and contemporary accounts and analyses of a variety of forms of personal harm inflicted within prison walls. We have tried to collect readings that reflect the meaning of violence within the prison world from a variety of perspectives. Individual and collective violence are explored in depth. Finally, we present a group of selections that offer creative suggestions for reducing the amount of individual and collective violence that people suffer in American prisons.

Michael C. Braswell
Reid H. Montgomery, Jr.
Lucien X. Lombardo

Table of Contents

Section I

Reflections on the Experience of Prison Violence

For many persons entering prison, the inscription on the gate of Danté's inferno—"Abandon all hope, ye who enter here" is becoming increasingly appropriate. Overcrowding, declining budgets, and decreasing or nonexistent program innovation and creativity are contributing to a growing sense of hopelessness and despair in prisons.

Two of the readings in this section attempt to reexamine prison violence from the experiential perspective of inmates. Another examines and challenges some long-held assumptions regarding the destructive effects of the prison experience. A final paper addresses the loss of any meaningful purpose for prisons and how such a condition influences the continued deterioration of prison life. Alternative metaphors are examined in an effort to restore social meaning in prisons and to create a new, more hopeful vision for the future.

1   Letter to Fay†††

George Jackson

My father is in his forties today; 35 years ago he was living through his most formative years. He was a child of the Great Depression. I want you to notice for later reference that I emphasize and differentiate *Great* Depression. There are many more international, national, and regional depressions during the period in history relevant to this comment.

There are millions of blacks of my father's generation now living. They are all products of a totally depressed environment. All of the males have lived all of their lives in a terrible quandary; none were ever able to grasp that a morbid economic deprivation, an outrageous and enormous abrasion, formed the basis of their character.

My father developed his character, convention, convictions, traits, and lifestyle, out of a situation that began with his mother running out. She left him and his oldest brothers on the corner of one of the canyons in East St. Louis. They raised themselves, in the streets, then on a farm somewhere in Louisiana, then in Civilian Conservation Corps (CCC) camps. This brother, my father, had no formal education at all. He taught himself the essentials later on. Alone, in the most hostile jungle on

†From SOLEDAD BROTHER by George Jackson. Copyright © 1970 by World Entertainers. Used by permission of Bantam Books, a division of Bantam Doubleday Dell Publishing Group, Inc.

††During the 1960s and early 1970s prisoners produced a large volume of high quality commentary on race, prisons, and society. George Jackson's letters published as *Soledad Brother* are some of the most eloquent of these prisoner writings. In the selection reprinted here, Jackson presents an analysis of race, economics, and generational change that provides a context for understanding the race component of prison violence. With African-Americans recently becoming the numerically dominant group in American prisons for the first time, and with the 1992 riots in Los Angeles, Jackson's focus on race and his analysis are as relevant today as they were when they were written over 20 years ago. George Jackson was killed at San Quentin on August 21, 1971. Fay Stender was Jackson's lawyer.

earth, ruled over by the king of beasts in the first throes of a bloody and protracted death. Alone, in the most savage moment of history, without arms, and burdened by a black face that he has been hiding ever since.

I love this brother, my father, and when I use the word "love" I am not making an attempt at rhetoric. I am attempting to express a refulgent, unrestrained emanation from the deepest, most durable region of my soul, an unshakable thing that I have never questioned. But no one can come through his ordeal without suffering the penalty of psychosis. It was the price of survival. I would venture that there are no healthy brothers of this generation, *none at all*.

The brother has reached the prime of his life without ever showing in my presence or anywhere, to my knowledge, an overt manifestation of *real* sensitivity, affection, or sentiment. He has lived his entire life in a state of shock. Nothing can touch him now, his calm is complete, his immunity to pain is total. When I can fix his eyes, which is not often because when they are not closed they are shaded, I see staring back at me the expressionless mask of the zombie.

But he must have loved us, of this I am certain. Part of the credo of the neoslave, the latter-day slave, who is free to move from place to place if he can come by the means, is to shuffle away from any situation that becomes too difficult. He stayed with us, worked 16 hours per day, after which he would eat, bathe, and sleep—period. He never owned more than two pairs of shoes in his life and during the time I was living with him, never owned more than one suit, never took a drink, never went to a nightclub, expressed no feelings about such things, and never once reminded any one of us, or so it seemed, never expected any notice of the fact that he was giving to us all of the life force and activity that the monster-machine had left to him. The part that the machine seized, that death of the spirit visited upon him by a world that he never influenced, was mourned by us, and most certainly by me, but none ever made a real effort to give him solace. How do you console a man who is unapproachable?

He came to visit me when I was in San Quentin. He was in his forties then too, an age in men when they have grown full. I had decided to reach for my father, to force him with my revolutionary dialectic to question some of the mental barricades he had thrown up to protect his body from what to him was an undefinable and omnipresent enemy. An enemy that would starve his body, expose it to the elements, chain his body, jail it, club it, rip it, hang it, electrify it, and poison-gas it. I would have him understand that although he had saved his body he had done so at a terrible cost to his mind. I felt that if I could superimpose the explosive doctrine of self-determination through people's government and revolutionary culture upon what remained of his mind, draw him out into the real world, isolate and identify his real enemies, if I could hurl him through Fanon's revolutionary catharsis [See Frantz Fanon's (1963) *The Wretched of the Earth*, New York, NY: Grove Press, for an analysis of the genesis of revolutionary violence in the context of colonialism in Africa.], I would be serving him, the people, the historical obligation.

San Quentin was in the riot season. It was early January 1967. The pigs had for the last three months been on a search-and-destroy foray into our cells. All times of the day or night our cells were being invaded by the goon squad: you wake up, take your licks, get skin-searched, and wait on the tier naked while they mangle your few personal effects. This treatment, fear therapy, was not accorded at all, however. Some Chicanos behind dope, some whites behind extortionate activities, were exempted. Mostly it came down on us. Rehabilitational terror. Each new pig must go through a period of in-service training during which he learns the Gestapo arts, the full range of anti-body tactics that he will be expected to use on the job. Part of this in-service training is a crash course in close-order combat where the pigs are taught how to use club and sap, and how to form and use the simpler karate hands, where to hit a man with these hands for the best (or worst) effect.

The new pigs usually have to serve a period on the goon squad before they fall into their regular role on the animal farm. They are always anxious to try their new skills—"to see if it really works"—we were always forced to do something to slow them down, to demonstrate that violence was a two-edged sword. This must be done at least once every year, or we would all be as punchy and fractured as a Thai Boxer before our time was up. The brothers wanted to protest. The usual protest was a strike, a work stoppage, closing the sweatshops where industrial products are worked up for two cents an hour. (Some people get four cents after they have been on the job for six months.) The outside interests who made the profits didn't dig strikes. That meant the captain didn't like them either since it meant pressure on him from these free-enterprising political connections.

January in San Quentin is the worst way to be. It is cold when you don't have proper clothing, it is wet, dreary. The drab green, barred, buttressed walls that close in the upper yard are 60 to 70 feet high. They make you feel that your condition may be permanent.

On the occasion I wish to relate, my father had driven alone all night from Los Angeles; he had not slept more than a couple of hours in the past two days.

We shook hands and the dialectic began. He listened while I scorned the diabolical dog—capitalism. Didn't it raise pigs and murder Vietnamese? Didn't it glut some and starve most of us? Didn't it build housing projects that resemble prisons and luxury hotels and apartments that resemble the Hanging Gardens on the same street? Didn't it build a hospital and then a bomb? Didn't it erect a school and then open a whorehouse? Build an airplane to sell a tranquilizer tablet? For every church didn't it construct a prison? For each new medical discovery didn't it produce as a by-product 10 new biological warfare agents? Didn't it aggrandize men like Hunt and Hughes and dwarf him?

He said, "Yes, but what can we do? There's [sic] too many of the bastards." His eyes shaded over and his mind went into a total regression, a relapse back through time, space, pain, neglect, a thousand dreams deferred, broken promises, forgotten ambitions, back through the hundreds of renewed hopes shattered to a time when he was young roaming the Louisiana countryside for something to eat. He talked for 10 minutes of things that were not in the present, people that I didn't know. "We'll have to take something back to Aunt Bell." He talked of places that we had never seen together. He called me by his brother's name twice. I was so shocked I could only sit and blink. This was the guy who took nothing seriously, the level-headed, practical Negro, the workaday, never-complain, cool, smooth, colored gentleman. They have driven him to the abyss of madness; just behind the white veneer waits the awesome, vindictive black madness. There are a lot of blacks living in his generation, the one of the Great Depression, when it was no longer possible to maintain the black self by serving. Even that had dried up. Blacks were beaten and killed for jobs like porter, bellboy, stoker, pearl diver, and bootblack. My clenched fist goes up for them: I forgive them, I understand, and if they will stop their collaboration with the fascist enemy, stop it now, and support our revolution with just a nod, we will forget and forgive them for casting us naked into a grim and deleterious world.

The black colonies of Amerika have been locked in depression since the close of the Civil War. We have lived under regional depression since the end of chattel slavery. The beginning of the new slavery was marked by massive unemployment and underemployment. That remains with us still. The Civil War destroyed the *landed* aristocracy. The dictatorship of the agrarian class was displaced by the dictatorship of the manufacturing capitalist class. The neoslaver destroyed the uneconomic plantation, and built upon its ruins a factory and 1,000 subsidiaries to serve the factory setup. Since we had no skills, outside of the farming techniques that had proved uneconomic, the subsidiary service trades and menial occupations fell to us. It is still so today. We are a subsidiary subculture, a depressed area within the parent monstrosity. The other four stages of the capitalist business cycle are: recovery, expansion, inflation, and recession. Have we ever gone through a recovery or expansion stage? We are affected adversely by inflationary trends within the larger economy. Who suffers most when the prices of basic, necessary commodities go up? When the parent economy dips into inflation and recession we dip into subdepression. When it goes into depression, we go into total desperation. The difference between what my father's generation went through during the *Great* Depression and what we are going through now is simply a matter of degree. We can sometimes find a service to perform across the tracks. They couldn't. We can go home to Mama for a meal when things get really tight. They couldn't. There's welfare and housework for Mama now. Then there was no such thing as welfare.

Depression is an economic condition. It is a part of the capitalist business cycle, a necessary concomitant of capitalism. Its colonies—secondary markets— will always be depressed areas, because the steadily decreasing labor force, decreasing and growing more skilled under the advances of automation, casts the unskilled colonial subject into economic roles that preclude economic mobility. Learning the new skills, even if we were allowed, would not help. It would not help the masses even if they learned them. It would not help because there is a fixed ceiling on the labor force. This ceiling gets lower with every advance in the arts of production. Learning the newer skills would merely put us into a competition with established labor that we could not win. One that we don't want. There are absolutely no vacuums for us to fill in the business world. We don't want to capitalize on people anyway. Capitalism is the enemy. It must be destroyed. There is no other recourse. The system is not workable in view of the modern, industrial, city-based society. Men are born disenfranchised. The contract between ruler and ruled perpetuates this disenfranchisement.

Men in positions of trust owe an equitable distribution of wealth and privilege to the men who have trusted them. Each individual born in these Amerikan cities should be born with those things that are necessary to survival. Meaningful social roles, education, medical care, food, shelter, and understanding should be guaranteed at birth. They have been part of all civilized human societies—until this one. Why else do men allow other men to govern? To what purpose is a Department of Health, Education, and Welfare, or of Housing and Urban Development, etc.? Why do we give these men power over us? Why do we give them taxes? For nothing? So they can say that the world owes our children nothing? This world owes each of us a living the very day we are born. If not we can make no claims to civilization and we can stop recognizing the power of any administrator. Evolution of the huge modern city-based society has made our dependence upon government complete. Individually, we cannot feed ourselves and our children. We cannot, by ourselves, train and educate them at home. We cannot organize our own work inside the city structure by ourselves. Consequently, we must allow men to specialize in coordinating these activities. We pay them, honor them, and surrender control of certain aspects of our lives to them so that they will in return take each new, helpless entry into the social group and work on him until he is no longer helpless, until he can start to support himself and make his contribution to the continuity of the society.

If a man is born into Amerikan society with nothing coming, if the capitalist creed that runs "The world doesn't owe you a living" is true, then the thing that my father's mother did is not outrageous at all. If it is true that government shouldn't organize then the fact that my father had no place to seek help until he could help himself has little consequence. But it would also mean that we are all in the grip of some monstrous contradiction. And that we have no more claim to civilization than a pack of baboons.

What is it then that *really* destroyed my father's comfort, that doomed his entire generation to a life without content? What is it that has been working against my generation from the day we were born through every day to this one?

Capitalism and capitalist man, wrecker of worlds, scourge of the people. It cannot address itself to our needs, it cannot and will not change itself to adapt to natural changes within the social structure.

To the black male the losses were most tragic of all. It will do us no good to linger over the fatalities—they are numberless and beyond our reach. But we who have survived must eventually look at ourselves and wonder why. The competition at the bottom of the social spectrum is for symbols, honors, and objects; black against itself, black against lower-class whites and browns, virulent, cutthroat, back-stabbing competition, the Amerikan way of life. But the fascists cooperate. The four estates of power form a morbid, lone quadrangle. This competition has destroyed trust. Among the black males a premium has been placed on distrust. Every other black male is viewed as the competition; the wise and practical black is the one who cares nothing for any living ass, the cynic who has gotten over any principles he may have picked up by mistake. We can't express love on the supposition that the recipient will automatically use it against us as a weapon. We are going to have to start all over again. This next time around we will let it all hang out, we will stop betraying ourselves, and we will add some trust and love.

The great Amerikan bison or buffalo—he is a herd animal, or social animal if you prefer, just like us in that. We are social animals, we need others of our general kind about us to feel secure. Few men would enjoy total isolation. To be alone constantly is torture to normal men. The buffalo, cattle, caribou, and some others are like folks in that they need company most of the time. They need to butt shoulders and butt butts. They like to rub noses. We shake hands, slap backs, and rub lips. Of all the world's people we blacks love the company of others most, we are the most socialistic. Social animals eat, sleep, and travel in company, they need this company to feel secure. This fact means that socialistic animals also need leaders. It follows logically that if the buffalo is going to eat, sleep, and travel in groups some coordinating factor is needed or some will be sleeping when others are traveling. Without the leader-follower complex, in a crisis the company would roar off in 100 different directions. But the buffalo did evolve the leader-follower complex as did the other social animals; if the leader of a herd of caribou loses his footing and slips to his death from some high place, it is very likely that the whole herd will die behind the leader-follower complex. The hunter understood this. Predatory man learned of the natural occurrence of leadership in all of the social animals; that each group will by nature produce a leader, and to these natural leaders falls the responsibility for coordination of the group's activity, organizing them for survival. The buffalo hunter knew that if he could isolate and identify the leader of the herd and kill him first, the rest of the herd would be helpless, at his mercy, to be killed off as he saw fit.

We blacks have the dependence problem the buffalo had; we have the same weaknesses also, and predatory man understands this weakness well.

Huey Newton, Ahmed Evans, Bobby Seale, and hundreds of others will be murdered according to the fascist scheme.

A sort of schematic natural selection in reverse: Medgar Evers, Malcolm X, Bobby Hutton, Brother Booker, W.L. Noland, M.L. King, Featherstone, Mark Clark, and Fred Hampton—just a few who have already gone the way of the buffalo.

The effect these moves from the right have had on us is a classic textbook exercise in fascist political economy. At the instant a black head rises out of our crisis existence, it is lopped off and hung from the highest courthouse or newspaper firm. Our predetermined response is a schizophrenic indifference, withdrawal, and an appreciation of things that do not exist. "Oh happy days. Oh happy days. Oh happy days." Self-hypnotically induced hallucinations.

The potential black leadership looks at the pitiable condition of the black herd; the corruption, the pre-occupation with irrelevance, the apparent ineptitude concerning matters of survival. He knows that were he to give the average brother an M-16 this brother would not have anything but a club for a week. He weighs this thing that he sees in the herd against the possible risks he will be taking at the hands of the fascist monster and he naturally decides to go for himself, feeling that he can't help us because we are beyond help, that he may as well get something out of existence. These are the "successful Negroes," the opposite of the "failures." You find them on the ball courts and fields, the stage, pretending and playing children's games. And looking for all the world just as pitiable as the so-called failures.

2

Violence from Without and Within: Safety†

Hans Toch

What people need around them often depends on what goes on within themselves. We prize conditions that help us to control our feelings, to govern our thoughts, and to achieve our aims. Requisites for our external environment relate to pressures in our internal environment.

The search for safety is, in some respects, the extreme version of the pursuit of privacy. In both cases, the person's equilibrium hinges on finding sanctuary from others. With the high-privacy person the issue is over-stimulation, and the stimulus content is crowding. The issue with safety is violence.

The contents of the safety concern are those of danger and fear. The aim of high-safety persons is to escape conflict. Their external threat is violence from others, and their internal press is violence from within.

The threat to safety is external danger and the impact it makes on the person who experiences it. The danger and its impact are both sources of discomfort. The combined source is sometimes referred to as "tension" of the environment:

> **GH N 5***: It's the general atmosphere in here. It's like an explosive atmosphere, you know what I mean? It seems like everybody is at everybody else's throat, and it's not easy to live with. You walk up and down the hall, and everybody's shooting daggers at everybody. It's hard to hold a civil conversation with anybody....

*Codes refer to the prison where the inmate was incarcerated at the time of the interview.

11

It's more visible here, it's more visible here than in another institution that I've been in.... Tense at all times. And you don't know how to make your next move. If you should make it.

Att R P: Sure, there's always tension. You can walk down the corridor and see static electricity in the hall from the tension. It's only a figure of speech, but you know what I mean.

* * *

Att R 15: There is also a lot of tension there, not only between the officers and the inmates, but also among the inmates too. There is a lot of static jumping off down there. And a lot of the things that they did that I saw there got me emotionally involved, things that are terrible.

Tension must be controlled or discharged; if it is not monitored it accumulates and explodes. High-safety persons tend to see environments as not having enough checks on explosiveness and violence. Inmates in widely different prisons thus often make the point that their respective institutions are excessively "loose" or "lax":

Au N B: You take a young kid coming in a penitentiary, as loose as Auburn is here, he's pretty certain to be taken off pretty fast. Because these kind of people, they'll take you off in a minute.... There are animals running around this place. This is not one of these seminaries where you got a highly educated bunch of people. You got a bunch of animals in here. And it's too lax.

* * *

GH N 14: This was a cream puff. Everybody wanted to come in here.... Things just got too lax, too loose. You couldn't—like, even now, I've been down five and one-half years, and I'm walking down the corridor. If I hear running, I have a tendency to check it out. Because the only time a man is running in the hallways, when I say a man I don't mean these jitterbugging kids that are fucking around playing tag or something like that. I'm talking about when a man is running he's either chasing somebody or somebody's chasing him. There's got to be something to it.

* * *

Cox S 1: They have a lot more liberty and they can go around carrying shivs and if someone don't like you that's all there is to it.

Where lack of control is not a pervasive feature, it is seen as a feature of particular people within the environment. In this view, there are groups of people whose self-control is manifestly negligible or weak. Such people are feared because they are apt to explode promiscuously. They may attack or victimize upon slight and unpredictable provocation. They may be mentally ill or emotionally unbalanced:

Att R 37: I'll tell you the truth, this is the only institution that I've seen in my life, how people that they are sick mentally, walking around with other people that are in the right state of mind. They have these people over here that they's sick, I mean they're supposed to be in the hospital, not in an institution like this.... They've got them walking around here. You can see, like, let's say lifting weights, right? You got to be watching your back. You don't know when this man might break out and you got three hundred or some pounds on top of you, and he might kick your head off or throw something. You got to be looking for these people, looking out for these people.

* * *

Att R 38: You can understand, they get in here, and they get locked up and they get depressed, they get depressed. They get violent.... I say, everybody in here is sick to a certain extent. Everybody in this institution is sick. Even I'm sick, I know I'm sick.... I know that I was like this, so when I see a guy like this here, I just say, well, I was like that too. You try to stay away from them, but you can't. There's so many here like them.

* * *

GH R H: I had to get off the tier because a guy that sets fire to a book for nothing, there must be something wrong, and I can't figure out what's in his mind, so I had to get off.... I said, "Captain, this was where I was before, and I had trouble here, you know, and I wanted to go to another jail, man, because this other guy, he must think it's a joke to him to burn things." Guy comes down and sets everything on fire, and everybody starts laughing, and stuff like that. So I told him, "I got to get off here, man." ... I told another shift that I didn't like this tier either, because I don't like it...it was a homicide tier, you know what I mean?

Emotional disequilibrium or loss of control in others may sometimes be ascribed to stress. In this model, the environment acts on dangerous people, and it subjects them to pressure that makes them dangerous:

> **GH R P**: Well, the lifers make it difficult, because you can never tell when they are going to be tired of doing their time, and they don't go nowhere, because this institution keeps them here.... They either escape as you see they have done before, or they turn against another inmate.

* * *

> **GH R P**: See, but something may jump off, and your wife may die, and you may not receive the letter, and you will turn on me, and I wouldn't understand that. You would be grouchy one day, and I feel good, and why should you be grouchy? Or we are both in grouchy moods, then you may have static.

A double control issue is posed where the environment contains controllers who may (as the fearful person sees it) run out of control themselves. A prison or hospital inmate can begin to see his keepers as potential sources of violence. This view is harrowing, because it (1) removes the most prominent source of institutional stability and control, (2) makes for an environment that has a person totally at its mercy, and (3) places danger at the doors of men who are potentially effective threats:

> **GH N 7**: You always have the impression that any time of the night they might hit your cell for some reason, and something might happen to you. You never know. That makes you very uncomfortable also. That existed in Comstock and it existed in Clinton. You never know when they're going to hit your door and for what.

* * *

> **GH N 21**: I left there in 'sixty-seven. They never had to worry about me coming back to a mental institution. Because I had never knew that stuff like that could ever exist. I used to hear about it, and I used to say, "Well, these guys have got to be lying for what they're saying," but when I seen it there, forget about it. It's the only place I've seen where a person gets sick and they try to kill you. I couldn't believe it. I saw things, like I tell you, they don't have to worry about me, because every day when I was in the bughouse, I went to work just to get off the hall. They had no prob-

lems out of me.... The officers are mean. I was doing pushups one day, and the officer says, "What, are you getting ready for me?" I couldn't do no more pushups.... I was scared to death over there. And, like I say, I've never seen nothing like it before in my life. I seen guys, one old man about sixty-five years old, I seen four young hacks put this guy in a strait jacket and beat the living hell out of this guy, and then throw him down the stairs. And I tell you, when I saw that, every time they came up to me it was, "Yes, sir" and "No, sir" and "Do you want to go off the hall to work?" Yeah, man, every day.

* * *

Att R P: There was a guy in a cell with blood all over the place. They took him out of his cell and put him in the hospital, and when he got out of the hospital they put him in the box. And they had the audacity to say that he had done it to himself. There aren't too many inmates that'll take a razor blade to their face.

Total institutions pose another threat in the control that they can exercise—and can fail to exercise—over life-preserving or life-sustaining functions. From a fear-ridden perspective, malevolent neglect by staff or peers can place an inmate's physical existence at risk:

Att R 38: The doctors they got here, right? They tell me that in the last six months or something, ten guys have died.... If a guy's dying and a doctor could save him, he won't get saved.

* * *

Cox S 8: And that mess hall, I was back there one day, and these guys back there, they're the type of guys, if you don't know what they're doing back there, you could wind up eating something that you're not supposed to eat. I seen guys back there, they be cleaning the food, they're only halfway cleaning that food. They just throw it in, cook it up some old way, drop it right on in there, and take it and give it out to somebody.

* * *

GH R P: Us inmates are worried that they are going to lock this place up, because the food is getting so short in this prison, and they are worried about they might lock this goddamned place up for that.

The Impact of Perceived Threat

The high-safety person lives in a world of low trust, high vigilance, uncertainty, and discomfort. Danger occupies his mind, circumscribes his actions, and governs his awareness. The anticipation of cues to danger makes the environment a map of open areas one must traverse between precarious and very temporary sanctuaries. It makes life a matter of being tensely and continuously on guard against dangers one cannot hope to locate, to anticipate, or to guard against:

> **Cox S 2**: Here if you go in your cell, you got to think about the next day, how's it going to go? If you go in a shop, is some guy going to be waiting for you with a pipe, is something going to happen? When you come back to your cell, is your stuff going to be in your cell?

* * *

> **Au R DD**: In a place like this you don't know who to trust. The main thing is you don't know who to trust, and with the small population you know everybody, you get to know everybody, and you know who to stay away from, but every day I see faces that I never seen before, and I have been here for two months.

With accumulating tension the link between external and internal violence may become explicit or manifest. The individual finds himself harboring violent thoughts and feelings or may sense himself nearing an explosion point. He may feel a need to seek protection from himself or may become concerned about harm he might do:

> **El R BB**: This is when all the tension just builds up in you over the months, and one day you feel tense, and you put the earphones on, and bam, too late though, you break down, and bam, you beat on the wall. It be all that tension, you know.... Well, it's just tension. The tension builds. You know, if too much tension builds up in you, and you get tired of beating your walls, and it still don't come out, then sometimes you might get that urge to do something evilish then. To relieve that tension, regardless of what it is. So you might get in that keep lock, so you don't get in no trouble. That's the safe way. When it comes down you're ready to do something, you say, "Give me a keep lock," and relax.

> **Att R 38**: Just like the riot, that's what messed me up. When I got out on the street I started having nightmares from when I seen the dudes get killed and stuff like that, and I started drinking. I tried

to avoid drinking, but, see, when I drink I forget about the problems.... Take a guy here, you come here—right?—when you're young. You come here, and there's older people here. He listens, and he don't never hear nothing good. He only hears that they killed somebody, they're going to rob this here, they're going to do this here, they call a woman a bitch. And a guy, subconsciously, he inherits all of this in his mind. And he starts acting like this too. Not that he wants to, but he be around day and night, around people like this here, and he start acting like this too. Acting like an uncivilized people. And when he gets out, the impression that he had built up in here, and when he gets out it explodes. Especially if he drinks, and all the problems that was in here, whether people knows it or not, all the problems that a dude gets in here, when they get in the streets, see, they freak.

Sometimes a frustration-aggression mechanism is at work, where the person feels retaliatory urges (particularly against controlling agents in the environment), which threaten to break through messily or violently:

GH N 19: I've been talking to the doctor, and, like I told him, just like I told you, life can get to a point where I'm not going to be able to control myself. And, like, if I do anything in here, I'm not going to be held responsible for it.

I: *Would this be like violence against other people, or against yourself?*

GH N 19: Against either. Because, you know, I keep thinking, like, man, they accuse me of assaulting an officer, which I didn't do. They accuse me of assaulting a doctor, which I didn't do. Maybe I should do it. Get a payback or something.

* * *

GH R R: If you just keep a man confined, so much pressure builds up on him, and the least little thing happens, he's like a time bomb, he blows up. He holds it in, he keeps holding it in. He's responding to a negative thought coming from a correctional guard. It's one of them things like, if you hit him now, they're going to take you off the count. So what you do, you just hold your head, be cool. And you just wait. But some guys can't hold it down too long.

A more immediate issue is posed by the option of responding or not respond-ing to violence with violence. Safety is very often seen in fight-flight terms. Fight, however, may entail (1) the threat of retaliation from one's victim, (2) a potential loss of self-control, and (3) a response of the larger environment, with a loss of sta-tus or safety:

> **CH N 21:** The man has never really threatened me, but to avoid a problem for him and I—see, that's why I did ten years before, a lot of problems like hitting guys. I knew if the man approached me it would be a serious thing. I'm not running out of fear from him. I'm just running, I'm afraid if he does approach me some-body's going to be hurt very bad, in this crowd or the crowd that I'm in. Put it like this, I don't want to do anything because I still have eight and one-half years to be in jail.... See, my brother, he's with organized crime, I'll put it to you that way.... You're not by yourself. So I know if I go out there it's going to be a war. And I know, whether I get hurt or not, it's going to jam me up bad, where I'm going to wind up CR [Cell Restricted], and I'm trying to avoid this.

Exercising the Flight Option

Despite its perceived liabilities, the flight option may be exercised by the high-safety inmate. He may seek physical sanctuary in a subenvironment (should it exist) in which he is protected, or where the peer group is low-pressure and nonthreatening:

> **GH N 15:** I wouldn't leave this place if they offered me a thou-sand dollars, or a million dollars. It wouldn't pay to leave. Because there is a sense of security here.

* * *

> **EI N 1:** I'm away from the population and I have peace of mind. I'm not always looking over my shoulder. In here you never know what is going to happen next.
>
> **I:** *So you feel that your job assignment is beneficial?*
>
> **EI N 1:** Yes, very beneficial.

Another flight option is to withdraw from social intercourse or to restrict con-tact to a subgroup that is nondangerous:

Au R AA: Just mind my business, man.... You know, avoid unnecessary static.... If you mind your own business and don't fuck with nobody, you won't have no trouble.... Me, personally, I don't have no trouble.

* * *

EI R BB: If you're stupid enough to get involved with it, and knowing that you can get in trouble doing this and doing that there. If you're that dumb enough to go ahead and do it, then you deserve— if you stick your hand in the fire that's hot, you're going to get burned.

A third retreat option is psychological and involves restricting the range of intimacy of communication. While maintaining himself in physical circulation, a man may insist on superficiality and reserve in all of his contacts with others:

Au R DD: I am out in the streets, and the people that I hang around with, I trust them. I am not used to this, you know—like wanting to know who you talk to, you know, and all that. I have to change now, and I have to be careful what I tell someone, and most things I can't even tell to people, because I might be in a spot, you know.

Any retreat option has two liabilities. One is that a person may find it hard to reconcile a flight strategy with a self-image of autonomy or potency. The second liability revolves around the person's public image.

A person with high-safety concerns may be stigmatized to begin with, because victimization tends to go hand in hand with a reputation for weakness, cowardice, or explosiveness. In this connection, flight can ameliorate physical danger, but it can also exacerbate a man's stigma. Where a sanctuary protects, it also poses the question of how a man is to view himself when he leaves or when he rejoins the outside world:

GH N 21: I've always had a good name for myself, what they consider in jails and everything. And it's hard.... Maybe my mistake was the way I was brought up, with so-called wise guys. And I always got stuck in prison with them. Maybe if I got stuck with the so-called creeps, who I think are the best guys, maybe I would have never come back to jail again.... Well, what they consider like a creep is a guy that's not with the so-called guinea mob, a guy that's not pushing dope or who thinks like that. A guy that just came in for a jive crime, he ain't with nobody in the street, so he's supposed to be a creep.... It's hard, because, when

you come to protection, right away everybody puts you down—
you're a stool pigeon. And it's uncomfortable, and you really
can't talk when people know—it's hard to explain, it's just that
you get a name. "I don't know why he's up in protection, but I think
he's a stool pigeon, he ratted on somebody." It's not easy, especially when, like I said, you been a good guy all your life, with
the so-called good people. People start saying "I can't believe
Denny—".... They'll make you feel it, because a lot of times
you'll walk into a room or something, and guys will be talking
in a corner, and right away everybody will stop. And right away
you feel like a weasel. If you feel, like I said, like, me, I'm right
from the old school, where I say it was tough. If a guy was a rat,
he was hurt.

The Safety Cycle

A review of one individual case may help us to better understand the safety concern of the obsessed inmate. The case is relevant here, because it highlights the relationship of environmental "threats" to individual "concerns" and environmental
"solutions."

Our victim is a 20-year-old white property offender serving a four-year sentence
at Auburn prison. He is a parole violator with a juvenile record whose institutional
experience includes three years in an orphanage. He is tall (6 feet), of normal build
(153 pounds), with some education and normal intelligence.

Auburn is an institution with a substantial client age range, and it can make a
young inmate conscious of his youth. "Here I am, like, younger than everybody out
there," our man tells us, "and I just got to watch myself more, you know. I just can't
slip. I just can't say the wrong thing."

Constant vigilance reaps its perceptual result in the shape of repeated "evidence" of danger:

> Well, see, the first day I came in here—I walked in the reception
> area, and I was standing down there, and I seen this guy, you
> know. This black guy just staring at me—just staring at me from
> about 6 feet away. And he started smiling. And I knew—I have
> been around, you know, and I have been through all of this before.
> And he started smiling, and I see him go away and talk to some-
> body else, and he was whispering, and I knew right off what was
> going on.

* * *

No one actually approached me, but I heard things running around, like so and so would say something, and they would come back and tell me, but a few instances like that—nothing that I would really worry about, but I had to watch out for it.

* * *

Like my hair was long and everything, and I looked about 16 years old, so I used to go to the mess hall and everybody would stare at me. I don't have no complex, but, gee—when everybody is staring at you—how can you miss it, you know? So I figured that the best thing would be to do was to cut my hair, so the next morning I got up and cut it.... It eased up after awhile, and I realized that there are certain people that stare at you all the time....

You try to be calm if you can, but you can't, because it really bothers you. Like, I will see some people out there talking, and they look my way, and right away—they are talking about me, and I don't know what to think.

As fear builds up, the young man has thoughts of trying to escape into a segregation setting, possibly permanently. He holds this gambit in reserve, but rejects it as an immediate option. His reasoning here follows lines similar to those we have already discussed:

When I first came, I wanted to go to protection, and then I started to think, and I found that if I do that, you know, once they transfer you out it will be on your record that you were in protection...and then you have a bad name, and they make you look like a punk or something, so I figured that I had just better stick it out. So that is why I didn't go to protection....

Like, I have been taking chances all my life—like going out there and steal and petty stuff, you know, and I am in jail—just by taking chances. So that I am taking a chance being in the population, you know. And, like, if I hear today—if my friend comes up and tells me that he heard they are going to jump on me—I will go and lock right in. I won't come out. Why take a chance, you know? I have been taking chances all my life.

To be sure, there are some saving factors in the picture. For one, the presence of guards is reassuring because it reduces the chances of a physical attack. There is also the fear-reducing counsel of friends, who raise questions about the seriousness of actual danger:

Like, I will go and call up my friend, and I will go and tell him,
and he will say, "Don't worry about it—they ain't going to bother
you." I guess that I am paranoid. I tell everybody that I am not,
but I guess that I am, you know.

On the other hand, the help one gets is not all equally helpful. There are those
who increase one's distrust by raising questions about the credibility of other men.
And there are those (both among staff and peers) who stipulate the inevitability of
violence, and who advocate a "fight-fire-with-fire" approach to the problem:

Like, this one guy that I was talking to out there, he seemed like
he was all right. He was an Italian dude like me. A little bit older,
but we are both Italians and we should look out for each other. So
he looked out for me. And then I had this other guy come up
and say, "What is happening? Don't turn your back on him,
because he might do something to you, you know." I don't know
what to think, because here this guy is going and being nice to me,
and this guy is telling me to watch out for him. Like, I don't
know what to think....

I: *So you have had an opportunity to discuss this with one of the
officers? And he understands the problems?*

Yes. He told me—I told him that, like, when I came I had a knife
and all that, and he told me that I had better put it up or better use
it. "Just don't pull it out, you know, because if you pull it out and
scare somebody—it will make them leave, but the next time they
come up on you they will have something, and you might not have
yours, and that is that. So if you are going to pull it out—use
it."...

And then, like, I met this one guy from New York and he was a
nice guy. He was about 24—not much older than me—and I
found out that I could trust him, you know. And he had apparently
the same kind of problem, but not as bad as me. And we would
talk and talk, and he would say, "Don't worry about it. If anything
comes of it—just jump on the guy who bothers you, you know."

Both types of advice dovetail with one's concerns. They reinforce the sense of
one's impotence and add to the disquieting feeling of being outmanned and outgunned.
They increase one's awareness of the violence and malevolence of others, compared
to one's babe-in-the-woods innocence.

One here buys the assumption that violence is the only way of countering or preventing the violence of others. If one is unsure of one's fighting prowess one can at least appear capable of violence by acting circumspectly, by behaving seriously, and talking tough:

> I would say that it is making me act a lot more older, act more mature and everything. Like, really, on the streets I am immature, but in here I don't do those things like fooling around and stuff like that, because the first wrong move that I make it costs me, you know....

> Like, I don't fool around. I don't say nothing. If you just walk up and don't say nothing, they won't bother you, because they won't know what to expect. You know, like karate or black belt or something like that. But if you are always fooling around and playing around, they know that you are nothing but a talker and, you know, you are always trying to make people think you are a tough guy, but when they know what you are they will try to put it over on you. But if you keep quiet and don't say nothing, they don't know what to expect, and they don't bother with you. So that is mainly what I am trying to do....

> Like, I will be standing in line like so. I will stand up straight and put my chest out a little bit to give them like a good impression that I am not a little kid and all that stuff, you now. I make sure that my hair is straight up and everything, and I am always thinking. Every time that I walk by the mess hall I say, "I wonder how many are looking at me, and I don't want them to see me then like this." I say this to my friends—when one of them is fooling around I literally punch them back, because there are always people there to see that.

This pose is carefully thought out but has two serious defects: (1) It deviates from a self-image of carefree playfulness, suppresses urges, and causes strain; also (2) how can one convince others with a performance about whose credibility one has one's own serious doubts?

> In here you have got to perform. I am not myself in here. If everybody just left, I would be out there fooling around and playing basketball, but now I just walk around and keep my mouth shut....

> Here I consider myself a phony, you know. If I am in camp, I run around and have a good time, and here I just walk around with my head down, and I don't hardly say anything to anybody.

The strain of such a pose exceeds its benefits. To secure relief, one must resort to the seeking of staff help. To reduce the implication of dependence this entails, one claims that violence induces one's advertised potential for lethal retaliation:

> I went to him to see if he could call someone—the service unit, because I had been dropping slips, and nobody was talking to me or nothing. And I had to talk to somebody, you know, because I was afraid that something was going to happen, but this way— like, if I hurt somebody bad I had some type of reflex. I could tell the guard to say—come to the adjustment committee, and, "I told him what would happen if you did not get me a transfer"— and, "I told you what would happen and now you can't blame me for it."

A staff member receives a plea for help. When we talk to him later, he remembers his solution, which consists of removing the inmate from population and placing him in a succession of "niches":

> He had been approached by unknown individuals, if he would be interested in homosexual activity. The way it occurred is, when he came into the program committee, I don't know—a feeling or sixth sense just said to me, you know—"This is a weak one, and I think, you know, that he can have problems." So on a direct question he had admitted to me that he had a problem, and he wanted to—he didn't want protective custody—he didn't want to have the population think that he was coming back out of the situation, but he just wanted to be put off to the side someplace. So at his request we marked him in idle for about two weeks, and then I called back for the program committee, and he was assigned to the storehouse butcher, which is one of these isolated sections. And after about a week he came back to me, and he said, "Well, I think I have got it under control, and I would like to now go to another area," so he is presently up in the silk screen shop learning the silk screen process.

In considering environmental options, the advantages (in this case, safety) must be balanced against the liabilities, such as stigmatization. Ultimately, some compromise can be achieved:

> And (Idle Company) is kind of good, you know. You know, really, I wanted to stay there, but I figured that I wouldn't ever get a chance to get transferred if I stayed in Idle. It looks bad, you know.
>
> I: *It looks like you are a fuck-up.*

Yeah. It goes on your work record. So I got out of there, and they offered me another good job in the butcher shop, and I turned it down, you know. So I went back and I went and told my friend of the offer, and he said, "What, are you crazy? That is a good job that he offered you," so I went back, and they gave it to me....

You know, it is not too bad in the utility room. It is all white people, and it is pretty good.

I: *So when you are working, do you feel relatively relaxed about this?*

Uh, yeah, because, like, I work in the utility room, and I know that nobody is going to run up on me. And, like, there is always something to grab around there if I have to protect myself. I feel safer up there. I have been up there about three weeks, and there has been no problems.

The solution that is achieved for this inmate includes not only freedom from external danger, but also congruence of self. The inmate speaks to us of an environment in which "you can be yourself and you can talk to people and you can trust people."

Admittedly, the cards in this case are somewhat stacked, because the situation is much less extreme than are others we could review. On the one hand, the "objective" danger is less than that encountered by inmates who are subjected to overt threats (Chapter 9). On the other hand, there is less struggle with violent impulses, less of a freedom issue, and more openness to support than in other case histories.

The dynamics of the situation, however, are reasonably representative. A man is presensitized to violence and scans the world for cues to danger. He feels powerless, fears the unpredictability of other men, and withdraws. He also feels tension and must struggle with feelings about himself. Violence and its control become the main theme of the inner and outer environment. The man-environment match that must be achieved includes not only physical safety but the facilitation of an adjustment mode that permits self-modulation, relaxed impulse control, and trust.

3

Empty Bars: Violence and the Crisis of Meaning in Prison†

Peter Scharf

John Dewey wrote in 1896 that in education there are two central questions that must be addressed if the profession is to progress beyond the "rule of thumb" phase: (1) What should be taught? and (2) How do children learn? Corrections, it can be argued, must also address two central questions if it, too, is to progress beyond the "rule of thumb" phase: (1) Who should be sent to prison or receive other criminal sanctions? and (2) What should be the educational, rehabilitative, or other social purposes of the prison?

This paper deals primarily with the second question, and I will argue that the correctional profession during the past decade has virtually abdicated dialogue on this key question. Chastised by criticism of medical model rehabilitation, it has failed to develop any concept of what purposes the prison is to serve. I will further argue that this failure affects virtually every aspect of prison life and that the only salvation of the prison lies in a rediscovery of some coherent meaning system to guide interactions with inmates.

While prison treatment programs of the 1960s and early 1970s faced major psychological, ethical, and empirical contradictions, they resulted in prisons quite different from those one might visit today, anywhere. A visitor to a California treatment prison might have encountered scenes implausible today in almost any prison in the United States. Using transactional analysis (TA) or rational emotive therapy (RET), inmates would gather in groups to discuss their relationships with staff members, parents, or among themselves. Inmates would be assigned counselors with whom

†This article was published in the *Prison Journal,* Vol. LXIII, No. 1, 1983, and is reprinted here by permission of the Prison Society. Although this article was originally published in 1983, the malaise that Scharf described still exists 10 years later.

they would meet on a regular basis. Staff members would commonly express genuine concern regarding inmates (at least some staff members and some inmates) and engage in weekly analyses of their progress.

While it is not my intention to express nostalgia or to bring back the therapeutic prison, it is useful to compare it with the prison reality one encounters roughly a decade later. In virtually no prison in the country is there anything analogous to a treatment philosophy that structures staff member and inmate relationships and goals. While in 1968, one might have expected the "transactional analysis" or "daytop" prison to evolve into another set of purposes, it is disturbing to consider that the treatment philosophy of the late 1960s, in 15 or so years, has resulted in a doctrinaire (and absurd) notion that the prison should serve no social purposes whatsoever.

This rejection of any purpose for corrections is evident at all levels of the penal enterprise. The prison directors of most state systems (with some exceptions—for example, Ellis MacDougal of Arizona) have largely rejected the notion that prisons have the capacity to positively reform the inmates under their charge. The public discussion of prisons has revolved around such issues as new prison construction, the prevention of riots, and the rejection of the "liberalism" of previous administrations. The tone set at the top permeates all levels of the system. Prison wardens, counselors, and guards express little, if any, confidence that anything they might do has any impact upon the prisoners in their charge. A comment by a warden colleague of mine well expresses the climate of the day:

> We are in the business of babysitting, warehousing, or whatever you prefer to call it. I think that the public is pretty well fooled if they think anything goes on here besides keeping the meat cool. Programs are fine if it keeps them busy. The best days we have are during the football season. That's when they are busy...

The Malaise of the Prison

The reality of the failure in the prison is a common theme for reforms in almost all eras. Rather than delay the argument with a long rendition of failure, let me simply list the most obvious realities of the prisons of 1983:

1. **The prisons are hopelessly overcrowded.** Since 1974, prison populations in more than 40 states doubled; prison institutions in most states are filled beyond their maximum **emergency** capacities.

2. **Prisons are largely unable to protect the physical safety of their inmates.** Rapes, beatings, knifings, and killings are common occurrences in many prisons.

3. **Prisons have abandoned systematic efforts at rehabilitative, educational, and vocational training.** In many states coherent efforts at rehabilitation (of whatever variety) are simply nonexistent.

4. **There has been an almost complete divorce of interaction between professional correctional and academic disciplines.** At the 1982 American Correctional Association meeting, there were fewer than one dozen academic professors of criminology or corrections in attendance. Practitioner presence at academic criminology meetings (e.g., the American Society of Criminology meeting) has been similarly negligible.

5. **There has been an obvious decrease in the quality of correctional practice, evidenced in public discussion of techniques used in correctional management.** It should be obvious that few correctional professionals claim, use, or can describe any skills unique to the profession.

6. **There has been an almost total abandonment of experimentation in corrections. While in the late 1960s there were literally dozens of experiments to innovate new methods of correctional care and rehabilitation, one is hard-pressed to name a single experiment in a given state which proposes some new form of correctional treatment.**

7. **There has been an increased unwillingness to consider corrections as a social invention in which the premises of the institution must be subjected to ongoing review and reinvention.** There is almost no correctional philosophy under debate and review at any level of the profession; nor is there any concern to initiate correctional dialogue on other than the most pragmatic level of professional practice.

8. **There is almost no consensus as to a rational correctional purpose. In a real sense, the profession seems to have lost its moral defense—its sense of purpose.** Corrections appears to have become an institution without an ideal—a set of practices without purpose or direction.

The causes of these trends are less than obvious. Many contend that corrections' decline may be traced to such factors as the loss of LEAA funding, the wave of critiques from Jessness (1972) to Martinson (1974) which shed doubt upon the efficacy of efforts at prison rehabilitation, and the movement to formalism (e.g., fixed sentencing) in sentencing, paroling, and other correctional decisions. However, there are more spiritual causes as well (see Fogel, 1975).

Following the reaction to 1960s style correctional progressivism emphasizing medical model and behaviorist treatment programs, there was a failure by the corrections profession to conceptualize anything other than the warehouse model of corrections as an alternative to the treatment prison. The medical model treatment prison was, as almost all correctional professionals realized, riddled with both moral and psychological contradictions. The demise of simplistic treatment models should have yielded a spirit of inquiry in which new purposes of the prison were sought and developed.

The response by the profession, however, was reactive and almost vindictive. Academic criminologists abandoned any concern with rehabilitation, treatment, or education as quickly as they had embraced it 10 years earlier. The practitioners followed by abandoning any active search for new program models, aided of course by politicians concerned with the costs of correctional programs and a public convinced that inmates were being coddled by psychiatrists and prison liberals.

The Consequences of This Malaise

The failure to define any rational purposes in the prison may be seen in every aspect of prison life:

The loss of purpose dominates all social processes within the prison. While the prisoner of the 1960s might feel that the therapeutic prison was a sham and that he was being manipulated by its treatment agents, there was in the treatment ideology a mutuality of goals that might bind the staff member and the inmate. In Maxwell Jones' (1953) therapeutic community or in the reform program proposed by the author and Joseph Hickey (see *Prison Journal*, Winter 1971; Winter 1977), there was an ideological commitment to the inmates' and staff members' mutual betterment and hope for every inmates' personal growth—if not rehabilitation. Similar mutuality is evident in any program that seeks the improvement of the inmate (e.g., prison education programs, vocational training, etc.).

The prison of today offers no basis for virtually any mutual goals that both the inmate and the prison might mutually seek. The inmate is simply to exist and to obey. There is nothing expected of him other than cooperation and good behavior. There is no reason for him to adhere to the regime of his captors other than the threat of more time or the loss of privileges.

Further absent are many of the prison sacraments that have, in the past, made prison endurable for the inmate. The "silent" system of the eighteenth-century Quakers held open the notion that through penitence and prayer, salvation might result. Maconochie's mark system held open the notion of release based on effort. The Auburn prison sought a form of Calvinist redemption through work. In the prison of today, there is virtually no form of redemption possible.

The loss of common values and of the possibility of social redemption have profound consequences for both inmate and staff members. The inmate, psychologically, is given no reason to identify with the authority of the prison other than in terms of instrumental interest or fear. As evidenced by prison literature (for example, Jack Abbott's 1981 book, the haunting *In the Belly of the Beast*), there is an almost absolute polarization of the world view of the prisoner and the prison and larger society. In earlier prison literature, there is always some part of the prison that makes some bond with the inmate. In Cleaver's *Soul on Ice* (1968), similarly, there is described a teacher who cries when the inmates fail to understand a literary point. This almost complete alienation from the prison is evident to almost anyone who has visited a prison in the past several years and can compare it with the prison culture of a decade earlier.

The failure of the prison to ritualize redemption in any form means psychologically that inmates must seek their own meaning for imprisonment. At times, inmate-manufactured meaning systems may be disturbing. An inmate on work release in Washington recently sought out his victim from an earlier crime and killed her along with her child and a neighbor. One wonders about the private meaning system this inmate found for himself in prison.

The failure to define any rational meaning for imprisonment has consequences for staff members as well. In many states the "best and brightest" staff members have simply left the field. Those who have entered the field of corrections as a form of social service, of course, find the greatest disappointment. In many prisons staff stress levels are evident in high blood pressure, obesity problems, and use of drugs and alcohol. One hypothesis to explain the high rates of staff burnout and health problems might relate to the inherent meaninglessness of the job.

Politically, the failure to define rational purposes for the prison has become a major political liability. In several states during 1982, legislatures have insisted that the prisons institute rehabilitation programs—a novel twist from legislative hearings a decade earlier in which prison administrators had to beg for funding for a variety of programs. Rather than seeking to convince a skeptical public about its programs, in the past several years prison officials have been more cynical about their ability to implement meaningful programs than the public. This is ironic in that institutions that have no faith in their ability to impact the persons they work with rarely inspire faith from the public. While educators are obviously optimistic about their ability to teach, the police are usually confident in their ability to catch criminals, and medical doctors are sure of their ability to cure disease, it is those in the corrections profession who are most convinced of their inability to impact the inmates in their charge.

Violence and Meaning in the Prison

A special consequence of meaninglessness may be found in the case of prison violence. A close analysis of many cases of prison violence may be related to the gang phenomenon of loss of purpose we have described.

Gang violence is on the increase in virtually every large prison and may be interpreted as an effort to create a meaningful community in an anomic prison environment. As Toch (1977) points out, one of the most important functions served by therapeutic communities or programs in prison is to provide social cohesion and support for inmates. In the absence of organized efforts at community, ersatz groups such as the prison gang emerge. Faced with other prison gangs in the context of the prison, the result is an almost relentless cycle of violence and vengeance.

Another type of violence results from prison "horseplay," almost always because of efforts by adolescents to combat the hopeless boredom of the prison. A dorm wrestling match may literally be the major diversion of the day for many inmates. The intensity of this type of horseplay—sometimes resulting in injury on hard concrete floors—is related both to the absence of any other channels to vent energy and the absence of immediate privileges (such as a good educational or rehabilitative program) which might be lost through the result of such activity.

Baiting by guards—at times resulting in altercations (at times physical)—might be seen as the result of the meaninglessness of the prison experience. Prison guards, themselves without role or purpose, will at times effectively and intentionally seek to frustrate or irritate a particular inmate—at times simply because there is no other realistic mode of relating and also because the prison guard is almost as bored as the inmate. Often "tickets" will be delivered in the most humiliating fashion or inmates will be left waiting for many minutes simply because the staff member is bored and wants to see the inmates "react."

In maximum security sections (e.g., administrative segregation), one often sees almost pathetic efforts to define meaning in a context devoid of common social value. In one prison an inmate serving a 99-year sentence for multiple murders would every day throw his excrement at the guards, who, in turn, would mace him or throw it back. When a guard observed this once he asked the inmate why he did this, and the inmate replied quietly: "Hell, there ain't nothing else in here to do."

Often suicidal behavior has an element of socially intelligible meaning to it in terms of the anomie of the prison of 1983. In one prison, an inmate swallowed two razor blades, explaining to the author and a physician that he "thought it was a way to get out of the prison for awhile."

This type of violence is far from atypical. A cycle exists in many prisons where the warehouse prison creates frustrations which Toch (1977) and Sykes (1956) suggest create psychological deprivations, fears, and frustrations which make violence more likely. Fearing assault, inmates group in protective dyads, friends' "homes bands," and gangs. Beginning as defense groups, these groups often eventually initiate violent attacks against others. Abdul Mu'Mn (1981) suggests that such collective groups are most common among inmates who fail to involve themselves among other tasks, religious, or educational groups in the prison.

Violence in the prison, of course, becomes an obstacle to the discovery of meaning, as well as a result of the anomic reality of the prison. Abraham Maslow, for example, suggests that when safety is a personal reality for a human being, higher order psychological functioning is impossible. Concerned with safety (rape, beatings, or killings), long-term problem solving, life planning, or program development become improbable or impossible. Thus, violence as it becomes an institutionalized reality of prison life hinders the type of conscious evolution of purpose that would make life in prison livable, if not productive.

Hope and Alternatives

What is the hope for the prison? What new metaphor might emerge to restore some useful social meaning to the prison—its inmates and staff members? The history of corrections is the history of social metaphors of the prison emerging and asserting themselves. (Metaphor is used as a general concept; the specific cases are posed as similes.)

Prison as Monastery

The creation of the American prison in Pennsylvania (The Walnut Street Jail) presented a metaphor of the prison as monastery. As the monk retreated from the world into the private experience of prayer and silence, so, too, the first prison "rehabilitation program" assumed a retreat from the world in an antinomian Quaker search for redemption and the return of grade. In this sense, the first metaphor of the prison was that of penitence set in the context of the monastery.

Prison as Workshop

The congregate work prison (Auburn prison model) assumed a notion of the prison as workshop. As portrayed in Ignatieff's *Just Measure of Pain* (1979), the metaphor of the congregate prison approached the reality of the cottage and workshop industry of the era. The regulation of work and discipline used to enforce work approached in many respects the types of work conditions "free labor" experienced in the mid-nineteenth-century nonmechanized workshop—hence the metaphor of prison as workshop.

Prison as Schoolhouse

During the 1850s clergy began visiting the prison in a systematic manner, with the goal of teaching inmates to read and discuss the Bible. By the end of the century, some form of school was common in most prisons. During the past five years, the prison as school metaphor has been revived with the Alaskan University Within

Walls program and the Canadian University of Victoria prison education program. Two distinct versions of the prison as schoolhouse exist. There is the metaphor of prison as liberal arts academy with a full curriculum in philosophy, literature, and often the social sciences. A vocational/technical version of the schoolhouse exists— with the well-known Chino (California) Diving Program as an example. What unifies the metaphor is the notion that the goal of the prison should be to educate the inmate in either liberal arts perspectives or vocational skills.

Prison as Hospital

The dominant metaphor of the prison reform era of the 1950s and 1960s was the medical model version of prison as "hospital." As Adolphson, a 1950s reformer reasoned, the inmate should be treated much as one who has a physiological disease. If we treat a man with infected adenoids by placing him in a hospital, he reasons, so, too, we should treat a person with a criminal disease by placing him in a hospital for criminals—the treatment prison. Ideas such as differential treatment, case management, prescriptions, etc.—common in this reform era—all in effect derive from the metaphor of prison as hospital with treatment being administered for specific criminal problems and release being determined by the degree of the inmate's "cure."

Prison as Commune

Another metaphor exists in the gemeinschaft image of the prison commune. In Maxwell Jones' (1953) therapeutic community and perhaps in Joseph Hickey's and the author's *Toward a Just Correctional System* (1980), there is the notion that the prison should reflect many of the communal values found in the nineteenth century communes. Inmates are expected to feel a bond with one another and make sacrifices for the group; and there is an attempt to create a community within the prison itself that will have greater harmony, communal spirit, and order than the outside society. This metaphor also may be exemplified in many drug programs that existed in prisons, at least through the 1970s, such as Synanon and Daytop.

Prison as Polis

Reformers Thomas Mott Osborne (1916) and W.E. George (1904) conceived of the prison as a democratic state. In the Osborne Mutual Welfare League (see *Prison Journal*, Winter 1977), inmates constituted a republic with 56 representatives elected from the inmate population-at-large. In the George Junior republic, a minisociety was created to mirror the major legal institutions of the larger society. Murton

(1975) and others have recently attempted to reimplement this civic metaphor of the prison finding, as did Osborne, that such efforts, perhaps hopelessly, conflicted with the bureaucracy of the prison and correctional system.

Prison as Enterprise

It is perhaps the sign of the times (i.e., the Ronald Reagan era) that the newest metaphor of the prison and the one most in vogue is that the prison should become a capitalist enterprise. Labeled "free venture" programs, this metaphor assumes that the inmate should learn capitalist values by participating in entrepreneurial business ventures housed in the prison. The key assumptions include the notion that the inmate should "pay his way" in the prison and that participation in such programs (which are "seeded" by outside capital sources) will teach inmates capitalistic entrepreneurial work values.

The Evolution of a New Metaphor for the Prison

The question that should be asked is, of course: What metaphor might guide the prison during the coming decade? It might further be asked: What process needs to be undertaken if an alternative to the warehouse is to be found?

An answer to the first question requires a sense of correctional reform revolutions in the past—and, perhaps, a bit of clairvoyance. As Weber (1948) has suggested, most organizational changes begin with a charismatic vision of an alternative mode of operation. Maconochie, Osborne, and Jones, for example, share a passionate commitment to what might be called "correctional" prophesy or the ability to move from "what exists" in prisons to "what could be." What is needed to revive corrections at this juncture is a new correctional vision—an idea with which to restructure the terrible monstrosity of an undifferentiated warehouse that we have allowed to dominate our correctional agencies. Currently prisons are terrible storage facilities for people, whose individualities do not matter and are not taken into consideration.

As to the content of the next correctional revolution, it will certainly mirror larger political and cultural realities. Much as Alexander Maconochie reflected the spirit of the European revolution of 1848, the democratic prison reform movement of Osborne (1916) was rooted in American progressivism, and the prison therapy movement was contexted by the analytic "couch culture" of the 1960s, so, too, the next correctional revolution will be grounded in the politics and culture of the larger polity.

In the short term, the pragmatism, austerity, realism, and apoliticism of the day will surely be reflected in any new correctional metaphor that emerges. Viewed from this perspective, the prison metaphor of the year 1990 will probably be politically palatable, inexpensive, and provide clear and immediate benefits to the inmates.

Less important, however, than the specific metaphor that will evolve is the restoration of creative thinking, vision, and imagination in corrections. Critical, I suspect, will be the infusion of new personalities into corrections—the present leadership in the field appears to be both morally and intellectually bankrupt. The specific malaise of corrections—violence, overcrowding, boredom, etc.—is inherently related to the fact that in the words of a friend of mine (a clergyman and former member of a state parole board), "there is not an honest principle (or fact or number) in the whole field." Unless a new principle and vision comes into being, the prisons will become worse and the people they house will emerge damaged and embittered from their incarceration. The present mentality of "keep the lid on" will incur a horrendous cost to society both in terms of violence within the prison and from those creatures who will emerge from confinement without purpose and goals. The price of almost any rehabilitation program will appear to be a bargain compared with the costs of controlling the graduates from the 400,000-person human "warehouse" system we have created. A true "cost" model is needed to understand the price of keeping people in human suspension for endless periods of time.

The alternative to this vision of the future is obvious. Only by creating an alternative to drift can the present inertia be reversed. Society must have the courage to admit it has failed and to reinvent the future. From this perspective, the "first client" of corrections must be corrections itself. Much as the criminal who drifts into crime and the criminal justice system, corrections itself has sleepwalked itself into its present plight. It must reawaken if it is to survive.

Any change given this perspective begins with a serious self-analysis by the corrections profession and also requires what Weber (1948) called a sense of charisma on the part of the correctional reformer. In many ways corrections in its present state is a prime candidate for the emergence of a new charismatic vision to guide it (hopefully, sensibly) over the next decades. My best guess, of course, is that this vision will be a quiet, stoic one, but hopefully a vision that weighs such considerations as the responsible balance of risk to citizens with the cost (both financial and human) incurred by the maintenance of the prison system. Critical in the emergence of this charismatic vision are effective educational and vocational models that will restore a sense of dignity and purpose to both correctional staffs and inmates.

The biggest obstacle to any reemergence of a new metaphor of the prison is corrections' poor self-image. In this sense, corrections' image of itself is much like its image of the prisoner. Much as the corrections professional of 1983 does not believe the inmate can change, so, too, it does not believe it, as an institution, can change. Once the prison believes it can create itself, perhaps it will have the faith that it can reform the inmate.

References

Abbott, J. (1981). *In the Belly of the Beast*. New York, NY: Random House.

Adolphson, H. (1960). *Crime and Insanity*. New York, NY: Holder.

Cleaver, E. (1968). *Soul on Ice*. New York, NY: McGraw-Hill.

Dewey, J. (1966). *Democracy and Education*. New York, NY: The Free Press.

Fogel, D. (1973). *We are the Living Proof*. Cincinnati, OH: Anderson Publishing Co.

George, W.E. (1904). *The Junior Republic*. Ithaca, NY: George, Jr. Republic Institute.

Hickey, J. and P. Scharf (1980). *Toward a Just Correctional System*. San Francisco, CA: Jossey-Bass.

Ignatieff, M. (1979). *Just Measure of Pain*. Cambridge, England: Cambridge University Press.

Jessness, K. (1972). Evaluation of Oh Close and Karl Holton school therapeutic programs. Stockton, CA: Northern California Reception Center.

Jones, M. (1953). *Therapeutic Community*. New York, NY: Basic Books.

Kohlberg, L., P. Scharf and J. Hickey (1971). "The Justice Structure of the Prison—A Theory and an Intervention." *Prison Journal*, 51, 3-14 (Autumn-Winter).

Martinson, R. (1974). "What Works?" *Public Interest*, 5, 22-54.

Maslow, A. (1968). *Towards a Psychology of Being*. New York, NY: Van Nostrand.

Mu'Mn, A. (1981). "Ethnic and Religious Characteristics of Chino Prison Inmates." Unpublished dissertation. University of California at Irvine.

Murton, T. (1975). *Shared Decision-Making as a Treatment Technique in Prison Management*. Minneapolis, MN: Murton Foundation for Criminal Justice.

Osborne, T.M. (1916). *Society and Prisons*. New Haven, CT: Yale University Press.

Scharf, P. and J. Hickey (1977). "Thomas Mott Osborne and the Limits of Democratic Prison Reform." *Prison Journal*, 57, 3-15.

Sykes, G. (1956). *Society of Captives*. Princeton, NJ: Princeton University Press.

Toch, H. (1977). *Living in Prisons*. Glencoe, IL: The Free Press.

Weber, M. (1948). *From Max Weber*. New York, NY: Oxford Press.

4

Reexamining the Cruel and Unusual Punishment of Prison Life[†]

James Bonta & Paul Gendreau[††]

Historically, prisons have been described as barren landscapes devoid of even the most basic elements of humanity (cf. Sykes, 1958) and detrimental to the humanity of the offender (Rector, 1982). Perhaps one of the best known descriptions of the inhumanity of prison is Cohen and Taylor's (1972) description of long-term inmates in a British maximum security prison. Such notions about prison life have been pervasive whether from the perspective of investigative journalists (Mitford, 1973) or academics writing for basic criminology texts (see Fox, 1985).

Mitford (1973), in her very effective polemical style, painted a scathing indictment of prisons. Not only does imprisonment strip offenders of civil liberties, but also prison reforms are nothing but rhetoric and rehabilitation initiatives are despotic. Goffman (1961) also has been equally harsh in his assessment of the prison as a "total institution."

Careful empirical evaluations, however, have failed to uncover these pervasive negative effects of incarceration that so many have assumed. Mitford (1973) and Cohen and Taylor (1972) did not provide empirical evidence for psychological or behavioral deterioration. We need to be reminded that even Goffman (1961) did not collect data directly from prisons. His conclusions were based upon a review of the prison literature combined with data gathered from "asylums." Furthermore, earlier reviews of empirical studies also failed to uncover the widespread harm that is presumed inherent to prisons (Kilmann, 1980; Walker, 1983).

[†]Reprinted from *Law and Human Behavior*, Vol. 14, No. 4, 1990 by permission of Plenum Publishing Corporation.
[††]Authorship is alphabetical and the opinions expressed in this chapter do not necessarily represent Ministry policy. Reprint requests should be addressed to James Bonta, Chief Psychologist, Ottawa-Carleton Detention Centre, 2244 Innes Road, Ottawa, Ontario, Canada K1B 4C4. We would like to thank Don Andrews for his critique of an earlier draft of this manuscript.

For some, the quantitative data, gathered as much as possible under conditions of objectivity, must not be believed. The failure of such data to confirm popular expectations has led to a number of responses. One is an increased dependence upon a phenomenological approach (e.g., Flanagan, 1982), or, at the very least, a shift from quantitative psychology to a process that examines prison existence in a qualitative and interpretative manner (see Sapsford, 1983).

Another expression of disbelief in the data comes from critics (Mohr, 1985) who have argued that the failure to find damaging effects of incarceration has been due to the "false reality" of the researchers concerned. This false reality has apparently been ascribed to the fact that government researchers have vested interests in reporting results uncritical of the penal establishment.

A final concern, in this case emanating from researchers who have not yet embraced phenomenology, has been that much of the research has reached a "dead end." Historically, incarceration research examined informal social organizations within prisons and did not speak persuasively to the actual effects of imprisonment itself. In addition, the methodological problems in much of the early work were considerable and a number of researchers have been rather critical of the early simplistic approaches to imprisonment research (Porporino & Zamble, 1984; Wormith, 1984). That is, much of the early research was guided by the "all or none" views of the deprivation (Clemmer, 1940; Sykes, 1958) and the early importation theorists (Irwin & Cressey, 1962). Thus, the complex nature of incarceration was not addressed.

In the past, most prisons were maximum security, and psychoeducational programming was minimal. Daily prison life featured 10-hour lockup for a few and highly regimental and monotonous work duties for the rest. Until recently, approaching the examination of prison life from a uniform perspective made eminently good sense. Now, however, the realities of prison life are far different. It is now appropriate to reexamine the effects of incarceration with special attention to the specific conditions of confinement. Although prisons may appear similar on the surface, closer examination finds them varying widely in security, living conditions, and the degree of programming.

Prison overcrowding, almost unknown in the early 1970s, is now very evident. Today, both very long-term and short-term periods of incarceration have dramatically increased. The number of offenders incarcerated is over 700,000 (U.S. Department of Justice, 1988). Current government crime control strategies, in the United States at least, will likely ensure that imprisonment will be the preferred option for the time being (Currie, 1989). In addition, one of the most extreme forms of prison life, solitary confinement, is still frequently employed.

Thus, research examining the effects of prison life is critically important. More knowledge must be generated and analyses of prison life must take into account the deprivation and importation literature, while also recognizing the great variety of structures and experiences that incarceration currently includes.

Selection and Organization of Studies

This review focuses on quantitative studies about effects of imprisonment. Qualitative or phenomenological studies were not included. To be included in the review, a study was required to employ objective measures of the variables of interest and to evaluate the relationship between them by means of statistical tests.

Thus, the majority of studies were of a correctional or quasi-experimental nature. The only truly experimental studies (i.e., random assignment) were found in the solitary confinement literature. Some studies appeared to straddle both the quantitative and qualitative camps. In these instances, we made a judgment call and only included them for discussion where appropriate.

The studies were identified with the aid of a computer search of the prison adjustment and penal literature. Other reviews (e.g., Bukstel & Kilmann, 1980; Gendreau & Bonta, 1984; Wormith, 1986) and a review of recent criminological journals identified additional studies.

We viewed imprisonment as an independent variable and the behavioral and psychological observations of inmates as dependent variables. This organization appeared to work well with the studies dealing with specific conditions of confinement (e.g., solitary confinement). There is, on the other hand, a voluminous and frequently reviewed literature that has the independent variable, imprisonment, less clearly defined and investigates dependent variables such as attitude and self-esteem changes. These later studies were not included in the present review.

Finally, a further comment on the dependent variables in the review is in order. Our interest was on the evaluation of assumed negative effects due to incarceration, and therefore, we reviewed topics that were most likely to evidence such effects. We did not review the literature on rehabilitation and educational programs in prisons (see Gendreau & Ross, 1987) because their stated purpose is to actively promote positive behaviors. In general, *negative effects* were behaviors that threatened the physical welfare of the offender (e.g., aggressive behavior, suicide) and indicators of physiological stress levels (e.g., elevated blood pressure) and psychological distress (e.g., depression).

We examined specific aspects of confinement—crowding, long-term imprisonment, solitary confinement, short-term detention, and death row. We make one departure from this format and provide a commentary on the health risks associated with imprisonment, which follows from our discussion of prison crowding. In our review of the prison crowding literature, we were able to use meta-analytic techniques because there were both an identifiable theoretical perspective and sufficient studies that could be subjected to analysis. With respect to the other aspects of confinement, either there were too few studies (e.g., death row) or they consistently failed to show negative consequences (e.g., solitary confinement), or, as in the case of long-term confinement, the cross-sectional methodology with multiple groups did not make the data amenable to meta-analytic techniques.

Crowding

Crowding is invariably perceived negatively. It is seen by many correctional managers as *the* major barrier to humane housing of offenders despite an estimated 170,000 additional new beds since 1980 (*Corrections Digest*, 1986). This population explosion has prompted court interventions (Angelos & Jacobs, 1985; Call, 1983), sentencing reforms (Kennedy, 1985), and innovative classification systems intended to reduce prison populations (Clements, 1982).

Researchers view crowding as a complex phenomenon. Stokols (1972) distinguished *density*, a physical condition, from *crowding*, a psychological condition involving the individual's perception of constraints imposed by limited space. Loo (1973) further differentiated physical density into *spatial density* (number of people constant but the available space varies) and *social density* (space is constant but the number of people vary). For example, prison renovations might reduce the amount of space available to a number of inmates (spatial density), but the effects of this spatial rearrangement on the inmates may differ from the effects of a sudden influx of new inmates into the institution (social density).

Despite these distinctions, corrections research has been inconsistent in the use of the concepts of crowding and spatial and social density. Studies have described crowding as both an independent and a dependent variable, and the distinction between social and spatial density has infrequently been noted.

Most researchers agree that crowding describes a psychological response to high population density which is often viewed as stressful (Altman, 1978; Paulus, 1988). Although high population density is a necessary condition for crowding, it is not a sufficient condition, and other variables may be required to produce the perception of crowding. Sundstrom (1978) described crowding as a sequential process resulting from an interaction of person variables, high population density, correlates of high density (e.g., increased noise levels), and situational variables (e.g., duration of exposure).

Following Sundstrom's (1978) model, we would expect that the behaviors observed under high population densities would vary in intensity and variety with length of exposure. For example, under brief exposure we may see elevated blood pressure, followed by reports of anxiety as exposure increases, and ending with violent behavioral outbursts under prolonged exposures. To test this hypothesis, a longitudinal design is required, and, to the best of our knowledge, there is only one study that has approximated this goal (Ostfeld, Kasl, D'Atri & Fitzgerald, 1987). Indirect support of the model may be gathered from comparisons of the relative strength of the relationships between population density and a variety of outcomes. That is, we would expect that reports of physiological and psychological stress would be relatively easy to come by and that the findings would be robust, whereas observations of violent behavior would be more infrequent and equivocal.

To explore this model, we undertook both a qualitative and quantitative review of the prison crowding literature. Studies that provided sufficient statistical information on the relationship between population density and the dependent variable were subject to a meta-analysis. The dependent variable was arranged into three categories: physiological, psychological, and behavioral. Some studies reported more than one measure within a category. In these situations, we gave priority to systolic blood pressure for the physiological category, a paper-and-pencil measure of perceived crowding described by Paulus (1988) for the psychological category, and misconduct for the behavioral category. These measures were the most frequently used. We would have liked to categorize the measures of crowding into aggregate, social, and spatial density, but to have done so would have drastically reduced our samples in each cell.

The strength of the relationship, or effect size, was measured by Cohen's d (1977) and calculated using the statistical conversion formulas described by Glass, McGaw, and Smith (1981). In our analysis, d indicated the size of the difference in standard units between crowded and noncrowded conditions. Standardizing the measures (d) allowed us to compare results from different studies. For studies that reported nonsignificant results, d was set at zero. The results of this meta-analysis are shown in Table 4.1.

As can be seen from Table 4.1, physiological and psychological stress responses (Outcomes A and B) were very likely under crowded prison conditions. The majority of studies employing such measures found significant results. The one inconsistent finding was the *inverse* relationship between crowding and blood pressure ($d = -.70$) reported by McCain, Cox, and Paulus (1980). This may have been a spurious result because there was no relationship between blood pressure and crowding for the institution in question for the previous year (1978). If this size effect is removed from the calculation of the mean, then we obtain a mean of $d = .51$ for Outcome A, which is quite consistent with the model. In the case of behavioral acting-out, the strength of the relationship diminished to the point of being relatively insignificant as the studies ranged in effect size from -.90 to +.87.

While the results outlined under Outcomes A and B seem straightforward, some clarification is required. That is, although physiological stress in response to population density was the rule, reports of psychological stress concomitant with physiological stress were not always observed and, for the most part, rarely studied. When the two were observed together, the relationship was usually dependent upon other variables. In 1973, Paulus, McCain, and Cox reported (no data were presented) that social density was related to a physiological measure of stress (palm sweat) but not to a subjective appraisal of feeling crowded. However, in a subsequent study (Paulus, Cox, McCain & Chandler, 1975), which considered length of exposure, there was an increased perception of feeling crowded for inmates in dormitories (high social density) but not for inmates in cells (low social density). Other studies have noted the moderating effect of length of exposure on physiological and psychological measures of stress (D'Atri, 1975; D'Atri, Fitzgerald, Kasl & Ostfeld, 1981; Paulus, McCain & Cox, 1978, 1981; McCain, Cox & Paulus, 1976).

Table 4.1. Effect Size of Outcome for Prison Crowding*

Study	Sample	A	B	C
			Outcome	
D'Atri (1975)	34 adults (M)	1.19		
D'Atri & Ostfeld (1975)	91 adults (M)	1.06		
	126 adults (M)	1.05		
D'Atri et al. (1981)	37 adults (M)	.79		
Ostfeld et al. (1987)	128 adults (M)	.54	n.s.	
McCain et al. (1976)	64 adults (M)		.53	
Paulus et al. (1975)	121 adults (M)		.34	
McCain et al. (1980)	206 adults (M)	n.s.		
	183 adults (M)	n.s.	.82	
	87 adults (M)	-.70		
	121 adults (M)	n.s.		
	212 adults (M/F)		.51	
Ray et al. (1982)	115 juveniles (M)	n.s.		
Ruback & Carr (1984)	561 adults (F)			.37
Jan (1980)	4 adult prisons (M/F)			.43
Megargee (1977)	1 adult prison (M)			.87
Nacci et al. (1977)	37 adult prisons (M/F)			.47
Bonta & Kiem (1978)	1 adult prison (M)			n.s.
Bonta & Nanckivell (1980)	1 adult prison (M)			-.52
Clayton & Carr (1984)	21,500 adults (?)			n.s.
	1,203 adults (?)			.70
Porporino & Dudley (1984)	24 adult prisons (M)			-.90
Ekland-Olson et al. (1983)	14 adult prisons (M/F)			n.s.
N of studies		10	5	11
Means		.39	.44	.13
SD		.62	.30	.52

*A = Physiological measures (blood pressure, heart rate); B = Psychological measures (reports of crowding, discomfort); C = Behavioral measures (assaults, misconducts). Samples may employ male (M) or female (F) inmates or both (M/F). Sometimes the composition of the sample was unclear (?).

In the one longitudinal study reported in the literature, Ostfeld and his colleagues (1987) followed 128 inmates through their incarceration to release and post-release. Physiological and psychological measures were taken at regular intervals and controls were introduced for other confounding variables such as weight and criminal history. They found changes in blood pressure associated with population density but no statistically significant changes for anxiety, hostility, and depression.

These studies, nevertheless, suggested a positive relationship between social density and physiological indicators of stress and subjective reports of discomfort. Indications of physiological stress appear as immediate consequences to high social density, and it is possible that with increased exposure to such a situation other cumulative consequences such as psychological distress may follow (Paulus et al., 1975).

It is most important, however, from a policy perspective, to evaluate whether population density is related to severe, disruptive behavior that may jeopardize the physical safety of the inmates. The findings as shown in Table 4.1 do not support an overall relationship between crowding and disruptive inmate behavior.

Megargee (1977) was the first to empirically study the relationship between crowding and reported disciplinary infractions. He collected data over a three-year span at a medium security prison for youthful offenders (aged 18 to 25). Spatial density was more highly correlated with institutional misconduct than was social density, but social interaction factors (e.g., friendship ties) may have played an important role. Density, without distinction to spatial or social density, and disciplinary infractions are, according to some investigators, positively related (Cox, Paulus & McCain, 1984; Jan, 1980; Nacci, Teitelbaum & Prather, 1977; Paulus, McMain & Cox, 1971, 1981; Ruback & Carr, 1984), but no such association was found by others (Bonta & Kiem, 1978; Bonta & Nanckivell, 1980; Clayton & Carr, 1984; Ekland-Olson, Barrick & Cohen, 1983; Porporino & Dudley, 1984).

From our appraisal of the empirical literature we cannot conclude that high population density is always associated with aggressive behavior. Most researchers agree that other variables play important moderating roles (Bonta, 1986; Cox et al., 1984; Ellis, 1984). One important moderator variable is age of the inmates. The relationship between misconduct and population density has been more pronounced in institutions housing young offenders (Ekland-Olson et al., 1983; Jan, 1980; Megargee, 1977; Nacci et al., 1977). Even in studies that failed to uncover a general positive relationship, the introduction of age as a moderator showed a correlation between population density and misconduct (Bonta & Kiem, 1978; Bonta & Nanckivell, 1980; Clayton & Carr, 1984; Ekland-Olson et al., 1983). In the Ekland-Olson et al. study (1983), when institutions with a relatively young population (median age of 27) were selected for analysis, a highly significant correlation was found ($r = .58$ or a $d = 1.43$). The authors concluded that age is a much better predictor of disciplinary infractions than prison size.

Only one study (Gaes & McGuire, 1985) discounts the importance of age. Gaes and McGuire (1985) assessed a variety of predictors along with age and under these conditions age became relatively less important. The authors observed that most studies of overcrowding and misconduct typically assess few variables and may overestimate the importance of any one variable.

Interpreting the behavioral consequences of prison overcrowding is further confounded by the use of aggregate level data. As Table 4.1 clearly shows, almost all the studies under Outcome C are aggregate level data. The problem with this level of analysis is that many other factors (e.g., age, release policies) may play more important roles than population density. Clayton and Carr (1987) have shown that aggregate data analysis overestimates the relationship between crowding and behavior (a point already made in the preceding paragraph). In their study investigating the relationship between prison overcrowding and recidivism (2 years post-release), age was the critical variable. The only other study that used recidivism as an outcome measure was by Farrington and Nuttall (1980), and they found a significant relationship between crowding and post-release recidivism. However, Gaes (1983) has suggested that other extraneous variables (e.g., age, staff-inmate ratios) could better account for the results.

Although age has consistently been identified as an important moderating variable, explanations of why this is so have not been carefully researched. Are the young simply impulsive, lacking in coping skills, and more easily susceptible to stress? MacKenzie (1987) found oppositional or "assertive" attitudes and fear of victimization rather than coping ability as most relevant to misconducts. Clearly further research on this issue is desirable.

The identification of person variables as moderators in the experience of prison crowding raises the enduring issue of importation versus deprivation. That is, are the behaviors observed in prison reflective of behavioral patterns that were present prior to incarceration or a response to the deprivation of liberties imposed by confinement? As Freedman (1975) wrote, "crowding has neither good nor bad effects but rather serves to intensify the individual's typical reactions to a situation" (1975:89). Thus, the disciplinary infractions observed in crowded prisons may be the result of either high population densities or a continuation of behaviors that existed before incarceration, or both. As Ruback and Innes (1988) have remarked, there are no studies that have partitioned inmates with violent histories from nonviolent inmates. This is very important because it is usually the maximum security settings that are crowded, and they are also the settings most likely to house violent inmates. The possibility of an interaction can be seen in Smith's (1982) account of how assertive inmates became more aggressive and the passive inmates more submissive under crowded conditions.

There are other factors, besides person variables, that may influence aggressive behavior in crowded prisons. For instance, crowded prisons may be poorly managed (Gaes, 1985). Although prison populations may fluctuate widely, corresponding changes in the number of supervisory staff, counselors, and programs rarely occur. When the population is large, there are fewer correctional staff to monitor behavior and provide inmates with the opportunities to learn adaptive coping skills. The management of prisons and prison systems may account for some inmate disturbances. A case in point is the occurrence of sudden changes in the population membership (Ellis, 1984). Porporino and Dudley (1984), in reviewing evidence from 24 Canadian penitentiaries, found high inmate turnover more important than population density in the prediction of inmate disruptions. The authors speculated that inmates are required to deal with newly arrived inmates more frequently and this may be extremely stressful. For example, in the 1980 New Mexico prison riot, the inmate population was not at its peak but there was a sudden influx of new inmates in the months preceding the riot (Colvin, 1982).

Another factor appears to be the chronicity of the situation (Megargee, 1977). That is, as sentence length or exposure to crowded situations increases so does the risk for misconduct (Bonta & Nanckivell, 1980; Nacci et al., 1977). This is a tentative conclusion because of other confounding factors such as age and type of institution (Jan, 1980; Paulus, 1988).

In summary, crowded prisons may produce physiological and psychological stress among many inmates. More disruptive effects, however, depend upon moderating person variables such as age, institutional parameters (e.g., sudden shifts in the inmate membership), and the chronicity of the situation. In addition, aggressive behavior may be a cumulative effect of high population densities. More research into the parameters that govern this effect is required.

Two theoretical models have been advanced in an effort to explain the inmate's response to prison overcrowding. The social-interaction demand model favored by Paulus and his colleagues (Cox et al., 1984; Paulus, 1988) assumes that social interactions interfere with goal attainment and increase uncertainty and cognitive load. That is, it is the nature of the social interactions that may produce negative effects and high population densities are important only to the degree that they affect social interactions. The second model is based on a cognitive social-learning model (Bonta, 1986; Ellis, 1984; see also Cox, Paulus & McCain for a critique of this model).

This latter model places greater emphasis on individual differences (person variables) and stresses two processes: attribution and learned coping behavior. Increases in population density produce changes not only in social interactions but also changes in noise level, temperature, etc., and these in turn produce physiological arousal. When inmates attribute this arousal to violation of their personal space rather than some other factor they then report feeling crowded. Once the attribution is made, existing coping behaviors are activated with the goal to reduce arousal and feelings of crowding.

Except for MacKenzie's (1987) findings, penal researchers have found that coping behavior plays a significant role in the inmates' response to incarceration and that inmates vary in the effectiveness of their coping behaviors (cf. Zamble & Porporino, 1990). Clements (1979) has suggested that coping behavior may be influential in the inmates' adaptation to prison overcrowding, although some of these behaviors, such as assault and suicide (Cox et al., 1984; Megargee, 1977), are clearly not adaptive. Unfortunately, poor coping skills are all too prevalent among inmate populations and this is reflected in their disruptive behavioral responses to high population densities. However, other behaviors can alleviate crowding-induced arousal and at the same time be adaptive. For example, classroom attendance (Jan, 1980; Lawrence, 1985) and psychological interventions (Karlin, Katz, Epstein & Woolfolk, 1979) have been shown to decrease feelings of being crowded. Besides searching for ways to control the prison population growth we can also develop programs to teach individual inmates more effective skills to cope with high prison populations.

Health Risks

As we have seen with the prison crowding literature, it is not uncommon to observe physiological and psychological distress associated with high population densities. Such outcomes are also commonly associated with stress and physical disorders. In fact, many studies of prison overcrowding will use illness complaints as a dependent measure. Thus, we now turn our attention to a related topic and ask ourselves if imprisonment threatens the health of the confined.

Most of the research has dealt with the identification and description of illnesses reported by prisoners (cf., Novick & Al-Ibrahim, 1977). Available data fail to clearly indicate whether inmates display more or less health risks than the general population. When threats to health come from suicide and self-mutilation, then inmates are clearly at risk. Though it is widely believed that the risk of homicide is greater within prison than in the community, the evidence is mixed. In Canadian penitentiaries, the homicide rates are close to 20 times that of similar-aged males in Canadian society (Porporino & Martin, 1983). In the United States, deaths due to homicide are actually less likely within prison (Ruback & Innes, 1988). With respect to self-injurious behavior, the results are more consistent. Inmate suicides for a 20-year period in the United States were at a rate of 17.5 per 100,000 inmates in contrast to 11 per 100,000 people in the general population (Austin & Unkovic, 1977). Self-mutilations are at an even higher rate (Ross & McKay, 1979).

When one examines the incidence of physical illnesses, the findings are less conclusive. One of the classic studies comes from Jones (1976) who surveyed the health risks of Tennessee prisoners and compared them where possible to probationers and data existing on the general adult male U.S. population. The patterns of results are rather complex but, by and large, a variety of health problems, injuries, and selected symptoms of psychological distress were higher for certain classes of inmates than probationers, parolees, and, where data existed, for the general population.

In contrast to Jones (1976), a number of other researchers have failed to find deleterious effects on health. Goldsmith (1972) followed 50 inmates over a two-month period and found no major health problems as assessed by physical examinations. On a larger inmate sample (N = 491), Derro (1978) found that only 12 percent of the symptoms reported on admission related to a significant illness. This is an important point because many studies "count" health care contacts without differentiating the nature of the contact. Inmates may seek the aid of health care professionals for reasons other than a physical illness.

Two studies also reported a significantly lower incidence of hypertension among inmates compared to the general population. Culpepper and Froom (1980) found the incidence of hypertension among a prison population at 6 percent. In another study (Novick, Della-Penna, Schwartz, Remlinger & Lowenstein, 1977), the incidence of hypertension among 1,300 inmates was 4.5 percent. This finding, however, relates to the effects of incarceration in general and not to specific conditions such as prison crowding where the results are different (Gaes, 1985).

One of the problems with the interpretation of the above data has been that there is so little use of adequate control groups especially with respect to age and race (see Ruback & Innes, 1988 for a notable exception). Also, Baird (1977) found that many prisoners with physical complaints were displaying a variety of health risks well *before* incarceration. As a case in point, Bentz and Noel (1983) found that upon entering prison, inmates were reporting a higher incidence of psychiatric disorder than a sample of a rural population in North Carolina. This finding is also of interest in light of Gibbs' (1987) claim that incarceration aggravates psychological symptomatology (we will elaborate on this in the discussion on short-term detention).

A final consideration is that many prisons may actually be conducive to good health. In a number of cases, illness complaints have either decreased with time served (MacKenzie & Goodstein, 1985) or remained unchanged (Wormith, 1986). In most prisons, inmates have regular and nutritious diets, access to recreational exercise, and opportunity to sleep. Furthermore, offenders can obtain fairly immediate health care. Because of this last possibility, health risks could easily be overreported in prisons with extensive health services and thus bias some of the research findings.

In summary, the current findings recall Glueck and Glueck's (1950) comparison of 500 delinquents with 500 nondelinquents: In training school, the boys were generally healthy and physically fit, whereas in the community, as a result of their adventurous lifestyles, they were prone to more serious accidents. More than 35 years later, Ruback and Innes (1988) make this same observation based upon information from adult inmates. Thus, as far as physical health is concerned, imprisonment may have the fortuitous benefit of isolating the offender from a highly risky lifestyle in the community.

Long-Term Incarceration

In 1984 there were approximately 1,500 offenders serving life sentences in Canadian prisons (Wormith, 1984) and with recent legislation defining minimum sentences (25 years) without parole for first and second degree murder, those numbers are expected to increase significantly. Similar trends have also been noted in the United States, where mandatory and lengthy prison terms have been widely implemented (cf., Cullen & Gilbert, 1982). What happens to these people as a result of such lengthy sentences? Most of the research has focused upon time spans not longer than 2 or 3 years, and our knowledge regarding offenders serving sentences of 5, 10, or more years is less adequate.

Using cross-sectional designs, Heskin and his colleagues measured inmates' performances on cognitive tests (Banister, Smith, Heskin & Bolton, 1973), personality measures (Heskin, Smith, Banister & Bolton, 1973), and attitudinal scales (Heskin, Bolton, Smith & Banister, 1974). Four groups of prisoners, all sentenced to at least 10 years, were studied. The average time served was 2.5 years for the first group of inmates, 4.9 years for the second group, 6.9 years for the third, and 11.3 for the fourth group. No differences were found among the groups in intellectual performance, although there was a decline in perceptual motor speed on the cognitive tasks (Banister et al., 1973). On the personality and attitudinal tests, there were increases in hostility and social introversion (Heskin et al., 1973) and decreases in self-evaluations and evaluations of work and father (Heskin et al., 1974).

Subsequently, Bolton, Smith, Heskin, and Banister (1976) retested 154 of the original 175 inmates in the Heskin research (average retest interval was 2 years). Their findings showed no evidence of psychological deterioration. In fact, verbal intelligence improved over time and hostility decreased. The findings with respect to hostility are in contrast to the cross-sectional studies, but, as the authors noted, there was a significant drop-out rate. Furthermore, the initial testing occurred during a period of institutional tensions, which may have produced artificially high hostility scores.

Sapsford (1978) administered a psychometric test battery to 60 prisoners sentenced to life imprisonment. The prisoners formed three groups: (1) reception (newly received), (2) middle (6th year of sentence), and (3) hard core (average sentence served was 14 years). Some matching was attempted but it is not clear the extent to which the procedure was successful. From the results, only three inmates could be described as having failed to cope with their sentence. The only deteriorating effects observed were increases in dependency upon staff for direction and social introversion. In fact, depression and anxiety were lower for inmates serving longer sentences.

Reed's (1978) geriatric prisoner research also has relevance to the issue. His aged prisoners (mean age of 60 years), with an average sentence served of 23 years, reported fewer life problems than their peers in the outside community. Furthermore, they reported active interests and feeling younger than their age.

Similarly, Richards (1978) also failed to note negative differences between British prisoners who had served at least 8 years of their sentence and inmates who had served more than 10 years. The two groups were matched on age at sentencing and type of offense. The inmates were asked to rate the frequency and severity of 20 different problems that may be initiated by incarceration (e.g., missing social life, sexual frustration). The results showed no differences in the perception of problems by the two groups, and there was agreement by the inmates that coping could be best accomplished by relying on "myself."

Utilizing Richard's (1978) problem-ranking task, Flanagan (1980a) assessed American inmates who had served at least 5 years and compared his results to those reported by Richards (1978). He found that the American inmates perceived similar problems to those reported by the British prisoners in that they also did not perceive the problems as particularly threatening to their mental health. Furthermore, they preferred to cope with their sentences on their own rather than seek the aid of others. In another study, Flanagan (1980b) compared misconduct rates of 701 short-term prisoners (less than 5 years) and 765 long-term inmates. Even after controlling for age, the misconduct rate among the long-term inmates was approximately one-half that of the short-term offenders.

Rasch (1981) assessed lifers who had served 3, 8.5, and 13.5 years and found no deterioration in health, psychiatric symptoms, or intellect. The results of MMPI testing documented decreased pathology over time, replicating Sapsford's (1980) findings. Another German study, cited by Wormith (1984a), apparently found similar results. Moreover, when long-term inmates (20 years) displayed pathology, such behaviors were apparent long before incarceration.

A series of studies conducted by Wormith (1984; 1986) observed a differential impact from long-term incarceration. In the first study (Wormith, 1984), 269 inmates who had served from one month to 10 years were administered a psychometric test battery. Once again those inmates who had served the most time displayed significantly less deviance. This relationship remained even after the introduction of controls for sentence length, age upon admission, and race. Improvement over time was also noted on attitudinal measures and nonpathological personality characteristics. Finally, changes in intelligence did not vary with length of incarceration.

The second study by Wormith (1986) consisted of a random sample of 634 male prisoners stratified according to sentence length and time served. Long-term inmates (8 years to life), compared to short-term inmates, demonstrated better adjustment on measures of self-reports of emotions and attitudes (e.g., anger) and institution discipline. On measures of criminal sentiments, long-term offenders displayed a U-shaped function while short-term offenders became more antisocial. As expected, long-term inmates had deteriorating community relationships over time but made greater use of institutional programs (e.g., education), which was likely important for a successful adaptation to prison life.

MacKenzie and Goodstein (1985) reported findings similar to those described by Wormith (1984; 1986). Long-term inmates (more than 6 years served) found the earlier portion of their sentences more stressful, but with time they learned to cope effectively. Of particular interest was their differentiation of two subgroups of long-term offenders. Using prison experience as a discriminating factor, they identified two groups, inmates with minimal prison experience (lifers) and inmates with extensive prison experience (habituals). Both groups showed the same adjustment patterns, contrary to the expectation that habituals would evidence disruptive behaviors. Similar findings with respect to female offenders have also been reported by MacKenzie, Robinson, and Campbell (1989). In fact, long-term inmates were more bothered by boredom and lack of activities than by anxiety.

Most of the above studies have been cross-sectional. A publication by Zamble and Porporino (1990) on how inmates cope with prison assumes importance for two reasons. First, it is longitudinal. Of their sample (N = 133), 30 percent were serving sentences of more than 10 years. They were assessed within one month of admission and one and one-half years later. Zamble and Porporino found no *overall* indication of deterioration of coping skills over time, even for inmates serving their first incarceration. As well, there was no increase in identification with "criminal others" and their "view of the world" did not change. The authors surmise that as prisons, by and large, constrain behavior and do little to encourage changes in behavior one way or the other, inmates typically undergo a "behavioral deep freeze." The outside-world behaviors that led the offender into trouble prior to imprisonment remain until release.

Secondly, it is important to emphasize that Zamble and Porporino do not in the least deny the fact that individual differences are meaningful. They reported that how some inmates coped with incarceration correlated with postprison recidivism. For example, some of the significant factors were changes in perceptions of prison life, degree and type of socialization with incarcerated peers, planning for the future, and motivation regarding work and educational goals. We will return to this point later.

In summary, from the available evidence on the dimensions measured, there is little to support the conclusion that long-term imprisonment necessarily has detrimental effects. As a caution, however, Flanagan (1982) claims that lifers may change upon other dimensions that have yet to be objectively measured. For example, family separation issues and vocational skill training needs present unique difficulties for long-term inmates (Wilson & Vito, 1988). Unfortunately, cross-sectional designs and, until recently, small subject populations have been characteristic of these studies.

Solitary Confinement

In Jackson's (1983) scathing denouncement of the use of solitary confinement for prisoners, he wrote that solitary confinement is "the most individual destructive, psychologically crippling and socially alienating experience that could conceivably exist within the borders of the country" (1983:243). The commonly accepted definition of prison solitary confinement is maximum security lock-up, usually for punitive reasons. Sensory stimulation is very limited. The inmate may have a book to read and access to one half hour of "recreation" (alone). Conditions of prison solitary confinement should not be confused with other forms of protective segregation (cf., Gendreau, Wormith & Tellier, 1985) where admission is usually voluntary, and the inmate has access to programming, TV, and so forth. No doubt, if any prison experience is evidence of cruel and unusual punishment, then surely that experience is prison solitary.

In contrast to the popular notions of solitary's negative effects, there exists extensive experimental literature on the effects of placing people (usually volunteer college students) in solitary, or conditions of sensory deprivation, which has been ignored in the penology literature. It should be noted that the conditions in some of the sensory deprivation experiments are more severe than those found in prison solitary (cf., Gendreau & Bonta, 1984). In fact, this literature (cf., Suedfield, 1980; Zubek, 1969) has much relevance to prison solitary confinement. Considerable research has also been undertaken with prisoners themselves (Gendreau & Bonta, 1984), and many of these studies are, methodologically, the most rigorous of all the prison studies. Therefore, conclusions drawn from this source are especially informative.

Experimental studies (Ecclestone, Gendreau & Knox, 1974; Gendreau, Freedman, Wilde & Scott, 1968, 1972; Gendreau, Horton, Hooper, Freedman, Wilde & Scott, 1968; Gendreau, McClean, Parsons, Drake & Ecclestone, 1970; Walters, Callaghan & Newman, 1963) have found few detrimental effects for subjects placed in solitary confinement for periods up to 10 days. All but one of these studies employed random assignment and most employed a double blind assessment of dependent variables. Perceptual and motor abilities were not impaired, physiological levels of stress were lower than for the control groups, and various attitudes toward the environment and the self did not worsen. Individual differences have also been observed. Experience with prison life, conceptual ability, anxiety, diurnal adrenal levels, and EEG patterns were related to some of the results reports, although it should be noted that results are based upon very small sample sizes. Some of the experimental studies even reported beneficial results (cf., Suedfield, 1980). In certain respects, the prison literature (Gendreau et al., 1972) is quite consistent with the experimental sensory deprivation laboratory data (e.g., Suedfield, 1980; Zubek, Shepard & Milstein, 1970).

In contrast to the studies that used volunteer subjects, Weinberg (1967) looked at 20 inmates who were involuntarily placed for 5 days in solitary confinement. Using measures such as cognitive and personality tests, language usage, and time estimation, he, too, found no deleterious effects. Suedfield, Ramirez, and Baker-Brown (1982), also studying inmates involuntarily in solitary confinement, also failed to find detrimental effects. Their data were collected from five prisons in Canada and the United States, and they found that, in general, inmates found the first 72 hours the most difficult but after that they adjusted quite well. The authors reached this conclusion: "Our data lend no support to the claim that solitary confinement...is overwhelmingly aversive, stressful, or damaging to the inmates" (1982:335).

In contrast, Cormier and Williams (1966) and Grassian (1983) recorded signs of pathology for inmates incarcerated in solitary for periods up to one year. No objective measures or control groups were used. In the former study, most of the inmates exhibited substantial pathology prior to solitary confinement. In the second study, all subjects were involved in a class action suit against their keepers at the time of the interview, and the author actively encouraged more disclosure when the inmates were not forthcoming with reports of distress. Similarly, the experimental literature on sensory deprivation demonstrates that once controls are set and expectancies are introduced, bizarre experiences, under even the most severe conditions (immobilization and sensory deprivation for 14 days), were minimal for the majority of subjects (e.g., Zubek, Bayer & Shepard, 1969).

The real culprit may not necessarily be the condition of solitary per se but the manner in which inmates have been treated. There is evidence suggesting that this is the basis for most inmates' complaints (Suedfield, 1980; Vantour, 1975). Jackson (1983) himself acceded to this fact. When inmates are dealt with capriciously by management or individual custodial officers, psychological stress can be created even in the most humane of prison environments. Therefore, solitary confinement may not be cruel and unusual punishment under the humane and time-limited conditions investigated in experimental studies or in correctional jurisdictions that have well-defined and effectively administered ethical guidelines for its use.

We must emphasize that this is *not* an argument for employing solitary and certainly not for the absurdly lengthy periods as documented by Jackson (1983). Gendreau and Bonta (1984) have outlined several research issues that urgently need to be addressed. Some of these are studies investigating individual tolerance of solitary confinement, its possible deterrent effect, and a compelling need to find alternatives to humanely restrain those who are a danger to themselves and others while incarcerated. With rare exceptions (Barak-Glantz, 1983), the necessary research has not been conducted.

Short-Term Detention

In 1972, nearly 4,000 jails in the United States processed one million male and female offenders per year (Miller, 1978). The offenders were charged with a variety of crimes and approximately 75 percent of them were awaiting trial. Despite the extensive use of jails, little is known about the effects of short-term detention. Perhaps this is the area that requires most attention, as it is the initial adjustment phases that are important in assessing the impact of incarceration. For example, 50 percent of suicides occur in the first 24 hours of imprisonment (Hayes, 1983).

A common belief is that waiting for trial and sentencing produces a considerable amount of anxiety (Cholst, 1979; Dy, 1974; Gibbs, 1982; Schneider, 1979). More specifically, anxiety increases as the trial and sentencing dates approach and then decreases after sentencing when the uncertainty surrounding trial has passed.

A study by Dyer (reported in Krug, Scheier & Cattell, 1976) is difficult to evaluate because of the lack of information provided. Dyer administered an anxiety scale to adolescent females and found a decrease in anxiety over time in detention. However, no information regarding the number of subjects, the setting, and the interval between tests was provided. Oleski (1977) administered the same scale to 60 male inmates (ages 18 to 26) in a Boston city jail. All were awaiting trial and all had limited prior prison experience. The tests were administered one week after admission and again eight weeks later. Anxiety levels were found to be higher at posttest.

Bonta and Nanckivell (1980) administered the same anxiety scale used in the previous studies to four groups of inmates selected without age and court status limitations. Group 1 inmates were remanded into custody and sentenced by the time they were retested. Group 2 were still awaiting sentencing. Group 3 inmates entered the jail already sentenced, and Group 4 was a control group for the effects of testing. The test was administered within one week of reception and again three to four weeks later. No changes in anxiety over time or after sentencing were observed.

Gibbs (1987) assessed psychopathology among 339 jail inmates. The inmates were asked to rate symptoms prior to incarceration, 72 hours into confinement, and again 5 days later. He found symptoms to increase between pre-incarceration and 72 hours of imprisonment and interpreted this finding as showing that detention per se affects symptoms. However, the interpretation is not entirely convincing. First of all, symptomatology prior to incarceration was based upon the inmates' recollections of their difficulties before detention and thus subject to memory and reporting biases. Second, at the 5-day retest, symptoms actually diminished, and third, the finding that those without prior hospitalizations did worse was a puzzling finding and not consistent with the prison as stress model.

There is another intriguing, albeit tangential, aspect to the short-term detention literature, and that is the use of short-term detention as a deterrent. Three common strategies are "Scared Straight," "boot camp," and shock probation programs. The assumption is that prison life is aversive in some form or other and that exposure to it will decrease the probability of future criminal behavior, particularly for young, impressionable offenders.

The classic evaluation of "Scared Straight" by Finckenauer and Storti (1978) found only one of nine attitudinal measures significantly changed for juveniles as a result of brief exposure to hardened prisoners and no reduction in recidivism (Finckenauer, 1979). Other variations on the original program have also found no overall deterrent effect (Buckner & Chesney-Lind, 1983; Lewis, 1983), although some individual differences were noted. Similarly, there is now general consensus that shock probation (i.e., short prison terms prior to probation) has also failed to demonstrate significant deterrent effects (Boudouris & Turnbull, 1985; Friday & Peterson, 1973; Vito, 1984). There is even one report (Vito, Holmes & Wilson, 1985) suggesting that shock probation for a subgroup of probationers increased recidivism!

Some jurisdictions have received media attention by employing quasimilitary, boot camp regimes for offenders. In the only evaluation with a follow-up that we are aware of—although more will be forthcoming in the near future (MacKenzie, personal communication)—juveniles taking part in such a program did not have reduced reconviction rates compared to nonparticipatory youths (Thornton, Curran, Grayson & Holloway, 1984). Curiously, older adolescents reported an easier time in the program compared to their previous experiences with incarceration.

Death Row

Once an issue of little importance, the pragmatics of how best to deal with inmates awaiting capital punishment is now of particular concern. The rate of death penalty commitments between 1981 and 1983 ranged from 228 to 264 per year in the United States, and these rates are expected to remain in the same range (Cheatwood, 1985). Since the rate of executions is far lower, a considerable number of offenders are on death rows waiting out lengthy appeal applications. In fact, psychiatrists are now being asked to assess the death row inmate's appreciation of the appeal process and competency for execution (Kenner, 1986). In 1985, nearly 1,500 inmates were in this situation (Cheatwood, 1985). The growing numbers have led to crowded conditions on some death rows, and, in one incident, apparently motivated two condemned prisoners to take hostages as a sign of protest (*The Citizen*, 1986).

Very little evidence is available on how inmates adjust to death row. Perhaps the first study reported is that by Bluestone and McGahee (1962). They interviewed 19 inmates (18 men and one woman) awaiting execution at Sing Sing prison. Expecting to find intense anxiety and depression, they found none. Gallemore and Panton (1972) tested eight men awaiting execution at reception and several times thereafter up to a period of two years. Five men showed no observable deterioration upon the measures employed whereas three reported symptoms ranging from paranoia to insomnia. In a further study of 34 inmates on death row, Panton (1976) compared their MMPI profiles with a large prison sample. Death row inmates showed increased feelings of depression and hopelessness. Severe disturbances (e.g., psychosis) were not observed.

Johnson (1982) interviewed 35 men on death row and found them concerned over their powerlessness, fearful of their surroundings, and feeling emotionally drained. Younger inmates were more susceptible to these concerns. However, no comparison group was employed and the prevalence of these feelings among inmates in general is unknown.

Smith and Felix (1986) conducted unstructured psychiatric interviews of 34 death row inmates. Most of their sample exhibited well-intact defenses regarding their alleged guilt. Only seven inmates evidenced a depressed mood and might have required further counseling intervention. Debro, Murty, Roebuck, and McCann (1987) interviewed 25 death row inmates and found that *all* slept well and felt relatively good about themselves. None requested or received tranquilizers. Finally, in a rare study of death row inmates who had their sentences commuted to life imprisonment, 23 inmates (46%) showed no change in personality functioning as measured by the MMPI (Dahlstrom, Panton, Bain & Dahlstrom, 1986). Furthermore, 18 (36%) showed an improvement while only nine (18%) deteriorated.

This literature, inadequate as it is, is meaningful for what it fails to produce—evidence of severe psychological reactions to a tragic fate. Why this is so is unclear. Some (Bluestone & McGahee, 1962; Smith & Felix, 1986) have suggested that death row inmates have particularly well-developed defense mechanisms, but this hypothesis has been based solely on subjective clinical impressions. In fact, it may be those associated with the condemned inmate (family, prison staff, etc.) that suffer more (Smykla, 1987). The limited data are a testimony to the ability of men to cope with the worst of consequences.

Summary and Conclusions

When it comes to scholarly inquiry in the field of criminal justice, a pernicious tendency has been to invoke rhetoric over reality and affirm ideology over respect for empirical evidence. We have witnessed this sad state of affairs in the debates over the effectiveness of rehabilitation, personality and crime, and the relationship between social class and criminal behavior (Andrews & Wormith, 1989; Cullen & Gendreau, 1989).

If we are to make progress in understanding what it is our prisons do to inmates, then we must respect the available evidence. We do not discount the importance of phenomenology in assessing prison life; this line of inquiry does provide valuable insight (e.g., Toch, 1977). But, if we stray too far from the epistemic values that are crucial to a vigorous social science then we run the risk of making disastrous policy decisions. Therefore, if we are to have a more constructive agenda we must face the fact that simplistic notions of the "pains of imprisonment" simply will not be instructive and will mitigate against the inmate's well-being.

The facts are that long-term imprisonment and specific conditions of confinement such as solitary confinement, under limiting and humane conditions, fail to show any sort of profound detrimental effects. The crowding literature indicates that moderating variables play a crucial role. The health risks to inmates appear minimal. Unfortunately prisons, in a way, may minimize some stress by removing the need to make daily decisions that are important for community living (Zamble & Porporino, 1990).

If we approach prison life with sensitivity, however, we will foster a much more realistic and proactive research and policy agenda. Our literature review revealed considerable support for this notion. We repeatedly found that interactions between certain types of individual differences and situational components explained a meaningful percentage of the variance. To illustrate, we found that age, changes in the prison population, and the chronicity of the situation had profound influences on the responses of inmates to high population density. There also appear to be some cognitive and biological individual differences that may influence adjustment to solitary confinement.

In regard to the above, it is important that the assessment of environments reach the same level of methodological sophistication as the assessment of individuals. There have been some promising developments toward that end. Wenk and Moos (1972) have developed the Correctional Institutions Environment Scale; Toch (1977), the Prison Preference Profile; and Wright (1985), the Prison Environment Inventory. These are initial steps and it is hoped that research along these lines will continue.

Our final comments are in regard to theory development. To date, the incarceration literature has been very much influenced by a "pains of imprisonment" model. This model views imprisonment as psychologically harmful. However, the empirical data we reviewed question the validity of the view that imprisonment is *universally* painful. Solitary confinement, under limiting and humane conditions, long-term imprisonment, and short-term detention fail to show detrimental effects. From a physical health standpoint, inmates appear more healthy than their community counterparts. We have little data on the effects of death row, and the crowding literature indicates that moderating variables play a crucial role.

On a brighter note, the stress model does provide a positive agenda for ameliorative action. In the long-term incarceration literature, researchers (Zamble, 1989; Zamble & Porporino, 1988, 1990) have found that some inmates cope successfully with prison but others do not and that the type of coping is modestly related to future recidivism. Furthermore, on the basis of their analysis, if emotional distress is reported by inmates, it is more often early on in their incarceration. It is at this point that they may be receptive to treatment. The implications for the timing of prison-based treatment programs is obvious. The crucial point is that on the basis of this evidence, we can now develop a variety of cognitive-behavioral and/or skills training programs that could assist prisoners in dealing with their experiences in the most constructive manner possible. There is accumulating and persuasive evidence, moreover, that certain types of offender programming strategies in prison can reduce subsequent recidivism (Andrews, Zinger, Hoge, Bonta, Gendreau & Cullen, 1989). This proactive agenda, we wish to emphasize, was not forthcoming from those who viewed prisons as invariably destructive. Unfortunately, their recommendations were for almost total deinstitutionalization, which is not only an extreme view, but also one that is totally unpalatable given North American cultural values and the current sociopolitical reality (see Currie, 1985; Glazer, 1989).

In our view, a social learning perspective (cf. Bandura, 1977) provides a more comprehensive explanation of the evidence. Social learning theory examines behavior (attitudes, motor actions, emotions) as a function of the rewards and punishments operating in a prison environment. There is an explicit acceptance of person variables moderating the responsivity to imprisonment. Several questions emerge from this perspective: *Who* perceives prisons as stressful? *What* aspect of imprisonment shapes behavior? And *how* do individuals respond to imprisonment? Answers to these questions would provide insight into the individuals who do not perceive their environments as stressful while imprisoned and what aspects of imprisonment attenuate the prison experience. In addition, this perspective would clarify the links between emotions, attitudes, and behavior.

From this review, we also see a clear research agenda. Further efforts to understand the effects of prison overcrowding should focus on individual levels of analysis along with multiple measures of the three outcome variables (emotions, attitudes, and behavior). Longitudinal designs (e.g., Zamble & Porporino, 1990) should be the rule. The inherent difficulties in interpreting aggregate level data appear only to confuse our understanding of the impact of crowded conditions on the individual. We need to know under what conditions an individual feels crowded, becomes emotionally distressed, and copes with this distress in a maladaptive manner. For example, Ruback, Carr, and Hopper (1986) suggested that perceived control is a possible mediator. The solution to prison overcrowding is not to embark on a prohibitively expensive prison construction program (Funke, 1985) but rather to alter the rate of intake and release (Skovron, 1988). One way of accomplishing this task is to increase community correctional treatment programs that would allow the diversion of inmates away from prisons (Bonta & Motiuk, 1987). Despite the reluctance of many correctional administrators to develop such programs, there appears to be considerable public support not only for community treatment initiatives (Skovron, Scott & Cullen, 1988) but for rehabilitation in general (Cullen, Skovron, Scott & Burton, 1990).

The application of longitudinal designs using data collected at the individual level is also needed in the other areas we have discussed. This is especially so with long-term imprisonment and health risks where the data suggest that if anything, the prison system may actually prevent deterioration. However, only longitudinal designs will allow us to make such a conclusion with any high degree of certainty. If future research leads us to the same conclusion, then the next step would be to identify the system contingencies that support such an environment, for certainly we can learn something positive from this type of result. Finally, and remarkably, we know so little about the psychological impact of a system that houses over one million individuals: the jails. Here, almost any type of reasoned research would be a step in the right direction.

All of the above is easier said than done. The host of issues that need to be researched seem infinite. The methodological complexities in examining both person and situation interaction are pronounced. But, it appears to us to be a positive agenda in order to gain knowledge addressing a vital question.

References

Altman, I. (1978). "Crowding: Historical and Contemporary Trends in Crowding Research." In A. Baum and M.Y.M. Epstein (eds.) *Human Response to Crowding* (pp. 3-29). Hillsdale, NJ: Erlbaum.

Andrews, D.A. and J.S. Wormith (1989). "Personality and Crime: Knowledge Destruction and Construction in Criminology." *Justice Quarterly*, 6, 289-310.

Andrews, D.A., I. Zinger, R.D. Hoge, J. Bonta, P. Gendreau and F.T. Cullen (1989). "A Clinically Relevant and Psychologically Informed Meta-Analysis of Juvenile Correctional Treatment Programs." Paper presented at the Research Seminar of National Associations Active in Criminal Justice, Ottawa.

Angelos, C. and J.B. Jacobs (1985). "Prison Overcrowding and the Law." *The Annals*, 478, 100-112.

Austin, W.T. and C.M. Unkovic (1977). "Prison Suicide." *Criminal Justice Review*, 2, 103-106.

Baird, J.A. (1977). "Health Care in Correctional Facilities." *Journal of the Florida Medical Association*, 64, 813-818.

Bandura, A. (1977). *Social Learning Theory*. Englewood Cliffs, NJ: Prentice-Hall.

Banister, P.A., F.V. Smith, J.J. Heskin and N. Bolton (1973). "Psychological Correlates of Long-Term Imprisonment: I. Cognitive Variables." *British Journal of Criminology*, 13, 312-323.

Barak-Glantz, I.L. (1983). "Who's in the 'Hole'?" *Criminal Justice Review*, 8, 29-37.

Bentz, W.K. and R.W. Noel (1983). "The Incidence of Psychiatric Disorder Among a Sample of Men Entering Prison." *Corrective & Social Psychiatry and Journal of Behavior Technology*, 29, 22-28.

Bluestone, H. and C.L. McGahee (1962). "Reaction to Extreme Stress: Impending Death by Execution." *American Journal of Psychiatry*, 119, 393-396.

Bolton, N., F.V. Smith, K.J. Heskin and P.A. Banister (1976). "Psychological Correlates of Long-Term Imprisonment: IV. A Longitudinal Analysis." *British Journal of Criminology*, 16, 36-47.

Bonta, J. (1986). "Prison Crowding: Searching for the Functional Correlates." *American Psychologist*, 41, 99-101.

Bonta, J. and T. Kiem (1978). "Institutional Misconducts in a Jail Setting: Preliminary Findings and a Note of Caution." *Crime and Justice*, 6, 175-178.

Bonta, J. and L.L. Motiuk (1987). "The Diversion of Incarcerated Offenders to Correctional Halfway Houses." *Journal of Research in Crime and Delinquency*, 24, 302-323.

Bonta, J. and G. Nanckivell (1980). "Institutional Misconducts and Anxiety Levels Among Jailed Inmates." *Criminal Justice and Behavior*, 7, 203-214.

Boudouris, J. and B.W Turnbull (1985). "Shock Probation in Iowa." *Offender Counseling, Services, and Rehabilitation*, 9, 53-61.

Buckner, J.C. and M. Chesney-Lind (1983). "Dramatic Cures for Juvenile Crime: An Evaluation of a Prison-Run Delinquency Prevention Program." *Criminal Justice and Behavior*, 10, 227-247.

Bukstel, L.H. and P.K. Kilmann (1980). "Psychological Effects of Imprisonment on Confined Individuals." *Psychological Bulletin*, 88, 469-493.

Call, J.E. (1983). "Recent Case Law on Overcrowded Conditions of Confinement." *Federal Probation*, 47, 23-32.

Cheatwood, D. (1985). "Capital Punishment and Corrections: Is There an Impending Crisis?" *Crime and Delinquency*, 31, 461-479.

Cholst, S. (1979). "The Effects of Long-Term Detention." *International Journal of Offender Therapy and Comparative Criminology*, 23, 210-213.

Citizen, The (1986). "Killers Release Hostages After Death Row Siege." (March 18).

Clayton, O. and T. Carr (1984). "The Effects of Prison Crowding Upon Infraction Rates." *Criminal Justice Review*, 9, 69-77.

Clayton, O. and T. Carr (1987). "An Empirical Assessment of the Effects of Prison Crowding Upon Recidivism Utilizing Aggregate Level Data." *Journal of Criminal Justice*, 15, 201-210.

Clements, C.B. (1979). "Crowded Prisons: A Review of Psychological and Environmental Effects." *Law and Human Behavior*, 3, 217-225.

Clements, C.B. (1982). "The Relationship of Offender Classification to the Problems of Prison Overcrowding." *Crime and Delinquency*, 28, 72-81.

Clemmer, D. (1940). *The Prison Community*. New York, NY: Rinehart.

Cohen, J. (1977). *Statistical Power Analysis for the Behavioral Sciences.* New York, NY: Academic Press.

Cohen, S. and L. Taylor (1972). *Psychological Survival.* Harmondworth, England: Penguin Books.

Colvin, M. (1982). "The New Mexico Prison Riot." *Social Problems,* 29, 449-463.

Cormier, B.M. and P.J. Williams (1966). "Excessive Deprivation of Liberty as a Form of Punishment." Paper presented at the meeting of the Canadian Psychiatric Association, Edmonton.

Corrections Digest (1986). 17, (June), 1-2.

Cox, V.C., P.B. Paulus and G. McCain (1984). "Prison Crowding Research: The Relevance of Prison Housing Standards and a General Approach Regarding Crowding Phenomena." *American Psychologist,* 39, 1148-1160.

Cox, V.C., P.B. Paulus and G. McCain (1986). "Not for Attribution: A Reply to Bonta." *American Psychologist,* 41, 101-103.

Cullen, F.T. and P. Gendreau (1989). "The Effectiveness of Correctional Rehabilitation." In L. Goodstein and D.L. MacKenzie (eds.) *The American Prison: Issues in Research Policy* (pp. 23-44). New York, NY: Plenum Publishing Corp.

Cullen, F.T. and K.E. Gilbert (1982). *Reaffirming Rehabilitation.* Cincinnati, OH: Anderson Publishing Co.

Cullen, F.T., S.E. Skovron, J.E. Scott and V.S. Burton (1990). "Public Support for Correctional Treatment: The Tenacity of Rehabilitative Ideology." *Criminal Justice and Behavior,* 17, 6-18.

Culpepper, L. and J. Froom (1980). "Incarceration and Blood Pressure." *Social Services and Medicine,* 14, 571-574.

Currie, E. (1985). *Confronting Crime: An American Challenge.* New York, NY: Pantheon Books.

Currie, E. (1989). "Confronting Crime: Looking Toward the Twenty-First Century." *Justice Quarterly,* 6, 6-26.

Dahlstrom, G.W., J.H. Panton, K.P. Bain and L.E. Dahlstrom (1986). "Utility of the Megargee-Bohn MMPI Typological Assessments: Study with a Sample of Death Row Inmates." *Criminal Justice and Behavior,* 13, 5-17.

D'Atri, D.A. (1975). "Psychophysiological Responses to Crowding." *Environment and Behavior,* 7, 237-252.

D'Atri, D.A., E.F. Fitzgerald, S.V. Kasl and A.M. Ostfeld (1981). "Crowding in Prison: The Relationship Between Changes in Housing Mode and Blood-Pressure." *Psychosomatic Medicine,* 43, 95-105.

D'Atri, D.A. and A.M. Ostfeld (1975). "Crowding: Its Effects on the Elevation of Blood Pressure in a Prison Setting." *Preventative Medicine,* 4, 550-566.

Debro, J., K. Murty, J. Roebuck and C. McCann (1987). "Death Row Inmates: A Comparison of Georgia and Florida Profiles." *Criminal Justice Review,* 12, 41-46.

Derro, R.A. (1978). "Administrative Health Evaluation of Inmates of a City-County Workhouse." *Minnesota Medicine,* 61, 333-337.

Dy, A.J. (1974). "Correctional Psychiatry and Phase Psychotherapy." *American Journal of Psychiatry*, 131, 1150-1152.

Ecclestone, J., P. Gendreau and C. Knox (1974). "Solitary Confinement of Prisoners: An Assessment of Its Effects on Inmates' Personal Constructs and Adrenalcortical Activity." *Canadian Journal of Behavioral Science*, 6, 178-191.

Ekland-Olson, S., D. Barrick and L.E. Cohen (1983). "Prison Overcrowding and Disciplinary Problems: An Analysis of the Texas Prison System." *Journal of Applied Behavioral Science*, 19, 163-176.

Ellis, D. (1984). "Crowding and Prison Violence: Integration of Research and Theory." *Criminal Justice and Behavior*, 11, 277-308.

Farrington, D.P. and C.P. Nuttall (1980). "Prison Size, Overcrowding, Prison Violence, and Recidivism." *Journal of Criminal Justice*, 8, 221-231.

Finckenauer, J.C. and J.P. Storti (1978). *Juvenile Awareness Project: Evaluation Report #1*. Newark, NJ: School of Criminal Justice, Rutgers University.

Finckenauer, J.C. (1979). *Juvenile Awareness Project: Evaluation Report #2*. Newark, NJ: School of Criminal Justice, Rutgers University.

Flanagan, T.J. (1980a). "The Pains of Long-Term Imprisonment." *British Journal of Criminology*, 20, 148-156.

Flanagan, T.J. (1980b). "Time Served and Institutional Misconduct: Patterns of Involvement in Disciplinary Infractions Among Long-Term and Short-Term Inmates." *Journal of Criminal Justice*, 8, 357-367.

Flanagan, T.J. (1982). "Lifers and Long-Termers: Doing Big Time." In R. Johnson and H. Toch (eds.) *The Pains of Imprisonment* (pp. 115-128). Beverly Hills, CA: Sage Publications.

Fox, V.G. (1985). *Introduction to Corrections*. Englewood Cliffs, NJ: Prentice-Hall.

Freedman, J.L. (1975). *Crowding and Behavior*. New York, NY: Viking Press.

Friday, P.C. and D.M. Peterson (1973). "Shock of Imprisonment: Comparative Analysis of Short-Term Incarceration as a Treatment Technique." *Canadian Journal of Criminology*, 15, 281-290.

Funke, G.S. (1985). "The Economics of Prison Crowding." *Annals of the American Academy of Political and Social Science*, 478, 86-89.

Gaes, G.G. (1983). Farrington and Nuttall's "Overcrowding and Recidivism." *Journal of Criminal Justice*, 11, 265-267.

Gaes, G.G. (1985). "The Effects of Overcrowding in Prison." In M. Tonry and N. Morris (eds.) *Crime and Justice: Vol. 6* (pp. 95-146). Chicago, IL: University of Chicago Press.

Gaes, G.G. and W.J. McGuire (1985). "Prison Violence: The Contribution of Crowding Versus Other Determinants of Prison Assault Rates." *Journal of Research in Crime and Delinquency*, 22, 41-65.

Gallemore, J.L. and J.H. Panton (1972). "Inmate Responses to Lengthy Death Row Confinement." *American Journal of Psychiatry*, 129, 81-86.

Gendreau, P. and J. Bonta (1984). "Solitary Confinement is Not Cruel and Unusual Punishment: People Sometimes Are!" *Canadian Journal of Criminology*, 26, 467-478.

Gendreau, P., N.L. Freedman, G.J.S. Wilde and G.D. Scott (1968). "Stimulation Seeking After Seven Days of Perceptual Deprivation." *Perceptual and Motor Skills*, 26, 547-550.

Gendreau, P., N.L. Freedman, G.J.S. Wilde and G.D. Scott (1972). "Changes in EEG Alpha Frequency and Evoked Response Latency During Solitary Confinement." *Journal of Abnormal Psychology*, 79, 54-59.

Gendreau, P., J.G. Horton, D.G. Hooper, J.L. Freedman, G.J.S. Wilde and G.D. Scott (1968). "Perceptual Deprivation and Perceptual Motor Skills: Some Methodological Considerations." *Perceptual and Motor Skills*, 27, 57-58.

Gendreau, P., R. McLean, T. Parsons, R. Drake and J. Ecclestone (1970). "Effects of Two Days Monotonous Confinement on Conditioned Eyelid Frequency and Topography." *Perceptual and Motor Skills*, 31, 291-293.

Gendreau, P. and R.R. Ross (1987). "Revivication of Rehabilitation: Evidence From the 1980s." *Justice Quarterly*, 4, 349-407.

Gendreau, P., S.J. Wormith and M.C. Tellier (1985). "Protective Custody: The Emerging Crisis Within Our Prisons?" *Federal Probation*, 49, 55-63.

Gibbs, J.J. (1982). "The First Cut is the Deepest: Psychological Breakdown and Survival in the Detention Setting." In R. Johnson and H. Toch (eds.) *The Pains of Imprisonment* (pp. 97-114). Beverly Hills, CA: Sage Publications.

Gibbs, J.J. (1987). "Symptoms of Psychopathology Among Jail Prisoners: The Effects of Exposure to the Jail Environment." *Criminal Justice and Behavior*, 14, 288-310.

Glass, G.V., B. McGaw and J.L. Smith (1981). *Meta-Analysis in Social Research*. Beverly Hills, CA: Sage Publications.

Glazer, S. (1989). "Can Prisons Rehabilitate?" *Congressional Quarterly's Editorial Research Report*, 2, 430-433.

Glueck, S. and E. Glueck (1950). *Unravelling Juvenile Delinquency*. New York, NY: Commonwealth Fund.

Goffman, E. (1961). *Asylums: Essays on the Social Situation of Mental Patients and Other Inmates*. Garden City, NY: Anchor Books.

Goldsmith, S.B. (1972). "Jailhouse Medicine—Travesty of Justice?" *Health Services Report*, 87, 767-774.

Goodstein, L. (1979). "Inmate Adjustment to Prison and the Transition to Community Life." *Journal of Research in Crime and Delinquency*, 16, 246-272.

Grassian, S. (1983). "Psychopathological Effects of Solitary Confinement." *American Journal of Psychiatry*, 140, 1450-1454.

Hayes, L.M. (1983). "And Darkness Closed In...A National Study of Jail Suicides." *Criminal Justice and Behavior*, 10, 461-484.

Heskin, K.J., N. Bolton, F.V. Smith and P.A. Banister (1974). "Psychological Correlates of Long-Term Imprisonment: III. Attitudinal Variables." *British Journal of Criminology*, 14, 150-157.

Heskin, K.J., F.V. Smith, P.A. Banister and N. Bolton (1973). "Psychological Correlates of Long-Term Imprisonment: II: Personality Variables." *British Journal of Criminology*, 13, 323-330.

Irwin, J. and D.R. Cressey (1962). "Thieves, Convicts, and the Inmate Culture." *Social Problems*, 10, 142-155.

Jackson, M. (1983). *Prisons of Isolation: Solitary Confinement in Canada*. Toronto, CN: University of Toronto Press.

Jan, L.J. (1980). "Overcrowding and Inmate Behavior: Some Preliminary Findings." *Criminal Justice and Behavior*, 7, 293-301.

Johnson R. (1982). "Life Under Sentence of Death." In R. Johnson and H. Toch (eds.) *The Pains of Imprisonment* (pp. 129-145). Beverly Hills, CA: Sage Publications.

Jones, D.A. (1976). *The Health Risks of Imprisonment*. Lexington, MA: D.C. Heath.

Karlin, R.A., S. Katz, Y.M. Epstein and R.L. Woolfolk (1979). "The Use of Therapeutic Interventions to Reduce Crowding-Related Arousal: A Preliminary Investigation." *Environmental Psychology and Nonverbal Behavior*, 3, 219-227.

Kennedy, E.M. (1985). "Prison Overcrowding: The Law's Dilemma." *The Annals*, 478 (March), 113-122.

Kenner, W.D. (1986). "Competency on Death Row." *International Journal of Law and Psychiatry*, 8, 253-255.

Krug, S.E., I.H. Scheier and R.B. Cattell (1976). *Handbook for the IPAT Anxiety Scale*. Champaign, IL: Institute for Personality and Ability Testing.

Lawrence, R. (1985). "Jail Education Programs: Helping Inmates Cope with Overcrowded Conditions." *Journal of Correctional Education*, 36, 15-20.

Lewis, R.V. (1983). "Scared Straight—California Style: Evaluation of the San Quentin Squires Program." *Criminal Justice and Behavior*, 10, 204-226.

Loo, C. (1973). "Important Issues in Researching the Effects of Crowding in Humans." *Representative Research in Psychology*, 4, 219-226.

MacKenzie, D.L. (1987). "Age and Adjustment to Prison: Interactions with Attitudes and Anxiety." *Criminal Justice and Behavior*, 14, 427-447.

MacKenzie, D.L. (1989). Personal Communication, March 30.

MacKenzie, D.L. and L. Goodstein (1985). "Long-Term Incarceration Impacts and Characteristics of Long-Term Offenders: An Empirical Analysis." *Criminal Justice and Behavior*, 13, 395-414.

MacKenzie, D.L., Robinson, J.W. and C.S. Campbell (1989). "Long-Term Incarceration of Female Offenders: Prison Adjustment and Coping." *Criminal Justice and Behavior*, 16, 223-238.

McCain, G., V.C. Cox and P.B. Paulus (1976). "The Relationship Between Illness Complaints and Degree of Crowding in a Prison Environment." *Environment and Behavior*, 8, 283-290.

McCain, G., V.C. Cox and P.B. Paulus (1980). *The Effect of Prison Crowding on Inmate Behavior.* Rockville, MD: U.S. Department of Justice.

Megargee, E.I. (1977). "The Association of Population Density, Reduced Space, Uncomfortable Temperatures with Misconduct in a Prison Community." *American Journal of Community Psychology,* 5, 289-299.

Miller, E.E. (1978). *Jail Management: Problems, Programs and Perspectives.* Lexington, MA: Lexington Books.

Mitford, J. (1973). *Kind and Unusual Punishment.* New York, NY: Knopf.

Mohr, J.W. (1985). "The Long-Term Incarceration Issue: The Banality of Evil and the Pornography of Power." *Canadian Journal of Criminology,* 27, 103-112.

Nacci, P.L., H.E. Teitelbaum and H. Prather (1977). "Population Density and Inmate Misconduct Rates in the Federal Prison System." *Federal Probation,* 41, 26-31.

Novick, L.F. and M.S. Al-Ibrahim (1977). *Health Problems in the Prison Setting.* Springfield, IL: Charles C Thomas.

Novick, L.F., R. Della-Penna, M.S. Schwartz, E. Remlinger and R. Lowenstein (1977). "Health Status of the New York City Prison Population." *Medical Care,* 15, 205-216.

Oleski, M.S. (1977). "The Effect of Indefinite Pretrial Incarceration on the Anxiety Level of an Urban Jail Population." *Journal of Clinical Psychology,* 33, 1006-1008.

Ostfeld, A.M., S.V. Kasl, D.A. D'Atri and E.F. Fitzgerald (1987). *Stress, Crowding, and Blood Pressure in Prison.* Hillsdale, NJ: Erlbaum.

Panton, J.H. (1976). "Personality Characteristics of Death Row Prison Inmates." *Journal of Clinical Psychology,* 32, 306-309.

Paulus, P.B. (1988). *Prison Crowding: A Psychological Perspective.* New York, NY: Springer-Verlag.

Paulus, P., V. Cox, G. McCain and J. Chandler (1975). "Some Effects of Crowding in a Prison Environment." *Journal of Applied Social Psychology,* 5, 86-91.

Paulus, P., G. McCain and V. Cox, (1971). "Prison Standards: Some Pertinent Data on Crowding." *Federal Probation,* 45, 48-54.

Paulus, P., G. McCain and V. Cox (1973). "A Note on the Use of Prisons as Environments for Investigation of Crowding." *Bulletin of the Psychonomic Society,* 6, 427-428.

Paulus, P., G. McCain and V. Cox (1978). "Death Rates, Psychiatric Commitments, Blood Pressure, and Perceived Crowding as a Function of Institutional Crowding." *Environmental Psychology and Nonverbal Behavior,* 3, 107-116.

Porporino, F.J. and K. Dudley (1984). *Analysis of the Effects of Overcrowding in Canadian Penitentiaries.* Ottawa: Solicitor General Canada.

Porporino, F.J. and J.P. Martin (1983). *Strategies for Reducing Prison Violence.* Ottawa, CN: Solicitor General Canada.

Porporino, F.J. and E. Zamble (1984). "Coping with Imprisonment." *Canadian Journal of Criminology,* 26, 403-421.

Porporino F.J., E. Zamble and S. Higginbottom (unpublished). "Assessing Models for Predicting Risk of Criminal Recidivism." Kingstone, Ontario: Department of Psychology, Queen's University.

Rasch, W. (1981). "The Effects of Indeterminate Sentencing: A Study of Men Sentenced to Life Imprisonment." *International Journal of Law and Psychiatry,* 4, 417-431.

Ray, D.W., A.W. Wandersman, J. Ellisor and D.E. Huntington (1982). "The Effects of High Density in a Juvenile Correctional Institution." *Basic and Applied Social Psychology,* 3, 95-108.

Rector, M.G. (1982). "Prisons and Crime." *Crime and Delinquency,* 28, 505-507.

Reed, M.B. (1978). *Aging in Total Institution: The Case of Older Prisoners.* Nashville, TN: Tennessee Corrections Institute.

Richards, B. (1978). "The Experience of Long-Term Imprisonment." *British Journal of Criminology,* 18, 162-169.

Ross, R.R. and H.B. McKay (1979). *Self-Mutilation.* Lexington, MA: Lexington Books.

Ruback, R.B. and T.S. Carr (1984). "Crowding in a Women's Prison: Attitudinal and Behavioral Effects." *Journal of Applied Social Psychology,* 14, 57-68.

Ruback, R.B.,T.S. Carr and C.H. Hopper (1986). "Perceived Control in Prison: Its Relation to Reported Crowding, Stress, and Symptoms." *Journal of Applied Social Psychology,* 16, 375-386.

Ruback, R.B. and C.A. Innes (1988). "The Relevance and Irrelevance of Psychological Research: The Example of Prison Crowding." *American Psychologist,* 43, 683-693.

Sapsford, R.J. (1978). "Life Sentence Prisoners: Psychological Changes During Sentence." *British Journal of Criminology,* 18, 128-145.

Sapsford, R.J. (1983). *Life Sentence Prisoners: Reaction, Response and Change.* Milton Keynes, England: Open University Press.

Schneider, M.A. (1979). "Problems in Short-Term Correctional Settings." *International Journal of Offender Therapy and Comparative Criminology,* 23, 164-171.

Skovron, S.E. (1988). "Prison Crowding: The Dimensions of the Problem and Strategies of Population Control." In J.E. Scott and T. Hirschi (eds.) *Controversial Issues in Crime and Justice* (183-199). Newbury Park, CA: Sage Publications.

Skovron, S.E., J.E. Scott and F.T. Cullen (1988). "Prison Crowding: Public Attitudes Toward Strategies of Population Control." *Journal of Research in Crime and Delinquency,* 25, 150-169.

Smith, D.E. (1982). "Crowding and Confinement." In R. Johnson and H. Toch (eds.) *The Pains of Imprisonment* (pp. 45-62). Beverly Hills, CA: Sage Publications.

Smith, C.E. and R.R. Felix (1986). "Beyond Deterrence: A Study of Defenses on Death Row." *Federal Probation,* 50, 55-59.

Smykla, J.O. (1987). "The Human Impact of Capital Punishment: Interviews with Families of Persons on Death Row." *Journal of Criminal Justice,* 15, 331-347.

Stokols, D. (1972). "On the Distinction Between Density and Crowding." *Psychological Review*, 79, 275-279.

Suedfield, P. (1980). *Restricted Environmental Stimulation: Research and Clinical Applications*. New York, NY: Wiley.

Suedfield, P., C. Ramirez, J. Deaton and G. Baker-Brown (1982). "Reactions and Attributes of Prisoners in Solitary Confinement." *Criminal Justice and Behavior*, 9, 303-340.

Sundstrom, E. (1978). "Crowding as a Sequential Process: Review of Research on the Effects of Population Density on Humans." In A. Baum and Y.M. Epstein (eds.) *Human Response to Crowding* (pp. 31-116). Hillsdale, NJ: Erlbaum.

Sykes, G. (1958). *The Society of Captives: A Study of a Maximum Security Prison*. Princeton, NJ: Princeton University Press.

Thornton, D., L. Curran, D. Grayson and V. Holloway (1984). *Tougher Regimes in Detention Centres*. London: Prison Department, Home Office.

Toch, H. (1977). *Living in Prison: The Ecology of Survival*. New York, NY: The Free Press.

United States. (1988). *Report to the Nation on Crime and Justice*. Washington, DC: Bureau of Justice Statistics.

Vantour, J.A. (1975). *Report of the Study Group on Dissociation*. Ottawa, CN: Solicitor General Canada.

Vito, G.F. (1984). "Developments in Shock Probation: A Review of Research Findings and Policy Implications." *Federal Probation*, 48, 22-27.

Vito, G.F., R.M. Holmes and D.G. Wilson (1985). "The Effect of Shock and Regular Probation Upon Recidivism: A Comparative Analysis." *American Journal of Criminal Justice*, 9, 152-162.

Walker, N. (1983). "Side Effects of Incarceration." *British Journal of Criminology*, 23, 61-71.

Waller, I. (1974). *Men Released from Prison*. Toronto: University of Toronto Press.

Walters, R.H., J.E. Callaghan and A.F. Newman (1963). "Effects of Solitary Confinement on Prisoners." *American Journal of Psychiatry*, 119, 771-773.

Weinberg, M.M. (1967). "Effects of Partial Sensory Deprivation on Involuntary Subjects." Unpublished doctoral dissertation, Michigan State University.

Wenk, E.A. and R.H. Moos (1972). "Social Climates in Prison: An Attempt to Conceptualize and Measure Environmental Factors in Total Institutions." *Journal of Research in Crime and Delinquency*, 9, 134-148.

Wilson, D.G. and G.F. Vito (1988). "Long-Term Inmates: Special Needs and Management Considerations." *Federal Probation*, 52, 21-26.

Wormith, J.S. (1984). "The Controversy Over the Effects of Long-Term Imprisonment." *Canadian Journal of Criminology*, 26, 423-437.

Wormith, J.S. (1986). "The Effects of Incarceration: Myth-Busting in Criminal Justice." Paper presented at the 94th Annual Convention of the American Psychological Association. Washington, DC, August.

Wright, K.N. (1985). "Developing the Prison Environment Inventory." *Journal of Research in Crime and Delinquency,* 22, 259-278.

Zamble, E. (1989). "Behavior Change During Long-Term Imprisonment." Paper presented at the Annual Meeting of the Canadian Psychological Association. Halifax, Nova Scotia.

Zamble, E. and F.J. Porporino (1988). *Coping Behavior and Adaptation in Prison Inmates.* New York, NY: Springer-Verlag.

Zamble, E. and F.J. Porporino (1990). "Coping, Imprisonment, and Rehabilitation: Some Data and Their Implications." *Criminal Justice and Behavior,* 17, 53-70.

Zubek, J.P. (ed.) (1969). *Sensory Deprivation: Fifteen Years of Research.* New York, NY: Appleton-Century-Crofts.

Zubek, J.P., L. Bayer and J.M. Shepard (1969). "Relative Effects of Prolonged Social Isolation and Behavioral and EEG Changes." *Journal of Abnormal Psychology,* 74, 625-631.

Zubek, J.P., J.M. Shepard and S.L. Milstein (1970). EEG Changes after 1, 4, and 7 Days of Sensory Deprivation: A Cross-Sectional Approach." *Psychonomic Science,* 19, 67-68.

Section II

Interpersonal Violence

In his classic work *Society of Captives* Gresham Sykes noted that prisoners indicated that one of the worst things about being in prison was being around other prisoners. What Sykes identified as a "deprivation of security," and Hans Toch, in *Living in Prison* refers to as an environmental concern for "safety," is psychologically and behaviorally a reflection of various forms of interpersonal victimization. The readings in this section provide descriptions and analyses of various contexts of interpersonal prison violence. Here macro-level political and cultural contexts move us beyond the "violent individual" explanations of prison violence. Such analyses allow us to situate our understanding of the behavior of individuals within the context of forces and processes that mediate between macro-level conditions and the individual behavior of both the victimizer and the victimized.

In Part A of this section various authors provide descriptions and analyses of inmate violence directed against other inmates. One theme that runs through this section is that interpersonal violence in prison takes many forms. In addition, we learn that interpersonal prison violence must be viewed as a reflection of the correctional organizations, the cultural values that are brought into prison and developed in reaction to the conditions of confinement, as well as the personal characteristics of the inmates involved in the violence.

The readings in Part B of this section explore the involvement of prison administration and staff in interpersonal prison violence. Here, issues of power and control are explored as they are manifested from the macro-level political culture within which prison administrators operate to the micro-level decisions of correctional officers deciding whether and how to respond to interpersonal violence. In addition, these readings provide analyses of themes associated with correctional staff both as targets and as perpetrators of violence.

Section II

Interpersonal Violence

A: Inmate-on-Inmate Violence

5   Scenes of Violence†

Mark Fleisher

Prison Violence

There is a great deal of research on the correlates and causes of prison violence. Surveys have been conducted in state and federal prisons, examining the roles of age (Mabli et al., 1979; MacKenzie, 1987), overcrowding (Ekland-Olson, 1986; Ellis, 1984; Farrington & Nutall, 1980; Gaes & McGuire, 1985; Nacci et al., 1977a, 1977b), boredom and idleness (Sykes, 1958; Sykes & Messinger, 1960), ethnic and racial rivalries (Carroll, 1974; Davidson, 1974; Irwin, 1980; Jacobs, 1977, 1983:61-79; Jacobs & Kraft, 1978; Sylvester et al., 1977), and sexual jealousy in generating violent behavior among convicts (Cohen, 1976:53-58; Lockwood, 1980, 1982, 1986; Nacci & Kane, 1982, 1983, 1984; Wooden & Parker, 1982). The presence of rival street gang members or of local prison gangs appears also to contribute to prison violence (Irwin, 1980; Jacobs, 1974a; Park, 1976). And of course, sociopsychological issues have been widely studied as causes of violent behavior (Toch, 1969, 1975, 1977; Toch & Adams, 1986; Toch et al., 1987; Walkey & Gilmour, 1984).

The general conclusions of all this research are that violent convicts commit violent acts; that convicts who feel powerless, mistreated, idle, bored, sexually frustrated, and cramped also commit violent acts; and that for all these reasons, prison violence will continue (Jacobs, 1976:80). Toch (1978:21) extends these views:

---

†Reprinted from *Warehousing Violence*, pp. 197-219, 1989. Reprinted by permission of Sage Publications, Inc.

There are two favored perspectives relating to prison violence. One...centers on *violent inmates*....Some inmates are consistently violent persons, who happen to be explosive in prison, but are likely to act out in almost any setting....A second portraiture conceives of inmate violence as at least partly a *prison product*. The most extreme version of this view is that of abolitionist critics who see prison aggression as a natural (and presumably, legitimate) reaction to the frustration of being locked up. Other critics also argue that prison incidents denote lax security, and thus suggest negligence. This view is to some extent shared by prison administrators, who think of controlling violence through perimeter architecture, ingenious hardware and deployment of custodial personnel. This context-centered view is a negative one, because it seeks to prevent violence by reducing the opportunities for aggression, rather than by trying to affect the motives and dispositions of violence participants.

After being personally involved in or seeing violent acts, from fistfights to homicide, and after interviewing perpetrators and victims, I have come to believe that convict violence at USP-Lompoc is at least partly the result of inmates' street culture. Inmate-on-inmate attacks were promoted most often by face-to-face rivalries, retaliation, machismo, disrespect, and drunkenness. The motivation for Lompoc's one homicide, during my research, was "political," but all other violent incidents might have occurred just as easily on the street, and for the same reasons.

Convict violence was self-rewarding behavior (see Bowker, 1980). In my experiences with penitentiary violence, assailants often looked and talked as though they had enjoyed committing violence. Violence reinforces a convict's status and prestige and adds macho-value to his mainline image. In turn, this image is currency with which to buy "social space," power, control, contraband, sex, and so on.

Hacks use violence also, and in ways similar to convicts. But for hacks, prestige accrued in dealing with or meting out violence can be transformed into promotions and pay increases.

Violence at Lompoc

There are three "official" ways of dying in the Federal Prison System: an inmate is either killed, commits suicide, or dies of natural causes. From 1981 through 1986, with an average daily population of 1,139 inmates, USP-Lompoc has averaged 1.02 homicides per year.

Assessing the nature of assaults is a more difficult problem. Table 5.1 shows USP-Lompoc's 1985 and 1986 assaultive incident rates; this analysis includes all aggressive acts initiated by an inmate toward another inmate or staffer, as reported in USP-Lompoc incident report logs. These logs record inmate infractions and include the violation code (101, assault; 201, fighting), the inmate's name and unit, and the date on which the incident report was filed. These logs are the crudest level of reporting violations. Incident report logs do not differentiate types of assault or any significant details. Staffers may cite an inmate for fighting if he is just threatening to fight another inmate; or with assaulting staff if he throws a carton of milk, a cup of urine, or urine mixed with feces, or if he tosses a food tray at a hack. Some new hacks cite verbally aggressive convicts with assault. But in the log books, fights are fights and assaults are assaults.

Table 5.1. **Assaultive Infractions Rate at USP-Lompoc, 1985-86**

| Infraction Type | 1985 | | 1986 | |
	(n)	Rate/100 Inmates Per Month	(n)	Rate/100 Inmates Per Month
100-Level				
Killing	(1)	.01	(1)	.01
Assault	(54)	.37	(120)	.86
Possession of a Weapon*	(66)	.46	(65)	.46
200-Level				
Fighting	(59)	.41	(79)	.56
Threatening Staff	(27)	.19	(43)	.31
Total Assaultive				
Infractions	(n = 207)		(n = 308)	

SOURCE: USP-Lompoc Report Logs, 1985-86.
*NOTE: Possession of a weapon isn't an assaultive "incident," but since it's often directly related to assault, I've included it here.

A closer look at these incident reports reveals that few assaults on staff or inmates result in bruises, broken bones, or serious lacerations. Assaults resulting in any degree of injury are reported by each federal institution in their monthly correctional services report. Table 5.2 shows physical assault rates.

During my research two inmate-on-inmate unarmed assaults resulted in severe injuries to the victims, and the others had injuries no more serious than bruises and cuts. In several cases of inmate unarmed assault on line staff, staffers' black eyes, bloody noses, and contusions were not "injuries," by staffers' definitions, but simply obvious (and proud) signs of "not taking any bullshit from convicts," said a line hack.

Two inmate-on-inmate armed assaults were serious, resulting in multiple shank punctures; two others involved shank lacerations; one resulted in a non-life-threatening shank puncture; another inmate was smashed in the head with a weight

Table 5.2. Physical Assault Rates at USP-Lompoc, 1983-86
(Per 100 Inmates Per Year)

	1983		1984		1985		1986	
	Rate	(n)	Rate	(n)	Rate	(n)	Rate	(n)
Inmate-on-inmate								
armed	1.62	(17)	1.05	(12)	.66	(8)	1.03	(12)
unarmed	.19	(2)	.09	(1)	.41	(5)	.94	(11)
Inmate-on-staff								
armed	.10	(1)	.17	(2)	.17	(2)	.09	(1)
unarmed	.10	(1)	.26	(3)	.25	(3)	.94	(11)
total		(21)		(18)		(18)		(35)

SOURCE: USP-Lompoc Monthly Report of Assault Data and the Correctional Services Report, July 1986.
NOTE: Average Daily Population, 1983 (1,049), 1984 (1,146), 1985 (1,208), 1986 (1,167).

lifter's triangular barbell; the other armed assaults caused either no injuries or minor cuts. There was one inmate-on-staff armed assault during my research; this resulted in no injuries, either to the hack or to the inmate.

Victims of armed assaults are "stuck" or "shanked," not stabbed, and the events themselves are called "stickings" or "shankings."

According to Big Brother, short shanks are not killing weapons, but are used to "teach loud-mouth motherfuckers some manners." To use a strap-on shank (which is made by embedding a galvanized nail into a melted plastic handle, such as that of a plastic dining hall utensil), the attacker ties the strap firmly around his wrist. Ideally, this prevents the attacker from losing his weapon and having it used against him by the victim or by someone else who may jump into the fray. Convicts call this "strapping down with a shank" or "filling your hand." Not all weapons have fastening straps, but, says convict Doyle, "when a guy is hell-bent on killing somebody, he'll tape the shank in his hand with masking tape or electrical tape, or whatever kind of tape he can steal." According to convicts, aluminum shanks with a tightly wound cloth handle and lace strap can get past the penitentiary's metal detectors.

At the Scene

At the ring of a triple-deuce phone or at the high-pitched squeal of a body alarm, lieutenants look as though an electric current has just passed through them. They react almost involuntarily as they dash out of the office and run to central control, where the control-room officer tells them the location of the emergency situation.

Emergencies are quiet events. The rattle and jingle of security keys, bounding on hips and echoing in the hollow main corridor, is the only noise. No yelling. No buzzers. No bells. To the sound of keys, men dash out of their offices along the main corridor and stand for just a moment to see the direction in which others are running. All office doors are locked; corridor grills slam and lock; inmates working in, or walking along the main and work corridor stop in their tracks to stare at sprinting and panting staffers.

Up front, a buzzer rings for an instant—a half second, if that long. When staffers in the personnel office and the business office hear it, they, too, stop whatever they are doing and begin their sprint toward the inside. These men, clad in business suits, push into the central control sallyport, waiting for the main corridor grill to slide open. When it does, Gene Gill or Chuck LaRoe is standing there, directing them to the lieutenant's office; they are a backup crew. A backup crew is a precaution against diversionary violence or a false alarm. A call from Unicor, for example, which is one-quarter mile away from central control, may be a planned diversion to get staffers away from an incident occurring somewhere else.

A Special Operation Response Team ("riot squad") is prepared to respond to riot or hostage situations, but there is not a tactical squad, or an emergency response team ("goon squad"), that handles routine emergencies such as fights, stabbings, and killings. It is the responsibility of all male employees to respond to emergencies; women never respond.

On the day watch, 40 to 45 men respond; on the evening watch, eight to nine; and on the morning watch, about four. Staffers who are directly supervising inmates do not abandon them to respond to an emergency. Inmate work-crew supervisors, food-service stewards in the kitchen, or cellblock correctional officers, for example, will not respond, because doing so will leave inmates unsupervised. Similarly, Unicor staffers will not respond unless they are requested to do so by correctional services.

In my experience at scenes of violence, I found that whatever the degree of an inmate's injuries (from cuts to fatal stabbings), staffers' reactions are fundamentally the same: faces are exemplars of dispassionate concern, expressionless with eyes open wide; they efficiently assist injured inmates; they effectively manage inmates who are hanging around, watching. They never panic, raise their voices, or lose control.

The physical damage inflicted to an inmate during a serious assault is treated as if it were invisible: no one shows visible emotional reactions to pools of blood running on the floor, blood splattered and dripping on the walls, and a writhing, injured person—at least, not at first. Once the initial tension of the scene wanes and control is regained, staffers relax, cigarettes are lit, laughing begins, and comments about the event are bantered about among staffers.

In a minor emergency, a loud but not violent inmate-to-inmate confrontation, a lieutenant (usually one who knows one or both inmates) will take charge of the scene. The goal is to handcuff the inmates, to take them off to I-unit, and to begin their investigation. Such an encounter may last only five to ten minutes.

A September 1987 minor incident in K-unit was controlled by Lt. Hammer. Jesse Jennings, K-unit's counselor, called Lt. Hammer and asked for assistance. I joined in. When we walked into the unit, convict Rulan was hanging from the C-range tier railing, leaning over the flats, and waving a steel mop wringer in one hand and threatening to use it on convicts Jones and Stockie. Jones and Stockie (who are cousins) were standing on the flats. Jones was holding a pool cue tightly in his right hand, and Stockie had both hands full of billiard balls. Hammer was talking to Rulan, trying to convince him to put down the mop wringer and to talk about the problem. Meanwhile, Jones and Stockie never took their eyes off of Rulan.

I walked between Jones and Stockie. "Come on, put that shit down, walk out quietly," I suggested to them. "No fucking way, man, not until that fucker puts that wringer down," said Stockie.

Rulan's cell was on D-range at the front of the tier, directly overlooking the pool table. Rulan decided to mop his cell as well as the tier's front end. According to Jones, who was playing pool with Stockie directly below Rulan's mopping, Rulan yelled down to them, "Push the table out of there."

Jennings said that Rulan "didn't want to get water on the table top, as he mopped up the tier." Rulan grumbled at Hammer: "They didn't pay no attention to me. They looked up at me, and didn't pay no attention. So I told them again, "Push that fucking table out of the way so it don't get wet."

Jennings said that, "Rulan went down to the flats, grabbed the table and pushed it under C-tier. Jones and Stockie said something to Rulan, Rulan said something back, and then I heard yelling. When I looked, there was Rulan hanging off the tier with a wringer in his hand, and Jones and Stockie had cues and pool balls."

Hammer talked to Rulan for about 10 minutes, and finally got him to put down his wringer; only then did Jones and Stockie put down their billiard equipment. Later, a staffer told me that Rulan "was a fag, and he was trying to defend his honor in there. Everyone knows he's a punk." This is the most common postscript, offered by staff and inmates alike, to most incidents.

In a more serious emergency, a no-weapons fight, the combatants are separated and checked for injuries: if one or both are injured, they are taken immediately to the hospital; if they are able to walk, they do so, or, if one of them is seriously hurt, a physician's assistant and a gurney are brought to the scene.

A Sunday evening meal in May 1987 had just begun. Lines were forming at each steamtable; there were perhaps 200 inmates in the mess hall. Lts. Brooks, Mahan, and I were shooting the breeze at the mess hall doors, standing just outside them in the main corridor. As we talked, I glanced into the mess hall and saw two inmates pushing and grabbing each other's clothing. Their chow line did not disperse, but the line bowed, giving them more room to fight; no one else joined in the fracas. I tapped Lt. Brooks on the arm: "There's a fight." He looked in, saw it, and the three of us ran in; the inmates in line moved aside for us. The dining hall then became dead silent.

At the scene, Brooks and Mahan jumped between the fighting convicts, separating them. Brooks grabbed his inmate from behind in a bear hug, pushing him away from his opponent toward a table, where he shook him down and cuffed his hands behind his back. As this happened, Lt. Mahan took his inmate in the opposite direction, out of the mess hall and down to the hospital to have his bloody nose checked.

Within 45 seconds both inmates were removed, the meal lines had reformed, and the noise increased to its normal Super Bowl level. Brooks asked me to watch the mess hall door, as he tended to his inmate in the main corridor, asking him about any possible injuries. As I stood there, an inmate walked by me, shaking his head from side to side, and said with a laugh: "Fried chicken make men go crazy."

In December 1985, at about 11:50 one morning, I was standing at the entry doors to the dining hall with a lieutenant and Captain Collins. The main corridor was filled with inmates going to lunch, coming from lunch, and sauntering up and down the corridor before work recall.

A call came over the lieutenant's radio from central control: "Body alarm in K-unit!" The dining hall doors were slammed closed and locked by the main corridor officer. The operations lieutenant yelled to the captain, who was next to me: "Body alarm in K-unit!" We turned and started running. As we ran, Captain Collins yelled repeatedly, "Get out of the way," to inmates who, in the noise of hundreds of inmates in the corridor, did not hear us coming.

As we entered K-unit's open door, the counselor, standing expressionless just inside the door, said: "It's upstairs, TV room," His tone of voice and the look in his eyes told me it was the "real thing."

The captain, who was one step ahead of me, hurtled the six flights of steel stairs two at a time. Up we went, into the TV room. As we entered the room, I saw Carl Lowen kneeling over inmate Ralston who was rolling from side to side in pain. Lowen, who ran upstairs after hearing the rumbling of fighting inmates from his office three floors below on the flats, had Ralston wrapped in an army blanket, knees slightly elevated. He was holding Ralston's head on his forearm, keeping it off the concrete floor, and telling him, "They're going to be here in just a minute. The PA is coming, they'll take good care of you."

Lying in an expanding pool of blood coming from a badly lacerated forehead and smashed face, Ralston moaned, rocking back and forth in pain. Radiating from the pool of blood were several streams of it that had squirted from the inmate's head and face, hitting the walls about six feet from the point of the assault.

Ralston was a big man, well over six feet tall and weighing more than 200 pounds. The severity of his injuries, the position of blood on the floor and walls, and the quantity of blood raised the possibility that more than one convict had assaulted him. The severity of Ralston's injuries also suggested to some onlooking staffers that a blunt weapon was used to beat him. "He was probably sitting and watching television," said a lieutenant, "when he was attacked. Looks like they used something on him, maybe a chair. Check 'em for blood." The television was still on, blaring early afternoon soap operas.

Within several minutes the room was filled with hacks, lieutenants, and unit management staffers. Ralston was taken to the hospital, and John Sams ordered me to "rack them all in their cells, right now." A formal investigation was beginning.

I walked down each range, beginning on E-range, telling each inmate to get in his cell: "Let's go, get in your cell!" I said over and over. Inmates responded, "What happened?" "What's going on?" "Nothing," I said, "Let's go, get in your house." They all went peacefully and without too much hesitation. After I got a range of inmates in their cells, the CC racked the cells closed.

Remarkably, of the 40 to 50 inmates who were in K-unit at the time of the assault, not one of them knew anything at all, most did not know that an assault had occurred, they said. Then I joined a team of staffers shaking down all public areas of the unit, searching for a weapon. We looked behind vending machines; behind and under the washer and dryer; in the shower room under sinks and in shower drains; in full trash cans that were dumped out on each tier; and, in every possible place where a pipe or a shank could be hidden. We found nothing.

After finishing this, I walked into the K-unit office. "That fucking thug is a chicken-hawk," exclaimed a staffer, who was reading Ralston's jacket. "He was picking up kids on the street and molesting them in the back of his van. That slimy fuck deserved what he got. They should'a killed him."

Captain Collins, John Sams, Gene Gill, and Rudy Marks discussed proceeding to the next step of the investigation, which was to interrogate all inmates who were in K-unit during the assault. Four two-man interrogation teams were assembled from various unit management teams. I worked with Carl Lowen.

Once interrogation teams were assembled, we decided among ourselves how inmates would be selected for each team's interviews. We went range by range, cell by cell, until all the inmates had been interviewed.

Lowen and I sat in his office. Each interview team used a standardized inter-view form. Inmates were not told what had happened in the television room. They were asked, "Where were you at approximately 11:50 a.m.? Whom were you talk-ing to? Did you see anyone standing near the television room entrance?" and so on. As each inmate sat in front of us, we scrutinized the skin on his face and hands, look-ing for bruises, scratches or blood, and we look carefully at each man's clothing and shoes, looking for bloodstains.

As the interrogation teams worked, about six hacks, each working alone, went from cell to cell. Each inmate was ordered to strip to his underwear, to raise his arms straight out to the side, and to stand with his legs spread. The officer checked for visible fresh scratches and bruises on the inmate's chest, back, arms, and legs.

After this, each inmate was ordered to stand on the tier outside his cell, as the officer shook down the cell, looking for bloody clothes, a weapon, or both. According to lieutenants, inmates at USP-Lompoc have flushed bloody clothes down their toilets and tried to flush assault weapons. Lt. Baker said that, in some serious cases, officers have been stationed at the penitentiary's sewer outlet pipe, waiting for evi-dence to flow past.

After the interviews, data sheets were collected. Those inmates who seemed to know more than they were willing to discuss in the interrogation were earmarked for later interviews. The investigation lasted several hours, and K-unit remained locked down for the remainder of that afternoon, opening again after the four o'clock count.

Lowen's intuition was that one of our interviewees, convict Clyde, was probably the assailant, and Lowen suspected that convict Motta, a known partner of Clyde's, was his jigger (an inmate lookout). Lowen was right. During our interview with Clyde, he was calm, but a bit more impatient than other interviewees, claiming he disliked being in Lowen's office. He said, "I don't want any of them guys to think I'm telling you anything." Lowen said, "How are they going to know what you say?" "They'll know," said Clyde.

Within hours of the assault, Clyde and Motta (with the help of snitches) were serious suspects, and were locked away in I-unit pending SIS (Special Investigative Supervisor) investigation. Over the next several days staffers picked up information silently from K-unit inmates. When the details were collected, including the motive, Clyde was charged with assault.

Sex is the first motive cited by most staff and inmates as the explanation for inmate-on-inmate brutality. The next most common explanation is bad debts. Clyde was not talking, though. I asked him about it: "It's something that happens, that's all."

For days afterward, staffers talked about this incident. Men described and redescribed Ralston's injuries, and some men compared this assault to others: "That was the worst beating I've ever seen without a weapon. He must have used his boots on that guy's face to split it open that way. About 15 years ago in [Texas], I saw one that was close to this, but the convict's head wasn't split open like this guy's was," said one Unicor staffer.

Lower I-unit didn't stop Clyde's violence. While in a rec cage several months later, he punched inmate George in the face, "exploding" (shattering) his cheekbone, causing one eye to hang from its socket. George's surgeon, a friend of mine, told me that George's injuries would require extensive reconstruction of the cheek, and that there was a high probability that George would lose his vision in the injured eye. After months of medical care, George's vision was restored. Despite the seriousness of George's injuries, one staffer at the scene described it this way: "He just got smacked. He'll [George] be all right."

On March 6, 1986, a Marielito killed another Marielito. The victim, Julio, was murdered when Bernardo shoved a foot-long shank under Julio's rib cage, pushing into his heart. Bernardo also shanked Julio's side, stomach, arm, and chest.

The F-unit killing occurred between E-range and F-range. I was there just after it happened, and I got a chance to talk to the FBI agent. Apparently, Bernardo and Julio were playing dominoes. Their fight began in the E-range dayroom, but only a few drops of blood were on the dayroom floor. During their initial struggle, Bernardo and Julio overturned a very heavy wooden table, which took up most of the space in the dayroom. Their fight moved to the E-range tier, and ended in death at the tier's front end. A thick pool of blood lay on the concrete floor, where it dripped and oozed from Julio's chest wounds. After shanking Julio, Bernardo ran down to his cell on A-range. On his way down, Bernardo passed his CC, who was running up to the third tier, after he heard the ruckus while working in the unit office.

We followed the same procedure here as we did in the Ralston assault. A new hack (in his late twenties, with three years of military corrections experience) and I worked separately, shaking down convicts in their cells and searching each cell for bloody clothes and a murder weapon; a weapon was not found that day. My partner was first on the scene. He said, "I seen him laying there. He had a big hole in his stomach on the side opposite to the appendix. I looked down and seen it and couldn't believe it at first. He was breathing, he took one big breath. I knew he was going to die. I wish I didn't run up here so fast."

Carrying Julio in a blanket, three staffers brought him down the narrow, winding staircase connecting each tier, to a waiting stretcher and a physician's assistant. He died in the penitentiary hospital about one hour later. His body was taken to the Lompoc Community Hospital, where he was pronounced dead by a physician (an FPS physician's assistant cannot sign a death certificate). A staffer told me that Julio was handcuffed when they rolled him outside the perimeter of the penitentiary, since he was not "officially dead" yet. A penitentiary hospital employee said that was "stupid."

It was discovered later that Bernardo dropped his shank into his cell's heating duct outlet. It took several days to dig it out from the heating system under F-unit. Investigators said, incidentally, that a victim's shank wounds can sometimes identify the killer as Marielito. Their shanks are bifacially sharpened, whereas Havana Cuban criminals' shanks are unifacially sharpened; each type of weapon leaves a distinctive wound.

After our work was done we all stood around, telling stories, joking and laughing, not about the killing, but about anything else. "I'm my best at times like these," said one staffer. "If an outsider had walked in and watched us, he never would have guessed that this was a murder scene and that we had just been involved in a murder investigation." There was no sense of violence or killing or death at the scene. Once the victim had been taken to the hospital, a procedure had to be followed. Policy had to be maintained, work had to be done.

Inmates milling around outside the cellblock knew there had been a killing. Their mood was light, excited, cheerful, airy, and friendly, almost as if to express a sense of relief, knowing that now a murder might not happen again for quite some time.

Why did Bernardo kill Julio? Sex and drug debts were the first rumors circulating among staff and inmates alike. Slim, who lives across the corridor in C-unit, told me his version of the killing. He sounded as if he had seen it on videotape. "They got into a little beef over their dominoes; some guys take it real serious, you know. Julio had a pipe and Bernardo pulled his shit. These things happen. I hear Julio was getting out in June. He got out all right, but he went through the door flat, and feet first."

A final rumor came from a senior custody staffer: "Bernardo was supposed to be transferred to Atlanta, on his way back to Castro's prisons. I guess he didn't want to go, huh? You know, Julio was going to be paroled this June [1986]. Tough break, huh. Ah, shit, we got a lot of Cubans.

Bernardo was housed in lower I-unit. Not long after arriving there, he tore his way through a rec cage's anchor fence which forms its perimeter. After getting out, he scurried to the roof of the main penitentiary building, where he was spotted by a rookie tower officer. A call for assistance went out. We chased him around the rear compound and cornered him within minutes. When he was asked why he ran off, he smiled and said, "I was testing institution security." During the rest of my research, Bernardo was relatively quiet—he did not assault or kill anyone.

But on July 4, 1987, Bernardo, now back on the mainline, tried to kill convict Bobby. A staffer gave me this account:

> Bernardo had a shank hidden in the gym toilet. He got into a skirmish with a black [Bobby] in the gym, over basketball or something. He went after Bobby and tried to stab him. Bobby ran out of the gym and down the gym corridor, heading for the main corridor. As Bobby ran, Bernardo kept swiping at him with the shank. Bobby ran into the main corridor, but Bernardo still came at him. Bobby ran into the lieutenant's office, but Bernardo didn't stop. He ran in after him, and even tried to stab him in front of the lieutenants. They grabbed him and got the shank.

Testing Mettle

A penitentiary culture systematically excludes outsiders, and in doing so creates an ethos among staffers. This ethos forces staffers to prove their worthiness. It binds men to other men who are in the same situation, and it keeps them from sharing their lives and stresses with noncorrectional people. Even their wives, who, they say, cannot possibly understand what it is like on the inside, are excluded (see Blau et al., 1986:148, on marriage and correctional officer stress). "Wives don't understand," said Lt. Brooks. "They don't know what a triple deuce is or a body alarm; forget about the shank that's got your name on it. As wives grow older, they begin to understand. New hacks' wives don't understand anything."

A penitentiary culture also systemtically isolates insiders from insiders. The time-honored inmate expression, "do your own time," also applies to line staff. This is not a "sharing" culture: close, personal relationships (both among correctional staffers and inmates) are not easily formed or maintained. A penitentiary culture compartmentalizes people, isolating staff and inmates alike from interpersonal relations and from counsel. These men do not freely allow other men to enter into their personal lives unless they have earned their entrance. Violence opens the door.

"Working in this penitentiary," said a line hack, who had come to USP-Lompoc from a California prison, "is just babysitting a bunch of thugs, until the shit hits the fan." Experienced staffers understand that "new men don't know what's going on, for the first few months," said Gary Charles. "But they better learn in a hurry. If a hack doesn't respond to an emergency or if he backs away from action at the scene, he's a wimp, a coward, a chicken-shit."

Charles continued:

> Trust in fellow officers is a fragile thing. You're trusting them with your life. I know that two men here are cowards. I've seen them back off. One guy did it in two fights and the other in three fights. Then you have untried rookies. I have four and a half years in the Arizona State Prison, and I still had to prove myself to my fellow officers here. It's a great thing here. Out in the corridor, Larry [Bert] is a man I'd trust with my life. Everybody was a rookie, but they got to prove themselves. It's like being blood relatives. Experience trusts experience. If you've got seven or eight years in federal institutions, it follows you along. Rookies have to prove that you can trust them: his actions, his willingness to work; he isn't bashful, he'll give orders; how he looks and how he acts when inmates are around. You know [GS-6 hack] Mahony in H-unit? An inmate will deck him, then he'll be an outstanding officer.

Testing a new hack's mettle begins with blood. GS-8 George Sand:

> Hacks have to earn their bones. I don't respond to [new] guys until I see blood on them—his or an inmate's. I want to see blood. Older hacks have been around for the trash truck escape and killings. The new guys are untested. New guys are stuck in towers or units. They may look good, but you can't trust them until there's an emergency, when you can see them in action. Emergencies aren't common, but when they come, they hit hard and heavy.

In the man's world of the penitentiary, the unwritten rule among the keepers and the kept is simple: Anybody can work in prison, but only "men" should be on the line in a penitentiary. Because of the organizational culture's emphasis on avoiding conflict, GS-8s and lieutenants do not talk openly about men who do not jump into a convict melee or men who subtly encourage and instigate fights with convicts.

Cowards and chicken-shits are quietly evaluated and discouraged informally, and with negative performance evaluations, from pursuing a career in correctional services. There is always competition for prestige among aggressive hacks. If a hack wants to stand out during a fight, all he has to do is wait around long enough; violence will find him.

Leon Mahony waited for months to earn his bones. Even before he got involved in his first knockdown, drag-out convict brawl, he had already been judged as "a good one," by Charles and by other lieutenants, who had seen him react to several triple deuces. Mahony always reacted quickly; he ran fast at the head of the pack;

and he never failed to talk about how much he enjoyed the action, and how disappointed he was about missing "the good ones," the bloody fights/assaults.

Mahony let everyone know that he was ready at anytime, to "rock'n'roll with thugs." After a few months on the job, he got his first chance. This story of the J-unit brawl was told to me the next day by the participants: Lt. Houser, Charles, and Mahony.

It was early evening, around 6:15, during an up-to-then-quiet weekday evening watch. As the J-unit officer was walking on E-range, he passed a cell and spotted four inmates, hanging around inside. There was a "smell of homebrew and they sounded loaded," said the unit hack.

J-unit's new hack called central control, saying that he had two drunken convicts in cell E-10, E-range. Lt. Houser, the operations lieutenant, walked out of the lieutenant's office and told Charles, who was main corridor officer, to come with him. They walked into J-unit. Charles said that "Seventy-five, eighty inmates were hangin' off the tiers, hootin' and hollerin', so it had to be handled carefully without any extra-curricular activities."

They walked up three flights of dimly lit steps, arriving at E-10 to find the rookie unit hack standing in front of now empty E-10, pointing to the drunks, standing on F-range. Houser yelled to convicts Leiser and Peltzer: "Stop." They ignored the order and started walking down the tier. Again, Houser ordered them to stop and again they refused his order.

Houser and Charles then walked around to F-range. Charles approached Leiser: "I ain't gonna be here long. I'm gonna make the big time," said Leiser, according to Charles. "What's the big time? He thinks he's hot shit. He wants to make [USP] Marion. Ah...they think it's good for their reputations to do time in the control unit. He's a punk." Charles continued:

> I ordered Leiser to turn around to put on cuffs and he refused. I
> ordered him for a second time to turn around and again he refused
> the order. Leiser pushed me backward and tried to get away from
> me and Houser. Houser grabbed his right arm and I grabbed his
> left arm and tried to put handcuffs on him.

By this time, Leon Mahony was on his way up to the third tier, from his corridor two post, outside J-unit.

> I was walking down the flats. Then I looked up and saw Houser
> and Charles on E-range. I went up the F-range side and by the time
> I got there, Houser had Leiser. The three of us grabbed him. He
> was fighting, screaming and kicking. Peltzer came towards us and
> Charles said, "Stay back," and he said, "Fuck you, I'm gonna
> kill you motherfuckers" and jumped on Charles's back and
> punched at me [hitting him in the eye]. By then there was a pile

of us on the tier, stacked four high. [Another officer] was holding one cuff. Leiser broke free and tried to kick me, and they
jacked his ass on the wall.

Charles continued: "I broke the glasses off Peltzer's face and I wanted to break
his fuckin' neck. I had a four-battery Mag Light on my hip. I reached for it once and
chose not to go after it. If I used it, we might have had to fight 85 other convicts."

By then, yet another officer appeared, cuffing inmate Peltzer. Houser and
Charles cuffed Leiser.

Mahony took Peltzer, walking him down from the third tier, followed by inmate
Leiser, who was guided by Charles. On the way down the steps, Leiser again started
to fight. Charles said that "Peltzer tried to kick Mahony in back of the legs on the
way down the steps. I jammed him up against the wall. Then he tried to break
away from me and jump Mahony who was about three stairs ahead of us. I put
him on the wall to regain control."

The melee ended. Inmates Leiser and Peltzer were locked away in I-unit.
Mahony had a nasty black eye, Charles had been kicked several times in the ribs and
armpit, but he loved every minute of it, he said. Charles talked about Mahony. "I
told Mahony he was gonna get his cherry broke before too long. That was 15 minutes before it happened. Mahony got a big shiner; he was proud of it. It was hard,
hot, and heavy, that's how violent it was up there. It was fun!"

Mahony thought about the fight, too.

> The next day, I'm working I-unit rec yard. Whenever I turned my
> back somebody yelled, "Please don't hit me again, officer" or "What
> did they teach you at Glynco?" A couple of guys just came up and
> laughed at me. [Convict] Donnie came up and said, "Can I touch
> it [the black eye]?" and, "What's the matter with you, hurt your
> neck, too?"

Mahony continued: "So I had to look at 'em and listen to it. They gave me a
Peanuts cartoon of Charlie Brown with a black eye, lying on the ground, asking "Why?"
As he thought about the night before, Mahony commented:

> It was loud in there, ninety of them screaming and hollering. We
> got the guys and Charles said, "Let's get the hell out of here!" It
> was exciting. A sense of camaraderie with the three of us. Charles
> is a wild man, he loves it. I wanted to beat the shit out of them.
> Charles had boot prints on his shirt, and I didn't feel getting hit.
> I almost rolled off the tier, I reached up and grabbed a bar [of the
> tier's rail] and held on.

The result: no deaths and only minor injuries. The next day the convict rumor
mill buzzed about the brawl. Rumor had it that it was a good, fair fight. According
to Slim, who had an acquaintance in J-unit, a bunch of J-unit convicts were armed

and prepared to attack and kill the officers if they thought that the fight had been conducted with unnecessary staff brutality. Slim's comment, even with its apocryphal origin, suggests a prevailing attitude held by inmates and staff: a prison fight like this one should be conducted by fair fighting rules.

Staff and inmate spectators enjoyed this one. Both staffers and inmates bolstered their prison reputations. The inmates may have gotten their wish, to be transferred to USP-Marion, and they will carry with them a proud record of assaulting staff.

Staffers were satisfied, too. Charles added new bruises and scars to a body and face already scarred and damaged from countless brawls with convicts. Houser improved his prestige as a knowledgeable supervisor by handling a potentially dangerous situation professionally. And Mahony strutted amid inmates and peers, exhibiting his shiny black eye proudly, a valuable badge of courage among rookie hacks.

An upper-echelon administrator, on the other hand, was not happy with the way the officers had handled that volatile situation. "With all the experience those guys have, they should have known better than to chase down drunks with 80 or 90 convicts hanging over the rails and yelling and screaming. They should have locked down the unit before dealing with the drunks. They could have gotten really hurt in there." "Yeah," I said, "but it sounds like they had fun, huh?" With a slight smile on his face, he said: "I bet they did, too."

Unlimited macho talk floats around the mainline after a cellblock brawl. According to Charles, after the J-unit fight "a couple of convicts came up and told me that guys think I'm a bad motherfucker. They think we did a good job down there [J-unit]." I replied: "You are a bad motherfucker, huh?" "I can be!" said Charles. Such a reputation can lead to yet another way of proving one's macho qualities.

Contracts

Within several weeks of this fight, Charles told me that the "ABs have a certified contract on me." Several snitches independently identified the hitters and the contract's source. The validity of the contract was verified by the SIS and the FBI, according to Charles. "The captain wanted to pull me [off the main corridor] and stick me in I-tower for about a week until things calmed down. They've tried this before. When it gets tough, I don't want to be pulled out. I told the captain: "Cap, either play me or trade me!"

Charles didn't want to hide from the convict hitters. "I asked around and I found out who was going to try to take me out. I stopped each one in the corridor, and I told him: 'If I see you coming up behind be or near me with a hand in your pocket, I'll take you out right then.' I love this. My wife thinks I'm crazy."

Murder contracts on staffers are powerful messages. If a convict wants to kill a staffer or an inmate, and cannot or does not want to do it himself, he may "put a contract" out on the target. The target may be in the same or different prison, on the street, or anywhere in the country.

Big Brother describes the contract arrangement:

> Say I put out the word that I want some dude hit and will give $1,500. I'll send my ol' lady to see a hitter [in another prison]. Or the word can go out by telephone, in a letter or to your ol' lady in the visiting room. You got to be real careful when you talk on the phone or mail out a letter. They listen to calls and the SIS reads the mail. If the FBI finds out you set up a contract, you'll never get out of here. The best way to do it is send the word with some dude who's being transferred to the joint where the guy is, who you want hit. He can set it up, and you can pay him. After the hit, you have your ol' lady put the money in the hitter's account.

The cost of a contract varies according to target (convict or staffer), social status of the target, and expertise of the hitter. At USP-Lompoc, "some ol' dope head will do it," said Slim. "It'll cost you one-half ounce of heroin. Some guys might charge $500 to $1,000, or less, a couple hundred. A slight professional would cost $1,000 or a bit more. They use discretion." A contract "on the inside [penitentiary] may go for $200," said a senior lieutenant, "but in the [FPC] camp, it may cost $1,000 to $2,000," since camp inmates, who do not have histories of violence, will have to contract with someone else who will do the hit at the camp.

As deadly as contracts can be, they are factors in mettle testing and sources of prestige for hacks, who take a sense of pride in being considered a worthwhile target. Once a contract has been verified, hacks take an even greater risk by remaining on the mainline. But greater risk yields greater prestige.

Assaulting Each Other

> Do you ever wonder why staff run in an emergency? Do you ever think about if a convict or staff is down? No one gives a shit if convicts kill each other, but it's scary to think that a staff member is down [A line hack].

In the 50-year history of the Bureau of Prisons, five staffers have been killed by inmates. Three of the five killings occurred between 1980 and 1985. These killings, particularly the two correctional officers' killings at USP-Marion, are still on the minds of USP-Lompoc's line staff. Of these three convict killers, two were housed at USP-Marion, and the third coperpetrator in the "piping" (bludgeoning someone with a piece of pipe) and near decapitation of an FCI correctional officer is housed at USP-Lompoc.

Charles:

> We don't give a shit if they kill each other, but the golden rule is,
> "They don't touch me and I don't touch them." 'Cause if they do,
> we go to the dirt. When something is done to a staff member, some-
> thing got to be done to the convict. I don't mean beat the hell out
> of them. They got to know the staff members are off-limits: they
> can do what they want to each other, but they've got to leave
> staff alone, physically.

The few serious inmate-on-staff assaults at USP- and CFI-Lompoc are remembered well. Two serious assaults are noted here, one in 1982 at USP-Lompoc and
the earlier one in 1978 at SCI-Lompoc. The staff victim of the 1982 attack, a J-unit
counselor, has since retired, but a staffer who responded to the body alarm offers
his own account.

> The counselor was piped by a convict because his transfer was turned
> down and it was handled by the counselor. We went in and found
> him on the tier, his head was caved in and he was in a big pool
> of blood. An inmate pushed his body alarm, he came up behind
> him and pushed his button; the convict saved his life. The next
> day they bused him [the attacker] out. The staff were serious
> about killing him.

The victim of the 1978 incident, correctional officer John Burland, now a case
manager at USP-Lompoc, had his throat cut by a convict assailant on January 30,
1978. Burland recalls,

> I had been out of the institution for two weeks with walking
> pneumonia. I worked D-unit for two days and was assigned to L-
> unit to cover sick and annual post on evening watch. I hadn't
> worked L-unit in a long while. When I checked in, no one told me
> about [the attacker]. He had giant eyes, he had been burned out
> from drug usage. In those days they had a racking system: A
> guy could put his name on a chart to be racked out to watch TV
> after the 10:00 p.m. count. Some other inmate put [his] name on
> this chart and I racked him out. He thought that devils were after
> him and other inmates. I was raising the door on the lock box, and
> I felt a brush, like hair, on the side of my neck. I turned around
> and I could see blood hitting the wall, about five feet away. At first,
> I thought an inmate had been cut on the third tier. I saw this
> inmate standing in front of me with two razor blades in leather thongs,
> and a crazed look in his eyes. I said, "What the hell are you

doing?" He lunged at me again and that's when he cut my little finger all up. I backed up and hit my alarm button. I heard the keys in the corridor. He dropped the weapons to his side, turned around and walked to his cell. He put the weapons in his locker, took all his clothes off and went to bed.

Assaults without weapons occurred in a variety of situations during my research. In one incident, a convict, later reported to have been high on a hallucinogen, was frantically trying to escape from his cellblock, claiming spacemen were outside the cellblock and were coming for him. He smacked a rookie hack in the side of the head, when the hack refused to give the inmate his security keys. In another incident, an emotionally unstable inmate punched two staffers who tried to stop him for a shakedown.

In the only armed assault, convict Julian tried to stab George Sand, the main corridor officer. It happened just before noon on a weekday, directly in front of the mess hall.

According to Lt. Houser,

He tried to get into the mess hall, wearing a headband, two or three times. We stopped him at the door, and told him to take that thing off. He turned around and walked back to his unit. Then the last time, he came back again, still wearing the headband. I followed him into the mess hall and got him up by the steamline. I escorted him out, and turned him over to Sand for a shakedown. We were going to lock him up.

Officer Sand said: "I had him against the wall with his hands up against it, shaking him down. There was no problem, then he broke. He spun around and I pushed up against him and held him against the wall. I didn't know he had a shank, until Mike grabbed him."

And Mike Rizo added: "I was walking down the corridor and saw Julian up against the wall with a shank in his hand. I ran down there and grabbed his arm."

The details of this event remain fuzzy. No one knew if Julian had the shank on him or if someone handed it to him as he spun around. Because of the attack's high visibility, some staffers thought that it was a "lockup" move (an attempt to get off the mainline and subsequently transferred). (Toch, 1977:125, suggests that inmates remove themselves from the mainline population to seek safety and privacy, and to find their way out of stressful situations, p. 193; I have seen this happen repeatedly, and some inmates talk about I-unit as a "vacation.") Said a GS-8: "It was a lock-move all the way. His fucking ugly brother is in [USP] Marion and that fucking slime wanted to join him. Fuck him, get him out of here."

A unit staffer told me: "Julian had just gotten a letter from [a relative] telling him that his brother had been killed [in a shoot-out]. He tried to get an emergency call, but no one would give him one, so he went off."

Slim had a version, too.

> Mark, did you see that? Just like "Miami Vice." That guy came
> running down the corridor and grabbed that shank just in time. Sand
> would have got it good, man. Just like TV, huh? Julian was paid
> off by [convict Grey Feather] to off Sand. Yeah, they don't give
> a shit about Sand. He wanted to get the warden. They're still
> pissed off about the headbands. Eagle didn't have the balls to do
> it himself, so he got that crazy fucking Julian to do his shit for him.

The formal penalties for assaulting staff are serious: loss of all good time, disciplinary transfer, and an additional sentence of one to five years. Why do convicts
assault staff? Slim said,

> An officer could have disrespected you or the officer could be an
> asshole and you get fed up with it, and it get to the point where
> you want to do something to him. Some of them have a shitty atti-
> tude or think you a lower form of dude 'cause you're on this
> side of the wall. It's petty stuff, really. Let's say the phone. You
> call your people, they accept the charges, then hacks cut you off.
> If they're so tough, let them take off that radio and let's step in
> that little room; then they not be tough.

Slim said he had a run-in with his black supervisor in food service, who called
him a "nigger." Slim said he recognized his supervisor's friendly intention, and, even
though they had a good relationship, up to that point, he became angry. "If I've got
to go to I-unit for busting you in the motherfucking mouth I'll do that," Slim said
he told his supervisor. I guess I can't blame him. Association brings on simulation,"
commented Slim about a black hack's use of the epithet.

Slim suggested also that convicts who have done time before have learned to
distrust staff in situations like this one:

> When I was down in [state prison] in '79, we did a racial thing.
> A white guard let whites get to the bats, and they rolled on us. What
> we did was get strapped down. We were in a dorm. They rolled
> off in the dorm and was swinging bats. They locked us down
> for couple of weeks. We got out and decided we were going to ride.
> We rode on two white guys watching TV. We rode on them and
> one of them died, and the other was pretty bad. Imagine yourself
> in that situation. That you got buddies laid up in the hospital and
> you got a few bruises. You roll up on these guys, your buddies got
> knives and you say, "Let's hit these motherfuckers." Anger leads

you. You got anger out front there. You try to hit them a multi-tude of times. They curl up in a ball and you hit them from every angle. We don't know if they were involved in the original thing or not; they were vulnerable, two of them, eight of us. If you leave yourself vulnerable, you're an easy mark. They had a lot of guards that keep stuff stirred up between tips. One guard might like the ABs more than Nazis. The guard who let them get the bats was a white broad, too, a sergeant's wife.

Frankie was the only inmate who agreed to discuss an assault on staff that he himself had submitted. This event happened at USP-McNeil Island.

In 1975, I caught a beef, a hassle with inmates and staff. Since then, when they read my jacket, they see me as a different dude. Five convicts moved on a partner of mine; they came up on him, and I got into it. We wiped a couple of them, others ran off. My part-ner was stabbed through the mouth into his neck, his tooth was missing and he was bleeding. I didn't know he was hit in the neck. I didn't know it was that serious until the blood came squirting out his mouth. When staff came, they broke it up, but they didn't take him to the hospital. So in the scuffle, we were busted for fighting with staff. I got six years for it, but they wanted to give him 45 years for assaulting staff and conveying a weapon.

Lt. Baker talked about working the line in USP-Marion's control unit. As America's only penitentiary monitored by Amnesty International, reports of occa-sional staff-to-convict abuse reach the media.

"Baker, did you ever abuse any convicts at Marion?" I asked him. He thought quietly about his answer for quite a while: "No, I wouldn't call it abuse. We didn't abuse them; we adjusted their attitudes."

Abuse is one thing, convict attitude adjustment is another, according to custody staffers. They talk of attitude adjustment in other institutions when an assaultive con-vict "accidentally" hits his head on a wall or "trips" going down steel steps or has his cuffs put on too tightly.

Experienced men do not talk about "abuse." Conventional wisdom on the sub-ject is: "equal force for equal force," "deadly force for deadly force," and "once a convict is in control, don't use force."

If an inmate claims that excessive force was used against him, he has the option of filing an administrative remedy against the offending officer(s). During my research, there was one case of alleged excessive force. Since I did not see the event, I compiled the story from details discussed at a meeting of the American Federation of Government Employees.

A struggle occurred in the hospital between an inmate and several hacks and a physician's assistant. This inmate was being placed in soft restraints: leather cuffs for wrists and ankles. As the physician's assistant leaned over the inmate to fasten the final restraint on his wrist, the inmate spat in his face. The physician's assistant responded by stepping on the side of the inmate's face, pushing his head aside as he fastened the leather cuff on his wrist.

A lieutenant, who was supervising the event, reported it. After an investigation, it was concluded that the physician's assistant had used excessive force in controlling the inmate.

"This is a complex situation governed by the heat of the moment and the convict's frame of mind," said an experienced custody staffer who was familiar with this case. He agreed that the physician's assistant's behavior was inappropriate for that particular situation. In a broader sense though, he asks,

> If you're fighting a convict who has a shank and you throw him into a wall, is that excessive force? Is he threatening my life, or is that just part of my job? Some guy throws shit on me, so I smack him. He files against me. We go to court and the jury finds that convicts throwing shit on hacks is part of the job, an occupational hazard. Is stepping on the face of an inmate who just spit on you, an appropriate control mechanism? Was it excessive force? When in this situation here was the inmate controlled? Do you mean to tell me that being spit on or having shit and piss thrown on you by some convict in I-unit is part of a correctional officer's job? If people on the street or people in courts think that catching shit and piss on your face and all over your clothes should be part of our job, then let *them* come in here and watch these convicts!

References

Bowker, L.H. (1980). *Prison Victimization*. New York, NY: Elsevier.

Carroll, L. (1974). *Hacks, Blacks, and Cons: Race Relations in a Maximum Security Prison*. Lexington, MA: Lexington Books.

Cohen, A.K. (1976). *"Prison Violence: A Sociological Perspective."* In A.K. Cohen et al., *Prison Violence*, Pp. 3-22. Lexington, MA: Lexington Books.

Cohen, A.K., G.F. Cole and R.G. Bailey (eds.) (1976). *Prison Violence*. Lexington, MA: Lexington Books.

Davidson, T. (1974). *Chicano Prisoners: The Key to San Quentin*. New York, NY: Holt, Rinehart, and Winston.

Ekland-Olson, S. (1986). "Crowding, Social Control, and Prison Violence: Evidence from the Post-*Ruiz* Years in Texas." *Law & Society Review*, 20(3):289-421.

Ellis, D. (1984). "Crowding and Prison Violence." *Criminal Justice and Behavior*, 11(3):277-307.

Farrington, D.P. and C.P. Nutall (1980). "Prison Size, Overcrowding, Prison Violence and Recidivism." *Journal of Criminal Justice*, 8(4):221-231.

Gaes, G.G. and W.J. McGuire (1985). "Prison Violence: The Contribution of Crowding Versus Other Determinants of Prison Assault Rates." *Journal of Research in Crime and Delinquency*, 22(1):41-65.

Irwin, J. (1980). *Prisons in Turmoil*. Boston, MA: Little, Brown and Co.

Jacobs, J.B. (1974a). "Street Gangs Behind Bars." *Social Problems*, 21:395-409.

Jacobs, J.B. (1976). "Prison Violence and Formal Organization." In A.K. Cohen et al. (eds.) *Prison Violence*, Pp. 79-87. Lexington, MA: Lexington Books.

Jacobs, J.B. (1977). *Stateville. A Penitentiary in Mass Society*. Chicago, IL: The University of Chicago Press.

Jacobs, J.B. (1983). *New Perspective on Prisons and Imprisonment*. Ithaca, NY: Cornell University Press.

Jacobs, J.B. and L.J. Kraft (1978). "Integrating the Keepers: A Comparison of Black and White Prison Guards in Illinois." *Social Problems*, 25:304-318.

Lockwood, D. (1980). *Prison Sexual Violence*. New York, NY: Elsevier.

Lockwood, D. (1982). "The Contribution of Sexual Harassment to Stress and Coping in Confinement." In N. Parisi (ed.) *Coping with Imprisonment*, Pp. 45-64.

Lockwood, D. (1986). "Target Violence." In K.C. Haas and G.P. Albert (eds.) *The Dilemmas of Punishment*, Pp. 116-133. Prospect Heights, IL: Waveland Press.

Mabli, J., C.S. Holley, J. Patrick and J. Walls (1979). "Age and Prison Violence: Increasing Age Heterogeneity as a Violence-reducing Strategy in Prisons." *Criminal Justice and Behavior*, 6(2):175-186.

MacKenzie, D.L. (1987). "Age and Adjustment to Prison: Interaction with Attitudes and Anxiety." *Criminal Justice and Behavior*, 14(4):427-447.

Nacci, P.L. and T.R. Kane (1982). "Sex and Sexual Aggression in Federal Prison." Federal Bureau of Prisons, Progress Report.

Nacci, P.L. and T.R. Kane (1983). "The Incidence of Sex and Sexual Aggression in Federal Prison." *Federal Probation*, 47(4):31-36.

Nacci, P.L. and T.R. Kane (1984). "Sex and Sexual Aggression in Federal Prisons." *Federal Probation*, 48(1):46-53.

Nacci, P.L., H.E. Teitelbaum and J. Prather (1977a). "Population Density and Inmate Misconduct Rates in the Federal System." *Federal Probation*, 41(2):27-38.

Nacci, P.L., H.E. Teitelbaum and J. Prather (1977b). "Violence in Federal Prisons: The Effect of Population Density on Misconduct." National Institute of Justice/National Criminal Justice Reference Service.

Park, J.W. (1976). "The Organization of Prison Violence." In A.K. Cohen et al. (eds.) *Prison Violence,* Pp. 89-96. Lexington, MA: Lexington Books.

Sylvester, S.F., J.H. Reed and D.O. Nelson (1977). *Prison Homicide.* New York, NY: Spectrum Publications.

Sykes, G.M. (1958). *The Society of Captives.* Princeton, NJ: Princeton University Press.

Sykes, G.M. and S.L. Messinger (1960). "The Inmates Social System." In D. Cressey (ed.) *Theoretical Studies in Social Organization of the Prison,* Pp. 5-19. New York, NY: Social Science Research Council.

Toch, H. (1969). *Violent Men: An Inquiry into the Psychology of Violence.* Chicago, IL: Aldine.

Toch, H. (1975). *Men in Crisis.* Chicago, IL: Aldine.

Toch, H. (1977). *Living in Prison: The Ecology of Survival.* New York, NY: The Free Press.

Toch, H. (1978). "Social Climate and Prison Violence." *Federal Probation,* 42(4):21-25.

Toch, H. and K. Adams (1986). "Pathology and Disruptiveness Among Prison Inmates." *Journal of Research in Crime and Delinquency,* 23:7-21.

Toch, H., K. Adams and R. Greene (1987). "Ethnicity, Disruptiveness, and Emotional Disorder Among Prison Inmates." *Criminal Justice and Behavior,* 14(1):93-109.

Walkey, F.H. and D. Ross Gilmour (1984). "The Relationship Between Interpersonal Distance and Violence in Imprisoned Offenders." *Criminal Justice and Behavior,* 11(3):331-341.

Wooden, W.S. and J. Parker (1982). *Men Behind Bars: Sexual Exploitation in Prison.* New York, NY: De Capo Press.

6   Issues in Prison Sexual Violence[†]

Daniel Lockwood

Although exaggerated claims have confused the issue, recent research indicates that sexual harassment is a major punishment for some prisoners. While discussion of prison sexual violence has focused on homosexual rape, a rare event, sexual harassment, affecting far more men, has been a neglected topic. In contemplating such decisions as sentencing and release from confinement, in weighing the suffering of imprisonment in a particular case, the stress associated with being the target of sexual aggressors should always be considered. While, indeed, prison managers should carry out measures to reduce the problem, it remains a strong possibility that sexual harassment, an inherent situation in the American prison of today, is not likely to be much reduced by administrative measures.

In the last few years, research has allowed for accurate estimates of the extent of this problem in the New York State and federal prison systems (Lockwood, 1980; Nacci, 1982). Contrary to the claims of some writers, who have claimed without much evidence, that high rates of prison rape prevail throughout the nation, these studies show that low rates of sexual assault exist in the prison systems examined. These same surveys, however, have indicated that large numbers of men have been sexually propositioned in confinement. Sexual approaches perceived as offensive, thus, should be seen as the most important basis of the problem of prison sexual violence. Peter Nacci, a researcher with the Federal Bureau of Prisons, carried out a large study of prison sexual behavior, following a rash of sex-related murders at the Lewisburg Penitentiary. While the Nacci study found that .6 percent of federal inmates surveyed, or 2 out of 330, have been compelled to perform undesired

[†]This article was originally published in the *Prison Journal* and is reprinted here by permission of the Prison Society.

sex acts, 29 percent of these men had been propositioned in their institutions (Nacci, 1982). Similarly, the random survey I carried out in New York showed that 28 percent of the men selected had been targets of aggressively perceived approaches at some point in their institutional career. One man among these 76 had been the victim of a sexual assault. Thus, one may conclude that to the degree this situation prevails in other prisons, the problems created by sexual propositions in prison affect far more men than those suffering the devastating consequences of sexual assault.

The impact of sexual approaches on targets has been described in my previous work (Lockwood, 1980). To summarize these findings, sexual harassment, that is, sexual approaches perceived as offensive by their targets, leads to fights, social isolation, racism, fear, anxiety, and crisis. Others report the same. Sylvester (1977) claims that homosexual activity is a leading motive for inmate homicides. Nacci and Kane (1982) report that of 12 murders occurring during a 26-month period among a population of federal prisoners, five had a sexual basis, that is, sex pressuring, unrequited love, or jealousy. Hans Toch (1969), among others, describes similar findings. One can conclude, therefore, that of all the sources of prison violence, sexual pressuring, as Nacci and Kane state, can be "potentially the most dangerous conflict in prison."

In 1968, a government investigation was described in the "Report on Sexual Assaults in the Philadelphia Prison System and Sheriff's Vans" (Davis, 1968). This report, receiving widespread media coverage at the time, has influenced popular and scholarly writing on the topic. Often, as writers have generalized the finding of this report to other prison systems, we can trace errors in the criminological literature to reliance on this single source. Prison and jail conditions vary widely over place and time. Concerning rates of victimization, it is quite improper to extrapolate findings from one prison system to another.

Another source of error has been misinterpretation of the definition of sexual assault used in Davis' report. While writers defined "sexual assault" to mean "prison rape," in actuality the Philadelphia Report included in its definition of sexual assault "solicitations accompanied physical assault or threats, and other coercive solicitations" (Davis, 1968:2). The high rate of sexual assault in the Philadelphia Report was thus defined as prison rape, and, used as a basis for estimating rates of homosexual rape in other prisons, resulted in a false picture of the actual situation in many places.

Individual case studies in the prison literature have also been used to generalize about the dynamics of sexual pressuring in prison. In reviewing these accounts, and attempting to use them as primary sources to examine prison sexual violence, one should always be cautious. Popular writers, prison reformers, and even prisoners themselves, such as those in "Scared Straight," the 1978 film made in Rathway that attracted the nation's interest, have been perpetuating certain ideas about prison sexual violence that are not supported by systematic research on the topic. Let us review some of these.

One myth is that sexual aggressors tend to be successful, that targets of sex pressure, after enough threats or physical force, becoming willing "kids" of prison "daddies." Even among prisoners, there is the belief that many partners in consensual relationships were at one time "turned out" by "booty bandits." My research contradicts this notion. My findings show targets coping with the experience by making demonstrations of violence that cause others to leave them alone or by developing protective lifestyles. In most cases, in my study, targets were only targets once. Then they managed to deal with the problem. Others, although pressured over time, did not give in to the urging of the aggressors. In no case was I able to document a change of sexual behavior caused by aggression and encountered no consensual arrangements begun by aggressive overtures against heterosexual men.

Another unfounded inference is the notion that victims of sexual harassment, embittered by the experience, commit crimes upon their release as they turn their hate and hostility toward the public. In actuality, there is little reliable data about the effects of any specific prison experiences on subsequent behavior in the free world and no empirical information about the postrelease criminal behavior of former targets of sexual aggression. To claim, without evidence, that prison victimization results in increased recidivism is a disservice to former prisoners seeking acceptance by employers, neighbors, and family members. Especially when combined with the fantasy of high rates of sexual assault, the claim that many men leave prison with strong motives for antisocial behavior is a damaging myth.

Another popularly held notion, also unfounded, is the idea that targets of sex pressure in prison are primarily sex offenders against children or other "low status" criminals, according to the convict code. In reality, at least according to my research, the crime one commits has little to do with one's selection to be a target. Other factors are far more important in target selection, especially race, nature of the home neighborhood, and other indicators of subculture. The nature of the commitment offense per se is a poor predictor of victim selection in prison.

Having examined some of the myths regarding sexual pressuring in prison, let us look at some of the realities. Fear is the most common emotion accompanying the target experience. Fear can be a general feeling or a specific apprehension of being physically harmed, sexually assaulted, or killed. Fear can shift from the arena of the incident and its players to encompass feelings about the entire prison milieu. Such fear often becomes intensified by the inability of targets to easily remove themselves from the presence of aggressors. Regardless of force in an incident, fear can be an intense emotion, persisting over time and governing subsequent lifestyles. For example, here are some typical comments from men interviewed:

> **ARE 4:** I would live in apprehension. Every time I would unlock that door or lock out till the time I went back in it was constant pressure of watch out for this man.

> **ARE 36:** Whenever I see him around I am consciously aware of
> it. No matter what I am doing I have to keep in the back of my
> mind where he is. Not that he would try anything out there in the
> yard or anything, but the thing is, you never know...I have always
> got it in my mind whenever he is around to be well aware.

Not all men emerge from incidents feeling fearful. About 50 percent of our targets said they did, although we do suspect underreporting because men in prison do not readily admit to feeling fearful. The nature of the target's fear differed from man to man, depending more on personal characteristics than on incident characteristics. We rated the severity of incidents looking at the level of force. We also rated the intensity of the psychological reaction. When compared statistically, it was shown that a prisoner's individual reaction to victimization has as much to do with personal factor as it does with the level of force deployed.

Anger is also a common reaction and includes accumulated frustration venting from persistent unwanted approaches. Men who have trouble controlling feelings are particularly sensitive to this response. Other prisoners are vulnerable because confinement causes frustration, to which the feelings about the sexual approach must be added. Anger can result in explosive reactions or can be narrowly held in check, contributing to the prisoner's tensions and anxiety.

Anxiety was reported for about one-third of the incidents in my study. The stress accompanying this tension frequently was signaled by physical indicators. Fear was the primary feeling bringing on anxiety, which could persist far beyond the end of the incident. Men with previous mental health problems seemed particularly vulnerable.

Crises can follow from sexual approaches as men react to these feelings. These crises are commonly signaled by emotional upset, along with requests for medication or isolation. Suicidal thoughts and gestures sometimes accompany these crises when men feel their fate as future victims is sealed or when men wish staff to move them to a safe area. The following excerpt from an interview with a prisoner who cut his wrists with broken glass following an aggressive sexual approach illustrates this possibility:

> **CR 26:** I was just so confused and everything because of that I
> just didn't care anymore and I felt to myself if they are going to
> rip me off for my ass, I am going to cut up and go over to the hos-
> pital and they can't get me over there. I just didn't care. I had been
> put away most of my life and half of my life was ruined anyways
> so why should I live with the pain and all.

There is also an impact on social relations. Targets, or those who believe themselves to be potential targets, become suspicious, avoid making friendships (which are a way of coping with prison aggression), and often isolate themselves in their cells, coming out only when necessary. Sexual aggression is also a cause of racial polarity, as whites band together in their fear of black aggressors. The impact of sexual aggression on men's lives seems to be accentuated by inmate beliefs that sexual assault leads to permanent identity change, that aggressors are successful, and that homosexual activity is reprehensible. These beliefs add to the intensity of the target experience.

Planned Change to Correct the Problem

In considering policy to alleviate the situation, Nacci and Kane (1982) have proposed a plan of "target hardening," in which inmates are advised to change mannerisms that attract aggressors, e.g., avoiding "feminine" hairstyles, gestures, and clothing, and staying away from others, especially homosexuals, who may suggest to others that they are available for sexual activity. Such an approach, based on the factors in target selection, is logical and can be recommended. However, one should also consider that this approach may lend itself to "blaming the victim" and may place an unfair burden on potential victims for altering life habits and styles.

Nacci and Kane (1982) have also suggested, quite correctly, that "an infusion of morality is required" to correct the basis of the problem. Since prison sex aggression, ultimately, is caused by values and attitudes, this plan could be successful. In brief, what is called for is the moral reform of the prison, with special regard to "normalizing" sexual relations and attitudes. For example, prisoners would not be allowed to refer to other men by female referents, it would not be permitted for males to be accepted as female surrogates, and consensual homosexual activity would not, as it now is, be condoned. This may be a good plan for making institutions safer. However, from the view of prisoner's rights, there may be some difficulty in implementing the coercion to virtue implied by such a program. One must also consider the difficulty of creating a moral community among men with histories of immoral and predatory behavior.

Following my own field research, I have recommended the violence-reduction plan of AVP, or the Alternatives to Violence Project, of the American Friends (Lockwood, 1980). In addition, I have suggested that properly applied notions of the therapeutic community, carefully tied to the dynamics of the situation, would also be helpful (Lockwood, 1982). However, even though one applies all methods of planned change available today to the problem, the position I took in the mid 1970s, when my research on prison aggression began, is a tenable one: the causes of prison sexual aggression are fundamentally the same as the causes of sexual aggression and sexual harassment in the free world. Both behaviors spring from male values and attitudes regarding women (or, as is the case of prison, men placed in female roles). Since it is unlikely that such conduct norms, so widely ingrained throughout our culture, will change, sexual aggression and sexual harassment must be viewed as a permanent factor in the sentence of imprisonment. While, indeed, some men within our society exhibit little sexual aggression, it is also true that members of such subcultures are not as likely as others to end up in prison. The most violent people among us, who tend more than others to end up in prison, are also the most sexually abusive. When confined, they will continue to harass weaker men.

As for research implied by the studies undertaken in the last few years in the field of prison sexual aggression, we must consider that the types of men who commit acts of sexual aggression in prison are the same men who commit acts of criminal violence on the street. To examine big city mugging, armed robbery, and rape is also to study the behavior of sexual aggressors in prison. Thus, general studies of violence, applied to the portrait now in existence of prison sexual violence, should prove to be useful.

Additionally, one should also bear in mind that criminal behavior continues when criminals are sent to prison. Prison populations are a laboratory for the study of violent behaviors of all types. Findings about the specific topic of sexual aggression, thus, should make a general contribution to criminology. At the current time, for example, I am examining patterns of interaction that typically develop in incidents marked by sequences escalating to violence. While the research sites are correctional institutions, the findings are generally applicable. In conclusion, prison sexual violence should be seen as a manifestation of more general forces in our society, and as we progress toward understanding and correcting violence among us, we shall progress toward a more thorough understanding of prison victimization.

References

Davis, A.J. (1968). "Sexual Assaults in the Philadelphia Prison System and Sheriff's Vans." *Transaction*, 6, 13.

Lockwood, D. (1980). *Prison Sexual Violence*. New York, NY: Elsevier.

Nacci, P.L. (1982). "Sex and Sexual Aggression in Federal Prisons." Unpublished manuscript. U.S. Federal Prison System: Office of Research.

Sylvester, S., J. Reed and D. Nelson (1977). *Prison Homicide*. New York, NY: Spectrum.

Toch, H. (1969). *Violent Men*. Chicago, IL: Aldine.

7

The Violent and Victimized in the Male Prison[†][††]

Kevin N. Wright

A review of the literature on prison violence identifies two types of studies concerning violent and victimized inmates. One, typified by Irwin's *Prisons in Turmoil*, is rich in descriptive detail but is generally based on one person's observations and assessment of what is taking place in the prison setting. The second set consists of empirically generated profiles of either violent or victimized inmates and tends to be limited in scope. This study seeks to expand existing empirical research by testing some of the propositions posed in the descriptive literature. Specifically, the study examines the differences and similarities of violent and victimized inmates and explores whether environmental factors affect these inmates' behavior.

The methodology consists of a cross-sectional analysis of patterns of inmate adjustment in ten prisons. Using several indicators of violence and victimization, the distinctiveness of these two groups is explored, and profiles using background variables, personality types, and environmental concerns are developed. To test whether violent and victimized inmates experience incarceration differently, the study examined whether they rate their environmental situation differently.

Profiles of aggressive inmates conform to the descriptions of state-raised youth found in the literature. These institutionally experienced individuals are considered to be among the most violent individuals in prison and are a source of considerable disruption. However, this research revealed two types of predatory inmates: a group

[†]Reprinted from *Journal of Offender Rehabilitation*, Vol. 16 (3/4), 1991. Copyright © 1991 by The Haworth Press, Inc., 10 Alice St., Binghamton, NY 13904. Reprinted by permission.

[††]The research described in this chapter was supported by Grant 83-IJ-CX-0011 from the National Institute of Justice.

that has trouble relating to other people and another that is assaultive. Personality types helped explain the differences in these two groups.

> Findings concerning victimized inmates were consistent with the literature. They are the "lambs" within the population, lacking experience to cope with the predatory environment. They, too, have distinctive personalities.

> Contextual factors were found to be related to troubled adjustment to prison. Both violent and victimized inmates have specific environmental needs and rate the prison setting as worse than do nonviolent or non-victimized criminals.

Incarceration is traumatic for almost all inmates; it symbolizes the unworthiness of the individual to live among the law abiding and the failure of the person to contribute to society in a meaningful and acceptable way. It strains ties to the free world and suspends career and personal goals. Rejected by society, the inmate is placed in the stark, impersonal, and often volatile environment of the prison, where he must function in a subservient, dependent role with few opportunities for demonstrating self worth. Within this context, incarceration poses a substantial emotional challenge to which the inmate must respond to survive. As Robert Johnson (1976) states, "the pressures of prison threaten to undermine the convict's image of himself as a self-sufficient, respectable adult male."

Within the twisted confines of an all-male institution, the personal threat of incarceration often becomes defined and reconciled as an issue of manhood. Doubts about one's identity are simplified to questions of manliness, and the status of inmates as men is played out by a ritual of testing to identify weaker individuals, a process which in turn substantiates the strength of those who dominate them. As a consequence, inmates face the "ever-present fear of failure and humiliation at the hands" of their keepers and their peers (Johnson, 1976), and physical and psychological aggression are an inevitable aspect of the prison environment.

Some inmates face this challenge with hard, silent stoicism. Outward composure allows them to ward off threats of emasculation. They accept their punishment without emotion and give the appearance of withstanding the pains of incarceration. Other inmates withdraw into themselves. They engage in few social activities and constrict their environment; they find a niche, be it the prison library, the school or their cell, where they feel relatively safe and secure. A minority of inmates opt for more extreme forms of adaptation. Some prove their masculinity by exaggerating it. These are the aggressive inmates who prove their worth by confronting those who confine them and by dominating weaker peers. At the opposite extreme are the exploited, who are unable to withstand the threats of others and are victimized. It is the latter two types of inmate with which this study is concerned.

Prison Violence

Hans Toch (1985) identifies in the literature two perspectives for explaining the prevalence of prison violence: one view holds that "some inmates are consistently violent persons, who happen to be explosive in prison, but are likely to act out in almost any setting." The other claims that violence is a prison product.

The literature is less clear about who becomes a *victim*. Are they unfortunate individuals who happen to be in the wrong place at the wrong time, or do they possess special characteristics or play particular roles that lead to their victimization? This review will begin by exploring the individual characteristics of violent inmates, then consider the contextual elements that contribute to prison violence and conclude with a discussion of the small body of research on victims.

Bowker (1985) claims that some people who are sentenced to prison "are violence prone in that they have not generally been socialized to reject violence as a way of solving problems" and may have histories of participation in subcultures of violence before incarceration. Irwin (1980) shares this perspective in his description of the background of most male prisoners, claiming that many are "drawn from a social layer that shares extremely reduced life options, meager material existence, limited experience with formal, polite, and complex urban social organizations, and traditional suspicions and hostilities toward people different from their own kind." Consequently, inmates bring with them to prison their violent pasts and draw on their experiences as they shape the culture of the facility. Johnson observes (1987) that "the wors[t] of society's rejects create a world in which the prospect and often the reality of violence are facts of everyday life. In the convict world, toughness and the capacity for violence define power, status, and honor." Gibbs (1981) describes the process whereby the adoption of a masculine persona helps ensure survival and status within the inmate society:

> This is a world in which legitimate authorities are seldom appealed
> to, and disputes are settled by vendetta. It is a world in which "male"
> no longer simply connotes certain anatomical characteristics. As
> in many all-male groups, manliness becomes a status contin-
> uum. One's place on the continuum is of great importance, and
> may be determined by demonstrations of "toughness" during the
> first weeks of confinement.

Clear and Cole (1986) identify four characteristics of the incarcerated population that make this group particularly violence prone: (1) age, (2) certain social attitudes such as "machismo," (3) membership in a free world gang, and (4) racism. Similarly, Bennett (1975) found violent offenders in the California prison at San Quentin to be younger and more often nonwhite, less well-educated, and from broken homes than nonviolent inmates. They tended either to have had no father figure or a succession of father figures; and, if a father figure was present, he was likely to be alcoholic, criminal, or abusive. They were arrested at a young age, had been incarcerated previously, and had histories of institutional violence. Myers and Levy (1978) found a similar profile of inmates labeled as chronic disciplinary problems in the Southern Ohio Correctional Facility.

Toch (1985) argues that violence in prison must be viewed as the intersection of violence-prone people with situational stimuli that invoke those predispositions. In studying the violent incident involving the victimization of one inmate by another, Mueller, Toch, and Molof (1965) found that several factors, including extortion, homosexual relations, debts, stealing, and routine disputes often resulted in the escalation of an "incident" to a violent encounter.

Johnson (1987) describes the ecology of the contemporary prison as "strikingly parallel to that of our dangerous and yet highly differentiated urban slum." Prison populations are composed of predominantly poor, lower-class segments of society who differentiate themselves along ethnic lines and are generally hostile to one another. Many residents of the prison, like those of the urban slum, lack commitment to public morality which promotes a safe and violence-free setting. Consequently, residents must either withdraw from social relations or form strong bonds with individuals from similar backgrounds for mutual protection. The formation of coalitions for mutual protection, since intergroup conflict may be used to demonstrate intragroup loyalties (Irwin, 1980), further promotes a climate that permits violence.

Relatively recent changes in the inmate society have rendered prisons even more violent (see Irwin, 1980; Johnson, 1987; Jacobs, 1977; Conrad, 1982; Bowker, 1982; Carroll, 1974; Sheehan, 1978; Stastny & Tynauer, 1982). A decade or two ago, the informal culture of inmates promoted stability and helped contain violence. The inmate code discouraged exploitation of other inmates and promoted an individualized form of adaptation. In return for greater privileges and the most desirable jobs, high-status inmates joined the custodial staff in keeping peace in the facility. Without the limitations imposed by recent federal court decisions, troublemakers could be sequestered by prison officials in special housing for long periods (Jacobs, 1977).

Johnson (1987) identifies several factors thought to contribute to the demise of the "repressive but reasonably safe" traditional prison. The rise of professional administrators and their attempts to reduce oppression and to "initiate" treatment programs undermined the system of rigid discipline found in traditional prisons. Concurrently, it came to be thought that individual change could not occur in highly authoritarian settings and that discipline must be relaxed. Power shifted away from custody personnel to the new treatment staff. The rise of the Black Power movement, at a time when the black prisoner population was increasing, led to escalation of racial tensions and violence. Finally, and perhaps most importantly, exploitive and violence-prone state-raised convicts gained power.

Johnson (1987) describes the influence of state-raised convicts on prison life as follows:

They have made today's prison a dangerous place for staff and fellow prisoners alike. It is they who, by their violence, find themselves embroiled with the custodial staff. They are the prison's bastard children, and this unhappy status brings out the worst in both the prisoners and the prison. They are easily provoked to violence by the stresses of prison life, and in turn they provoke the prison staff to use violence and even brutality to maintain law and order behind bars.

From this review, one might infer that victims are often weaker inmates who cannot withstand the threats and aggressive advances of stronger inmates. They succumb to the constant pressure applied as masculinity is tested and may lack the physical and ego strength or social abilities to avoid conflict. However, in the exploitive environment found in today's prisons, victims may simply be the unfortunate prey of exploitive, state-raised convicts or ethnic cliques. They may also be aggressors who lose in contests of will.

Little research has been conducted on the victims of violence. However, one finding that has emerged is that who becomes a victim is related to the motivation for the attack. Bowker (1982) identifies four types of victimization: economic, social, psychological, and physical. Each may lead to violence. Inmates involved in the "underground economy" may be victimized to settle debts. Violence may result from racial antagonism associated with social victimization. Also, inmates who have been threatened may retaliate to regain status or prestige, or out of frustration. Finally, retaliatory violence often follows violent attacks in each of these situations. The characteristics of the victims vary from situation to situation.

Some research (Bowker, 1982a, 1982b; Gibbs, 1981) identifying the characteristics of victims tends to focus on physical victimization and, in particular, sexual victimization. Victims are described as "lambs" within the prison population, in contrast to their assailants who are labeled "wolves." They tend to be white, small, young, and middle class. They lack mental toughness and are not "street-wise." Lambs often have been convicted of sex crimes, particularly against children, or of comparatively minor property offenses. Toch (1977) found that many victims have histories of emotional disturbance.

Fuller and Orsagh (1977), in their study of the correlates of victimization, made two important observations: the primary precipitating event of victimization was an assault, and the principal cause of an assault was an inmate interaction of some sort, most commonly over economic matters. Wolfson's (1978) study of prison homicide corroborates these findings. Economic retaliation was the most frequent cause of murder in prison. Prison homicides were often premeditated and, contrary to claims found in the literature, were seldom the result of racial warfare. Victim precipitation commonly played a role.

The purpose of the present study is to expand existing research by exploring two broad questions: First, the similarities and differences between violent and victimized inmates will be considered to see if there are, in fact, two distinct groups as implied by the literature. Second, it will consider whether environmental factors affect the adoption of particular responses to incarceration and if the factors identified in the literature contribute to these outcomes.

Methods

Design

To learn more about patterns of inmate adjustment, a cross-sectional analysis of individuals who engage in extreme forms of adaptation was conducted. Several indicators taken from official records and self-reports were used to classify inmates as *violent* and/or *victimized*. Since these attributes involve a matter of degree rather than distinction, those individuals who fall at the extreme ends of a continuum indicating these behavioral traits were selected.

The literature generally suggests that those individuals who are violent and those who are victimized constitute two distinct groups. But, since it is possible that individuals who are victimized or threatened may respond violently to protect themselves, this study explored the distinctiveness of the two groups. Having classified subjects into these groups, profiles were developed (using background variables, personality, and environmental concerns) to distinguish these individuals from inmates who do not engage in extreme forms of adjustment.

Recognizing not only that individual characteristics determine response patterns but that the social context affects outcomes, the possible impact of social environments on inmate behavioral responses was examined. Subjects were asked to assess their prison setting on eight environmental characteristics to determine whether violent and victimized inmates ranked their settings differently than inmates not so classified.

Measures

Two sources of information were used to identify violent and victimized inmates: official records and self-reports. From the disciplinary records maintained at each facility, a complete history of rule infractions was obtained for every inmate in the sample. Data were collected for a three-year period from August 15, 1980 to August 15, 1983. *Violent* inmates were considered to be individuals who had been charged with an assault on an inmate or a staff member. *Victimized* inmates were identified as those who had attempted suicide or had inflicted an injury on themselves.

The Prison Adjustment Questionnaire (PAQ) was developed to measure self-perceptions of adjustment (see Wright, 1985a for a full explanation of the instrument and its development). This instrument consists of 20 questions that explore nine adjustment problems that inmates may experience during incarceration. In designing the instrument, it was recognized that people in prison have problems coping; they may have long histories of adjustment problems in school, in their personal lives, and with the law. Since this study was concerned with the adverse effects of incarceration, it was necessary to control for this history; interest lay in those problems that were exacerbated or created by incarceration. To do this, the first question about a particular problem asked the respondent whether the problem was "worse" in prison than in the free world. Responses were then scored by frequency of occurrence.

Based upon psychometric analyses of the instrument, three interpretable dimensions were found, two of which were used in this component of the research. The first, the external dimension, includes items that indicate that the subject is experiencing problems relating to other people, that he fights and argues with fellow inmates and staff. Inmates who scored high on this dimension (in the top 10% of the sample) were considered highly aggressive. The second dimension includes very real and tangible physical problems (being hurt, sick, taken advantage of). In this study, rather than looking at the dimension as a whole, it was decided to examine the responses to two of the items individually: inmates who reported that they were at least occasionally hurt or taken advantage of.

To summarize, two measures of violence and three measures of victimization were used, some from the official records and others self-reported, resulting in classification of subjects as:

Assaulters: Those individuals who have been officially charged with assaulting a staff member or another inmate.

Highly aggressive: Those individuals falling into the top 10 percent of those who report on the external dimension of the PAQ that they fight and argue with fellow inmates and staff.

Self-injured: Those individuals who have been officially charged with self-inflicted injury or attempted suicide.

Hurt: Those individuals who report on the physical dimension of the PAQ that they have been hurt in prison.

Taken advantage of: Those individuals who report on the physical dimension of the PAQ that they are taken advantage of in prison.

Four questionnaires, including the PAQ, were administered to inmates. Toch's (1977) Prison Preference Inventory (PPI) was administered to determine each subject's environmental preferences on eight dimensions: freedom, emotional feedback, support, safety, privacy, activity, social stimulation, and structure. This 58-item, forced-choice instrument provides a ranking of environmental concerns as well as a numerical weight for each dimension. A new instrument for measuring the contextual attributes of prison settings was developed for use in this study, the Prison Environment Inventory (PEI). Toch's eight environmental factors were used as dimensions. Based upon an elaborate array of item and dimension analyses to test internal validity, a final, 48-item version of the questionnaire was formed (Wright, 1985).

The fourth questionnaire administered, the Minnesota Multiphasic Personality Inventory (MMPI), was used to obtain Megargee inmate classifications. This typology assigns inmates to one of 10 inmate personality types, each with its own unique attributes (Megargee & Bohn, 1979). A problem was encountered in collecting these data. Many inmates, after completing the first session, tired of the research, had other commitments, or had their curiosity satiated, and failed to return for the second session when the MMPI was administered. Other inmates, even though they began the questionnaire, were unwilling to complete it. For these reasons, only 55 percent of the sample completed the inventory.

In addition to the data obtained directly from the subjects, information about background was obtained from departmental records. Eighteen background variables including demographic, social, and criminal histories were collected for each subject.

To summarize, four sets of independent variables were obtained for each subject:

> *Background*: Eighteen variables from official departmental records included age, age at time of incarceration, ethnicity, employment status at time of arrest, military service, drug use, alcohol use, crime, crime class, second-time felon status, education, religion, previous contacts with the criminal justice system, county of commitment, conviction for a violent crime, counts, prior adult record, and marital status.

> *Personality*: Assigned as one of the 10 types identified by the Megargee typology based on the MMPI.

> *Environmental needs*: Determined using Toch's Prison Preference Inventory (PPI) for the following eight dimensions: freedom, emotional feedback, support, safety, privacy, activity, social stimulation, and structure.

> *Environmental assessments:* Determined using Wright's Prison Environment Inventory (PEI) for the same eight dimensions.

Sample and Data Collection

Data were collected from randomly selected samples of male inmates at five medium and five maximum security New York State prisons. The 10 prisons were randomly selected from all institutions within each security classification. A list of inmates incarcerated in the facilities was used to generate *random* samples. Populations were over-sampled to allow for attrition. Some inmates were unavailable for survey sessions because they were confined for disciplinary action or protection, or had sick-calls, visits, or court hearings. Other inmates preferred not to participate.

Inmates were notified they had been randomly selected, and a brief description of the study was given by prison staff. In some facilities, the call-out to the study was mandatory but *participation* was voluntary. In other facilities, both the call-out and participation were voluntary. In one prison, officials first determined if the inmates were willing to participate, then placed them on the call-out.

The entire survey session required an average of two two-hour sessions. Subjects were not financially compensated for their participation but were told a letter of appreciation would be sent to the institution and placed in their files. Questionnaires were administered in three ways: inmates who so elected could take a paper and pencil test in English, or if they preferred, taped versions in English or Spanish were also available. The total sample consisted of 942 subjects.

Findings

An Assessment of the Sample

To test for selection bias in the sample resulting from non-participation of some of the randomly selected subjects, the sample was compared to the population on the 18 background variables identified earlier. Significant differences were found on three variables: ethnicity, county of conviction, and number of counts. These results may restrict the population to which the findings of this study can be generalized.

A second sampling problem arose when a sizable proportion of the sample failed to complete the MMPI. To evaluate the extent to which sample attrition resulted in bias, completers and non-completers were compared on all independent and dependent variables. The two groups differed on only one independent variable: ethnicity. Whites completed the personality inventory most frequently, followed by blacks, then Hispanics. MMPI completers and non-completers also differed on only one dependent variable: Self-reports of external problems. The completers report a slightly higher rate of problem occurrence than the non-completers.

Identifying the Violent and Victimized

Eighty-nine of the 942 subjects (9.45% of the total sample) had been cited by prison officials for attacking either an inmate or a staff member during the three years prior to the study. By definition, 10 percent of the sample was also considered to be highly aggressive based upon their scores on the external dimension of the PAQ; that is, they reported fighting and arguing with inmates and staff more frequently than other inmates. The two indicators do not identify the same group of inmates (chi-square = 2.22, p = 0.14). Only 15 percent of the assaulters reported high rates of aggressiveness.

It is difficult to interpret these results and identify *truly* violent inmates within the sample. Not all assaults become officially recognized; consequently, some individuals who claim to be aggressive may have never been caught. Others charged with assaults may actually be victims who resisted the exploitive advances of more aggressive inmates, were involved in an ensuing fight, and charged with an assault as a consequence. It is also possible that some inmates who report that they argue and fight are never violent.

Three indicators were used to identify victims within the sample: Those officially cited for injuring themselves and those who report they are hurt or taken advantage of. Few individuals are charged with self-inflicted injury (8 of 942, or 0.85% of the sample). Thirteen percent report they are hurt, and 15 percent state that they are taken advantage of.

Of the eight individuals with records of self-injury, only one claimed to be hurt and none indicated that they had been taken advantage of. At first glance, this finding may appear inconsistent; however, Johnson (1976) reports that individuals who engage in self-injury do so to avoid being injured or exploited. Consequently, those individuals in the sample who have injured themselves may have avoided being hurt or taken advantage of by others.

Subjects who claim to be hurt or taken advantage of comprise a similar group (chi-square = 76.10, p = 0.0001). Thirty-five percent of those taken advantage of also report being hurt.

By examining the overlap between the violent and victimized groups, some questions regarding the classifications are clarified. Few assaulters report being hurt or taken advantage of; only 12 percent report being hurt (chi-square = 1.33, p = 0.25), and 9 percent indicate they are taken advantage of (chi-square = 0.04, p = 0.85). However, of those falling into the highly aggressive group, 30 percent report being hurt (chi-square = 63.33, p = 0.0001) and 21 percent being taken advantage of (chi-square = 21.66, p = 0.0001). Interestingly, self-inflicted injury is related to aggressiveness. Five of eight (62.5%) report that they fight and argue frequently (chi-square = 24.45, p = 0.0001), and three of eight (37.5%) have records of assault (chi-square = 7.42, p = 0.0006).

From these results, it appears that the measures used in this study identified several types of inmates experiencing problems adjusting to prison. One group is composed of *violent* individuals who assault other inmates and staff. Another, somewhat distinct group, is comprised of *aggressive* individuals who have problems relating to other people and are aggressive in response to threats of victimization. There is also a group of *victims* who are either hurt, taken advantage of, or both. Finally, there is a small group of inmates in the sample who suffer *severe distress* and attempt to hurt themselves or take their own lives. Many of these individuals also engage in violent or aggressive behavior directed toward others.

Profiles of the Violent and Victimized

Background

Profiles of the four groups of inmates with adjustment problems (the assaulters, the inmates who scored high on the external scale, and those who were hurt or taken advantage of) are summarized in Table 7.1. It was not possible to construct a comparative profile of the inmates who have been charged with self-inflicted injury because of the extremely small numbers of individuals falling into the category. These profiles were constructed by comparing troubled and non-troubled inmates on the 18 background variables.

Inmates who assault in prison are younger than their non-assaultive counterparts, with an average age difference of approximately three years. Besides being younger, assaultive inmates tend to have histories of unemployment, are less educated, and are more likely to be single. Interestingly, their criminal histories are not different from non-assaulters, but they were incarcerated for the first time at a younger age.

Table 7.1. **Background Profiles**

Significant Background Variables	Assaulter	Non-Assaulter	Highly Aggressive	Not Highly Aggressive	Hurt	Not Hurt	Taken Advantage Of	Not Taken Advantage Of
1. Ave. age	27 $t=4.20, p=.001$	30	26 $t=6.51, p=.001$	30	27 $t=4.00, p=.0001$	30		
2. Ave. age when incarcerated	24 $t=4.77, p=.0001$	27	23 $t=7.17, p=.0001$	28	24 $t=5.26, p=.0001$	27		
3. Unemployed at time of arrest	47% $x^2=18.15, p=.0001$	26%	44% $x^2=13.94, p=.0002$	26%				
4. Educational background	(No High School) 38% $x^2=0.80, p=.05$	27%					(High School Diploma) 38% $x^2=12.69, p=.005$	27%
5. Marital status (single)	73% $x^2=12.59, p=.01$	55%	75% $x^2=14.43, p=.01$	55%				
6. Convicted for a violent crime			88% $x^2=8.31, p=.004$	75%			85% $x^2=5.31, p=.02$	75%
7. Crime class			A 11% B 39% C 33% D 14% E 2% $x^2=10.89, p=.05$	16% 32% 24% 20% 7%				
8. Ethnicity			W 41% B 50% H 10% $x^2=25.93, p=.001$	22% 56% 22%				

This profile is consistent with the literature and provides empirical verification for the descriptions provided by Irwin (1980) and Johnson (1987) of the state-raised convict. Those inmates who attack others are young, institutionally experienced individuals, who have led unstable lives and show a strong tendency to exploit others. They exhibit a proclivity toward the use of violence to solve their problems and to acquire what they want.

Inmates who report that they fight and argue have profiles similar to those of the assaulters. They are younger, entered prison at a younger age, and are more likely to be unemployed and single. More of these highly aggressive inmates are incarcerated for violent crimes than those who fall into this characterization. They are incarcerated for serious felonies (rape, robbery, aggravated assault, and burglary) rather than granted larceny or possession of a controlled substance, but are no more likely to have been charged with murder.

Despite the fact that their backgrounds are similar to those of the assailants and consistent with the profile of state-raised convicts, *highly aggressive inmates* do not generally have assaultive prison records. What distinguishes the two groups appears to be personality, which will be discussed later.

Subjects who report that they are *taken advantage of* have a distinct profile in contrast to the violent and aggressive inmates. They are not younger than their counterparts and did not enter prison at a younger age. They are better educated and are more likely to be incarcerated for a violent felony. These attributes lead one to believe that these individuals come to prison less prepared to deal with its exploitive environment. They are probably more "middle class" than their counterparts and have not had to deal with similar circumstances in the free world. They lack "street" or institutional experiences to respond effectively to the predatory environment of prison.

Inmates who report being hurt tend to be younger and enter prison at a younger age. Interestingly, little else in their background distinguishes these individuals.

Personality

Assessment of the differences in personality was hampered by the low completion rate on the MMPI, which made it inappropriate to test statistically for differences between troubled and non-troubled groups using chi-square. However, some interesting differences among the groups can be noted in the frequency distributions shown in Table 7.2. As described earlier, Megargee has developed a typology of inmate personality types that he labeled A through J. These types can be categorized along a continuum from most normal to most disturbed as follows: I, E, B, A, G, D, J, F, C, and H.

In looking first at the *assaulters*, we note that the most normal inmates, Type Item, do not become assaulters. On the other hand, Types Able, Foxtrot, and Charlie are more likely to have histories of assaults in prison. This is consistent with Megargee's descriptions of these personalities. Type Able inmates are extroverted individuals who are outgoing, self-assured, and impulsive, but who can also be dominating and manipulative. They are characterized by high levels of hostility and alienation and are described as amoral and daring individuals who are willing to take risks. Type Foxtrot inmates are "obnoxious, 'streetwise' individuals who engender much interpersonal conflict" (Edinger, 1979). They display a broad range of problems and are one of the most violent groups. Type Charlie inmates are cold and bitter individuals who become hostile and violent when they perceive themselves to have been insulted. They have long histories of maladjustment related to their antagonistic attitude, poor sociability, distrust of others and conflict with authority (see Megargee & Bohn, 1979; Lillyquist, 1980; Edinger, 1979).

It is interesting that Type How inmates, the most deviant group, are not overrepresented among the assaulters. A sizable portion of the assaulters are characterized as Type How inmates (9%) but an even larger portion of the non-assaulters (13%) are Type How inmates. This finding is also consistent with the description of this type of personality. Type How inmates are not able to function on a social level and are unable to get along with other people. At times, they are introverted and withdrawn, but at other times they can be extremely aggressive (Megargee & Bohn, 1979; Lillyquist, 1980; Edinger, 1979).

Inmates characterized as highly aggressive have personality profiles similar to those of assaulters, with some important exceptions. Type Item inmates, the least deviant group, tend not to have interpersonal difficulties. Types Foxtrot and Charlie are overrepresented among the highly aggressive, just as they were among the assaulters. Type George and Delta inmates, who fall toward the more deviant end of the continuum, do not report having interpersonal problems. This is probably due to Type George inmates' effectiveness in interpersonal relationships and Type Delta's ability to charm and manipulate others to avoid aggressive conflicts. Type Able inmates are overrepresented among assaulters, but do not report themselves

Table 7.2. **Megargee Typology of Personality Types**

Adjustment Groups	Megargee Types from Least to Most Disturbed										
	I	E	B	A	G	D	J	F	C	H	n
Assaulter	0%	4%	0%	26%	4%	9%	9%	22%	17%	7%	23
Non-Assaulters	24%	2%	2%	17%	7%	5%	6%	13%	12%	13%	338
Highly Aggressive	11%	4%	0%	16%	2%	0%	7%	20%	20%	20%	45
Not Highly Aggressive	24%	2%	2%	18%	8%	6%	6%	13%	10%	12%	316
Hurt	20%	0%	0%	10%	8%	4%	8%	10%	16%	23%	49
Not Hurt	22%	2%	2%	19%	7%	6%	6%	14%	11%	11%	312
Taken Advantage of	21%	2%	3%	6%	6%	8%	2%	15%	19%	18%	62
Not Taken Advantage of	22%	2%	1%	20%	7%	5%	7%	14%	10%	12%	299

as highly aggressive. Perhaps this is due to their outgoing and self-assured nature and their ability to charm and manipulate others. While their daring and opportunistic nature leads them to assault others, their healthy self-image allows them to perceive themselves as not having interpersonal problems. Type How inmates, on the other hand, may not assault but clearly perceive themselves as engaged in interpersonal conflict (Megargee & Bohn, 1979; Lillyquist, 1980; Edinger, 1979).

The most deviant personality types, Charles and How, are clearly overrepresented among the victimized, as indicated by those who are hurt and taken advantage of. Both groups are considered to have extremely poor sociability and consequently believe others are "out to get them." In contrast, the streetwise and aggressive Type Foxtrot inmates avoid victimization. Type Able inmates, who Megargee and Bohn (1979) describe as "Artful Dodgers," are clearly underrepresented among the victimized.

Environmental Needs

Toch (1977) claims that people differ in what they need from their environments. When those needs are not met, distress, frustration, and violence are more likely to occur. Based upon this theoretical perspective, it would be expected that violent and victimized inmates and their non-troubled counterparts would need different contextual conditions. The findings support this hypothesis.

As indicated in Table 7.3, both assaultive and highly aggressive inmates express significantly lower needs for Structure and higher needs for Freedom than do non-violent inmates. The authoritarian and restrictive regime of prison may lead to incongruence between the contextual needs of these prisoners and the environmental provisions, a disparity which, in turn, results in distress, frustration, and, in some cases, violent reactions to relieve tension.

Table 7.3. Inmate Environmental Preferences

Significant PPI Variables	Average Scores							
	Assaulter	Non-Assaulter	Highly Aggressive	Not Highly Aggressive	Hurt	Not Hurt	Taken Advantage Of	Not Taken Advantage Of
1. Structure	6.51	7.14	6.53	7.14	6.70	7.13		
	t=2.53,	p=.01	t=2.58,	p=.01	t=2.00, p=.05			
2. Freedom	6.73	5.37	6.46	5.39				
	t=4.54,	p=.0001	t=3.70,	p=.0002				
3. Social					5.18	5.59		
					t=2.01, p=.04			
4. Safety							7.49	6.64
							t=3.42, p=.004	
5. Activity							6.87	7.47
							t=2.87, p=.004	

Inmates who are hurt also express a lower need for Structure than their counterparts. This may be explained by the fact that similar personality types, those falling at the deviant end of the Megargee typology, are *both* violent and victimized. It may suggest that the victimized require a less controlled, less autocratic setting that allows them the autonomy to establish their own niche. Inmates who are hurt also require less Social Stimulation than others do, which may indicate a desire to withdraw. Inmates who are taken advantage of (as one might expect) desire safer and less active settings than other inmates.

Contextual Effects of Prison Violence

A final consideration in the assessment of prison violence is the effect of the contextual setting on patterns of adjustment. There is a substantial body of research suggesting that the social environment affects behavior, yet most studies of violent and victimized inmates focus on the attributes of individuals. As seen in Table 7.4, inmates who have problems adjusting rate their situation as much worse than inmates who are not violent or victimized.

Inmates who assault perceive their environments as having less Activity, less Social Stimulation, and less Structure than do non-assaultive inmates. *Highly aggressive* inmates

Table 7.4 Inmate Environmental Evaluations

Significant PEI Variables	Assaulter	Non-Assaulter	Highly Aggressive	Not Highly Aggressive	Hurt	Not Hurt	Taken Advantage Of	Not Taken Advantage Of
			Average Scores					
1. Activity	17.20	17.78	16.89	17.87	16.68	17.87	17.05	17.85
	$t=1.96, p=.05$		$t=3.28, p=.001$		$t=4.77, p=.0001$		$t=3.40, p=.0007$	
2. Emotional feedback			13.83	14.57				
			$t=2.91, p=.004$					
3. Privacy			13.89	14.85	14.01	14.86	14.15	14.86
			$t=2.86, p=.004$		$t=2.48, p=.01$		$t=2.55, p=.01$	
4. Safety			15.82	13.73	15.17	13.76	15.03	13.74
			$t=-.605, p=.001$		$t=3.83, p=.002$		$t=-.40, p=.001$	
5. Social Stimulation	15.11	15.80	14.94	15.83	14.84	15.88	15.26	15.83
	$t=2.23, p=.05$		$t=2.99, p=.003$		$t=3.83, p=.0001$		$t=2.26, p=.02$	
6. Structure	18.77	19.51			18.72	19.54	18.78	19.56
	$t=2.30, p=.02$				$t=2.97, p=.003$		$t=3.01, p=.003$	
7. Support			11.31	12.71	11.37	12.75	12.65	12.66
			$t=4.52, p=.001$		$t=4.92, p=.0001$		$t=2.32, p=.02$	
8. Freedom					15.40	16.17		
					$t=2.42, p=.02$			

believe their settings provide less Activity, Emotional Feedback, Privacy, Safety, Social Stimulation, and Support. *Victimized* inmates rate their environments lower on six dimensions (Activity, Privacy, Safety, Social Stimulation, Structure, and Support) than do their counterparts. Inmates *who are hurt* also state they have less Freedom. Given these findings, we must conclude that the environment (or at least the individual's perception of his environment) plays a significant role in who takes drastic and unacceptable action in response to the pressures of incarceration.

Conclusions

From this research, it appears that violent and victimized inmates are generally distinctive. Profiles of the background characteristics of violent inmates (those who assault and those who rate themselves as highly aggressive) indicate that they fit Irwin and Johnson's descriptions of state-raised convicts. These individuals are younger, and most had marginal lifestyles in the community before their incarceration. They tend to have been involved in the criminal justice system at an earlier age too and have had institutional experience. What is intriguing is that those inmates who report that they are aggressive toward others in prison generally do not become assailants. Personality differences appear to distinguish the two groups. Type Able inmates were assaulters but not overrepresented among the highly aggressive, while Type How did not generally assault but were overrepresented among the aggressive. Only two of the most disturbed personality types, Foxtrot and Charlie, were overrepresented as both assaulters and the aggressive.

The findings concerning victimized inmates are consistent with the literature and indicate that these individuals are "lambs" within the population. They appear to be less involved in a criminal culture before incarceration and to have less institutional experience. Upon their incarceration, victimized inmates are seldom charged with assaultive behavior. This finding is contrary to the claim made by some in the literature that a segment of assailants are victims who are trying to protect themselves. However, a sizable proportion of victims report that they are aggressive. They argue and fight with other inmates and staff. This finding may suggest that victims precipitate the attacks upon themselves by their affrontive behavior.

Interestingly, Types Charlie and How inmates, the most disturbed personality types, are overrepresented among victims. Both are unable to get along with other people and have extremely poor social skills. Type Charlie inmates become hostile when insulted, and it is easy to imagine how that hostility leads to their victimization. Concurrently, Type Charlie inmates may also react violently when confronted in a social situation and thus are overrepresented among the assaulters. Type How inmates are incapable of getting along with other people. Sometimes they withdraw into themselves but can be hostile, a process which possibly precipitates their victimization.

These findings provide important information for prison administrators. They suggest that potential assaulters can be identified by both background and personality, but that background alone will not be sufficient, since assaulters and highly aggressive non-assaultive inmates have similar backgrounds. For this reason, risk assessment inventories alone are inadequate to identify potential assailants.

Knowing that highly aggressive inmates do not become assailants, but that their affrontive behavior often leads to attacks on them, is important in their management. An understandable response to their affrontive behavior would be to increase the security classification for these individuals in an attempt to prevent them from hurting other inmates or the staff, while a more appropriate response might be to offer some form of interpersonal relations training for these individuals to help them understand the role they play in their attacks. Furthermore, correctional staff may need to be trained to intervene quickly to prevent the escalation of incidents to violent confrontations.

Identifying Types How and Charlie inmates within the population recognizes a group of inmates who are likely to have significant problems adjusting to prison. These individuals need to be closely supervised, and possibly specially placed, so that their inability to function socially does not lead to their victimization or attacks on others.

The literature suggests that prison violence is related to the threat incarceration poses to the individual's identity and particularly his sense of masculinity. Both assaultive and highly aggressive inmates express significantly lower needs for Structure and higher needs for Freedom than do their counterparts. The traditional administrative response to violence and aggression has been to tighten controls. Inmates who are perceived as potentially violent or who engage in violence are removed from less secure settings and placed in more structured settings with less freedom. It is possible that this practice *compounds* the problem. If these individuals were given greater freedom and opportunities to substantiate their self worth and manhood, then violence might be reduced.

Similarly, inmates who are hurt express less need for Structure. They, too, may need a less controlled and autocratic setting to find a protective niche. Inmates who are taken advantage of need a safe and less active setting. This information suggests that attention to placements is important if inmates are to have the facilities to successfully adjust. The effect of failure to meet these needs is clearly evident in the inmates' ratings of their environments. Troubled inmates rate their settings lower on a variety of variables in comparison to non-troubled inmates.

References

Bennett, L.A. (1975). "The Study of Violence in California Prisons: A Review with Policy Implications." In A.K. Cohen, G.F. Cole and G. Bailey (eds.) *Prison Violence* (p. 150). Lexington, MA: Lexington Books.

Bowker, L.H. (1982). "Victimizers and Victims in American Correctional Institutions." In R. Johnson and H. Toch (eds.) *The Pains of Imprisonment* (pp. 63-76). Beverly Hills, CA: Sage Publications.

Bowker, L.H. (1985). "An Essay on Prison Violence." In M. Braswell, S. Dillingham and R. Montgomery, Jr. (eds.) *Prison Violence in America* (pp. 7-18). Cincinnati, OH: Anderson Publishing Co.

Carroll, L. (1974). *Hacks, Blacks, and Cons.* Lexington, MA: Lexington Books.

Clear, T.R. and G.F. Cole (1986). *American Corrections.* Monterey, CA: Brooks/Cole.

Conrad, J.P. (1982). "What Do the Undeserving Deserve?" In R. Johnson and H. Toch (eds.) *The Pains of Imprisonment* (pp. 313-330). Beverly Hills, CA: Sage Publications.

Edinger, J.D. (1979). "Cross-Validation of the Megargee MMPI Typology for Prisoners." *Journal of Consulting and Clinical Psychology,* 47, 234-242.

Fuller, D. A., and T. Orsagh (1977). "Violence and Victimization Within a State Prison." *Criminal Justice Review,* 2, 35-55.

Gibbs, J.J. (1981). "Violence in Prison: Its Extent, Nature and Consequences." In R. Roberg and V. Webb (eds.) *Critical Issues in Corrections* (pp. 110-149). St. Paul, MN: West Publishing.

Irwin, J. (1980). *Prisons in Turmoil.* Boston, MA: Little, Brown.

Jacobs, J.B. (1983). *Statesville: The Penitentiary in Mass Society.* Chicago, IL: University of Chicago Press.

Johnson, R. (1976). *Culture and Crisis in Confinement.* Lexington, MA: Lexington Books.

Johnson, R. (1987). *Hard Times: Understanding and Reforming the Prison.* Monterey, CA: Brooks/Cole Publishing.

Lillyquist, M.J. (1980). *Understanding and Changing Criminal Behavior.* Englewood Cliffs, NJ: Prentice-Hall, Inc.

Megargee, E.I. and M.J. Bohn, Jr. (1979). *Classifying Criminal Offenders.* Beverly Hills, CA: Sage Publications.

Mueller, R.F.C., H. Toch and M.F. Molof (1965). *Report to the Task Force to Study Violence in Prisons.* Sacramento, CA: California Department of Corrections.

Myers, L.B. and G.W. Levy (1978). "Description and Prediction of the Intractable Inmate." *Journal of Research in Crime and Delinquency,* 15, 214-228.

Sheehan, S. (1978). *A Prison and a Prisoner.* Boston, MA: Houghton Mifflin.

Stastny, C. and G. Tynauer (1982). *Who Rules the Joint?* Lexington, MA: Lexington Books.

Toch, H. (1977). *Living in Prison.* New York, NY: The Free Press.

Toch, H. (1985). "Social Climate and Prison Violence." In M. Braswell, S. Dillingham and R. Montgomery, Jr. (eds.) *Prison Violence in America* (pp. 37-46). Cincinnati, OH: Anderson Publishing Co.

Wolfson, W.P. (1978). "The Patterns of Prison Homicide." Unpublished dissertation, University of Pennsylvania.

Wright, K.N. (1985a). *Improving Correctional Classification Through a Study of the Placement of Inmates in Environmental Settings.* Final report, National Institute of Justice Grant, 83-IJ-CX-0011, Department of Justice.

Wright, K.N. (1985b). "Developing the Prison Environmental Inventory." *Journal of Research in Crime and Delinquency,* 22, (Aug.) 257-277.

Section II

Interpersonal Violence

B: Correctional Administration, Staff, and Prison Violence

8   Political Culture and Staff Violence: The Case of Hawaii's Prison System[†]

Agnes L. Baro

This is a study of staff violence within the Hawaii prison system. It is an unusual study in that the explanation for violence is sought in the external rather than the internal prison environment. In particular, the study includes an exploration of Hawaii's political culture and it seeks to establish a relationship between that culture and the development and maintenance of systemic staff violence.

Curiously, most of the history of the statehood era prison system could be told in terms of *inmate* rather than staff violence. In fact, between 1960 and 1981, the type of violence endemic to the system was that of inmates threatening and assaulting staff and each other (Nuremberg, 1960; Jones, 1963; Doi, 1975; McMurray, 1980). On Monday, December 14, 1981, that pattern changed dramatically. It did so largely because staff were allowed to "discipline" inmates with batons, police dogs, and their fists. This event is known locally as the "81 shakedown." It lasted five days, cost the state well over one-quarter of $1 million, and led to a series of investigations spanning a three-year period. In the process, staff learned that inmates could be controlled through the use of excessive physical force. They also learned that disciplinary action would usually not be taken against them even though state law and policy forbid such practices.

In order to explain this remarkable change in the Hawaii prison system, it will be necessary to fully describe the 1981 shakedown, explore the political culture, and link that culture to the post-1981 problems with continued staff violence. This is the purpose of the present study. Although it is exploratory, it is asserted that the study does yield enough evidence to suggest that political culture is an important variable

---

[†]Reprinted by permission of the author.

in understanding prison violence. Perhaps more importantly, the study is also an assertion that more questions need to be asked about the political environments in which
staff or inmate violence is tolerated. Regrettably, few prison scholars ask these
types of questions. As a result, and as Jacobs suggests "our understanding of corrections politics is too shallow to wade in" (1984:223).

McGee (1981) and DiIulio (1987) suggest that political appointees and other
correctional leaders are almost single-handedly responsible for the operation of
safe prisons. However, as will be suggested, those who are *ultimately* responsible are
those in the larger political environment including governors, state legislators,
courts, and the citizens of whatever polity is at issue.

Method

In this study, political culture is defined as an *affiliation with local values, customs, or relationships that influence political or administrative decisions.* To operationalize this concept, an extensive literature review of all the major works written
about Hawaii's political history and culture was conducted. In the process, salient
local values and customs were identified and will be discussed. Similarly, information
was obtained about the type of relationships that have had the most impact on the
political system. Essentially, these relationships are located in island, school, sports,
and extended family social networks.

Other study methods included gathering information from government archives,
media files, and agency reports. Interviews were also held with top prison officials, mid-level managers, legislators, and prison system consultants. These interviews were fairly open-ended but when questions were asked about the impact of
the political culture, those interviewed were provided with the study definition of
the term and with information about the types of customs, values, and relationships of most interest.

Participant observation was also an important study method. It began in 1982
when the author was employed by the Hawaii Corrections Division as a planner. From
1983 until 1985, the author also served as the chief planner. Further participant
observation took place between 1987 and 1990 when the author was reemployed
as the inmate education program administrator and then transferred to the position
of employee training administrator. The research was authorized by the agency
and the opportunities to participate in the internal, legislative, and public arenas did
not appear to be limited by official knowledge that a study was in progress. In fact,
those interviewed were quite willing to discuss even sensitive matters and seemed
genuinely interested in the study and its progress.

Nevertheless, it must be admitted that participant observation is a method that
is subject to considerable bias; it also involves ethical dilemmas. For example, bias
can be introduced when the participant has an impact on the social process under
investigation (Babbie, 1981:243). One way to avoid this type of bias is to refrain

from making suggestions that could have an impact on the usual process. Another is to refrain from objecting to or interfering with the process even if it is illegal or unethical. However, these were not viable options.

First, compliance with law, rule, and policy was both an ethical and an employee-employer contractual obligation. Second, the duties of the positions I occupied included reporting noncompliance and making recommendations for improvements. However, the duties did not include taking personnel action against prison line staff or even recommending that such action be taken unless the person was assigned to my·office or was a trainee. Fortunately, I never witnessed any illegal use of physical force so I had no reason to report related activity. I did, however, encounter inmates who had been injured but when I asked about their injuries they reported having "fallen" or that they just "had an accident." When staff were asked, they usually responded that an accident report had been filed or that the matter was "under investigation."

As it developed, beyond knowing what questions to ask, who to ask, and where to find important public records, very little of the study data came from participant observation. Most of it is available in local libraries, media files, and government archives. Because of this, subjective impressions could be checked against historical records. In addition, I maintained an active correspondence with local political scientist, Richard McCleery, who reviewed drafts and provided valuable criticism.

Political Culture

As previously indicated, political culture is defined as *an affiliation with local values, customs, or relationships that influences political or administrative decisions.* More broadly, political culture can be thought of as a bridge between culture and politics (Chodak, 1973). However, there is no commonly accepted definition for the term even though it has been used by western political philosophers for almost 300 years (Kincaid, 1982:1).

Political culture can also be thought of as a subset of a broader culture. Orientations to political action involving cognition and preference are passed on from one generation to another (Almond, 1956). Thus, political culture can be a set of basic assumptions that "govern behavior without self-conscious reflection" (Kincaid, 1982:6). It is this lack of self-conscious reflection that makes research on political culture such a difficult undertaking. In fact, research findings on the relationship between public attitudes and political culture have been weak (Kincaid, 1982).

The best known theory about American political culture was developed by Daniel J. Elazar (1972) who considered the religious, economic, and cultural values of large, migrating groups. According to Elazar, these groups transmitted three major political subcultures that one can find alone or in combination in various regions of the United States. Elazar categorized these three political subcultures as: (1) moralistic; (2) individualistic; and (3) traditionalist. The moralistic subculture originated among the Puritans of New England; the individualistic comes from a pioneering group with roots in the Middle Atlantic states; and the traditionalist is based on the history of those who lived in plantation economies among the southern states. Under Elazar's scheme, Hawaii has been categorized as both "individualistic" and "traditionalistic" (Kincaid, 1982:21).

According to Kincaid (1982), political cultures that have both individualistic and traditionalistic characteristics can be sub-cultures wherein political change is difficult to achieve. This is because the individualistic tendency is to seek political change only when there are high personal or political rewards for doing so (Kincaid, 1982:10). Likewise, the tendency in the traditionalistic subculture is to avoid any change that is not in the interest of powerful elites (Kincaid, 1982:11). These tendencies may help to explain why political change in Hawaii is remarkably difficult to achieve. For example, one political party dominates both the legislature and the governor's office and has done so for 30 years. Additionally, party factionalism or dissent is actively discouraged (Lind, 1987) and there are elaborate efforts made in both the executive and legislative branches to protect the status quo (Neubauer & Pooley, 1985).

A considerable amount of research has been conducted in various tests of Elazar's theory. Kincaid (1982) reviewed approximately 25 related studies and concluded that the strongest support comes from research on political behavior such as voting patterns and the types of decisions that are made by political and administrative leaders. Thus, it was expected that an affiliation with local values, customs, and relationships would influence decisions.

Sharkansky (1975), who studied the United States as a developing nation, also provides information about political cultures that is helpful in understanding the situation in Hawaii. Sharkansky created an index of cultural, economic, and political characteristics that were common among developing nations. In applying this index to polities within the United States, Sharkansky found strong similarities and created a rank ordering of what he called the "least developed states" (1975). In these states, cultural traditions and political loyalties are essential features of the political process. Because of this, political campaigns tend to be more culturally oriented than policy specific. Sharkansky also noted that candidates in developing nations and in "least developed" states use racial symbols, ethnic food and music, and other cultural strategies to evoke loyalty.

Hawaii was not on Sharkansky's (1975) list of "least developed states" mainly because two of his eight indices (i.e., very low levels of political party competition and substantial efforts to induce economic growth) did not apply to Hawaii at the time his study was conducted. However, the level of political party competition has fallen sharply since the early 1970s and a reapplication of Sharkansky's index revealed that Hawaii could indeed be considered a "least developed state" (Baro, 1990). Above all, it is a state where cultural traditions and political loyalties are essential features of the political process. In particular, the provision of ethnic food and music is an important campaign strategy.

Fuchs (1961) noted that the importance of ethnic food and music can be traced back to the 1920s when Hawaiians were an absolute majority of the voters. According to Fuchs, "No political speech could begin unless preceded by entertainment—rallies were song and hula opportunities" (1961:79). The continued need to provide food and entertainment was an opportunity seized by the state Judiciary in the 1970s and 1980s. In order to develop one of the most highly centralized, well-funded, and independent judiciaries in the nation (Sipes & Sipes, 1982), administrators formed a special "volunteer" organization of judiciary employees who provided low-cost catering services (Lind, 1985).

For many years, Hawaii's candidates relied on the state Judiciary to provide the food for political rallies. Eventually, civil servants complained that their promotions depended on "volunteering" to cook and serve food. This complaint was supported by evidence that they did so on state payroll time and in state-owned facilities. The resultant scandal is well documented in a special report by the Executive Director of Common Cause Hawaii (Lind, 1985) and in a year-long series of investigative articles published in the Honolulu newspapers (e.g. Burris, 1985; Dooley, 1985; Reyes, 1986).

A review of all the major works on Hawaii's political history and culture reveals that there is general agreement about the importance of ethnic affiliation and political loyalty. Other salient characteristics of the political culture about which most authors agree are: a relatively high level of tolerance for government ineptitude and corruption; elaborate social networks; and conflict avoidance (Fuchs, 1961; Daws, 1968; Coffman, 1973; Farrell, 1982; Cooper & Daws, 1985). Each characteristic will be briefly explained in terms of its history and the ways in which it has influenced the political process.

Ethnic Affiliation

First, one needs to consider and appreciate the fact that Hawaii is a multi-ethnic society. No one group is large enough to constitute an absolute majority. Since the late 1960s, caucasians (known locally as "haoles") have been the largest ethnic group (Farrell, 1982:216). They now comprise more than one-third of the total population. More recently, Caucasians also make up 75 percent of all immigrants, most of whom are young and highly trained or educated (Takeuchi, 1989). However, haoles are still outnumbered by a combination of other ethnic groups, the next largest of which is the Japanese-Americans. Although racial tensions do exist between the various ethnic groups, the most notable is the tension between the haoles and non-haoles. Non-haoles are referred to as "locals" while haoles (no matter how many generations their families may have inhabited the islands) are viewed as outsiders (Whittaker, 1986).

For "locals," the use of a pidgin is an important issue and it facilitates a type of cohesion that has more than a little anti-haole sentiment attached to it. Locals who speak standard English are sometimes criticized for "talking haole" or becoming "haole-fied." As Farrell points out, "To depart from the fold by using speech identified with the—haole is a serious threat to local cohesion (1982:222).

Even the most well-educated (appointed and elected) government officials use pidgin as a means of identifying themselves as "locals" and establishing rapport with their constituents. Thus, even in formal settings such as legislative hearings it is not unusual to hear officials switch back and forth between standard English and pidgin. Local haoles understand pidgin but are often ridiculed when they speak it (Whittaker, 1986:176).

Ethnic affiliation also affects voting patterns. Although ethnic "block voting" has become less apparent in more recent years, it is still very much a part of local political tradition (Borreca, 1990:A-3). Ethnic affiliation also helps to explain why the Democrats have enjoyed undivided control over the legislature and the governor's office for the past 30 years. Haoles are not particularly important to or powerful within this party. In fact, the lieutenant governor made this point quite candidly in a 1990 interview when he indicated that he had tried to talk political leaders into "letting these people in" because "they were not going to go away" (Lieutenant Governor, May 11, 1990).

With regard to the prison system, the employment of haoles as line staff is a relatively new phenomenon. For most of the territorial and statehood period, the few haoles who were employed were more likely to be found in administrative or central office positions. One of these administrators was Ray Belnap who was hired by the first and last statehood, Republican governor. By 1962, the local Democrats had gained control of both the governor's office and the legislature. This is when the territorial tradition of hiring mainland haoles to administer government agencies came to an abrupt end (Daws, 1968; Coffman, 1973).

Nevertheless, Belnap, who was recruited from the California prison system, did manage to survive as the Corrections Division Administrator for approximately 12 years. However, Belnap never had the authority to hire or fire wardens and his requests to recruit mainland wardens were denied (Deposition of Vinson Ray Belnap, *Belnap v. Chang et al.*, 1980). Despite this lack of authority or power, Belnap was deemed responsible for the conditions at the Oahu prison and he was forced to resign during a mid 1970s "takeover" by the Lieutenant Governor. Conversely, non-haoles (i.e., locals) who were directly responsible for prison operations and administration either kept their jobs or were transferred to other state jobs (Doi, 1975, 1976).

In attributing Belnap's forced resignation to the political culture, former prison system administrator, Edith Wilhelm (a Japanese-American), stated that "Belnap wasn't liked. Throughout the entire correctional community, he wasn't liked. They resented the fact that he was brought in from the mainland" (personal communication, July 19, 1990). Similarly, retired warden, Clarence Andrade stated that "the people who counted didn't believe him because he represented mainland arrogance and superiority. Some folks have an automatic suspicion of mainland folks" (personal communication, July 17, 1986). Belnap reports that even the legislators referred to him as a "West Coast Haole" and threatened to "send him back where he came from." (Deposition of Vinson Ray Belnap, *Belnap v. Chang et al.*, 1980:154).

Tolerance for Government Ineptitude and Corruption

Tolerance for government ineptitude and corruption is most obvious when one traces the remarkably successful careers of civil servants and other government officials who have maintained power despite their involvement in questionable activities. As will be discussed, this type of tolerance extends to prison officials. However, the most obvious example of tolerance for corruption is provided by Cooper and Daws (1985) who studied the relationship between political power and land development. Their research revealed that, throughout the statehood period, corruption and conflict-of-interest were the norm, not the exception. In concluding this ambitious study, the authors note that "it is worth stressing that whatever the Democrats in power did about land was done with at least the tacit consent of the great majority of the governed" (1985:446).

With regard to government ineptitude, almost every legislative session is accompanied by the publication of one or more special studies or audits on a state bureaucracy. The results of the related reports are well publicized and frequently contain evidence of ineptitude. However, public pressure to remove or discipline government officials is rare (e.g., Pratt, 1985; Legislative Auditor, 1989).

Social Networks

It is the networking aspect of Hawaii's political culture that may be the most interesting but also the most difficult to document. These networks are comprised of overlapping membership in sports, school, church, neighborhood, and family groups. Thus, political favors and protection cannot be explained simply as an outcome of party loyalty or membership activity. This point is summarized by Neubauer and Pooley who state that "observers of Hawaii politics note the primary role in the prevailing political calculus performed by personal loyalty and the 'kinship' groups of family, school, and island" (1985:24).

A former prison system administrator, Vernon Chang, discussed the issue of social network protection in a 1986 interview. When asked about the continued employment of Branch Administrators (i.e., wardens) who did not comply with policy or law, Chang responded that most had friends or relatives who were connected and provided protection. In Chang's words, "a guy really has to screw up but generally a friend or relative will come to your support" (personal communication, July 21, 1986).

The career of former youth facility administrator Kayo Chung provides a notable example of social network protection. Chung had a long history of allowing corporal punishment to be used against incarcerated youth despite the fact that the practice was prohibited by policy and law. Former Corrections Division Administrator, Ray Belnap, reported that he tried to remove Chung from the youth facility position but was prevented from doing so by the department director, William Among who was a close personal friend of Chung's. During the 1980s when Chung was nominated to the parole board, Belnap also reports that he testified against Chung at the Senate confirmation hearing. When Chung received confirmation, Belnap sought an explanation from the committee chairman who explained that "Kayo Chung was my football coach" (Ray Belnap, personal communication, July 3, 1986).

Conflict Avoidance

Authors who have studied Hawaii's political culture generally agree that there is a widespread pattern of conflict avoidance (Fuchs, 1961; Coffman, 1973; Farrell, 1982; Wang, 1982). This type of avoidance is understandable in an island culture but it is also supported by cultural values about humility and consensus (Coffman, 1973; Cooper & Daws, 1985; Whittaker, 1986). For this reason, public hearings are often of dubious political value (Farrell, 1982) and there is a marked preference for talking in small, informal groups. The former Mayor of Maui, Elmer Cravalho, made this point somewhat abrasively when he stated that "public meetings are for haoles" (Farrell, 1982:155).

Conflict avoidance also has a profound impact on Hawaii's bureaucratic sub-culture. Meetings to resolve critical problems are frustrating experiences for those who were born and raised on the mainland (Whittaker, 1986). My own experiences in attending prison system meetings were that problems were rarely solved, confrontation was generally not allowed, and those who pressed for confrontation were frequently chastised. Federale ran a local experiment involving interagency meetings. She found a marked "refusal to openly criticize another participant or agency" (1989:15).

Political Loyalty

Hawaii's ruling Democrats have stayed in power for over 30 years because they have been able to maintain a remarkable grass roots, political loyalty (Coffman, 1973; Cooper & Daws, 1985). This type of loyalty has both cultural and political roots.

First, it should be noted that the statehood era Democratic Party was organized largely by Japanese-Americans who are still "the backbone" of the party (Borreca, 1990:A-3). Japanese-Americans are also overrepresented in the legislature and in the government bureaucracies (Cooper & Daws, 1985). Political scientist Richard McCleery asserts that a Japanese cultural value called "on" (roughly translated as honor or obligation) is an "anachronism" that has produced strong political and government agency loyalty (personal communication, January 8, 1990).

Historically, the political loyalties of the Hawaiian people were obtained by the territorial era Republican Party through an elaborate spoils system. Most police, prison guards, fire fighters, and clerical workers were Hawaiian (Fuchs, 1961; Daws, 1968). Thus, the Republican Party became increasingly dependent on government workers to maintain political supremacy. This was a legacy that the Democratic Party has used to full advantage.

Since statehood, all three governors have relied heavily on public employees and their unions to provide funds and grass roots campaign workers (Wang, 1982; Cooper & Daws, 1985). State ethics law prohibits partisan political activity in the workplace. Nevertheless, those appointed by the governor to top-level positions are expected to contribute 5 percent of their salaries to his campaign. Even mid-level civil service people are expected to buy and sell campaign fund-raising tickets. And, Democratic Party candidates for the U.S. Congress or the governor's office, are traditionally introduced as such in the workplaces and under the watchful eyes of top-level administrators.

With regard to the previously mentioned case of former administrator, Ray Belnap, former State Senator, Neil Abercrombie asserted that Belnap was particularly vulnerable because he did not meet local expectations that one should be politically loyal in some absolute sense. According to Abercrombie, "blind obedience" is the "eleventh vote" in local Democratic Party politics. In explaining the "eleventh vote," Abercrombie recalled his own experiences of more than 15 years and insisted that "you can vote with them ten out of ten times but if they don't believe you will vote out of blind obedience, they will lock you out" (personal communication, July 27, 1990).

Hawaii also has an informal but highly effective "warm body" policy whereby workers are rarely dismissed or declared redundant. In fact, one mainland prison consultant who wishes to remain anonymous reported that he did recommend to the governor that certain prison officials be dismissed. Reportedly, the governor's response was that "in Hawaii, we have warm hearts; we don't fire people." More open recommendations to dismiss recalcitrant prison officials have been made by other mainland consultants (e.g., Environmental Safety and Sanitation Panel, 1987; Medical Panel, 1987) but those named were not dismissed.

During the statehood period, there have been two well-publicized attempts to replace or dismiss staff at two prisons (i.e., Oahu Prison and the Kulani Correctional Facility). Problems with staff safety, security, corruption, and contraband prompted both of the related "takeovers" by special task forces. However, in the previously discussed Oahu Prison case, the warden and his chief of security kept their positions and the worst that happened to the staff was that 45 were transferred to other state jobs (Doi, 1976). Within two years, the prison was as dirty and dangerous as it had been before the takeover (Wolf, 1967a:A-3; Mackey, 1976; "State Prison Woes," 1976).

The 1980s "Kulani takeover" resulted in the warden being suspended on full pay for at least one year after which he was transferred to another state agency at the same pay level. The chief of security fought his dismissal through the civil service appeals process and was placed back in his former position. When asked about his efforts to dismiss these employees, former Corrections Division Administrator, Ted Sakai, reported that officials in the Department of Personnel Services told him he was "on the cutting edge of a new technology" (personal communication, August 4, 1986).

Political Cultures and Prison Violence

Interestingly, one of the very few studies on the relationship between prison violence and the external political environment was conducted by Richard McCleery (1968) who examined the 1960 Oahu Prison riot. In explaining the crises that occurred within the prison and the external political system, McCleery noted that both environments appeared to be ruled by situational rather than structural authority. Within the prison, central authority had broken down; definitions or explanations of situations were often conflicting or simply not provided. Meanwhile, the transition from a territorial to a statehood political system was having the same effect on the external environment. Central authority had broken down, and neither political party was prepared for the task of organizing and controlling groups that had competing interests. These groups included a labor union trying to organize prison guards, territorial era prison managers and their supporters, and a newly appointed prison administrator who McCleery asserts "encouraged every disgruntled faction to seek political relief" (1968:137).

McCleery's study did establish a relationship between the structural aspects of a political system and prison violence. However, there are no similar studies and there are no previous studies that focus specifically on the relationship between a political culture and prison violence. Nevertheless, one can find indications in some studies that affiliations with local values, customs, or relationships did have an impact on decisions related to prison violence (e.g., Murton & Hyans, 1967; DiIulio, 1987; Martin & Ekland-Olson, 1987). It is also interesting to note that most of these studies are of prison systems located in the South where Sharkansky (1975) found that cultural traditions and political loyalties were essential features of the political process.

For example, Martin and Ekland-Olson (1987) and DiIulio (1987) noted that Texas Department of Corrections (TDC) employees demonstrated high levels of political loyalty to Directors George Beto and J.W. Estelle. These authors also note that Texans had, for many years, taken great pride in their relatively low cost, productive, and highly disciplined prison system. When TDC employees, and Texans in general, perceived that they were under attack by "outsiders" who expressed concern over the violence associated with the infamous "building tender" system (i.e., inmates serving as custodians of other inmates), they stubbornly rejected efforts to change the system.

In fact, it was largely affiliations with local values, customs, and relationships that created much of what Martin and Ekland-Olson called the "myth, misunderstanding, and misrepresentations that surrounded the Texas prison system" (1987:xxi). These were affiliations that even encouraged prison officials to lie abut compliance with law and policy. As Martin and Ekland-Olson (1987) document, their lies were accepted by state officials who refused to believe "outsiders" such as federal court monitors.

Social relationships also played a large role in what Texas prison board member Harry M. Whittington called a failure to place the TDC Director and his staff "under proper controls and in compliance with the law" (Martin & Ekland-Olson, 1987:xiv). Whittington charged that TDC Director, Jim Estelle had developed such close, personal relationships with other board members that he had, in fact, neutralized the oversight authority the board should have exercised.

The 1981 Shakedown

Between 1960 and 1981 the Oahu Prison experienced chronic problems with inmates threatening and assaulting staff. By June of 1980, the old cellblock area of this prison appeared to be in complete control of the inmates. Former Unit Manager, Michael Hess, reports that staff assigned to work in this area frequently called in sick and, when on duty, refused to enter the inmate dormitory areas. Hess also reports that inmate control over "the block" was so well established that they were even allowed to barbecue meat stolen from the kitchen and to move freely back and forth to an outdoor recreation yard. According to Hess, "you could smell the marijuana, fear, and tension" (personal communication, August 7, 1986).

Evidence of mounting tension included a June, 1980 battle between inmates that resulted in the deaths of two and the serious wounding of another. This battle was followed by three days of disturbances involving considerable damage (McMurray, 1980). By October of 1980, all of the inmate programs had been closed down (Altonn, 1980b). Problems controlling inmates had spread to the rest of the prison and to the Halawa High Security Facility where an August, 1980 riot caused $400,000 worth of damages (Altonn, 1980a).

Trouble started again in the Spring of 1981 when inmates forced correctional officers out of the cellblock and held it under siege for approximately 10 hours (Hartwell & Downes, 1981). In September, 1981, a mentally ill pretrial inmate was beaten to death by other inmates (Memminger, 1981). Two days later, officials abandoned the cellblock when attempts to recover drugs and a pistol failed, but not before a lieutenant was injured by an inmate wielding a two-foot long machete (Hartwell, 1981).

One of the most dangerous aspects of the old cellblock was the partitions made of plywood, cardboard, and sheets that inmates had erected to create private spaces in the dormitories. Despite constant complaints from the security force, the warden allowed the partitions. According to the prison system director, these partitions had been an issue for several years. However, the warden was given the latitude to remove them "at the right time" but "apparently that right time did not come before his retirement" (Senate Judiciary Committee, 1983:144). Curiously, neither the director nor the division administrator saw fit to *order* the removal of these security and fire hazards. It should also be noted that it was six months after the warden retired before the partitions were removed, but that was poorly planned and it occurred in the midst of a volatile shakedown.

The shakedown began in the early morning hours of December 14, 1981. It was accomplished with the help of the Hawaii National Guard, the Honolulu Police Department, and correctional officers from the Halawa High Security Facility (HHSF). These groups were given peripheral assignments such as using police dogs to search for contraband, and erecting military tents in the recreation yard. The high security officers were supposed to stay on the perimeter.

During the first day of the shakedown, approximately 350 inmates were moved out of the cellblock into a large recreation field where they would spend the night. Some drew attention to themselves by verbally harassing the high security officers on the perimeter and by setting fire to a large tent. The next morning, the warden of the HHSF asked the warden of the Oahu prison (OCCC) to "allow HHSF to conduct the strip-search of the cellblock inmates" and to allow HHSF to "discipline" those inmates who had harassed HHSF officers (Senate Judiciary Committee, 1983:387).

The request was granted. On the second day (December 15, 1983), OCCC officials relinquished operational control of the "4-way" (i.e., the area where inmates were strip-searched on the way back to the cellblock). Those present in the 4-way during the searches included the HHSF warden and four of his management staff. Closed-circuit television cameras and an intercom which linked the area to central control were turned off (Ombudsman, 1983:17).

While the strip-searches were going on, staff in the medical unit became concerned about the number and types of injuries they were seeing and treating; one inmate was beaten so badly that he had to be sent to the hospital (Ombudsman, 1983:19). Despite objections from the medical staff, there were also several inmates who were prevented from getting medical attention and were transferred directly to the HHSF. The OCCC physician reported pleading with the warden to stop the beatings but he was ignored (Ombudsman, 1983:20). By the end of the day, 17 inmates had been treated for injuries and some unknown number had been denied medical treatment.

The events of December 16, 1983 could be characterized as a correctional officer riot. On this day, the OCCC staff had command of the 4-way. The closed-circuit television cameras were covered with paper (Ombudsman, 1983:23) and officers moved approximately 300 inmates from other sections of the prison through the area. According to one officer-witness, it "was one chaos inside there, guys went berserk" (Ombudsman, 1983:25). Part of this "chaos" was officers beating inmates while another part consisted of fights between officers who disagreed about which (if any) inmates should be beaten (Ombudsman, 1983:25).

The OCCC Chief of Security and the Security Section Captains are reported to have spent very little time in the 4-way during the December 16 searches (Ombudsman, 1983:27). A training center instructor did try to stop the beatings but he was physically threatened and forced to leave (Ombudsman, 1983:24). Similarly, the social work and program staff were not allowed into the 4-way. However, one Unit Manager was in an adjacent area and reports that he heard "a fear and pain type of screaming" and that he did have the opportunity to view some of the people in the area. This person claims that he "saw two guards holding an inmate while a third beat him with a baton" and that the OCCC warden and two deputy attorneys general also witnessed this beating (Michael Hess, personal communication, August 5, 1986).

On December 17, 1983, the OCCC Chief of Security finally took command of the 4-way and the last two days of the shakedown were relatively peaceful. However, rumors about the beatings began to leak out of the prison. Over the weekend, media reporters started getting anonymous telephone calls and relatives allowed weekend visits reported seeing "bruised and battered" inmates (Senate Judiciary Committee, 1983:4). It was alleged that unreasonable force had been used against over 100 inmates (Ombudsman, 1983:89). Some of the injuries inmates received included serious dog bites incurred when Honolulu police officers failed to control the animals.

There were three major investigations of the shakedown. These were conducted by a governor's "blue ribbon panel," the Senate Judiciary Committee, and the Ombudsman's Office. There was also an internal investigation conducted by Assistant Corrections Division Administrator, Edith Wilhelm. Wilhelm's report was the most controversial, and the First Deputy Attorney General (who was present at the prison during the shakedown) tried to suppress it (Senate Judiciary Committee, 1983).

Wilhelm reported that she visited the inmates transferred to the HHSF immediately after the shakedown. She noted that they had been injured and called for an outside investigation (Senate Judiciary Committee, 1983:7). However, Governor George Ariyoshi appears to have ignored or not known about Wilhelm's request. Instead, he made a public announcement that "Initial assessments from the Attorney General and the Department indicate that there is no substantial evidence of any brutality at the prison" (Senate Judiciary Committee, 1983:9). Meanwhile, Edith Wilhelm was assigned to do an internal investigation. She did not complete her task until March 1982 at which time she sent her report to the Attorney General's Office. The First Deputy immediately released a summary of her report to the press. According to Wilhelm, this summary was altered and she maintains that Lilly put the word "minor" in front of her words describing injuries such as "lacerations" and "bruises" (personal communication, July 30, 1986). At this point, she insisted on a meeting with the Attorney General. Shortly after this meeting, the governor convened the "blue ribbon panel" to conduct the external investigation Wilhelm had requested back in December.

The report of the governor's panel was inconclusive and the members recommended further investigation. In fact, the governor assured the public that further investigations would be conducted. One year later, the Senate Judiciary Committee discovered that no such executive branch investigations had occurred (1983:390).

However, this committee did find that excessive force had been used and that disciplinary action should be taken against those in "responsible charge" (1983:386-387).

The Ombudsman's report was more detailed than that of the Senate or the governor's panel. After interviewing 398 people, the Ombudsman found enough evidence to support a finding that unreasonable force had been used against at least 44 inmates, and that 12 supervisory personnel (including both wardens) and 22 correctional officers should be disciplined. The report was turned over to the prison system officials "for action deemed appropriate" (Ombudsman, 1983:79).

Eight months later and after an in-house panel also recommended disciplinary action, the director of the department issued a press release indicating that all charges against officers and wardens were dismissed (Ombudsman, 1984:2).

The reaction from Ombudsman, Herman Doi, was unprecedented. For the first time in 15 years, he issued a special report. The report confronted the director and charged that his decision not to discipline employees represented a "lost opportunity to deliver a strong message" (Ombudsman, 1984:6). Doi also warned the director that his decision would "adversely affect the department and the public in years to come" (1984:15). The man who was called the "Dean of U.S. Ombudsman" (Hill, 1981:11), quoted Winston Churchill and reminded the prison system director that "we cannot say the past is past without surrendering the future" (1984:15).

Doi's special report was prophetic. The use of unreasonable force resulting in serious inmate injuries became a chronic problem that continued well into 1990. However, the balance of power in Hawaii's prison system had clearly shifted. Complaints about inmates intimidating or assaulting staff disappeared while complaints about staff escalated. Most of these complaints came from the OCCC and the HHSF but there was a system-wide effect on the behavior of inmates transferred to minimum security prisons. As late as 1989, conversations with line staff and inmates at these facilities indicated that there was a generalized fear of being sent back to OCCC or HHSF; fear that was related to the threat of corporal punishment.

Post-1981 Shakedown Violence

Although the prison system director had dismissed all charges arising from the 1981 shakedown, he also insisted that those officers who continued to use excessive or unreasonable force would be prosecuted. Some prosecutions did occur. The first (in the state's history) took place in February of 1984, three years after the alleged assault occurred (Catterall, 1984). The jury took 45 minutes to acquit the officers. Nevertheless, 18 prison employees were prosecuted for abuses (including sexual abuses) of inmates (Burris & Ong, 1984). However, over one-half of these people were acquitted.

Interviews with current and former employees revealed that there was a pattern of excessive and unreasonable force being used against inmates that continued at least until 1990. The former OCCC medical unit supervisor, Katherine Kreamer, reports that she continued to receive medical unit complaints about injured inmates long after the 1981 shakedown (personal communication, November 1, 1990). Similarly, former OCCC Unit Manager, Bruce Bikle reported that six months after the shakedown, "we had control of our inmates but not of our officers." According to Bikle, "just to stop an inmate beating was an accomplishment;" systemic or administrative remedies were not developed (personal communication, November 2, 1990).

When asked whether the unauthorized use of force was a systemic problem after the 1981 shakedown, one administrator replied that "there was a pattern in the holding unit at OCCC but most of the incidents at the Halawa facility surfaced during the past year. We all heard rumors that it was going on well before then. In fact, the unauthorized use of force was an issue in the 1986 supplemental agreement with the ACLU" (Ted Sakai, personal communication, July 13, 1990).

The United States Department of Justice supports the view that staff violence against inmates was a systemic problem. In investigating inmate complaints, the department informed Governor Ariyoshi that state prison officials were "failing to protect inmates against excessive and inappropriate" uses of force that resulted in "a pattern and practice of brutality" (William Bradford Reynolds, personal communication to Governor George Ariyoshi, July 8, 1983). The Department also sought permission to conduct a full investigation of the conditions inside OCCC. Permission was denied and the Department filed suit under the 1981 Civil Rights of Institutionalized Persons Act.

Once the suit was dismissed by the Federal District Court for Hawaii, the governor granted permission for a Department of Justice investigation. The department brought in mainland prison experts and took one year to complete its report. At the end of that year, the department announced that inmates at OCCC were controlled by "fear and violence" (Burris & Ong, 1984). In a letter to Governor Ariyoshi, Assistant Attorney General William Bradford Reynolds asserted "a pattern of unjustified staff violence at all levels throughout the facility" (Altonn, 1985). Reynolds further noted that one of the mainland consultants had reported that OCCC was the only prison he had ever seen where inmates had to be put in protective custody in order to protect them from staff.

The U.S. Department of Justice report was an important factor in the state's decision to settle out of court with the ACLU who had filed a class action suit. However, admissions that staff violence was a problem and promises to solve this type of problem were not included in the settlement agreement (*Spear v. Ariyoshi*, 1985). Nevertheless, this issue was raised by the ACLU both in its discovery requests and in the negotiations for a supplemental agreement. It should also be noted, that despite chronic noncompliance with various aspects of the consent degree, and despite continued inmate complaints about staff violence, the ACLU never did file a motion to complain to the court.

However, in 1989, the ACLU did complain to the newspapers and *threatened* to sue on behalf of inmates at the Halawa facility. The ACLU claimed that there were at least 20 separate inmate beatings that had occurred between November, 1988 and March, 1989. When the prison system director insisted that there was not enough evidence or reason to take disciplinary action against the correctional officers involved, the prison system doctor went to the press. Dr. Kim Thorburn told the press that she was alarmed by the violence against inmates at the two Halawa facilities. She also indicated that medical workers had treated 20 inmates who had "clearly been beaten" (Tswei, 1990).

In an interview for this study, Thorburn also indicated that both the administrator of the Halawa facilities and a deputy attorney general had recommended that no action be taken against most officers allegedly involved in 23 separate incidents. However, one officer was criminally indicted and another was told to enroll in a report writing class after he falsified a report about an inmate beating. Thorburn also reported that the strategy of top prison officials vacillated between ignoring complaints and "going after the least powerful person" (personal communication, July 17, 1990).

Impact of the Political Culture

In order to appreciate the impact of the political culture, one needs to remember that the warden in charge of the Oahu prison, from the early 1960s until his retirement in 1981, survived a 1975 "takeover" by a lieutenant governor's task force. Given the history of inmate violence and staff intimidation during his reign, questions need to be asked about how he managed to retain his position. Here it is asserted that it was the events that occurred during this warden's tenure that led to the staff violence during the 1981 shakedown.

The first attempt to put the prison under a different warden occurred in the 1960s when Corrections Division Administrator, Ray Belnap, asked Governor John Burns for permission to recruit an experienced warden from the mainland. Belnap reports that the governor denied his request and told him that Tony Olim, a correctional officer who had applied for the position, was the man who would be given the job (personal communication, July 31, 1986). This is the man who was selected and who held his position until 1981.

The second attempt to replace Olim occurred in 1973 when he became ill and took several months of sick leave. During this period, Belnap took over as the warden and convinced the governor to provide Hawaii National Guard assistance in disarming prisoners, ending the chronic intimidation of staff, and generally cleaning up the prison. Short-term order was restored but Olim insisted on returning to work. At this point, Belnap tried to convince Olim to retire but Olim called in a friend, state labor leader, David Trask, who threatened reprisals if Belnap did not stop pressuring his friend (Ray Belnap, personal communication, July 31, 1986). Olim returned to work in January of 1974; traditional problems with contraband and violence started again (Zalburg, 1974).

Although Olim insists that there were plans to replace him in 1975, there is no evidence of this in task force reports or in other public records. In fact, former state senator Neil Abercrombie reports that Olim and his staff were products of a "ward politics type of situation" and that "it was clear to me that Olim had connections" (personal communication, July 27, 1990). Abercrombie was in a good position to know because he was present at legislative, executive committee sessions (i.e., not open to the public) where the takeover was discussed.

When asked to provide examples of the impact of the political culture on the prison system, two former administrators (Wilhelm and Sakai) mentioned the administrative refusal to confront Olim (personal communication, July 13 and 18, 1990). Wilhelm even reports that top officials would telephone her to relay orders to Olim; no one wanted to confront him. Chief of Security John Smythe appears to have learned how to deal with Olim: "If I was going to lockdown or shakedown, I didn't tell him. Tony would leak it and we could get problems" (personal communication, July 16, 1990).

By 1981, staff resentment against those who refused to confront Olim and against inmates who continued to harass and threaten them had built up to a dangerous level. All that was required was an opportunity to ventilate and that opportunity came with the shakedown.

The warden in charge of the Oahu prison (OCCC) during the shakedown remained in that position until the late 1980s, even though staff violence against inmates continued to be a serious problem. No disciplinary action was taken against him or his chief of security. Similarly, staff violence continued at the Halawa facility but there was no indication that the warden was or would be rendered accountable. In fact, since the 1981 shakedown, both men have received promotions.

Both men are also members of elaborate social networks made up of island, school, and kinship groups. One is particularly active at campaign fund raising times while the other has a record of being able to rely on a remarkable degree of staff loyalty. Thus, they have managed to prosper and avoid professional consequences even when they refuse to comply with direct orders from the central office (Legislative Auditor, 1989; Medical Panel, 1987; Environmental Safety and Sanitation Panel, 1987; Corrections Panel, 1987).

By 1988, management deficiencies and a lack of staff discipline throughout the prison system had become a legislative issue. Hence, the Senate requested a management audit to be conducted by the Legislative Auditor (Senate Concurrent Resolution #57, 1988). The results of the audit indicated a lack of central control and leadership, a lack of responsible fiscal management, and a lack of discipline at all levels of the organization (Legislative Auditor, 1989). The Senate responded by appropriating $100,000 for the governor to hire a "Special Master" to assist the director in making management improvements. The governor refused to fire the director or any of the other managers (Borrecca, 1989). Thus, the taxpayers of Hawaii paid $80,000 for a director of corrections and another $100,000 for someone to watch over the director.

The Special Master was the former director of the Colorado prison system, Kip Kautzky. After six months, Kautzky reported that he had "run into hardpan" (i.e., dirt too hard to plow or turn) and that "it would be a serious error in judgment to think the mainland value of corrections management could translate here. It won't" (Altonn, 1990:A-1). In November of 1990, Kautzky resigned.

When asked about the impact of the political culture on his efforts to improve management, Kautzky replied that the "political culture is a cloud that hangs over every decision" and that "David Copperfield would have been at home in Hawaii because it is a world of illusion." Kautzky also insisted that "leadership is not important in Hawaii. Getting along with people is important" (personal communication, July 13, 1990).

According to Kautzky, there is such a widespread avoidance of conflict that "central authority had almost no impact on operations." He elaborated by noting that "People can't lose face, even the Chief of Security at OCCC is protected from losing face." Kautzky also maintained that the tolerance for ineptitude was a problem and that state officials were "extremely tolerant of lousy performance." Finally, Kautzky expressed concern over the informal custom of gubernatorial appointees donating at least 5 percent of their salaries to the governor's election campaign. This and other campaign fund-raising activities that he had witnessed led him to the conclusion that top administrators did not "even have to worry about their own survival" (personal communication, July 13, 1990).

Although Kautzky had witnessed decisions at several levels including the legislature and the governor's office, critics might charge that he was too new to the state to really understand or appreciate the complexities of administrative and political decisions. Perhaps he was only responding out of his sense of frustration at not being able to accomplish what he had hoped to accomplish? This is a fair criticism. Accordingly, Kautzky's perception was checked against the results of interviews held with two administrators who were born and raised in Hawaii and who had also witnessed decisionmaking at all levels of government.

The first of these two administrators was the deputy director (appointed by the governor) in charge of corrections. When asked to what extent, if any, administrative decisions were influenced by affiliations with local values, customs, or relationships, the deputy responded that there was a "profound influence" both in the legislative and executive branches of government. He also insisted that "local values have an impact in Hawaii more than in any other state" and that "I tell them, we should not lock the world out" or "be too soft hearted" (George Iranon, personal communication, July 12, 1990). The deputy also reported that attempts to discipline employees even at the line level were often interfered with by political leaders, including legislators.

The second administrator is a high-level civil servant (not appointed by the governor) who asserted that local loyalties, and membership in island-based social networks were frequently used to overcome central authority. Like Kautzky, this administrator also maintained that the impact of the political culture was such that "we tolerate ineptitude at the branches (i.e., prisons and jails) that we should not tolerate" (Ted Sakai, personal communication, July 13, 1990). This is the same administrator who tried to fire a warden in the mid 1980s and was told that he was "on the cutting edge of a new technology" (Ted Sakai, personal communication, August 4, 1986).

Conclusion

Although throughout most of Hawaii's statehood era, prison history could be written in terms of chronic problems with inmate violence, the last 10 years of that history have been marked by systemic staff violence. The turning point was the 1981 shakedown at the Oahu prison. When staff were not held accountable for the excessive and illegal use of force during the shakedown, a pattern of systemic violence began to emerge. That pattern and a pattern of not disciplining those responsible for the violence continued for many years.

If one were to take a "leadership" view of this situation, one might conclude that Hawaii has simply not found the leaders with the "right stuff." The problem with this perspective is that it ignores the political environment in which decisions are made about what the "right stuff" consists of and what type of leadership is actually being sought. Indeed, the leadership perspective can become what Kahn (1979:153), who studied police administration, calls a "zero sum game" or an attempt to establish and defend one-to-one relationships. In this way, all prison problems can be reduced to the search for the "great men" of prison administration (DiIulio, 1987:187-88) and scholars can avoid entering what McGee refers to as a "political jungle" (1981:59).

Although this study is exploratory and is subject to the biases that plague most participant observation work, it is supported by government and media reports and it does indicate that the political culture in at least one state has had a discernible impact on prison violence. For example, interviewees generally agreed that decisions not to discipline those who used or tolerated the use of violence against inmates could be attributed to affiliations with local values, customs, and relationships. More specifically, the local values about political loyalty, and a customary avoidance of conflict appear to have played a large role in decisions not to fire or discipline employees. Similarly, local relationships established in elaborate social networks appear to have provided a measure of protection for those subject to disciplinary action. And there is evidence that tolerance for government ineptitude, which other researchers have considered characteristic of the Hawaii political culture, has been extended to the prison bureaucracy. Above all, the careers of those responsible for controlling both the inmates and the staff were largely unaffected regardless of the level or type of violence that occurred during their administration of a particular prison.

References

Almond, G. (1956). "Comparative Political Systems." *Journal of Politics*, 18:(3), 391-409.

Altonn, H. (1980a, October 22). "Programs are Closed at Prison Here." *Honolulu Star-Bulletin*, p. A-1.

Altonn, H. (1980b, September 8). "Prison Riot Damage Put at $400,000." *Honolulu Star-Bulletin*, p. A-4.

Altonn H. (1985, January 3). "U.S. Claims Staff Violence at Oahu Prison." *Honolulu Star-Bulletin*, p. A-1.

Altonn, H. (1990, May 21). "Prisons Revamp: It Won't Be Easy." *Honolulu Star-Bulletin*, p. A-1.

Babbie, E. (1981). *The Practice of Social Research*. Belmont, CA: Wadsworth.

Baro, A. (1990). "*Effective Political Control of Bureaucracy: The Case of Hawaii's Prison System.*" Doctoral dissertation, Sam Houston State University, Huntsville, Texas.

Borrecca, R. (1989, February 21). "Isle Political Power Base is a Whole New Scene." *Honolulu Star-Bulletin*, p. A-6.

Borrecca, R. (1990, May 25). "Ethnic Questions are Raised." *Honolulu Star-Bulletin*.

Burris, J. (1985, September 18). "Cingcade Says It's No Accident Judiciary Involved in Politics." *Honolulu Advertiser*, p. A-3.

Burris, J. and V. Ong (1984, June 8). "Ariyoshi Defends Sunn on Shakedown." *Honolulu Advertiser*, p. A-1.

Catterall, L. (1984, February 1). "Three Standing Trial in Brutality Case." *Honolulu Star-Bulletin*, p. A-7.

Chodak, S. (1973). *Societal Development*. New York, NY: Oxford University Press.

Coffman, T. (1973). *Catch a Wave: A Case Study of Hawaii's New Politics*. Second Edition. Honolulu, HI: The University Press of Hawaii.

Cooper, G. and G. Daws (1985). *Land and Power in Hawaii*. Honolulu, HI: Benchmark Books.

Corrections Panel (1987). *Fall 1987 Report of Panels of Experts: Corrections Panel*. Honolulu, HI: Federal District Court #84-1104.

Daws, G. (1968). *Shoal of Time: A History of the Hawaiian Islands*. Honolulu, HI: University of Hawaii Press.

DiIulio, Jr., J. (1987). *Governing Prisons: A Comparative Study of Correctional Management*. New York, NY: The Free Press.

Doi, N. (1975). *Governor's Task Force on the Hawaii State Prison: Preliminary Report*. Honolulu, HI: Office of the Governor.

Doi, N. (1976). *Governor's Task Force on the Hawaii State Prison: Interim Report*. Honolulu, HI: Office of the Governor.

Dooley, J. (1985, August 30). "Legislators Ticket-Fixing a Tradition." *Honolulu Advertiser*, p. A-3.

Elazar, D. (1972). *American Federalism: A View from the States*. Second Edition. New York, NY: Basic Books.

Environmental Safety and Sanitation Panel (1987). *Fall 1987 Report of Panels of Experts: Environmental Panel*. Honolulu, HI: Federal District Court #84-1104.

Farrell, B. (1982). *Hawaii: The Legend that Sells*. Honolulu, HI: The University Press.

Federale, K. (1989). "Perceptions of Policy and Practice: Focus Groups on the Institutionalization of Juveniles in the State of Hawaii." Paper presented at the annual meeting of the American Society of Criminologists, Reno, Nevada.

Fuchs, L.H. (1961). *Hawaii Pono: A Social History*. New York, NY: Harcourt, Brace & World, Inc.

Hartwell, J. (1981, October 3). "Two Guards Injured Slightly in Drug, Pistol Retrieval." *Honolulu Advertiser*, p. A-1.

Hartwell, J. and S. Downes (1981, June 3). "Order is Restored at Prison After Inmates Seize Building." *Honolulu Advertiser*, p. A-1.

Hill, L.B. (1981). "Incremental Legal Reform: The Ombudsman, Bureaucracy, and Justice." Unpublished paper, University of Oklahoma, Norman.

Jacobs, J.B. (1984). "The Politics of Prison Expansion." In *The Annals of the American Academy of Political and Social Science*, 12:(1), 209-241.

Jones, B. (1963, December 12). "Jail Guards Knew Convicts Had Guns." *Honolulu Advertiser*, p. 1.

Kahn, R. (1979). "The Politics of Police Accountability: A Test of the Bureaucratic-State Approach to Political Change in Machine Cities." In F. Meyer and R. Baker (eds.) *Determinants of Law Enforcement Policies*, Lexington, MA: Lexington Books.

Kincaid, J. (1982). *Political Culture, Public Policy, and the American States*. Philadelphia, PA: Institute for the Study of Human Issues.

Legislative Auditor (1989). *Management Audit of the Department of Corrections of the State of Hawaii*. Honolulu, HI: Office of the Legislative Auditor.

Lieutenant Governor Campaigns (1990, May 11). *Honolulu Star-Bulletin*, p. A-1.

Lind, I. (1985). *Compromising the Courts: A Critical Report on the Political Activities of the State Judiciary*. Honolulu, HI: Common Cause Hawaii.

Lind, I. (1987, February 17). "In Hawaii, the Costs of Dissent Can Be High." *Honolulu Star-Bulletin*, p. 27.

Mackey, R. (1976). *Visits to Hawaii State Prison: February and July, 1976*. Honolulu, HI: Citizen's Corrections Inspection Committee.

Martin, S. and S. Ekland-Olson (1987). *Texas Prisons: The Walls Came Tumbling Down*. Austin, TX: Texas Monthly Press.

McCleery R. (1968). "Correctional Administration and Political Change." In L. Hazelrigg (ed.) *Prison Within Society*. New York, NY: Doubleday.

McGee, R. (1981). *Prisons and Politics*. Lexington, MA: Lexington Books.

McMurray, T. (1980, June 8). "Prison Melee Renewed: Doors, Lights Shattered." *Honolulu Advertiser*, p. A-1.

Medical Panel (1987). *Fall 1987 Report of Panels of Experts: Medical and Mental Health Panel*. Honolulu, HI: Federal District Court for Hawaii #84-1104.

Memminger, C. (1981, September 30). "Prisoner Was Beaten to Death, Examiner Says." *Honolulu Star-Bulletin*, p. A-1.

Murton, T. and J. Hyans (1967). *Accomplices to the Crime: The Arkansas Prison Scandal*. New York, NY: Grove Press.

Neubauer, D. and S. Pooley (1985). "The Politics of Hawaii's Economy in the 1980s." Paper presented at a meeting of the Western Regional Science Association, Molokai, Hawaii.

Nuremberg, M. (1960). *Nuremberg Report: Hawaii Prison System.* Honolulu, HI: Author.

Ombudsman (1983). Investigation of allegations of the use of unreasonable force against inmates during the shakedown of the Oahu community correctional center from December 14 through December 18, 1981. Honolulu, HI: Office of the Ombudsman.

Ombudsman (1984). Opinion of the Ombudsman regarding the decision of the director of the department of social services and housing to dismiss all cases from the 1981 Oahu community correctional center shakedown. Honolulu, HI: Office of the Ombudsman.

Pratt, R. (1985). "The Great Hawaiian Milk Crisis: Science, Policy and Economic Interest." *Social Process in Hawaii,* 31, 49-76.

Reyes, D. (1986, July 20). "After a Year of Controversy, Courts Doing Fine, Lum Says." *Sunday Star-Bulletin & Advertiser,* pp. A-1 & A-4.

Senate Judiciary Committee (1983). *Special Investigation.* Honolulu, HI: Author.

Sharkansky, I. (1975). *The United States: A Study of a Developing Nation.* New York, NY: David McKay Co.

Sipes, D. and L. Sipes (1982). *Managing the Hawaii Judiciary: An Era of Accomplishment 1966-1982, Executive Summary.* San Francisco, CA: National Center for State Courts.

"State Prison Woes." (1976, June 6). *The Sunday Advertiser* (editorial) p. B-2.

Takeuchi, J. (1989, February 21). "Isles' Population Face Will Change, Power Will Shift." *Honolulu Star-Bulletin,* p. 12.

Tswei, S. (1990, July 9). "Beatings, Abuses by Guards Alleged at 2 State Prisons." *Honolulu Star-Bulletin & Advertiser,* p. A-1.

Wang, J. (1982). *Hawaii State and Local Politics.* Hilo, HI: University of Hawaii.

Whittaker, E. (1986). *The Mainland Haole: The White Experience in Hawaii.* New York, NY: Columbia University.

Wolf, J. (1976) "Attempt to Change Prison Frustrating." *Honolulu Advertiser.*

Zalburg, S. (1979). *A Spark is Struck! Jack Hall and the ILWU in Hawaii.* Honolulu, HI: University of Hawaii.

Cases Cited

Belnap v. Chang et al., 77-0037 U.S.D.C.-Hi. (1977).

Spear v. Ariyoshi, 84-1104 U.S.D.C.-Hi. (1985).

Rape in Male Prisons: Examining the Relationship Between Correctional Officers' Attitudes Toward Male Rape and their Willingness to Respond to Acts of Rape†

9

Helen M. Eigenberg

Studies on male rape—the act of men raping men—suggest that rape in male prisons is relatively rare (Davis, 1968; Lockwood, 1980; Nacci & Kane, 1983, 1984a, 1984b; Wooden & Parker, 1982). However, these studies fail to clearly distinguish between consensual homosexuality, prostitution, and rape that may contribute to conservative estimates of rape. Furthermore, these studies suggest that correctional officers may inhibit reporting by treating victims insensitively or by ignoring coercive sexual behavior. Thus, despite evidence to the contrary, researchers fail to acknowledge that their estimates may underrepresent the amount of male rape that occurs in prison.

The purpose of this study is to explore correctional officers' attitudes toward male rape to determine whether these attitudes affect officers' willingness to respond to acts of rape in male prisons. This study does not examine the rape of women in women's facilities. Traditionally and historically, violence against women has been committed by men, not by other women. As a result, one would anticipate that the dynamics of rape in women's prisons would be very different from rape in men's prisons (see Propper, 1971). This chapter explores male rape in male prisons given the interesting contradictions that occur when men victimize other men in a way that is normally reserved for women. Research on rape in women's prisons is important, but beyond the scope of this examination.

This study concentrates on correctional officers for several reasons. First, correctional officers supposedly have some influence over inmates because of the amount of contact between the two groups (Guenther & Guenther, 1974; Peretti &

†Reprinted by permission of the author.

145

Hooker, 1976; Philliber, 1987).[1] Secondly, literature on female rape victims in the community suggests that police response has an impact upon reporting (Elias, 1986; Field, 1978; Feldman-Summers & Palmer, 1980; Griffin, 1979; Holmstrom & Burgess, 1978; Katz & Mazur, 1979; Karmen, 1990; Medea & Thompson, 1974; Robin, 1977; Russell, 1984; Schwendinger & Schwendinger, 1980; White & Mosher, 1986; Weis & Borges, 1973). It is reasonable to assume that correctional officers, like police officers, may affect reporting practices of inmate victims. And finally, correctional administrators can develop strategies that influence how correctional officers respond to rape. And even though affecting change is always problematic, it would seem logical to assume that the actions of correctional officers are more directly amenable to administrative control than are those of inmates. Thus, if officers appear to be part of the problem, if they appear to facilitate stigmatization of victims or if their actions facilitate victimization, then administrators may be able to devise strategies to rectify the problem.

Review of the Literature

Until the 1970s there was a remarkable void in the literature on rape in general (Gibbons, 1984; Wisan, 1979). Fortunately, there has been a tremendous increase in the number of publications addressing the rape of women in the community. However, very little is known about male rape. This topic has been virtually ignored both in and out of prison.

The earliest discussions of male rape in prison are found in the correctional literature dealing with homosexuality. These works (Buffum, 1972; Clemmer, 1958; Fishman, 1951; Kirkham, 1971; Sagarin, 1976; Sykes, 1958) focus on creating typologies of homosexuals. However, researchers fail to clearly distinguish between consensual sexual acts and acts of rape (Eigenberg, 1992). Homosexuality is defined so broadly that both rape victims and rapists are included in these classification schemes. As a result, the literature on homosexuality in prison discusses rape far more than it discusses consensual homosexuality. But more importantly, this literature demonstrates that researchers and inmates re-define acts of rape as consensual homosexual behavior which, in turn, may contribute to low estimates of rape in prison. Thus, just as female victims in the community have had rape re-defined as consensual sexual activity, male rape victims also are rendered invisible when sexual assaults are re-defined as consensual homosexuality.

More recent research tends to focus more on the act of rape and less on the "homosexual" nature of the problem (Davis, 1968; Lockwood, 1980; Nacci & Kane, 1983, 1984a, 1984b; Weiss & Friar, 1974; Wooden & Parker, 1982). These studies have gathered empirical data using victimization surveys, although the sparse amount of research makes it impossible to ensure the validity or reliability of any data (Eigenberg, 1989). Nonetheless, all of these studies suggest that rape occurs relatively infrequently; they report that as few as .3 percent or as many as 14 percent of inmates in male prisons are rape victims. However, it is difficult to determine what effect underreporting may have upon these estimates.

While all crime is underreported to some degree, rape has been called the "least reported and the least successfully prosecuted of all crimes of violence" (Stratton, 1975:5). Most authors agree that the Uniform Crime Report (UCR), which measures crimes known to the police, tends to underreport crime in general and rape in particular (Austin & Rodenbaugh, 1981; Brownmiller, 1975; Bureau of Justice Statistics [BJS], 1985; Dukes & Mattley, 1977; Ashworth & Feldman-Summers, 1981; Russell, 1984). This is because rape, like most crimes, rarely comes to the attention of the police unless the victim reports it and rape victims have been especially reluctant to report rape (BJS, 1985; Lizotte, 1985; Russell, 1984). And while the National Crime Survey (NCS) indicates that rape occurs almost twice as frequently as the UCR would suggest, there is reason to believe that the NCS also underestimates rape because of underreporting (Eigenberg, 1990; Koss, 1985, 1992; Russell, 1984). Thus, if both official figures and victimization surveys underestimate the amount of rape in the community, it would appear reasonable to assume that victimization surveys on rape in prison also underestimate the extent of the problem.

Reporting may be influenced by a wide variety of variables (i.e., age, race, relationship to the aggressor, nature of attack and injuries) (BJS, 1985; Koss 1985; Koss et al., 1985, 1987, 1988; Lizotte, 1985; Russell, 1984). However, some authors assert that negative social attitudes, those that stigmatize victims or suggest that the victim is to blame, play a critical role in reporting patterns (Brownmiller, 1975; Russell, 1984; MacKinnon, 1987; Schwendinger & Schwendinger, 1980; White & Mosher, 1986).

Male rape victims are stigmatized because they are victims in a society that is reluctant to accept the random nature of victimization (Elias, 1986; Karmen, 1990) and because of the homosexual connotations associated with the act (Kaufman, 1984; Weiss & Friar, 1974). Perhaps most importantly, inmates who report rape risk the stigmatization that accompanies informing (snitching). Here again, if social attitudes contribute to underreporting of rape in the community, it seems likely that the additional stigmatization associated with male rape would lead to underreporting. However, the literature on rape in prison has failed to address the impact of underreporting. It also has neglected to examine what effect, if any, officers might have upon reporting practices.

This study operates on the domain assumption that correctional officers' attitudes toward victims influence reporting by inmate victims. Research on female rape victims in the community shows that police responses affect reporting patterns (Elias, 1986; Field, 1978; Feldman-Summers & Palmer, 1980; Karmen, 1990; Katz & Mazur, 1979; Russell, 1984; White & Mosher, 1986; Weis & Borges, 1973). Training for police officers has been developed and implemented and officers appear to be processing rape investigations in a more sensitive manner (Karmen, 1990). At the same time, the number of rapes reported to the police has increased 42 percent since 1977 (FBI, 1987). It is reasonable to assume then that correctional officers, like police officers, affect the reporting practices of inmate victims. Therefore, it is important to examine correctional officers' attitudes toward male rape to determine whether they contribute to the stigmatization of victims.

It is also important to examine how officers react to rape because rule enforcement in prison is the primary responsibility of correctional officers. Officers introduce cases into the prison disciplinary system when they write incident reports; however, they also respond in less formal ways. For example, officers may receive information when inmates are at risk of rape (i.e., when they are being "pressured for sex"). As a result, officers may recommend that inmates be placed in segregation for their own protection. Or, officers may use their knowledge to increase patrols of areas as a way to prevent rapes.

An exhaustive search of the literature uncovered only one study that explicitly examined correctional officers and their attitudes toward male rape; however, it is rather limited as the main focus of the work was clearly on inmate victimization. Nacci and Kane (1983, 1984a, 1984b) surveyed 500 correctional officers in 17 federal institutions. They found that when officers were satisfied with their jobs, inmates were more likely to say there was less risk of rape, but when officers expressed high morale, inmates indicated a higher risk of rape (1983:49); however, the authors fail to clearly differentiate between job satisfaction and morale. Officers also indicated they were slightly more willing to prevent rape than to deter homosexuality, which is especially problematic if some rape is being committed under the guise of consenting homosexual acts. And while research indicates that bisexual and homosexual inmates are victimized more frequently (Lockwood, 1980; Nacci & Kane, 1983, 1984a, 1984b; Wooden & Parker, 1982), officers reported that they were more willing to protect heterosexual inmates from rape. The authors claim that officers appeared to equate bisexuality and homosexuality with voluntary participation.

In addition, Nacci and Kane report that officers overestimated the number of prisoners involved in both homosexual activity and rape when compared to estimates provided by inmates (1983:49). But if stigmatized inmates underreport both rape and consensual activities to researchers, then it is possible that the estimates provided by correctional officers were more accurate than those provided by inmates. The authors also asked officers whether rape victims were to be blamed for their victimization, yet no empirical results are reported. Instead, the authors state that when staff see victims as blameworthy because of appearance or their failure to protect themselves, inmates "sense greater danger in their environment" (1984a:49). This perception of danger may be real. Perhaps inmates are more at risk when officers focus on attributing blame to victims rather than assigning responsibility to perpetrators.

The paucity of research in this area made it difficult to identify factors that might affect either officers' attitudes toward male rape or their willingness to respond. As a result, the more general literature on correctional officers, homosexuality, and rape was consulted in order to identify other variables to include in this study. This literature indicates that several factors might be important. First, it is important to determine officers' attitudes toward inmates as it is possible that officers who view inmates negatively are less willing to respond to acts of rape because of their indifference toward inmates. Second, attitudes toward women are significant because prior research suggests that people with conservative attitudes toward women are more apt to accept rape myths as they apply to the rape of women in the community (Bunting & Reeves, 1983; Burt, 1980; Field, 1978; Klemmack & Klemmack, 1976). Thus, officers who endorse conservative attitudes toward women may be less willing to respond to rape in prison because of broader social definitions about rape and the role of women in society. Third, attitudes toward homosexuality are included because the literature suggests that researchers, inmates, and correctional officers may have difficulty distinguishing between consensual sexual behavior (i.e., homosexual) and coercive behavior (i.e., rape). Religiosity also was added as a control variable because prior research suggests that this variable is associated with attitudes toward homosexuality (Alston, 1974; Hansen, 1982; Nyberg & Alston, 1976; White, 1979). Finally, research on correctional officers frequently considers how both individual characteristics and organizational conditions affect correctional officers' attitudes (Crouch & Alpert, 1982; Cullen et al., 1989; Hepburn & Albonetti, 1980; Jurik, 1985; Klofas, 1986; Philliber, 1987; Poole & Regoli, 1980; Shamir & Drory, 1981; Smith & Hepburn, 1979; Whitehead & Lindquist, 1989). Consistent with this literature, the following variables also are included: age, race, education, sex, the security level of the correctional facility, amount of contact with inmates, and experience. The next section discusses operationalization and measurement in more detail.

Research Methodology

Sample

In October 1988, questionnaires were sent to 400 correctional officers employed by the Texas Department of Corrections (TDC). These officers were a simple random sample of all state correctional officers who were line officers employed in male correctional facilities. Surveys and a cover letter were distributed through the TDC's institutional mail system. No arrangements were made for a follow-up survey because of financial constraints. A total of 166 surveys were completed and one survey was undeliverable and was returned to the researcher. Thus, the response rate for the survey was 41.6 percent.

Data on gender, age, and race were used to evaluate the representativeness of the sample. The TDC data indicate that 80.7 percent of officers are male compared to 86.7 percent of the sample. And while males *appear* to be overrepresented in the sample, they may actually be underrepresented. This is because officers employed in female correctional facilities were not included in the sampling frame, but they are included in the TDC figures.[2] Data from the TDC also indicate that 75.3 percent of the officers are under age 40; while 70.9 percent of the individuals in this study are under age 40. Thus, respondents are slightly younger than the TDC employees. In addition, 63.1 percent of the officers working for the TDC are white, 27.3 percent are African-Americans, 9 percent are Hispanics, and less than 1 percent are other ethnic groups (.6%). In the sample, 72.1 percent of the sample are white, 17 percent are black and 10.9 percent are Hispanic. Hence, white male respondents and younger officers are overrepresented and black males are underrepresented.

Operationalization and Measurement

Individual characteristics (sex, age, race, education, religiosity) and organizational characteristics (experience, security level of facility) are measured using single items and measurement is rather straightforward. Coding is displayed in Table 9.1.

Officers' attitudes toward inmates are measured using Klofas and Toch's (1982) correctional orientation inventory. This instrument was selected because prior research suggests that it is reliable (Whitehead, Lindquist & Toch, 1987; Whitehead & Lindquist, 1989). The scale uses 17 items to measure four dimensions of officers' professional orientation (Whitehead, Lindquist & Klofas, 1987; Whitehead & Lindquist, 1989). The first factor measures counseling orientation, or the degree to which officers believe that their job orientation, should endorse rehabilitative goals. The second factor, concern for corruption of authority, assesses whether officers believe that inmates can be trusted. The third factor measures preference toward social distance; i.e., the degree of direct contact officers prefer to have with inmates. The final factor, punitive orientation measures whether officers believe that prison conditions should be harsh for inmates. Reliability coefficients for these measures are: .74 (counseling orientation); .77 (concern for corruption of authority); .74 (preference for social distance); and .64 (punitive orientation).[3]

Attitudes toward women are measured using 25 items that evaluate whether respondents endorse traditional or egalitarian views about the rights and roles of women. This unidimensional scale was developed by Spence, Helmreich, and Stapp (1973).[4] The reliability coefficient is .83.

Attitudes toward homosexuality are measured using a modified version of Herek's (1984) scale, which is designed to evaluate condemnation of homosexuality.[5] Herek's scale includes items that specifically assess attitudes toward both gay men and lesbians. In contrast, most researchers have used the word "homosexual" even though some literature suggests that respondents' attitudes differ depending upon the gender of the homosexual (Millham, San Miguel & Kellogg, 1976; Millham & Weinberger, 1977). However, Herek's scale was too long; therefore, items in his study dealing specifically with male homosexuality and with high factor loadings (.75 or higher) were included in this survey. The scale appears reliable (.86).[6]

Table 9.1. **Description of Variables**

Variable	Description
Sex	Male=0; Female=1
Age	Age to nearest year; M=34.22; SD=10.80
Race	Minority=0; White=1
Education	Some high school=1; High school graduate=2; Some college=3; BA/BS degree=4; Advanced degree=5; M=2.64; SD=.76
Religiosity	Not at all=0; Slightly=1; Somewhat=2; Extremely=3; M=1.87; SD=.70
Correctional Experience	Years of employment, M=4.05; SD=3.16
Contact with Inmates	None=0; 5 to 24% of the time=1; 25 to 49% of the time=2; 50 to 74% of the time=3; 75% or more of the time=4; M=3.77; SD=.70
Security Level of Facility	Minimum=1; Medium=2; Maximum=3; M=2.37; SD=.83
Social Distance	High score=preference for distance from inmates; Range=0 to 15; M=7.81; SD=2.79
Counseling Orientation	High score=preference for counseling orientation; Range=0 to 9; M=4.30; SD=2.30
Punitive Orientation	High score=preference for a punitive orientation toward inmates; Range=0 to 12; M=6.73; SD=2.76
Corruption of Authority	High score=concern with corruption of authority; Range=0 to 15; M=12.02; SD=2.62
Attitudes Toward Homosexuality	High score=condemnation of homosexuality; Range=0 to 44; M=36.10; SD=7.09
Attitudes Toward Women	High score=egalitarian attitudes toward women; Range=0 to 75; M=46.84; SD=10.00
Attitudes Toward Male Rape in Prison	High score=endorses stereotypical attitudes toward rape victims; Range=0 to 12; M=5.39; SD=2.47
Willingness to Respond	High score=willing to respond to acts of rape; Range=0 to 36; M=25.64; SD=5.03

Originally, seven items were included to assess officers' attitudes toward male rape in prison. Each of these questions evaluated stereotypical beliefs such as: some victims deserve rape, rape victims are weak or homosexuals, homosexual men falsely report rape, rapists are homosexuals, and rape is a sexual act. Three of these statements were used in the final analyses. Principle factor analysis with varimax rotation produced one factor that accounted for 15.9 percent of the variance. This factor appears to measure stereotypical attitudes toward rape victims. Specifically the factor is composed of statements that measure whether officers believe: inmates deserve to be raped if they had participated in prior consensual acts; rape victims are weak; and rape victims are homosexuals.[7] It has a reliability coefficient of .53.

Nine items measure the dependent variable—correctional officers' willingness to respond to rape. These items measure officers' support for a variety of responses including: writing disciplinary reports for rapes or for fighting when inmates are defending themselves from sexual assaults; encouraging inmates to report rapes; attempting to prevent sexual assaults; using cell assignments to safeguard inmates; protecting heterosexuals and homosexuals from rape; referring inmates to protective custody; and talking to inmates about the risk of rape. Principle factor analysis with varimax rotation suggests that this scale may be treated as a unidimensional scale.[8] The scale has a reliability coefficient of .67.

Findings

Means and standard deviations for each variable are displayed in Table 9.1. On the whole, officers seem willing to respond to acts of rape. Virtually all officers (97%) indicate that they should try to prevent rape. Likewise, most officers (92%) report that they should write disciplinary reports when inmates are pressured for sex and that they should encourage inmates to report acts of rape. In addition, most officers (93%) do *not* believe that it is acceptable to place inmates in cells where they might be raped. Officers are less overwhelming in their agreement when protection is the issue; 73 percent of the officers believe they should protect heterosexuals and 71 percent believe that they should protect homosexual inmates. About 69 percent of the officers believe that officers should place inmates in protective custody if they are being pressured for sex. However, only about one-half of the officers believe that they should write disciplinary reports to inmates who fight when they are being pressured for sex or that officers should talk to new inmates about the risk of sexual assault. The average score on the Response Scale also suggests that officers could be more responsive to rape in prison (see Table 9.1).

Mean values for the Male Rape Scale also suggest that officers are willing to endorse stereotypical attitudes toward male rape victims (see Table 9.1). About one-half of the officers (46.4%) believe some victims deserve to be raped; approximately one-third (33.7%) of the officers believe rape victims are weak; and about one-sixth (14.9%) of them believe male rape victims are homosexuals.

Zero-order correlations suggest that age, race, religiosity (RELIG), counseling orientation (COUN), social distance (DIS), punitive orientation (PUNIT), attitudes toward women (ATW), attitudes toward homosexuality (ATH) and attitudes toward male rape victims (MRAPE) influence officers' willingness to respond (see Table 9.2). Older officers and white officers are more willing to respond to acts of rape. Moreover, officers who are more religious, endorse a counseling orientation, prefer less social distance, reject a punitive orientation, have egalitarian attitudes

Table 9.2. Correlation Matrix

	AGE	RACE	SEX	EDUC	RELIG	SECLEV	CONTACT	EXPER	AUTH	COUN	DIST	PUNIT	ATW	ATH	MRAPE	RESPONSE
AGE	—															
RACE	-.05	—														
SEX	-.05	-.05	—													
EDUC	-.01	.13*	-.08	—												
RELIG	.09	.12	-.10	-.10	—											
SECLEV	-.16*	-.10	-.31*	.06	-.07	—										
CONTACT	-.11	.07	.07	.07	-.01	.02	—									
EXPER	.27*	.04	-.05	.04	-.08	-.08	-.02	—								
AUTH	-.23*	.02	.06	-.10	-.02	.15*	-.04	-.01	—							
COUN	.15*	.04	-.12	.11	.07	-.05	.08	-.02	-.36*	—						
DIST	-.24*	.02	.06	-.07	-.02	.07	-.01	.01	.28*	-.23*	—					
PUNIT	-.11	-.22	-.03	-.20*	-.03	-.09	-.10	.01	.28*	-.28*	-.23*	—				
ATW	-.04	.05	.23*	.10	-.14*	.00	.06	.06	-.07	.22*	.26*	-.22*	—			
ATH	-.03	-.06	-.08	-.05	.19*	.08	-.05	-.05	.15*	-.01	-.15*	.13	.14*	—		
MRAPE	.08	-.14*	-.14	-.08	-.08	.03	.07	.12	.17*	-.30*	.22*	.32*	-.25*	.14*	—	
RESPONSE	.12	.13*	-.01	.00	.19*	-.01	-.07	-.07	-.09	.31*	-.35*	-.25*	.29*	.10	-.29*	—

*p<.05.

Legend: EDUC = education; RELIG = religiosity; SECLEV = security level of the facility; CONTACT = contact with inmates; EXPER = correctional experience; AUTH = concern with corruption of authority; COUN = preference for counseling orientation; DIST = preference for social distance; PUNIT = endorse punitive orientation; ATW = attitudes toward women; ATH = attitudes toward homosexuality; MRAPE = attitudes toward male rape; RESPONSE = willingness to respond to acts of rape.

toward women, condemn homosexuals, or reject stereotypical attitudes toward victims are more willing to respond to acts of rape.

Officers' willingness to respond is also regressed on the variables representing individual characteristics, organizational conditions, and attitudinal perspectives.[9] With the exception of religiosity, however, individual and organizational variables do not impact upon officers' responses to male rape when all the variables are entered in the regression equation. However, zero-order correlations suggest that both age and race impact upon officers' responses and it is possible that the effect of these variables is masked by the small number of both older and black officers in the sample.

As shown in Table 9.3, the independent variables account for 28 percent of the variance in the regression equation. Five variables, religiosity, counseling orientation, social distance, attitudes toward women, and attitudes toward homosexuality have a significant, direct effect on officers' responsiveness. Officers who are more religious, endorse a counseling orientation, prefer less social distance, have liberal attitudes toward women, and condemn homosexuality are more willing to respond to rape. Attitudes toward male rape are not significant, although the direction is consistent with the theoretical orientation. Officers who have stereotypical attitudes toward victims are less willing to respond to acts of rape. Punitive orientation is significant when examining the zero-order correlations, although this variable is not significant in the regression equation.

Discussion

While officers appear to be willing to respond to acts of rape, it is possible that their answers to the survey items reflect what they think they would or should do under the circumstances (i.e., their responses fail to capture their actual behavior). The data offer some support for this interpretation. Questions that evaluated officers' formal duties (i.e., writing disciplinary reports, cell assignments, preventing infractions) produce higher agreement; however, questions that assess officers' discretionary power (i.e., talking to inmates about the risk of rape or ignoring violations in some instances) result in less agreement. Thus, officers appear to be willing to say that they will use formal means of social control but they are less cohesive in their approach when informal methods of control are examined. Classics in the correctional literature (Cressey, 1959; Sykes, 1958) suggest that formal methods of control are weak and that officers assert their limited power most effectively when they ignore misconduct. As a result, it may be premature to assume that officers are willing to respond to acts of rape. Future research should examine officers' discretionary power in more detail. Vignettes might prove useful in this respect.

Regression indicates that counseling orientation affects officers' willingness to respond to acts of male rape. It seems reasonable that officers who endorse a rehabilitative philosophy and who believe that officers should counsel inmates would proactively respond to acts of rape.

Table 9.3. **Regression of Officers' Willingness to Respond to Rape
on Independent Variables**

Independent Variables	Standardized Coefficients (All variables in the model)	Standardized Coefficients (Only with significant variables in the model)
Age	.08	
Race	.11	
Education	-.07	
Sex	-.09	
Religiosity	.14*	.17*
Security Level of Facility	.08	
Contact with Inmates	-.03	
Experience	-.06	
Corruption of Authority	.09	
Counseling Orientation	.16*	.13*
Social Distance	-.29*	-.30*
Punitive Orientation	-.05	
Attitudes Toward Homosexuality	.15*	.16*
Attitudes Toward Women	.24*	.23*
Attitudes Toward Male Rape	-.12	
Multiple R	.59	.56
R^2	.28	.27
F	5.27	11.81
Significance of F	.00	.00

*p <.05

In a similar vein, officers who prefer less social distance report a higher level of responsiveness to acts of rape. Thus, officers who prefer less social distance—those who do not mind contact with inmates—are more willing to respond to acts of rape. In contrast, officers who prefer social distance may isolate themselves from inmates and may not be in a position to discover acts of misconduct of any kind. However, social distance also may be associated with a rehabilitative orientation.

The concept of social distance originated in the role conflict literature (Klofas & Toch, 1982; Whitehead & Lindquist, 1989; Whitehead, Lindquist & Klofas, 1987). It asserts that officers experience difficulties when they are expected to perform both custodial and rehabilitative functions. Officers are expected to be humane and communicative with inmates if they are to effect rehabilitative goals; however, taking on this role may also compromise officers' custodial authority if they get "too close" to inmates (by violating the need for social distance) (Cressey, 1959; Hepburn & Albonetti, 1980; Sykes, 1958; Toch & Klofas, 1982). Thus, officers who prefer less social distance, like officers who favor a counseling orientation, embrace a rehabilitative role. In other words, officers who express compassion for inmates (by endorsing a counseling role and by maintaining less social distance) are more responsive to rape in prison.

In addition, this study indicates that correctional orientation may be useful when it is used as an independent variable, rather than as a dependent variable. Studies have concentrated on predicting officers' correctional orientation using demographic and environmental variables (e.g., job satisfaction, shift assignment, security level of facility, experience). This research (Whitehead & Lindquist, 1989; Whitehead, Lindquist & Klofas, 1987) is important; however, the real utility of the correctional orientation scale may lie in its ability to predict officers' attitudes toward a variety of inmate behaviors.

Attitudes toward women also predicted officers' willingness to respond. Officers who endorse a conservative role for women may be less willing to respond to rape because of the relationship between attitudes toward women and more general social definitions of rape. As discussed earlier, prior research suggests that individuals with conservative attitudes toward women are more apt to endorse stereotypical beliefs (rape myths) about the rape of women in the community (Bunting & Reeves, 1983; Burt, 1980; Field, 1978; Klemmack & Klemmack, 1976). Thus, attitudes toward women appear to provide a conceptual foundation that in turn predicts how individuals view rape in society. The data provide some support for this interpretation.

Officers with negative attitudes toward male rape—those who engage in victim blaming—are less willing to respond to acts of rape. And while this relationship is not significant, additional analyses indicate that attitudes toward male rape are significant in the regression equation when attitudes toward women are deleted from the model. As discussed above, perhaps attitudes toward women affect responses indirectly through attitudes toward male rape. However, this study also may have failed to fully capture the richness associated with the various dimensions of officers' attitudes toward male rape thereby weakening the effect of this variable. The scale factored rather poorly as evidenced by the small percentage of variance captured by the single factor (15.9%). It also was not as reliable as one would prefer (.53). Nonetheless, this study suggests that these attitudes toward male rape are important and that this variable should be examined in more depth in future research.

It was not anticipated that religiosity, a control variable, would have a direct effect upon correctional responses. Religiosity was included because some research suggests that religious individuals are more condemning of homosexuality. Perhaps, religiosity is capturing some variance associated with attitudes toward homosexuality —variance that the Attitudes Toward Homosexuality scale fails to capture. However, it is also conceivable that religiosity encourages a sense of compassion and a concern with humanity that makes religious officers more responsive to rape.

At first glance, it appears odd that officers who are more condemning of homosexuality are more willing to respond to male rape in prison. In this case, though, stereotypical attitudes may contribute to rigorous enforcement of rules. It is certainly possible that officers who condemn homosexuality are more willing to respond to rape because they view rape as a homosexual act. Ironically, officers with more liberal attitudes toward homosexuality may facilitate victimization. They may neglect to enforce policies prohibiting consensual sexual acts because they do not believe that this behavior is hurting anyone—that homosexual behavior between two consenting adults is none of their business. However, simply because an inmate does not have a knife at his throat at the time of the act does not mean that the act is, in fact, consensual.

To summarize, this exploratory study uses correctional officers as the unit of analysis to take a new approach to the study of male rape in prison. It suggests that officers respond to acts of rape based on their general views about inmates, definitions of rape, and beliefs about the role of women in society. It also indicates that officers' attitudes toward homosexuality are important because of the homosexual connotations associated with male rape and because of the problems associated with distinguishing between consensual homosexuality and male rape in prisons. And, it suggests that officers' attitudes toward male rape deserve further examination. Obviously, this research needs replication; the sample size is small and the attitudinal scales need to be evaluated in more depth to determine the reliability and validity of the various instruments. However, the data indicate that the approach used in this study deserves additional investigation. The remaining section discusses the implications of these findings.

Implications

This study has important implications in two areas. First, theoretical development on male rape needs to pay more attention to the literature on the rape of women in the community. Findings from this study suggest that we should attend to the ways in which male rape in prison reflects societal views about rape in general. Second, administrators must develop and implement policies that address male rape in prison. The data from this study indicate that correctional officers may (unwittingly) play a role in facilitating male rape in prison. Strategies need to be developed that encourage officers to become more proactive.

Theoretical Development

Feminist scholars have argued that male violence is an essential mechanism of social control which ensures that men maintain power over women (Brownmiller, 1975; Clark & Lewis, 1977; Edwards, 1989; Kelly, 1987; MacKinnon, 1987; Russell, 1984; Stanko, 1985). Rape plays a crucial role in this process. It promotes fear and helps keep women powerless. As Clark and Lewis (1977:28) note, "in order to preserve and enhance male supremacy, rape must be both possible and probable; it must remind women who has power over them and keep them solidly in their places."

Research on male rape suggests that it does not occur in response to sexual deprivation and that the sexual orientation of either the predator or the victim is not a factor (Cotton & Groth, 1984; Davis, 1968; Groth, 1979; Groth & Burgess, 1980;

Kaufman, 1984). In other words, male rape victims experience rape as an act of power—not an act of sex. But if male rape is conceptualized as an act of power, then it also is possible, if not probable, that our understanding of rape in the community would be affected. The entire myth system that serves to blur the distinction between rape and sex might be threatened if male rape is recognized as an act of power. Ultimately, this reconceptualization of rape might inhibit the degree to which rape could continue to function as a means of social control.

We live in a society where rigid gender socialization is enforced; one that dictates that women—not men—get raped. As a society, we deny the existence of male rape; we rarely discuss it, measure it, or publish research on it. And when we do, we reinforce estimates that, in all probability, underestimate the extent of the problem because we fail to discuss underreporting. Perhaps acknowledging the existence of male rape would threaten the very fabric of our society. Theoretical explanations should consider that male rape may be intricately related to societal views of rape in the community. In other words, male rape in prison cannot be analyzed in isolation, separate from the larger social structure.

Policy Initiatives

This study also suggests that officers might be more proactive in their responses to rape in prison. One way to increase responsiveness might be to encourage officers to be more rigorous in their enforcement of regulations that prohibit sexual activity. Ironically, officers with more condemning attitudes toward homosexuality are more willing to respond to male rape. It does not seem appropriate to encourage officers to develop negative attitudes toward homosexuality given the implications this type of a strategy would have upon officers' reactions toward homosexuals in the larger social arena. However, correctional administrators can encourage officers to respond to all types of sexual acts because it is frequently difficult (if not impossible) to distinguish consensual acts from coercive acts, merely by observing two inmates engaged in sexual behavior.

Administrators have a decided advantage over the larger criminal justice system because inmates who engage in "sexual activities" violate institutional policies, whether these acts are consensual or not. Thus, it is easier to "charge" and "convict" aggressors for misconduct because officials may use disciplinary sanctions against inmates caught engaging in sexual acts even in cases in which they cannot prove force (although consensual acts frequently carry a lesser sanction.)

A note of caution is warranted though as rigorous enforcement of policies prohibiting consensual acts might facilitate additional harm to victims. If officers write incident reports for consensual acts, both inmates are apt to receive misconduct reports, thus victims might be subjected to disciplinary actions. Rigorous enforcement could encourage reporting if victims are forced to choose between reporting a rape and receiving a disciplinary report for engaging in consensual sexual behavior. However, inmates reporting rape under these circumstances may not be believed and they may experience a second victimization by the prison disciplinary system. In the final analysis, inmate victims probably will be reluctant to report any type of victimization as long as they fear reprisals from other inmates in the general population (for snitching or informing). Thus, victims may suffer additional harm if administrators encourage officers to rigorously enforce policies prohibiting sexual activity; but if administrators fail to enforce these policies they appear to be abdicating control to the inmates. They seem to convey the message that rape is something they cannot or will not control, thereby leaving inmates to their own devices. In the prison vernacular, they seem to offer little assistance to inmates except the age-old advice of "fight or fuck."

Correctional administrators might also improve officers' willingness to respond to acts of rape through training. Because officers who endorse a rehabilitative philosophy are more willing to respond to rape, administrators might encourage officers to embrace this role. Training programs that emphasize interpersonal skills and counseling would offer officers the skills they need to perform this role more adequately.

Administrators might also consider designing and implementing training programs that specifically address sexual behavior in prisons. National training modules have been developed for virtually all aspects of the correctional officer's job. These modules are used extensively by state correctional systems. No national training module currently exists on the subject of male rape or homosexuality and this author has been unable to locate any state module that examines the subject in any depth.

Correctional officers might benefit from modified versions of "sensitivity training" programs that have been created for police departments. These programs could stress that officers may not be able to distinguish coercive sexual behavior from consenting sexual acts and emphasize the importance of enforcing disciplinary sanctions regardless of whether officers believe that these acts are consensual or not. Programs should also emphasize the importance of responding to rape victims in a compassionate way. Such training might help reduce the stigmatization accompanying male rape. In addition, trained officers may be more willing to engage in proactive responses that ultimately could help reduce the amount of rape in prison. Officers may encourage reporting through sensitive treatment of victims or through the skillful use of interpersonal skills. They might deter rape by warning new inmates about the risk of rape. At the very least, officers who are trained would be able to offer better assistance to victims. For example, officers could be trained to recognize the symptoms victims exhibit following a rape. Officers then would be in a position to provide crisis intervention and to refer victims for more in-depth counseling. Perhaps most importantly, they could ensure that victims receive medical treatment.

We need to develop strategies designed to address the problem of rape in prisons and training seems to be a logical place to begin. Furthermore, the current

AIDS epidemic makes it imperative that we begin to address this problem immediately. Rape in prison can no longer be "the most closely guarded secret of American prisons" (Weiss & Friar, 1974:x).

Notes

[1] Unfortunately, the complexity of the relationship and the nature of any interactions between the two groups have yet to be adequately researched (Philliber, 1987). Nonetheless, assuming a relationship between the behavior of officers and the behavior of inmates is certainly consistent with other research on correctional officers (Philliber, 1987:30).

[2] Data were not available from the TDC to ascertain the exact percentage of female officers who work in male facilities.

[3] Factor analysis of this scale has successfully reproduced this four factor structure several times (Whitehead & Lindquist, 1989; Whitehead, Lindquist & Klofas, 1987). Factor analysis of the current data was completed using principle factor analysis with varimax rotation. One question, however, failed to factor in accordance with prior research. (The specific item assessed whether officers should keep conversations with inmates short and businesslike.) The decision was made to use the original four-factor scale structure given its prior success despite this slight deviation. It is possible that some differences are a result of rotation techniques as the prior research does not describe what type of rotation was used in the factor analysis. However, additional analyses (including and excluding the questionable item) suggest that the final results were not affected by this decision.

[4] This is the short form of the ATW scale. Principle factor analysis with varimax rotation produced a multidimensional factor structure. Here again, however, the decision was made to use the original scale because homogeneous populations may fail to factor properly. The overwhelming majority of respondents in this sample were male, which probably affected the factor solution that is based on both male and female respondents.

[5] A modified version of Herek's scale was used because a thorough search of the literature failed to locate a better alternative. Several authors have created instruments to measure attitudes toward homosexuality (Hudson & Ricketts, 1980; Larsen, Reed & Hoffman, 1980; MacDonald & Games, 1974; Millham, San Miguel & Kellogg, 1976); however, reliability is rarely reported and dichotomous responses are frequently used.

[6] Principle factor analysis with varimax rotation resulted in two factors that appear to measure social condemnation and personal condemnation of homosexuality. Thus, these two factors seemed to capture a common concept—condemnation. Oblique rotation suggests that these two-factors are rather highly correlated (.65); therefore they should not be treated orthogonally (or as distinct subscales; Tabachnick & Fidell, 1990). As a result, this scale is treated as a unidimensional scale.

[7] Factor analysis produced four factors in the initial solution. Three of these factors had eigenvalues less than 1, two factors were composed of only one variable, and one variable had extremely low factor loadings (less than .30). All of these conditions suggest that these variables should be eliminated from the final factor solution (Tabachnick & Fidell, 1989). As a result, the final factor solution produced only one factor.

[8] Factor analysis resulted in two factors, only one of which had eigenvalue 1. However, the scatterplot and oblique rotation (factor correlation = .49) suggest that it is reasonable to treat the scale as an unidimensional one (Tabachnick & Fidell, 1989).

[9] Standard multiple regression with mean substitution is used. Violations of assumptions were evaluated. Correlation coefficients indicate that multicollinearity is not a problem. Linearity, homoscedasticity, and normality were evaluated through the use of scatterplots. The standardized scatterplot indicates that the data are relatively linear and homoscedastic. The normal probability suggests that there is some deviation from normality, although the observed values closely resemble a straight line. Thus, some assumptions have been violated. However, multiple regression is a robust technique although violation of assumptions may result in more conservative correlation coefficients (Tabachnick & Fidell, 1989).

References

Alston, J. (1974). "Attitudes Toward Extramarital and Homosexual Relations." *Journal for the Scientific Study of Religion,* 13, 479-481.

Austin, M. and B. Rodenbaugh (1981). *Sexual Assault: A Guide for Community Action.* New York, NY: Garland, STPM Press.

Brownmiller, S. (1975). *Against Our Will: Men, Women, and Rape.* New York, NY: Simon and Schuster.

Buffum, P. (1972). *Homosexuality in Prisons.* Washington, DC: U.S. Department of Justice, Law Enforcement Assistance Administration.

Bureau of Justice Statistics. (1985) *The Crime of Rape.* Washington, DC: U.S. Department of Justice.

Burt, M. (1980). "Cultural Myths and Supports for Rape." *Journal of Personality and Social Psychology,* 38(2), 217-230.

Clemmer, D. (1958). *The Prison Community.* New York, NY: Holt.

Cotton, D. and A. Groth (1984). "Sexual Assault in Correctional Institutions: Prevention and Intervention." In I. Stuart and J. Greer (eds.) *Victims of Sexual Aggression: Treatment of Children, Women, and Men* (pp. 127-155). New York, NY: Van Nostrand Reinhold Company.

Cressey, D. (1959). "Contradictory Directives in Complex Organizations: The Case of the Prison." *Administrative Science Quarterly,* 4 (June), 1-19.

Crouch, B. and G. Alpert (1982). "Sex and Occupational Socialization Among Prison Guards: A Longitudinal Study." *Criminal Justice and Behavior,* 9 (June), 159-176.

Cullen, F., F. Lutze, B. Link and N. Wolfe (1989). "The Correctional Orientation of Prison Guards: Do Officers Support Rehabilitation?" *Federal Probation,* 53 (March), 33-42.

Davis, A. (1968). "Sexual Assaults in the Philadelphia Prison System." In D. Peterson and C. Thomas (eds.) *Corrections: Problems and Prospects.* Second Edition (pp. 102-113). Englewood Cliffs, NJ: Prentice-Hall.

Dukes, R. and C. Mattley (1977). "Predicting Rape Victim Reportage." *Sociology and Social Research,* 62, 63-84.

Eigenberg, H. (1989). "Male Rape: An Empirical Examination of Correctional Officers' Attitudes Toward Male Rape in Prison." *Prison Journal,* 68, (2), 39-56.

Eigenberg, H. (1990). "Rape and the National Crime Survey: A Case of the Missing Question." *Justice Quarterly* (December).

Eigenberg, H. (1992). "Homosexuality in Male Prisons: Demonstrating the Need for a Social Constructionist Approach." *Criminal Justice Review* (in press).

Elias, R. (1986). *The Politics of Victimization: Victims, Victimology and Human Rights*. New York, NY: Oxford.

Feldman-Summers, S. and C. Ashworth (1981). "Factors Related to Intentions to Report a Rape." *Journal of Social Issues*, 37, 53-70.

Feldman-Summers, S. and G. Palmer (1980). "Rape As Viewed By Judges, Prosecutors, and Police Officers." *Criminal Justice and Behavior*, 7, 1-23.

Field, H. (1978). "Attitudes Toward Rape: A Comparative Analysis of Police, Rapists, Crisis Counselors, and Citizens." *Journal of Personality and Social Psychology*, 36(2), 156-179.

Fishman, J. (1951). *Sex in Prison*. London, England: John Lane, The Bodley Head.

Griffin, S. (1979). *Rape: The Power of Consciousness*. San Francisco, CA: Harper and Row.

Groth, N. (1979). *Men Who Rape: The Psychology of the Offender*. New York, NY: Plenum Press.

Groth, N. and A. Burgess (1980). "Male Rape: Offenders and Victims." *The American Journal of Psychiatry*, 137(7), 806-810.

Guenther, A. and M. Guenther (1974). "Screws vs. Thugs." *Society*, 11, 42-50.

Hansen, G. (1982). "Measuring Prejudice Against Homosexuality (Homosexism) Among College Students: A New Scale." *Journal of Social Psychology*, 117, 233-236.

Hepburn, J. and C. Albonetti (1980). "Role Conflict in Correctional Institutions: An Empirical Examination of the Treatment-Custody Dilemma Among Correctional Staff." *Criminology*, 17 (February), 445-459.

Herek, G. (1984). Beyond "Homophobia": A Social Psychological Perspective of Attitudes Toward Lesbians and Gay Men." *Journal of Homosexuality*, 10(1), 1-21.

Holmstrom, L. and A. Burgess (1978). *The Victim of Rape*. New York, NY: John Wiley.

Hudson, W. and W. Ricketts (1980). "A Strategy for the Measurement of Homophobia." *Journal of Homosexuality*, 5(4), 357-373.

Jurik, N. (1985). "Individual and Organizational Determinants of Correctional Officer Attitudes Toward Inmates." *Criminology*, 23 (August), 523-539.

Karmen, A. (1990). *Crime Victims: An Introduction to Victimology*. Monterey, CA: Brooks/Cole.

Katz, S. and M. Mazur (1979). *Understanding the Rape Victim*. New York, NY: John Wiley.

Kaufman, A. (1984). "Rape of Men in the Community." In I. Stuart and J. Greer (eds.) *Victims of Sexual Aggression: Treatment of Children, Women, and Men* (pp. 157-169). New York, NY: Van Nostrand Reinhold Company.

Kelly, L. (1988). *Surviving Sexual Violence*. Minneapolis, MN: University of Minnesota Press.

Kirkham, G. (1971). "Homosexuality in Prison." In J. Henslin (ed.) *Studies in the Sociology of Sex* (pp. 325-344). New York, NY: Appleton-Century-Crofts.

Klemmack, S. and D. Klemmack (1976). "The Social Definitions of Rape." In M. Walker and S. Brodsky (eds.) *Sexual Assault: The Victim and The Rapist.* Lexington, MA: Lexington Books.

Klofas, J. (1986). "Discretion Among Correctional Officers: The Influence of Urbanization, Age, and Race." *International Journal of Offender Therapy and Comparative Criminology,* 30, 111-24.

Klofas, J. and H. Toch (1982). "The Guard Subculture Myth." *Journal of Research in Crime and Delinquency,* 19, 238-254.

Koss, M. (1985). "The Hidden Rape Victim: Personality, Attitudinal, and Situational Characteristics." *Psychology of Women Quarterly,* 9, 193-212.

Koss, M. (1992). "The Underdetection of Rape: Methodological Choices Influence Incidence Estimates." *Journal of Social Issues,* 48 (1), 61-75.

Koss, M., T. Dinero, C. Seibel and S. Cox (1988). "Stranger and Acquaintance Rape: Are There Differences in the Victim's Experience." *Psychology of Women Quarterly,* 12, 1-24.

Koss, M., C. Gidycz and N. Wisniewski (1987). "The Scope of Rape: Incidence and Prevalence of Sexual Aggression and Victimization in a National Sample of Higher Education Students." *Journal of Consulting and Clinical Psychology,* 55,(2), 162-170.

Koss, M., K. Leonard, D. Beezley and C. Oros (1985). "Nonstranger Sexual Aggression: A Discriminant Analysis of the Psychological Characteristics of Undetected Offenders." *Sex Roles,* 12, 981-992.

Larsen, K., M. Reed and S. Hoffman (1980). "Attitudes of Heterosexuals Toward Homosexuality. A Likert Type Scale and Construct Validity." *Journal of Sex Research,* 16 (93), 245-57.

Lizotte, A. (1985). "The Uniqueness of Rape: Reporting Assaultive Violence to the Police." *Crime and Delinquency,* 31(2), 169-190.

Lockwood, D. (1980). *Sexual Aggression in Prison.* New York, NY: Elsevier.

MacDonald, G. (1981). "Misrepresentation, Liberalism, and Heterosexual Bias in Introductory Psychology Textbooks." *Journal of Homosexuality,* 6 (3), 45-60.

MacKinnon, C. (1987). *Feminism Unmodified: Discourses on Life and Law.* Cambridge, MA: Harvard University Press.

Medea, A. and K. Thompson (1974). *Against Rape.* New York, NY: Farmer, Straus, and Giroux.

Millham, J., C. San Miguel and R. Kellogg (1976). "A Factor-Analytic Conceptualization of Attitudes Toward Male and Female Homosexuals." *Journal of Homosexuality,* 2 (1), 3-10.

Millham, J. and L. Weinberger (1977). "Sexual Preference, Sex Role Appropriateness, and Restriction of Social Access." *Journal of Homosexuality,* 2 (4), 343-357.

Nacci, P. and T. Kane (1983). "The Incidence of Sex and Sexual Aggression in Federal Prisons." *Federal Probation,* 7, 31-36.

Nacci, P. and T. Kane (1984a). "Sex and Sexual Aggression in Federal Prisons: Inmate Involvement and Employee Impact." *Federal Probation,* 8 (March), 46-53.

Nacci, P. and T. Kane (1984b). "Inmate Sexual Aggression: Some Evolving Propositions and Empirical Findings, and Mitigating Counter-Forces." *Journal of Offender Counseling, Services, and Rehabilitation*, 9(1-2), 1-20.

Nyberg, K. and J. Alston (1976). "Analysis of Public Attitudes Toward Homosexual Behavior," *Journal of Homosexuality*, 2 (2), 99-107.

Peretti, P. and M. Hooker (1976). "Social Role Self-Perceptions of State Prison Guards." *Criminal Justice Behavior*, 3(2), 187-195.

Philliber, S. (1987). "Thy Brother's Keeper: A Review of the Literature on Correctional Officers." *Justice Quarterly*, 4 (March), 9-37.

Poole, E. and R. Regoli (1980). "Role Stress, Custody Orientation, and Disciplinary Actions: A Study of Prison Guards." *Criminology*, 18 (August), 215-226.

Propper, A. (1981). *Prison Homosexuality*. Lexington, MA: D.C. Heath.

Robin, G. (1977). "Forcible Rape: Institutionalized Sexism in the Criminal Justice System." *Crime and Delinquency*, 23, 136-153.

Russell, D. (1984). *Sexual Exploitation: Rape, Child Sexual Abuse, and Workplace Harassment*. Beverly Hills, CA: Sage Publications.

Schwendinger, J. and H. Schwendinger (1980). "Rape Myths in Legal and Theoretical Practice." *Crime and Justice*, 1, 18-26.

Shamir, B. and A. Drory (1981). "Some Correlates of Prison Guards' Beliefs." *Criminal Justice and Behavior*, 8 (June), 233-249.

Smith, C. and J. Hepburn (1979). "Alienation in Prison Organizations." *Criminology*, 17 (August), 251-262.

Spence, J., R. Helmreich and J. Stapp (1973). "A Short Version of the Attitudes Toward Women Scale (AWS)." *Bulletin of the Psychonomic Society*, 2, 219-20.

Stanko, E. (1985). *Intimate Intrusions: Women's Experiences of Male Violence*. London, England: Routledge and Keagan Paul.

Stratton, J. (1975). "Rape and the Victim: A New Role for Law Enforcement." *FBI Law Enforcement Bulletin*, (November), 3-6.

Sykes, G. (1958). *The Society of Captives: A Study of a Maximum Security Prison*. Princeton, NJ: Princeton University Press.

Tabachnick, B. and L. Fidell (1989). *Using Multivariate Statistics*. New York, NY: Harper and Row.

Weis, K. and S. Borges (1973). "Victimology and Case of the Legitimate Victim." In L. Schultz (ed.) *Rape Victimology* (pp. 91-141). Springfield, IL: Charles C Thomas.

Weiss, C. and D. Friar (1974). *Terror in the Prisons*. New York, NY: The Bobbs-Merrill Company, Inc.

White, T. (1979). "Attitudes of Psychiatric Nurses Toward Same Sex Orientations," *Journal of Sex Research*, 17 (1), 66-72.

White, B. and D. Mosher (1986). "Experimental Validation of a Model for Predicting the Reporting of Rape." *Sexual Coercion and Assault,* 1(2), 43-55.

Whitehead, J. and C. Lindquist (1986). "Correctional Officer Job Burnout: A Path Model." *Journal of Research in Crime and Delinquency,* 23 (February), 23-42.

Whitehead, J. and C. Lindquist (1989). "Determinants of Correctional Officers' Professional Orientation." *Justice Quarterly,* 6 (1), 69-88.

Whitehead, J., C. Lindquist and J. Klofas (1987). "Correctional Officer Professional Orientation: A Replication of the Klofas-Toch Measure." *Criminal Justice and Behavior,* 14 (December), 468-486.

Wisan, G. (1979)."The Treatment of Rape in Criminology Textbooks." *Victimology,* 4, (1), 86-89.

Wooden, W. and J. Parker (1982). *Men Behind Bars: Sexual Exploitation in Prison.* New York, NY: Plenum Press.

The Myth of Humane Imprisonment: A Critical Analysis of Severe Discipline in U.S. Maximum Security Prisons, 1945-1990[†][††][†††]

10

Mark S. Hamm, Therese Coupez,
Frances E. Hoze &
Corey Weinstein

Introduction

"Beating of inmates with clubs and fists was formerly common," wrote American penologist Donald Clemmer more than 50 years ago, "but occurs now only rarely..." (1940:204). Over the course of the past half-century this image of an increasingly humane system of U.S. penology has laid claim to a consensual validity among analysts of various political and academic persuasions (Bowker, 1985; Conrad, 1981; Jacobs, 1983; Glaser, 1964; Sherman & Hawkins, 1981; Newman, 1985). Indeed, one of today's leading penologists has been moved to proclaim:

> It is fair to say that, with a limited array of psychological stresses
> as the most horrible punishment we are willing to inflict upon our
> criminals, we are becoming both more civilized and more poten-
> tially civilizing in our punishments (Johnson, 1987:50).

It is of little wonder then, that the image of a humane American prison has found its way into criminal justice textbooks where students are taught, moreover, that: "The loss of privileges, loss of good time, and confinement in punitive segregation are the sanctions most often imposed for violations of the institution's rules. Twenty days

†Reprinted by permission of the authors.
††We wish to thank John Irwin, Marsha Rosenbaum, Milton Firestone, James Lincoln, and James Austin for their helpful comments on this chapter.
†††Portions of this chapter were presented at the annual meeting of the Academy of Criminal Justice Sciences, Nashville, TN, March 1991, and the Fifth International Conference on Penal Abolition, Bloomington, IN, May 1991.

of continuous punitive segregation is the maximum in many prisons..." (Clear & Cole, 1990:385-386) because "administrators have lessened the authority of correctional staff by humanizing the prison" (Travis, 1990:373). This social image, clearly drawn by esteemed criminal justice experts, has thus formulated a paradigm in the minds of a new generation of men and women who have learned to practice their trade as professionals in the field of corrections.

The present research will endeavor to suggest that penology has been misled by this "humane image" in fundamental ways. In so doing, we will develop quite a different portrait of prison discipline based on an extensive review of the literature and on an empirical snapshot taken during the late 1980s—a period when American penology underwent its most remarkable changes in history.

The Prison Discipline Literature

Between World War II and 1990, virtually hundreds of articles and books were written on the general subject of prison discipline. This vast body of literature primarily took one of three forms. First, inspired by the classic works of Sykes (1958) and Cressey (1965), academic criminologists adopted various socio-analytic models to explain the physical and psychological afflictions of inmates resulting from the stresses and power distributions that are an inevitable feature of prison life (Berk, 1966; Irwin, 1980; Jacobs, 1977; Johnson & Toch, 1982; Wheeler, 1968). The second body of literature on prison discipline was produced by government officials and the third, and largest, was recorded by prisoners themselves. We begin our analysis with a review of the academic research and then turn our attention to the writings of administrators and inmates.

The Criminological Evidence on Severe Prison Discipline

Here, our primary intent is to focus on quantitative studies related to the most egregious forms of prisoner discipline (e.g., physical and mental torture inflicted by staff, physical beatings and homicides by staff, and extended periods of solitary confinement). Thus, qualitative or phenomenological studies were not included in the present analysis. To be included, a study was required to meet three criteria: (1) the study must employ objective measures of victimization of prisoners by staff; (2) it must evaluate the relationship between prisoner victimization by staff and various prison conditions; and (3) it must do so by means of rudimentary statistical tests.

Hence, the studies reviewed were of a correlational or quasi-experimental nature. The studies were identified with the aid of a computer search of the prison victimization literature, other reviews (Bonta & Gendreau, 1990; Bowker, 1980), and an examination of recent criminology and criminal justice journals and books. We considered conditions of imprisonment as an independent variable and documented incidences of prisoner victimization by staff as dependent variables. Because our focus was on discerning the more brutalizing impacts of incarceration performed at the hands of prison staff members, we did not evaluate research on the indirect victimizing effects of imprisonment (e.g., physiological stress and psychological distress). Finally, because of their unique social and historical properties, we did not include studies of prison riots (see Useem & Kimball, 1989). Moreover, our review examines the levels of staff-on-prisoner victimization by two conditions of imprisonment: crowding and maximum security custody.

Crowding. Prison crowding is almost universally seen by correctional administrators and researchers as the major impediment to the humane treatment of criminal offenders. During the decade of the 1980s, nearly four out of five American states operated correctional systems in violation of the Eighth Amendment guarantee against cruel and unusual punishment (American Correctional Association, 1988) as the average state prison system functioned at approximately 120 percent of its rated capacity (Bureau of Justice Statistics [BJS], 1988). Among other developments, this unprecedented population explosion led to significant increases in disciplinary infractions and violence (Gaes & McQuire, 1985; Light, 1988; Nacci, 1977), increases in homicide and suicide rates (Paulus, 1988) and other negative impacts of imprisonment such as complaints about overclassification, ventilation, hygiene, noise, and insufficient programming (Cobb, 1985; Toch, 1985).

Following this research path, we would expect incidences of severe prisoner discipline to vary by the intensity, variety, and exposure to prison crowding. To test this hypothesis, we conducted a review of the prison crowding literature. Studies that met the present research criteria were then subjected to meta-analysis. The dependent variables were operationalized as: (a) physical assaults by staff against inmates (e.g., homicides and beatings); (b) the use of solitary confinement (e.g., confinement in isolated, maximum security lock-up cells where sensory stimulation is extremely limited); and (c) the use of severe mental discipline (e.g., actions taken by staff, usually for punitive reasons, that may jeopardize the physical safety and/or mental well-being of prisoners).

The strength of the relationships between crowding and the dependent variables was measured by Cohen's d (1977); a coefficient that represents the total "effect size" of crowding on the dependent variables. This coefficient was then converted to a Pearson's r using the statistical formula advanced by Lipsey (1990). Thus, standardizing the effect size (of Cohen's d) allows us to compare findings from a number of research projects in the area of prisoner victimization by staff (see Bonta & Gendreau, 1990). The results of this meta-analysis are displayed in Table 10.1.

As Table 10.1 makes clear, no empirical study of crowding has ever examined the incidence of physical assaults committed by staff (Outcome A). Table 10.1 also reveals that crowding has an insignificant effect on the use of severe mental discipline by staff—Outcome C (Bonta & Nanckivell, 1980; Paulus, Cox, McCain & Chandler, 1975). Finally, two studies (Ekland-Olson, Barrick & Cohen, 1983; Pelissier, 1987) produced insignificant coefficients between crowding and the use of solitary confinement (Outcome B), and one study (Jan, 1980) shows a strong positive relationship between the variables (d=1.79, r=.66).

Table 10.1. Staff-on-Prisoner Victimization by Conditions of Imprisonment using Cohen's d (Pearson's r reported in parentheses)

Study	Sample	Outcome		
		A	B	C
Independent Variable: Prison Crowding				
Bonta & Nanckivell (1980)	33 Adult Prisoners (m)			.28
Ekland-Olson et al. (1983)	10 Adult Prisons (m)		.24	(.14)
			(.11)	
Jan (1980)	1,096 Youthful Offenders (m)		1.79	
			(.66)**	
Paulus et al. (1975)	142 Adult Prisoners (m)			.34
				(.16)
Pelissier (1987)	922 Adult Prisoners (m)		-.01	
			(.00)	
Independent Variable: Maximum Security				
Glaser (1964)	1,449 Adult Prisoners (m)		-1.70	
			(-.64)**	
Jacobs (1977)	1,344 Adult Prisoners (m)		.07	
			(.03)	
Sellin (1967)	60 Adult Prisoners (m)	-1.87		
		(-.67)**		
Sylvester et al. (1977)	128 Adult Prisoners (m)	-2.69		
		(-.80)**		
Barak-Glantz (1983)	306 Adult Prisoners (m)		-.68	
			(-.32)*	
Marquart (1986)	3,000 Adult Prisoners (m)	2.34		
		(.76)**		

Note: A = Physical assaults by staff (including homicide)
       B = Use of solitary confinement
       C = Severe mental discipline
 *p < .01
**p < .001

In summary, the meta-analysis reveals that crowding has no effect on the use of severe mental discipline, has never been studied in relation to physical assaults by staff against prisoners, but may have significant effects on the use of solitary confinement. In this regard, two distinct features of the Jan (1980) study may have confounded the results.

First, Jan's significant findings were discovered among a population of youthful offenders. There is sufficient data to indicate that youthful offenders are simply more obstreperous than adults under any condition of confinement (see Mathias, 1984). Second, disciplinary infractions (the cause of solitary confinement in Jan's study) have been found by a number of investigators to be positively related to crowding (Cox, Paulus & McCain, 1984; Nacci, Teitelbaum & Prather, 1977; Paulus, McCain

& Cox, 1971; Ruback & Carr, 1984). In other words, it is difficult for us to discern whether the significant use of solitary confinement discovered by Jan was (1) a valid correlate of crowding, (2) a function of inmate age, high infraction rates, and/or crowding, (3) a function of a set of interactions among these factors, or (4) the relationship may simply be chance variation. There is, obviously, no basis for choosing among these alternative explanations of Jan's findings.

Maximum Security. Although the prison crowding literature provides little reason to believe that crowded prisons are associated with extreme forms of discipline, the same literature does show consistent, positive relationships between crowding and disciplinary infractions, inmate-on-inmate violence, homicide, and suicide (see Gaes [1985] for a concise review). These findings have been explained in terms of an array of managerial anomalies that have beset the field of corrections itself (Blumstein, 1983; Gottfredson & McConville, 1987). Perhaps most important among these anomalies is the problem of overclassification, which often leads to excessive—and from a security standpoint—an unwarranted number of inmates being confined to high-security institutions (DiIulio, 1987). Thus, we now turn our attention to a related topic and ask ourselves if certain organizational features of imprisonment threaten the physical and mental well-being of offenders.

Today, over 40 percent of the U.S. adult prison population are confined to maximum security institutions (ACA, 1989). Scholars have traditionally argued that maximum security prisons are often plagued by serious management problems (Gaes, 1985; Clarke, 1988), by violence directed toward inmates (Ward & Schoen, 1981), and by conditions that have been described as painful and inhumane (Goffman, 1961; Sykes, 1958; Toch, 1977). Confinement in maximum security is intended to incapacitate or control offenders whose criminal conduct is so violent or so chronic that no other alternative exists. Maximum security prisons are not established for the purpose of rehabilitation; rather, they are intended to be punitive. Surrounded by high stone walls, razorwire and gun towers, maximum security is a prison of last resort. What happens to people who are incarcerated under these conditions?

Six studies satisfied the criteria for inclusion into the meta-analysis. These included Glaser's (1964) study of 1,449 inmates at the U.S. Penitentiary, Terre Haute; Jacobs' (1977) investigation of 1,344 prisoners at Stateville; Sellin's (1967) national study of 60 prison homicide victims; Sylvester, Reed, and Nelson's (1977) national study of 128 prison homicide victims; Barak-Glantz's (1983) analysis of 306 prisoners at the Washington State Penitentiary, Walla Walla; and Marquart's (1986) analysis of 3,000 inmates at a maximum security prison in southern Texas. The results of this meta-analysis also appear in Table 10.1.

With respect to physical assaults committed by staff, two studies (Sellin, 1967; Sylvester et al., 1977) produced strong coefficients in the opposite direction. That is, maximum security inmates were more likely to be killers of each other, rather than the victims of homicide committed by staff. The third study to assess Outcome A, however, produced vastly different results.

Rather than study prison homicides, Marquart (1986) focused his attention on physical assaults committed at the maximum security Eastham Unit in Texas during 1981 and 1982 (Crouch & Marquart, 1989). Marquart discovered that "rather than being idiosyncratic or sporadic, guard use of physical coercion was highly structured and deeply entrenched in the guard subculture. Most importantly, guards who used physical force were rewarded for their behavior with improved duty posts or even promotions" (1986:347). Marquart goes on to explain this system of physical coercion:

> The...unofficial coercion was called (by inmates and officers alike) a "tune up." Tune ups consisted of verbal humiliation, shoves, kicks, and head and body slaps (1986:351).

Moreover, Marquart's research provides ample evidence to suggest that maximum security custody and prisoner victimization by staff are highly related (d=2.34, r=.76). Yet these strong coefficients disappear when we move to our analysis of Outcome B (use of solitary confinement). In fact, the research of Glaser (1964) and Barak-Glantz (1983)—like the studies of Sellin and Sylvester et al.—demonstrates a strong relationship in the opposite direction (d=-1.70, r=-.64 and d=-.68, r=-.32 respectively; meaning, therefore, that solitary confinement is used significantly less than other forms of discipline in maximum security). Similarly, Jacobs' (1977) investigation produced a nearly nonexistent relationship between maximum security and Outcome B (d=.07, r=.03). Finally, Table 10.1 shows that there has been, to date, no empirical attempt in the field of criminology to assess the relationship between severe mental discipline (Outcome C) and maximum security custody.

In summary, the criminological evidence on prisoner victimization by staff under conditions of maximum security is mixed. On one hand, research shows either no relationship or an inverse relationship between the variables. On the other, one study demonstrates that maximum security can have a profound effect on physical assaults committed by staff. We suspect that this disparity can be explained in terms of the research methodologies employed in the various studies.

For example, the Sellin (1967) and Sylvester et al. (1977) studies were based on official records provided by prison wardens from across the nation. Likewise, the works of Glaser (1964), Jacobs (1977), and Barak-Glantz (1983) were all based on official statistics. Together, these studies failed to produce a positive correlation between extreme discipline and maximum security custody. In fact, the overall correlation was negative and highly significant. However, Marquart's (1986) research produced a strong, positive correlation between the variables. Rather than relying on official figures, Marquart gathered data on severe discipline from his own observations as a maximum security prison guard.

Official and Inmate Evidence on Severe Prison Discipline

Much has been written by professionals and inmates on the severe disciplining of prisoners by staff prior to World War II (see Ayers, 1984; McKelvey, 1977;

Orland, 1975 for reviews). Thus our intent here is to concentrate only on those post-war accounts of severe discipline written by administrators, legislative bodies, judges (or all of their biographers) and prisoners (or their biographers).

We begin our analysis with a review of the literature emanating from the American South. We do so for two reasons. First, the Southern literature on this subject is the most plentiful; there are scores of books that mention discipline in Southern prisons. Second, the American South is the historical taproot of prisoner victimization by staff. That is, the earliest written accounts of beatings and torture in prisons came from the deep Southern states of Louisiana, Arkansas, and Mississippi (Bowker, 1980). After reviewing the Southern literature, we turn our attention to the writings that document severe discipline in California prisons because it is also plentiful and of compelling historical significance (Irwin, 1980; Wright, 1973). And last, we review the literature from other areas of the United States. Once again, our analysis excludes literature related to the indirect victimizing effects of incarceration and prison riots.

The Southern Literature

In the early days of 1951, a released convict from the Louisiana State Penitentiary told a New Orleans newspaper reporter that a number of inmates had deliberately slashed their heel tendons with razor blades to avoid field work and brutal forms of punishment by guards at the old maximum security prison in Angola (Carleton, 1971). The reporter printed the story, and in response, Louisiana Governor Earl Long empaneled a six-member Citizens Committee to investigate the allegations of prisoner mistreatment at Angola. In April 1951, the Committee released its official report stating that there had been 31 cases of heel slashing at the prison that "appeared conclusively to be the result of physical brutality inflicted upon convicts." The report observed that:

> ...the practice of brutality was established beyond question on
> several levels—physical, mental, emotional, and moral (Carleton,
> 1971:155).

This institutionalized system of brutality extended to other Southern states throughout the 1950s and 1960s. In his biography, Oscar Dees—former "Dog Warden" of the Alabama State Prison at Kilby during this era—described the common use of a "strap about six-feet long...that they use[d] to hit a man. The strap was used when a man committed a crime—say he cut another prisoner, they found him with a knife, or he quit work" (March, 1978:31). According to Dees, this form of discipline had a differential effect on inmates: "After a man's been spanked, a white man's buttocks turns blue, a nigger's buttocks turns white" (March, 1978:44). But the strap was not the only method of physical punishment under Dees' administration. "I carried a walking stick made out of hickory" said the former warden, "I'd hit a man anywhere I could...I didn't pick no certain place to hit him. If I took a notion to hit, I hit him" (March, 1978:50).

Solitary confinement (referred to as the "doghouse") was also a common feature of discipline at the Alabama State Prison. According to Dees:

> The doghouse...[didn't have] any windows in it. It's dark in there.
> [Prisoners were put] in there without any clothes...and hand-
> cuffed to a bar (March, 1978:33, 50).

Fred Dees, another Kilby warden (and son of Oscar), noted in his biography that the maximum amount of time spent in the doghouse was 21 days. "It'll kill you" said the former warden (March 1978:34). Moreover, these two Alabama prison officials—Oscar and Fred Dees—concluded that "Unjustified punishment might have gone on" (March, 1978:75).

Perhaps the most well-known case of "unjustified punishment" in Southern prisons was documented by Tom Murton, Superintendent of the Arkansas State Penitentiary at Cummins from 1967-1968, and Assistant Superintendent of the State Penitentiary at Tucker's Farm prior to 1967. Disciplinary practices at these maximum security prisons have been graphically depicted in the film *Brubaker*. Foremost among them was the use of the notorious "Tucker Telephone."

The "Tucker Telephone" consisted of a series of long electrical wires that extended from a hand-wrung telephone. A naked prisoner was strapped to a table and the electrical wires were attached to his big toes and his penis. Electrical charges were then sent through the inmate's body in a ritual played out by guards, called the "long distance call." In this ritual, guards tried to send electrical shocks into the toes and genitals of inmates until the inmates nearly became unconscious—thus prolonging the agony of suspected death. "Some men," recall Murton and Hyams, "were literally driven out of their minds" (1969:7).

One inmate known only as "Sam," who was "driven out of his mind" by the long distance call, lived on to describe yet another method of discipline used in the Arkansas prison system at the time:

> This old convict doctor [inmate trusty] had a pet coon down in the
> hospital and if you said anything insubordinate, he'd set the coon
> on you. That sonofabitch could tear your ass up. Coon's name was
> Oscar. I never will forget that mean sonofabitch. You could hit him,
> knock him all the way across the hospital...and he'd come right
> back at you (Jackson, 1977:189).

Bruce Jackson's (1977) research reveals that physical beatings were a common form of discipline in the Arkansas prison system during the 1960s. Says one former Tucker's Farm sergeant: "They used to kick 'em around pretty good back in the old days" (Jackson, 1977:193). And Robert Savor, former Arkansas prison commissioner, acknowledges to Jackson that "the strap and other methods of corporal punishment (including rubber hoses with spark plugs set on the end—the Arkansas "slapjack") were common throughout the Arkansas system" (1977:195, 227).

This institutionalized system of brutality was also widespread in Texas during the post-war years. As previously discussed, the former prison guard James Marquart (1986) observed that physical force as punishment was an important element of the overall control strategy of the Texas Department of Corrections between 1962 and 1982. The physical punishments in Texas prisons included outright beatings with clubs and fists, as well as the use of blackjacks, riot batons, and aluminum-cased flashlights. Then there was the practice of "tap dancing."

> On one such occasion, the inmate was thrown to the floor by several officers. One literally stood on the inmate's head (called the tap dance) while another "spanked" him on the buttocks and thighs with a riot baton (Crouch & Marquart, 1989:79-80).

* * *

In summary, there is sufficient reason to believe that the beating and torturing of inmates did occur in some Southern prisons between, at least, 1945 and 1970. It is also a commonly held belief that judicial interventions of the early-to-mid 1970s created effective limitations on the use of physical and mental abuse of prisoners by staff (Glick, 1973; Jacobs, 1983). But did these judicial remedies really cure the problem of brutality in Southern prisons? The historical record says that they did not. Old habits in the organizational life of corrections, it seems, are just as hard to break as those in the biological world.

• It was not until August of 1974, that the Mississippi Department of Corrections was forced to abolish its legendary prisoner trusty system. Until then, some 300 specially chosen white convicts were allowed to carry state-owned guns and whips (known as the "Black Annie"), and were recognized as legitimate instruments of prison law and order (McWhorter, 1981). This system of discipline was found "deplorable and subhuman" by the Federal District Court, Gainsville, Mississippi. The Court held that:

> The record is replete with numerable instances of brutality and abuses in discipline. The trusties who are armed, referred to as trusty shooters, perform guard duties in every camp facility. [Between 1972 and 1974] Thirty inmates received gunshot wounds and an additional twenty-nine inmates were shot at, and fifty-two inmates were physically beaten (McWhorter, 1981:95-96).

• Between 1970 and 1974, the Federal Court in Fort Smith, Arkansas, ruled three times that specific practices at the State Penitentiary at Cummins constituted cruel and unusual punishment. The first ruling dealt with the inhumane conditions of solitary confinement at the prison. The second dealt with cruel conditions related to the practice of chaining convicts to a fence for days at a time. And the third ruling dealt with the shooting of 120 unarmed, nonviolent inmates who were protesting prison conditions (Murton, 1976).

• It was not until March of 1975, that the Fifth U.S. Circuit Court of Appeals ruled that the use of solitary confinement (the doghouse) in Alabama's prisons constituted cruel and unusual punishment. The court further issued an injunctive order against the Alabama Department of Corrections to halt the use of the strap on state convicts (March, 1978).

• As late as 1976, Arkansas Warden A.L. Lockhart testified that physical brutality was still being used on inmates at the penitentiary in Cummins. And a number of guards testified to a continuing pattern of physical beatings, including the use of the slap-jack (Jackson, 1977).

• During 1976, prisoners at Cummins went on record testifying that guards had forced inmates to walk across broken glass, denied inmates in solitary confinement access to the courts by deliberately destroying writs, and had placed inmates in solitary confinement for periods up to 63 days (Jackson, 1977).

• On September 20, 1979—in the historic case of *Ruiz v. Estelle*—the federal district court, Eastern District of Texas, found the Texas prison system to be "unnecessarily harsh." "It is impossible," wrote the trial judges, "to convey the pernicious conditions and the pain and degradation which ordinary inmates suffer within the TDC;...the sheer misery;...the sense of abject helplessness felt by inmates" (Crouch & Marquart, 1989:25).

• In 1980, a legislative investigation of the Florida Department of Corrections found that guard brutality towards inmates was common in the State's prison system. Results of polygraph examinations administered to guards revealed widespread use of physical beatings, arbitrary use of solitary confinement, and three inmate homicides resulting from the brutality rendered by Florida's prison inspector (Ad Hoc Subcommittee on Management Oversight of the House Committee on Corrections, 1980).

• Following a disturbance involving a single inmate at the Atlanta Federal Penitentiary on the evening of November 1, 1984, some 85 Atlanta prisoners were handcuffed "hog style" (hands and feet cuffed behind their backs) and forced to lay on the cold ground for approximately six hours where they were beaten by baton-wielding guards (Subcommittee on Courts, Civil Liberties, and the Administration of Justice, 1986).

• During the week of February 3, 1986, nearly 300 Atlanta prisoners were handcuffed to hospital beds and intravenously force-fed. Another 20 inmates were fed through tubes in their noses. According to one inmate observer: "Milk was poured through the tubes which were oversized and gave the [prisoners] bloody noses. Their blood mixed with the milk and drained into their stomachs. Some guys almost drowned in their own blood" (McLain with Nehrstadt, 1988:239). Two months later, the U.S. House of Representatives issued a report characterizing conditions of imprisonment in Atlanta as "brutal and inhumane" (Subcommittee on Courts, Civil Liberties, and the Administration of Justice, 1986:7).

• On February 8, 1987, a prisoner at the Atlanta Penitentiary was strangled to death by 17 prison guards while the inmate's hands were cuffed behind his back (Armed Forces Institute of Pathology, April 21, 1987; Thompson, 1987).

• Finally, on July 15, 1988, Washington, D.C. Federal District Judge Barrington Parker ruled that the High Security Unit (HSU) at the Lexington Federal Prison in Kentucky afforded prisoners treatment that "skirted elemental standards of decency" (Amnesty International, 1988:2). At issue was the imprisonment of three female inmates who had been convicted of politically motivated criminal offenses and were serving terms of between 35 and 58 years. These female prisoners were held in solitary confinement where they were subjected to 24-hour camera surveillance. Situated in the basement of the Lexington prison, the HSU cells received no sunlight or ventilation; the floors, ceilings and walls were painted in "hot white" gloss and were bathed in artificial lighting at all times.

The Lexington women were systematically subjected to strip and body cavity searches far in excess of security needs, were forced to shower without a curtain, and were the objects of sexual abuse and humiliation. Experts from the American Civil Liberties Union and the General Board of the United Methodist Church, acting on behalf of the three female prisoners, concluded that the Lexington women had suffered "severe psychological harm which appears to be worsening" (Morgan, 1988:14). Moreover, these experts argued that the Lexington HSU was intended to be an experimental control unit and the Lexington women its first subjects.

The California Literature

According to officials and inmates, severe forms of prison discipline were by no means limited to the American South during the post-war years. Former California Warden Clinton T. Duffy described San Quentin's post-war solitary confinement units as "dungeons filled with forgotten men" (1950:59). "There was no appeal from a sentence to the hole," wrote the warden, "and men who complained were sapped with a rubber hose or whipped with the lash" (Duffy, 1950:59). Outright physical torture was also practiced as part of the prison routine in a special punishment cell block known as "Siberia," where:

> ...men were forced to stand on a nine-inch circle for hours at a time.
> If they moved or talked or turned around, they were dragged into
> a back room and beaten with a hose or leather strap (Duffy,
> 1950:59).

Volumes attest to the fact that similar practices continued in California maximum security institutions into the early 1970s. In 1966, the California Youth Authority testified during a Federal Court investigation of Soledad Prison that inmates were frequently kept is solitary confinement "strip cells" for as long as 58 days at a time (Minton, 1971). During this period, inmates at San Quentin wrote of "unmerciful beatings" administered to prisoners by guards (Saladin, 1971:98); of inmates being used as "target practice" for guards "wielding Thompson submachine guns" (Saladin, 1971:108); of "needless harassment and intimidation" (Hassan, 1972:29); of forced-feeding where "a tube was run up through my nose, down my throat, and into my stomach [for] twenty-four hours a day, for a week" (Myron, 1972:58). And from Soledad where "anything from pick-handles to panic stricken gunfire" was used to maintain control over prisoners (Jackson, 1972:64); where the disciplining of inmates included a restricted diet that officials described as "perhaps not palatable" (Yee, 1973:17). "Actually," wrote the trial judge in *Jordan v. Fitzharris* (1966), "the problems at Soledad [were] of a shocking and debased nature" (Yee, 1973:27).

Meanwhile, inmates at Folsom Prison wrote of "the escalating practice of physical brutality being perpetrated upon the inmates of California State Prisons," including "the teargassing of prisoners who [were] locked in the cells [which] led to the death[s] of [two inmates]," and "correctional officers [who] shoot inmates," and "agitation of race relations by prison administrators" (Berkman, 1979:184-185). Moreover, Folsom prisoners spoke of a series of events where inmates were "strangled, beat (sic), and kicked until the sadistic urge of officers had been satisfied" (Olsen, 1972:78).

As any observer of American penology knows full-well, these accounts were recorded during the romantic days of what has come to be known as the California prisoners' movement. Between January, 1970 and September, 1975, at least 59 persons were killed as a result of the battles between inmates and administrators inside California's maximum security prisons (Collier & Horowitz, 1988; DiIulio, 1987; Yee, 1973). Hence, the levels of extreme discipline witnessed in California may be seen as an artifact of the unique social and political contentions of the times; and not as a salient feature of California penology. Indeed, analysts point out that the prisoners' movement led to "a new system of prison rule...characterized by more open, formal, and representative political associations" (Berkman, 1979:3), and to sweeping prison reform legislation (Smith, 1973), to federal court decisions requiring that prison officials meet constitutional standards of due process of law before they severely punish a prisoner (*Clutchette v. Procunier,* 1971), and to the immediate decrease in California prison populations in the years following the tumultuous saga of the prisoners' movement (Wright, 1973). In a word, California prisons had become more humane. But had they? Unfortunately, there has been no contemporary examination of conditions in California prisons that may be used to answer this question.

Other Literature

Though not as well-known and frequently cited as the works emanating from the American South or California, officials and inmates have documented the existence of prisoner victimization under maximum security conditions in all parts of the nation. Former Missouri Commissioner of Corrections, Fred T. Wilkinson (1972), has documented numerous beatings and capricious uses of solitary confinement in his state during the 1960s. Also, Cartier (1986) provides evidence of numerous staff-on-inmate beatings at the Washington State Prison, Walla Walla, during the 1970s; and the New York State Commission of Investigation (1981) provides testimony of extensive staff-on-prisoner violence at New York's Green Haven Correctional Facility during the late 1970s. Finally, in 1988 Harvard University Press published the research of a former prison guard named Kelsey Kauffman. Kauffman is now a sociology professor at a small midwestern university. Kauffman's celebrated work uncovers evidence of hundreds of beatings that took place in the Massachusetts prison system during the 1970s and 1980s.

Summary

In the foregoing review we have shown that the quantitative evidence on severe forms of prisoner discipline is scarce. In fact, we could identify only one study (Marquart, 1986) in which there was a clear and institutionalized pattern of physical victimization of inmates by staff. When we turned to the writings of administrators and prisoners, however, we discovered a veritable explosion of rich information on the physical and mental abuse of prisoners at the hands of staff members. Although the various methods used in this body of penology do not allow us to assess the degree to which such information can be generalized to all correctional institutions in the United States, there is one important theme that undergirds this literature: Severe discipline appears to take place most often in maximum security institutions.

In the following section of this analysis, we will attempt to discern whether the use of severe discipline currently reaches the extremes observed by Marquart, Kauffman, Murton, and a host of administrators and prisoners who have commented on the subject since World War II. Yet discerning whether prisoners are, in fact, currently subjected to severe forms of discipline is not enough. Rather than simply enumerating the incidences of prisoner victimization by staff, we must discern its prevalence within U.S. prisons. In so doing, we must also delineate the essential features of this victimization (e.g., the use of clubs, fists, gas, solitary confinement, etc.), and the prisoner groups that are at greatest risk for such victimization. Finally, and most importantly, we must be able to explain how this victimization is currently supported and sustained by correctional bureaucracy.

Data and Methods: The Prison Discipline Study

To assess the extent and dimensions of severe discipline in contemporary prison settings, we constructed a combined forced-choice and open-ended survey questionnaire based on our review of the literature, our own experiences in prison, and upon advise from other penologists and prison officials. The instrument contained 15 questions concerning issues related to custody levels, disciplinary housing, severe punishment, and demographic information. The survey was disseminated to prison administrators, guards, prisoners, and their representatives in two phases.

First, in early 1989, we informed a large, nationwide mailing list of prisoner rights/advocacy and service organizations of the study and the availability of the survey questionnaire. As a result of that mailing, notices of our research were printed in five prison-oriented publications. Our most immediate response for questionnaires came from readers of the Santa Fe-based *Coalition for Prisoners' Rights*. As expected, the majority of these readers were prisoners, and they requested multiple copies of our instrument and also sent us extensive mailing lists of other individuals to whom we then sent additional copies.[1] In total, we mailed out approximately 2,500 questionnaires during this phase of the research. These questionnaires were sent to prisoners and their families, prison visitors, expert observers, lawyers, and correctional staff from around the nation.

The second phase began in late 1989 when we announced the study in the Prisoner Rights Union (PRU) newspaper, *The California Prisoner*, with a copy of the questionnaire enclosed in the mailing to 3,500 California prisoners. This mailing prompted another small round of requests for the survey. In total, then, slightly more than 6,500 questionnaires were disseminated throughout the United States with more than one-half going to prisoners in California.

Structural Barriers

Hundreds of prisoners indicated on their questionnaire that they were inhibited in responding to the survey out of fear of retaliation because the questionnaires were read by guards before return mailing from the prisons. This occurred despite the fact that the survey was careful not to elicit specific information on incidences or names of prison staff who were involved in extreme acts of discipline.

Of the 36 responding long-term prisoners personally known to us, we noted that they responded superficially to the questionnaire without referring to some of their worst experiences with staff. Others requested personal interviews, maintaining that they had too much information to squeeze into the brief questionnaire format. Yet we soon encountered even more serious problems with our research, including direct bureaucratic interference.

The Washington State Department of Corrections prohibited the dissemination of the questionnaire entirely, stating that they have laws against studies on prisoners without a prior review process. Nevertheless, we received 15 responses from prisoners at the State Penitentiaries in Walla Walla and Monroe. Administrators at Folsom Prison and the California Medical Facility at Vacaville destroyed all issues of *The California Prisoner* containing our questionnaire on the grounds that it was contraband. PRU attorneys quickly challenged and reversed that administrative decision in the courts. We then received many responses from both Folsom and Vacaville. Yet during the ban on our research, one Folsom prisoner who did manage to get his hands on a copy of the questionnaire reported that he was electrically shocked by a guard with a Taser (e.g., cattle-prod) for possession of the survey. Prisoners we visited at other California institutions reported similar cases of prisoners being Tasered for possession of the survey instrument.

A New York State prisoner's organization wrote to us asking for more information about our study and a detailed account of our intentions. Other prisoners and prisoner groups from across the country wrote declaring skepticism about our ability to find a respectable outlet for this research. Still others, getting more to the point, accused us of being "just another study for intellectuals only and a rip off of prisoners."

Sample Characteristics

We received a total of 605 usable surveys for a return rate of about 10 percent. Babbie (1989) would call this response rate *less than adequate*. Yet Babbie's text refers to research conditions that are free from the structural barriers of the Prison Discipline Study. Furthermore, as Babbie points out: "...demonstrated lack of response bias is far more important than a high response rate" (1989:242). We shall demonstrate such a lack of response bias in a moment.

Our 605 respondents were from 41 different states. Nearly one-third (31%) were from California. Another 29 percent were from the South, 19 percent were from Midwestern states, 12 percent came from Eastern states, and the remaining 9 percent were from the Northwest. Many questionnaires were accompanied by additional information including letters, copies of court documents, copies of newspaper articles and extensive accounts of personal experiences. Preliminary analysis of the data revealed one important finding: *The data show that the extent of severe discipline in prison is "flat"—or uniform—across the nation.* Hence, there appears to be no response bias in the present data.

Other respondent characteristics appear in Table 10.2. Although we extended invitations to administrators and guards to participate in the research, few responded to the survey. As such, the total sample is mainly comprised of prisoners (about 94%) and the remaining respondents were family members, visitors, expert observers, and lawyers. Table 10.2 shows that the majority of respondents (73%) reported on conditions in either maximum security or control unit custody. Last, Table 10.2 reveals that the majority of respondents had observed prison routine for more than four years. In fact, the mean for this variable was 9.08 years.

The data in Table 10.2 therefore permits the construction of a composite picture of the "typical" respondent in the Prison Discipline Study. This person is a long-term prisoner housed in maximum security confinement. Accordingly, the data do not allow us to generalize findings beyond this profile. Hence, in the analysis to follow, we will disaggregate the data to separate the responses of maximum security

Table 10.2. **Characteristics of Respondents (N=605)**

Characteristic	% of Sample
Status	
Guard	.2
Administrator	.5
Prisoner	93.7
Visitor	1.2
Family member	2.0
Expert observer	.8
Lawyer	1.6
Type of Facility Reported On	
Minimum security	3.3
Medium security	14.2
Maximum security	66.1
Control unit	6.9
Psychiatric unit	2.9
Medical unit	1.6
County jail	4.7
Juvenile facility	.3
Years of Observing Prison Routine	
Less than 1 year	2.8
1 to 3 years	16.8
4 to 10 years	50.3
More than 10 years	30.1

prisoners (N=441) from those of the other respondents. This maximum security sample will then become the focus of discussion and the other data will be used only for purposes of comparison.

Potential Limitations

Any research that attempts to discover the existence of severe correctional punishment will be plagued by methodological limitations (Bowker, 1980), and this study is no exception. In fact, the potential limitations of the present research are considerable. Most important, the universe of interest in this study is a self-selected sample of maximum security prisoners. Therefore, it is quite possible that those prisoners who had knowledge of severe discipline were the *only* ones who responded to the survey. If this limitation is operating in the current study, then we would expect nearly 100 percent of our 441 "self-selected" maximum security subjects to report experiences with severe discipline.

This potential limitation of the present research is equivalent to a study of persons interested in medical malpractice, that queries only victims of ineffective hospital service delivery. We would expect such victims to report a high prevalence of subsurface illegality in the medical profession. Yet such findings *would not* be representative of hospital service delivery systems as a whole. Likewise, if we find that nearly all of the respondents in this study claimed to have experience with severe correctional punishment, then the results may simply reflect a not-unexpected grousing by an embittered subgroup of prisoner activists.

The second potential limitation of this research lies in the demographic characteristics of subjects. The fact that a typical subject is a long-term prisoner would suggest that our subjects are more likely than other prisoners to experience severe punishment. Simply put, the longer a prisoner spends in the system, the more likely they are to experience some form of severe discipline. Adding to this research dilemma is the fact that the prison environment in many state systems has changed in recent years, and long-term prisoners may tend to view the increased restrictions brought about by these administrative changes as additional discipline, some of it severe. Hence, if this potential limitation is operating on the present data, we would once again expect nearly all of the respondents to report severe discipline.

Testing Potential Limitations

For both of the potential limitations posed by this research, there is a concomitant reason why such a study should be conducted. First, subservice illegality—wherever it exists in the public sector—must be approached etiologically. It is important to study the microsocial processes that support and sustain medical malpractice. By interviewing victims of ineffective health care, we may learn something about problematic surgery, inappropriate medications, and physician neglect of patients. Such a strategy has produced an impressive body of criminology. For example, the work of Straus, Gelles, and Steinmetz (1980), Kaufman Kantor and Straus (1987) and Walker (1979) has generated a coherent theory of domestic violence based exclusively on interviews with female victims of domestic assault. Likewise, we may learn something about the microsocial causes of severe discipline in maximum security prisons by focusing exclusively on its victims.

The experiences of long-term prisoners is also crucial to contemporary discourse in American penology. In perhaps the most exhaustive review of this subject ever conducted, Flanagan concluded that "the early view of the systematic destruction of the person as a result of long-term imprisonment is neither accurate nor heuristically helpful" (1981:205). If nearly 100 percent of the present sample are found to experience severe discipline, it would suggest that Flanagan's conclusion may be in need of further interpretation and analysis.

Findings

The incidence of prison discipline is displayed in Table 10.3. Here, we see that solitary confinement, loss of privileges (e.g., denial of visitation and mail privileges), and physical beatings are the most commonly observed forms of discipline by our sample of long-term maximum security prisoners. And to a somewhat lesser degree, these respondents noted the use of mental discipline within the various prisons. Below, these findings are examined in greater detail.

Table 10.3. **Incidence of Discipline (N=441)**

Type of Discipline	% of Sample Observing
Solitary confinement	61.2
Loss of privileges	57.5
Physical beatings	62.1
Mental discipline	40.0

Physical Beatings

We begin by reporting one of two central findings of the Prison Discipline Study. Mainstream penology holds that the physical beating of prisoners by guards is a rare occurrence in modern prison communities. Yet Table 10.3 shows that slightly more than six out of 10 respondents (62.1% of our 1989 sample) had in fact witnessed such beatings. Conversely, however, the Table implies that nearly four out of 10 subjects (37.9% of the sample) *had not* witnessed such beatings. This suggests that our findings are not an artifact of the study's methodology. That is, the present research *does not* appear to represent a study of only prisoners who had experience with severe punishment. Further, this discovery implies that the data are not constrained by the experiences of long-termers. Consistent with Flanagan's (1981) analysis, the data imply that offenders *are not* susceptible to "systematic destruction" as a result of extended incarceration.

Table 10.3 also shows that nearly the same percentage of prisoners had witnessed solitary confinement (61.2%) and loss of privileges (57.5%) as routine forms of prison discipline. Thus, physical beatings appear to be empirically connected to these other forms of discipline. To be sure, the statistical associations between the incidence of physical beatings, solitary confinement, and loss of privileges proved to be significant (Cramer's V=.25, p<.001 and V=.26, p<.001, respectively).[2] As such, solitary confinement, loss of privileges, and physical beatings constitute a definable "package" of disciplinary activities within the various maximum security prisons. Two questions ostensibly emerge from this discovery: (1) How frequently are these beatings carried out? and (2) How are these beatings performed?

Regarding the first question, Table 10.4 shows that of the 329 subjects who had knowledge of staff-on-prisoner beatings, more than three-fourths of them (76.2%) reported that these beatings were administered either routinely or occasionally. The remainder (24.8%) reported that beatings were a "rare" event.

Table 10.4. **Frequency of Prisoners Receiving Beatings by Staff (N=329)**

Frequency	% of Sample Observing
Rarely (once per year)	24.8
Occasionally (one time per month)	26.4
Routinely (as a matter of common practice)	49.8

Regarding the second question, Table 10.5 reveals that the beatings were performed in a combination of ways. That is, multiple methods of corporal punishment were employed. Foremost among these were the use of fists, boots, and clubs (in that order).

Table 10.5. **Methods Used in Physical Beatings of Prisoners by Staff (N=313)**

Method	% of Sample Observing
Fists	88.1
Boots	74.1
Clubs	71.8
Stun Guns (Tasers, etc.)	26.8
Other	32.5

Approximately 100 sample respondents indicated that they had witnessed beatings after a prisoner had been restrained with handcuffs or steel shackles. Another 40 testified that guards performed a "body slam" (e.g., being thrown to the floor or against the wall face first) after prisoners had been cuffed behind the back. Another 30 reported seeing "goon squad" beatings (e.g., a formal or informal group of guards assaulting a single, often handcuffed prisoner). Methods of administering these severe beatings were reported to include the use of mace, tear gas, Tasers, fire hoses, flashlights, riot batons, mop handles, rubber hoses, and wooden-bullet guns. Still others reported that prisoners had been dragged by the hair, dragged by a leash, or fired at with a shotgun. One prisoner reported being scalded with hot water by a guard; a paraplegic prisoner testified to being beaten unconscious by guards; two male prisoners reported homosexual rapes by guards; and one prisoner witnessed another prisoner hang himself to death while guards stood by laughing and watched.

A total of 25 female prisoners attested either to being beaten by male guards, being raped by male guards, or of being restrained to a bed naked and sexually ridiculed by guards. One female prisoner testified that she lost her baby after guards shot her with a stun gun.

Another 57 respondents reported what they called "hidden" physical abuse. These methods included setting up fights between prisoners by housing known enemies in the same cell or releasing enemies at the same time to a public area of the prison (referred to by guards as "dog fights" or "cock fights"). Respondents also reported that prisoners are frequently beaten in their cells or assigned to security housing for the purpose of administering a beating away from public view. Others complained of being forced to do hard labor while sick or infirmed.

Mental Discipline

Here we report the second major finding of the Prison Discipline Study. Mainstream penology insists that there are "a *limited array* of psychological stresses [that constitute] the most horrible punishment we are willing to inflict on our criminals" (Johnson, 1987:50, emphasis added). Table 10.3 shows that 40 percent of the respondents witnessed forms of mental discipline (operationalized in our survey as prolonged isolation, denial of visits, denial of mail, involuntary psychiatric treatment or medication, or "other"). This discovery provides another indication that our findings are not an artifact of research methodology. Fully 60 percent of the sample *did not* report experiences with this form of punishment; hence, once again the study does not appear to represent an examination of only prisoners who had experiences with severe discipline. Instead, the study seems to produce findings that reflect an underlying dimension of reality about life in maximum security prisons.

The prevalence of mental discipline is reported in Table 10.6. This table shows that the frequency of mental discipline follows a pattern similar to the reported frequency of physical beatings; the statistical relationship between these two sets of variables (mental discipline and physical beatings) was again significant (V=.33, p<.001). Once more, the majority of subjects who had knowledge of such discipline (81%) reported that it occurred on an occasional or routine basis. Only 18.3% described mental discipline as a rare event.

Table 10.6. **Frequency of Prisoners Receiving Mental Discipline by Staff (N=322)**

Frequency	% of Sample Observing
Rarely (once per year)	18.3
Occasionally (one time per month)	12.7
Routinely (as a matter of common practice)	68.3

Among the *wide array* of methods discovered in the study, nearly 40 percent of the sample witnessed prisoners receiving involuntary psychiatric treatment or medication. And nearly one-third (32%) attested to "other" incidents including verbal abuses and racial slurs, food tampering, frequent unnecessary shakedowns and body searches, false writeups, or death threats. Indeed, for a number of subjects, severe psychological abuse appeared to be at the very core of incarceration with the purpose being to "beat people down." The majority of respondents spoke of an environment permeated by "mind games" that they referred to as "the most debilitating part of imprisonment." In a letter to us, a longtime maximum security prison visitor summarized the common experiences of prisoners by reporting:

> Physical abuse has a beginning and end, psychological abuse is all-pervasive. It affects everything done, every decision. Even those who want to stay out of trouble are deeply affected often to

immobility over measuring every little detail of an interaction: a glance, a new routine, a letter a day late, a refused appointment, a change in the diet tray, a comment about the mail. Every small encounter may have multiple meanings and serious disciplinary repercussions.

The Victimology of Severe Prison Discipline

Two very pragmatic questions can be raised at this point in the analysis: Why are prisoners severely punished? and Which prisoners are at greatest risk for such victimization? Table 10.7 attempts to answer the first question and Table 10.8 sheds light on the second question.

Table 10.7 shows that there are multiple behaviors that bring about severe disciplinary action. It seems that the leading causes are: (1) prisoners being verbally hostile to guards, and (2) prisoners refusing to follow orders. It is important to note that the apparent leading "cause" of severe discipline—being verbally hostile to guards—is considered only a *minor* security infraction in most correctional institutions throughout the United States (BJS, 1989). It is also important to note that physical beatings *are not* a formally sanctioned punishment for rule violations in any U.S. prison system (BJS, 1989). Hence, prisoners are most likely to endure illicit beatings and mental harassments for personal, nonviolent (and otherwise petty) verbal responses to prison guards. Because of this, we see that severe punishment is driven by an informal or "sub-bureaucratic" social drama played out by two actors only: the guard and the prisoner. Within this unique informal relationship, therefore, seems to lie the answer for understanding why there is such widespread staff-on-prisoner abuse in maximum security prisons.

Table 10.8 shows that the primary victim of severe discipline is not a black man or woman, as might be suspected. The primary victim is not Hispanic, and certainly is not a gang member nor a political prisoner. The primary victim is not a homosexual or one suffering from AIDS. Rather, Table 10.8 reveals that the primary victim of severe discipline is a jailhouse lawyer.

Table 10.7. **Behaviors Bringing About Severe Disciplinary Action (N=353)**

Behavior	% of Sample Observing
Being verbally hostile to guards	67.4
Refusing to follow orders	58.3
Violating prison rules	46.7
Fighting with other prisoners	41.0
Objecting to cell changes	40.5
Possession of contraband	35.4
Refusing to take psychiatric medication	20.9

Table 10.8. Most Frequently Disciplined Groups of Prisoners (N=357)

Group	% of Sample Observing
Jailhouse lawyers	62.1
Blacks	51.2
Prisoners with mental handicaps	37.5
Political prisoners	33.3
Gang members	32.7
Hispanics	29.6
Homosexuals	24.0
Whites	20.1
AIDS patients	18.4
Prisoners with physical handicaps	17.3
Asians	5.0

We received hundreds of comments from prisoners explaining why jailhouse lawyers are differentially treated. These responses typically began with the assertion that prison officials "ignore grievances" and the "inmate appeal system is a farce" because of "unfair hearings and arbitrary discipline systems" based on "no true trial" or a "biased hearing." They proceeded to the idea that there were "inconsistent and everchanging rules" that were "vague" and "applied based on guards opinion of you." And so, these respondents arrived at the conclusion that there was "selective discipline with racial prejudice" and that "jailhouse lawyers can help you out of a jam." (Jailhouse lawyers assist prisoners, many of whom are illiterate, to participate on their own behalf in formal grievance and appeal procedures both within the prison and in the courts.) Because of this, these respondents observed that guards had a standard practice of "singling out jailhouse lawyers for discipline" in retaliation for challenging the status quo.

Two other insights into this "singling out" process can be achieved from a closer inspection of Table 10.8. First, we see that jailhouse lawyers, prisoners with mental handicaps, and political prisoners were all more likely to become the victims of severe discipline than were members of a prison gang. And second, we see that slightly more than one-half of the sample (51.2%) observed that blacks were singled out for severe discipline.

Our inspection of the substantive comments made on the questionnaire revealed that yet one-third category of people are singled out for severe discipline. These prisoners can be best described as those who exhibit *personal integrity*. According to our sample, they are prisoners "with principles or intelligence," or "those with dignity and self-respect." They are often "authors of truthful articles" or "motivated self-improvers" who are "verbally expressing one's opinion;" "wanting only to be treated as a human being" by "reporting conditions to people on the outside." Moreover, these data suggest that those maximum security prisoners who respond to their environment based on internal criteria and/or file grievances, lawsuits or think for themselves, or are different, are singled out for harassment, abuse and punishment.

The Organization of Prison Discipline: A Search for Correlates

Finally, we turn our attention to issues concerning prison management and attempt to identify the formal organizational forces that support and sustain severe discipline. We begin by asking a fundamental question alluded to, but never formally examined, by previous researchers (e.g., Sykes, 1958; Ward & Schoen, 1981): "Are maximum security prisons really more brutal than other prisons?" An analysis of variance (between maximum, medium, and minimum security respondents) reveals that they are indeed. Significant differences were found between maximum security and these other custody levels with respect to a prisoner's time spent in solitary confinement ($F=6.29$, $p<.001$), frequency of physical beatings ($F=2.99$, $p<.01$), and frequency of mental discipline ($F=2.22$, $p<.05$).

Our intuition tells us that these major differences can only be explained in terms of the specific features of the organizational apparatus that provides support for severe discipline. In other words, we would expect maximum security prisons to demonstrate a greater institutional capacity than minimum or medium custody prisons to: (1) confine prisoners in solitary, (2) exercise wide discretion on decisions to punish prisoners, and (3) have at its disposal greater means and propensity for acting out the drama of violence. This was not to be the case, however.

We found that maximum security prisons were no more likely than minimum or medium custody institutions to have isolation cells, strip cells, "behavioral adjustment units," security housing units, or control units within the various facilities ($F=.67$, $p=.50$). Simply put, nearly all prisons had these disciplinary housing units in equal proportions (see BJS [1989] for a replication of this finding). Likewise, maximum security prisons exercised no unusual discretion regarding decisions to incarcerate a prisoner in disciplinary housing ($F=.09$, $p=.90$). In most cases (and across custody levels), the decision to place a prisoner in disciplinary housing was made through a staff hearing process. Rarely was the disciplinary decision made solely by a guard or warden. Similarly, the decision to release a prisoner from disciplinary housing was made by these same staff committees, and rarely did guards or administrators interfere. On balance, maximum security prisons did not differ one bit from other custody levels in their exercise of discretion ($F=.01$, $p=.98$).

Maximum security staff also did not exercise any unusual tendencies toward victimizing the various prisoner groups, including jailhouse lawyers ($F=.07$, $p=.93$). (That is, these groups were equally victimized across custody levels in the frequency order displayed in Table 10.8. Maximum security prisons simply victimized all of these groups more often.) There were no specific behaviors that seemed to bring about severe discipline in maximum security prisons ($F=.19$, $p=.82$), and maximum security institutions were no more likely to rely on high technology methods of force such as the stun gun and the Taser ($F=.17$, $p=.80$).

So how do we explain the disproportionate use of extreme discipline in maximum security prisons? Among our limited array of organizational variables, we found only one that can even marginally account for this phenomenon: Maximum security prisons managed a greater percentage of prisoners serving long sentences (F=4.14, p=.052; the relationship between custody level and length of imprisonment was V=.19, p<.001). Fully 26 percent of the maximum security prisoners in our analysis had already been in prison for more than 10 years, and the remainder had already spent one-half of a decade behind bars. Yet this finding—once again—seems to tell us much more about the peculiar social world of maximum security prisoners, than it does about the formal organization of severe prison discipline.

This demands that we consider the nature of the maximum security setting itself. Prisoners are placed in maximum security because they have committed serious crimes or have been discipline problems in less secure settings. Hence, prisoners and employees alike know that maximum security is the "end of the line." Here, at the end of the line, there appears to be an institutional license to abuse prisoners.

Discussion

The image emerging from the Prison Discipline Study is akin to a picture taken by a photographer who moves ever so slightly during the final milliseconds of filming. The snapshot is mostly sharp, but the picture gets blurry near the edge. It is clear that solitary confinement, loss of privileges, physical beatings, and (to a somewhat lesser but harsher degree) mental discipline are all common disciplinary practices in U.S. maximum security prisons. According our sample, these practices are rendered routinely, capriciously, and brutally. It is also clear that severe discipline is a function of an informal ritual played out between guards and prisoners over complex issues related to personal *character* and *power*.

Yet the image becomes fuzzy when we try to discern the ways in which this severe discipline gets translated into public administration. Maximum security prisons exercise severe punishments more often than other custody levels, yet they do not provide the additional formal support for prisoner victimization that we would expect. But they do provide a less formal and highly entrenched institutional support for the victimization of prisoners.

Our findings both confirm and refute previous research. The pattern of guard brutality noted here is consistent with the vast and varied body of post-war literature demonstrating that "guard use of physical coercion [is] highly structured and deeply entrenched in the guard subculture" (Marquart, 1986:347). The unusually harsh treatment of jailhouse lawyers, blacks, and mentally ill offenders has been confirmed time and again in the literature (Balbus, 1972; BJS, 1989; Goetting, 1985; Thomas, 1988; Poole & Regoli, 1980; Swigert & Farrell, 1977; Toch & Adams, 1989). And our discovery that maximum security prisons are exceedingly cruel places will surprise no one (Cloward, 1960; Goffman, 1961; Sykes, 1958; Ward & Schoen, 1981).

Yet our study contradicts previous research in one important way. Previous studies have found guard brutality to be centered primarily around the issue of inmate labor. Carleton (1971), Crouch and Marquart (1989), Jackson (1977), Kauffman (1988), March (1978), Murton (1976), McWhorter (1981), and Wilkinson (1972) all found that guard force was most often sparked by a prisoner's refusal to work. Working was the rule. Prisoners who violated the rule got a "tune-up" or an "ass-whippin'" as they said in Texas. This was the way things went. But this is not what we discovered in the Prison Discipline Study.

We found "violating prison rules" to be a middle-ranking cause of severe discipline. In fact, hardly anyone in the sample even referred to problems associated with "work" as a possible correlate of severe punishment. Instead, we found "being verbally hostile to guards" as the probable cause. This came as a surprise to us in the same way that it surprised a young Texas prisoner in Crouch and Marquart's study.

> This experience [a "tune-up"] certainly got the inmate's attention, especially since he had believed that the officers would not hit him. He said, "Man, I didn't think you got fucked up for smarting off." Although the inmate had been at the unit for over six months and knew the guards used force, he mistakenly thought they would not hit him for such a "petty ass" violation (1989:79).

Conclusions

Although this research began as a study of severe prison discipline, the findings demand that it end with an analysis of prison guards and the relationships they form with prisoners. Historically, penologists have organized their thinking in this area around two distinct stereotypes: (1) the guard as a "hack" and (2) the guard as an "alienated professional."

The "Hack"

Under this traditional formulation, the prison guard is seen as incompetent, arbitrary, and sadistically brutal in his (or presumably her) control of prisoners. Essentially, the guard is viewed as "an ignorant, rigid, authoritarian individual who is vigorous only when demanding inmate compliance" (Ross, 1981:3). This stereotype further holds that "guards are more racially prejudiced than the average citizen...they do not like, and in fact often hate nonwhites" (Irwin, 1980:125; see also Carroll, 1982).

This bigoted "hack" looks upon prisoners as "heavy thugs" whose inherent violence can only be controlled through the use of abusive techniques. For their part, prisoners look upon the hack as "the lowest imaginable form of humanoid life, a species somewhere about the level of a gorilla" (Schroeder, 1976:151). According to this model, hacks hate prisoners and prisoners hate right back. This hatred then provides the common ground upon which the ceremony of prison violence is enacted.

The "Alienated Professional"

In contrast to the "hack" stereotype is the perception that guards are well-trained professionals who live out their organizational lives in deep alienation because of the occupational hazards of modern-day corrections. According to this stereotype:

> Guards are neither congenital sadists, rabid racists, nor ex-military officers looking for another uniform and more men to boss around. If their attitudes toward prisoners have anything in common, they are characterized not by hostility or dislike but rather by despair and disappointment (Johnson, 1987:122; see also Stojkovic, 1984).

This model further holds that these alienated guards are better trained (particularly in the use of high-tech security devices), and more effectively supervised than their occupational predecessors. Because of this,

> Prisons today are, in the main, less harsh and depriving than they were a generation ago (Johnson, 1987:120; see also Lombardo, 1982).

Thus, under this stereotype the victimization of prisoners by staff is a rare event occurring "*only* when the authority of the staff has been directly (and often violently) challenged" (Johnson, 1987:120 emphasis added; Bowker, 1980; Fleisher, 1989). This means that there is a distinct temporal ordering to severe discipline: Prisoners make unprovoked, violent attacks against guards, and guards respond with a judicious level of (high tech) discipline designed only to force rule-compliance and preserve prison security. There is nothing arbitrary, frequent, nor brutal about it. It is all done in a professional manner by alienated prison guards. This is the cornerstone of the *myth of humane imprisonment*.

Implications of the Prison Discipline Study

Our research implies that there is an inadequacy in only one of these stereotypes. We found that "hacks" certainly do exist in modern maximum security prisons, but we uncovered no evidence to suggest that a "new-improved" guard (e.g., the alienated professional) has emerged on the scene to correct the prevalence of prisoner victimization during the American 1980s. We found that prisoners still receive regular beatings in U.S. maximum security prisons; thus, we have no reason to believe that guards have quit hating prisoners and vice-versa.

So what is to be done about all of this? The stochastic trashing of a phenomenological metaphor (the guard as "alienated professional") is hardly enough to bring about meaningful changes in guard/prisoner relationships. Something more pragmatic is needed; indeed, something directly related to that unique social space wherein a prisoner exhibits personal integrity or verbal dissatisfaction, and a prison guard retaliates with excess force. In this regard, the Prison Discipline Study carries two sets of implications—those for administrators, and those for criminology.

Administrators

Given its institutionalized nature, we must assume that the severe discipline outlined in this research is common knowledge to all correctional staff of maximum security institutions. Administrators are certainly aware of the abuses we have uncovered. These overburdened executives must have a great deal of courage to face their situation and seek positive change. Yet even a courageous administrator will need society's support for programs designed to make solutions possible. Education, drug counseling, job training, visitor support and community networking are examples of needed programs. As one guard respondent put it:

> ...inmates are brutalized by guards who are themselves brutalized by prisoners and by administration. Remember, a prison is a self-sustaining, self-preserving institution. Such institutions exist mainly as places of employment, not as treatment facilities. Change threatens the status quo at such institutions. They had rather fire employees, than admit that change is needed.

For progressive administrators, our results imply that they take a more active role in supervising guards. Certainly, not all guards are "hacks" just as they are not all "alienated professionals." But identifying hacks through their reputation within the guard force and within the prisoner population is the first step toward improved administration, especially in maximum security prisons. This increased supervision can take many forms. For instance:

• Most administrators have the legal authority (and duty) to suspend or terminate the employment of any guard who beats a prisoner with fists, boots, or clubs (see Crouch & Marquart, 1989; Jacobs, 1983). This matter of law can be made clear in departmental policy and highlighted in staff training programs.

• Administrators can establish and maintain the prison equivalent of an international "peace council" where high-risk offenders (jailhouse lawyers, blacks, and mentally disturbed offenders) are allowed to interact with guards in a formal setting that is designed to eliminate hostilities and bring about peaceful forms of conflict resolution. This would require that the power relationships between prisoners and guards be equalized by an independent mediation body.

• Administrators can implement the use of psychometric examinations of guards during the hiring process. These measures must seek to identify the potential hack, and exclude him (or her) from employment (see Dillehay 1980 for such an instrument).

• Last, the administrator can adjust duty rosters so that known hacks are assigned to work only with well-seasoned officers who have "mellowed-out" and gained a reputation for fairness and decency in their treatment of prisoners. This strategy could effectively mitigate against the formation of "goon squads."

Criminology

We end our study with a plea to criminology in general. In 1980, John Irwin wrote that academic criminologists began to lose contact with the American prison after the mid 1960s. He argued that:

> ...most sociologists were white and not well received by hostile
> black, Chicano, and native American prisoner spokesmen (1980:88).

Because of this, Irwin observed that sociologists began to shift their attention away from prisoners and criminals to police, courts, and the general processing of offenders through the criminal justice system. To the extent that Irwin was correct, we must then assume that this shift depleted sociology of some of the necessary data to construct a cogent treatise on the American prison. Into this void, we suggest, came a *myth of humane imprisonment* based upon sociology's "loud" interpretation of second-and-third person accounts of the guard/prisoner relationship. This created not only an intellectual deficiency which served to undermine sociology's knowledge of the American prison, but this deficiency also worked to minimize the problem of severe prison discipline—and for this mistake, prisoners continued to suffer humiliation and pain rendered by the American prison system.

We have found Irwin's thesis to be only partially correct, however. The racial identity of the Prison Discipline staff was not a factor in our research. More important were the methods used to distribute the questionnaire. We relied on channels trusted by prisoners that were completely independent of prison administration or government. These prisoners, in turn, presented a minimum but healthy skepticism about our goals. In fact, many prisoners risked severe discipline to participate in the research and almost all of our respondents invited us to come for a personal interview.

Therefore, we find the maximum security prison a safe and interesting place to conduct research, in spite of (and because of) its institutionalized use of brute force.

To observe the drama of prison violence get played out, we believe, is of compelling significance to contemporary criminology. Our plea is for scholars to revive their interests in the classic models of penology set forth a generation ago by Cressey, Goffman, and Sykes, and begin applying them to the modern guard/prisoner relationship. Such an academic revival could possibly serve as a natural prophylactic against the racial hostility and violence in our prisons. This alone, it seems, would make an important contribution to prison governance.

Notes

[1] At no time were prisoners mailed bulk copies for distribution. In this way, we attempted to limit the number of questionnaires distributed to any one prison, and we attempted to limit the number of prisoner activists in the sample (e.g., those prisoners who may have been more attuned to or involved in challenges to official authority).

[2] All variables used in this analysis were measured at either the nominal or ordinal level. Therefore, the significance of the relationship between variables was examined by the x^2 statistic. Chi-squares were derived from tables larger than 2x2, however, precluding transformations into the more familiar phi coefficient as a measure of the strength of association between variables. Although Cramer's V is useful in its ability to express statistical relationships at the outer ranges of contingency table tabulation, it tends to produce deflated coefficients of the main effects (Jaccard, 1983). Because of this, the magnitude of association in Cramer's V should be compared to other measures of association with caution.

References

Ad Hoc Subcommittee on Management Oversight of the House Committee on Corrections (1980). *Final Report.* Tallahassee, FL: Florida Senate Corrections, Probation and Parole Committee.

American Correctional Association (1988). *Directory.* College Park, MD: ACA.

American Correctional Association (1989). *Directory.* College Park, MD: ACA.

Amnesty International (1988). *The High Security Unit, Lexington Federal Prison, Kentucky.* London: Amnesty International.

Armed Forces Institute Of Pathology (1987). Autcpsy Report of Santiago Peralta Ocana, April 21. Decatur, GA: Armed Forces Institute of Pathology.

Ayers, E.L. (1984). *Vengeance and Justice: Crime and Punishment in the 19th-Century American South.* New York, NY: Oxford University Press.

Babbie, E.R. (1989). *The Practice of Social Research.* Belmont, CA: Wadsworth.

Balbus, I.D. (1977). *The Dialectics of Legal Repression: Black Rebels Before the American Criminal Courts.* New Brunswick, NJ: Transaction Books.

Barak-Glantz, I. L. (1983). "Who's in the 'Hole?'" *Criminal Justice Review,* 8:29-37.

Berk, B. (1966). "Organizational Goals and Inmate Organization." *American Journal of Sociology,* 71:522-534.

Berkman, R. (1979). *Opening the Gates: The Rise of the Prisoners' Movement*. Lexington, MA: D.C. Heath and Co.

Blumstein, A. (1983). "Prisons, Population, Capacity, and Alternatives." In J.Q. Wilson (ed.) *Crime and Public Policy*. San Francisco, CA: ICS Press.

Bonta, J. and G. Nanckivell (1980). "Institutional Misconducts and Anxiety Levels Among Jailed Inmates." *Criminal Justice and Behavior*, 7:203-214.

Bonta, J. and P. Gendreau (1990). "Re-examining the Cruel and Unusual Punishment of Prison Life." *Law and Human Behavior*, 14:347-372.

Bowker, L. (1985). "An Essay on Prison Violence." In M. Braswell, S. Dillingham and R. Montgomery (eds.) *Prison Violence in America*. Cincinnati, OH: Anderson Publishing Co.

Bowker, L. (1980). *Prison Victimization*. New York, NY: Elsevier.

Bureau of Justice Statistics (1989). *Prison Rule Violations*. Washington, DC: U.S. Department of Justice.

Bureau of Justice Statistics (1988). *Prisoners in 1987*. Washington, DC: U.S. Department of Justice.

Carleton, M.T. (1971). *Politics and Punishment: The History of the Louisiana State Penal System*. Baton Rouge, LA: Louisiana University Press.

Carroll, L. (1982). "Race, Ethnicity, and the Social Order of the Prison." In R. Johnson and H. Toch (eds.) *The Pains of Imprisonment*. Beverly Hills, CA: Sage Publications.

Cartier, G.T. (1986). *Deadlock at Walla Walla*. Somerton, AZ: Somerton Press.

Clarke, J. (1988). *Last Rampage: The Escape of Gary Tison*. Boston, MA: Little, Brown.

Clear, T.R. and G.F. Cole (1990). *American Corrections*. Pacific Grove, CA: Brooks/Cole.

Clemmer, D. (1940). *The Prison Community*. New York, NY: Rinehart.

Cloward, R.A. (1960). "Social Control in the Prison." In D. Cressey (ed.) *Theoretical Studies in Social Organization of the Prison*. New York, NY: Social Science Research Council.

Cobb, A. (1985). "Home Truths About Prison Overcrowding." *Annals*, 478:58-72.

Cohen, J. (1977). *Statistical Power Analysis for the Behavioral Sciences*. New York, NY: Academic Press.

Cohen, S. and L. Taylor (1972). *Psychological Survival*. Harmondworth (UK): Penguin Books.

Collier, P. and D. Horowitz (1988). *Destructive Generation: Second Thoughts About the Sixties*. New York, NY: Summit Books.

Conrad J.P. (1981). "Where There's Hope There's Life." In D. Fogel and J. Hudson (eds.) *Justice as Fairness: Perspectives on the Justice Model*. Cincinnati, OH: Anderson Publishing Co.

Cox, V.C., P.B. Paulus and G. McCain (1984). "Prison Crowding Research: The Relavence of Prison Housing Standards and a General Approach Regarding Crowding Phenomena." *American Psychologist*, 39:1148-1160.

Cressey, D. (1965). "Prison Organizations." In J. March (ed.) *Handbook of Organizations*. New York, NY: Rand McNally.

Crouch, B.M. and J.W. Marquart (1989). *An Appeal to Justice: Litigated Reform of Texas Prisons*. Austin, TX: University of Texas Press.

DiIulio, J.J. (1987). *Governing Prisons: A Comparative Study of Correctional Management*. New York, NY: The Free Press.

Dillehay, R.C. (1978). "Authoritarianism." In H. London and J. Exner (eds.) *Dimensions of Personality*. New York, NY: John Wiley and Sons.

Duffy, C.T. (1950). *The San Quentin Story*. Garden City, NY: Doubleday.

Ekland-Olson, S., D. Barrick and L.E. Cohen (1983). "Prison Overcrowding and Disciplinary Problems: An Analysis of the Texas Prison System." *Journal of Applied Behavioral Science*, 19:163-176.

Flanagan, T.J. (1981). "Dealing with Long-Term Confinement: Adaptive Strategies and Perspectives Among Long-Term Prisoners." *Criminal Justice and Behavior*, 8:201-222.

Flanagan, T.J. (1982). "Lifers and Long-Termers: Doing Big Time." In R. Johnson and H. Toch (eds.) *The Pains of Imprisonment*. Beverly Hills, CA: Sage Publications.

Fleisher, M.S. (1989). *Warehousing Violence*. Newbury Park, CA: Sage Publications.

Gaes, G.G. (1985). "The Effects of Overcrowding in Prison." In M. Tonry and N. Morris (eds.) *Crime and Justice*, Vol. 6. Chicago, IL: University of Chicago Press.

Gaes, G.G. and W.J. McGuire (1985). "Prison Violence: The Contribution of Crowding Versus Other Determinants of Prison Assault Rates." *Journal of Research in Crime and Delinquency*, 22:41-65.

Glaser, D. (1964). *The Effectiveness of a Prison and Parole System*. Indianapolis, IN: Bobb-Merrill.

Glick, B. (1973). "Change Through the Courts." In E.O. Wright (ed.) *The Politics of Punishment: A Critical Analysis of Prisons in America*. New York, NY: Harper Colphon Books.

Goetting, A. (1985). "Racism, Sexism and Ageism in the Prison Community." *Federal Probation*, 49:10-22.

Goffman, E. (1961). *Asylums: Essays on the Social Situation of Mental Patients and Other Inmates*. Garden City, NJ: Anchor Books.

Gottfredson, S.D. and S. McConville (1987). *America's Correctional Crisis: Prison Populations and Public Policy*. New York, NY: Greenwood Press.

Hassan, A. (1972). "Letter to Fay Stender." In E. Pell (ed.) *Maximum Security*. New York, NY: E.P. Dutton.

Irwin, J. (1980). *Prisons in Turmoil*. Boston, MA: Little, Brown.

Jaccard, J. (1983). *Statistics for the Behavioral Sciences*. Belmont, CA: Wadsworth.

Jackson, G. (1972). "Letter to Fay Stender." In E. Pell (ed.) *Maximum Security*. New York, NY: E.P. Dutton.

Jackson, B. (1977). *Killing Time: Life in the Arkansas Penitentiary*. Ithaca, NY: Cornell University Press.

Jacobs, J.B. (1977). *Stateville: The Penitentiary in Mass Society*. Chicago, IL: University of Chicago Press.

Jacobs, J.B. (1983). *New Perspectives on Prisons and Imprisonment*. Ithaca, NY: Cornell University Press.

Jan, L.J. (1980). "Overcrowding and Inmate Behavior: Some Preliminary Findings." *Criminal Justice and Behavior*, 7:293-301.

Johnson, R. (1987). *Hard Time: Understanding and Reforming the Prison*. Monterey, CA: Brooks/Cole.

Johnson, R. and H. Toch (1982). *The Pains of Imprisonment*. Beverly Hills, CA: Sage Publications.

Kauffman, K. (1988). *Prison Officers and Their World*. Cambridge, MA: Harvard University Press.

Kaufman Kantor, G. and M.A. Straus (1987). "The 'Drunken Bum' Theory of Wife Beating." *Social Problems*, 34:213-231.

Light, S. (1988). "Individual and Contextual Effects on Inmate Assaults of Staff." Paper presented at Annual Meeting of the Academy of Criminal Justice Sciences, March.

Lipsey, M. (1990). *Design Sensitivity: Statistical Power for Experimental Research*. Newbury Park, CA: Sage Publications.

Lombardo, L.X. (1982). "Stress, Change, and Collective Violence in Prison." In R. Johnson and H. Toch (eds.) *Pains of Imprisonment*. Beverly Hills, CA: Sage Publications.

McKelvey B. (1977). *American Prisons: A History of Good Intentions*. Montclair, NJ: Patterson Smith.

McLain, D. with M. Nehrstedt (1988). *Strikeout: The Story of Denny McLain*. St. Louis, MO: The Sporting News Publishing Co.

McWhorter, W.L. (1981). *Inmate Society: Legs, Half-Pants and Gunmen A Study of Inmate Guards*. Saratoga, CA: Century Twenty One.

March, R.A. (1978). *Alabama Bound: Forty-Five Years Inside a Prison System*. University, AL: University of Alabama Press.

Marquart, J.W. (1986). "Prison Guards and the Use of Physical Coercion as a Mechanism of Prisoner Control." *Criminology*, 24:347-366.

Mathias, R.A. (1984). *Violent Juvenile Offenders*. San Francisco, CA: National Council on Crime and Delinquency.

Minton, R.J. (1971). *Inside: Prison American Style*. New York, NY: Random House.

Morgan, R. (1988). *High Security Unit for Women at Lexington Federal Prison, Kentucky, USA*. London: Amnesty International.

Murton, T. and J. Hyams (1969). *Accomplices to the Crime*. New York, NY: Grove Press.

Murton, T. (1976). *The Dilemma of Prison Reform*. New York, NY: Holt, Rinehart and Winston.

Myron (1972). "Letter to Fay Stender." In E. Pell (ed.) *Maximum Security*. New York, NY: E.P. Dutton.

Nacci, P.L., H.E. Teitelbaum and H. Prather (1977). "Population Density and Inmate Misconduct Rates in the Federal Prison System." *Federal Probation*, 41:26-31.

Newman, G. (1985). *The Punishment Response*. Philadelphia, PA: Lippincott.

New York State Commission of Investigation (1981). *Corruption and Abuses in the Correctional System—The Green Haven Correctional Facility*. New York, NY: New York State Commission of Investigation.

Olsen, M. (1972). "Letter to Fay Stender." In E. Pell (ed.) *Maximum Security*. New York, NY: E.P. Dutton.

Orland, L. (1975). *Prisons: Houses of Darkness*. New York, NY: The Free Press.

Paulus, P., V. Cox, G. McCain and J. Chandler (1975). "Some Effects of Crowding in a Prison Enviornment." *Journal of Applied Social Psychology*, 5:86-91.

Paulus, P., G. McCain and V. Cox (1981). "Prison Standards: Some Pertinent Data on Crowding." *Federal Probation*, 45:48-54.

Paulus, P.B. (1988). *Prison Crowding: A Psychological Perspective*. New York, NY: Springer-Verlag.

Pelissier, B. (1987). *Effects of a Rapid Increase in a Prison Population: A Pre- and Post-Test Study.* Washington, DC: U.S. Department of Justice, Federal Bureau of Prisons.

Poole, E.D. and R.M. Regoli (1980). "Race, Institutional Rule Breaking, and Disciplinary Response: A Study of Discretionary Decision-Making in Prison." *Law and Society Review*, 14:931-946.

Richards, B. (1978). "The Experience of Long-Term Imprisonment." *British Journal of Criminology*, 18:162-169.

Ross, R.R. (1981). "Introduction." In R.R. Ross (ed.) *Prison Guard/Correctional Officer*. Toronto, CN: Butterworth Publishers.

Ruback, R.B. and T.S. Carr (1984). "Crowding in a Women's Prison: Attitudinal and Behavioral Effects." *Journal of Applied Social Psychology*, 14:57-68.

Saladin, G. (1971). "Racism I." In R.J. Minton (ed.) *Inside: Prison American Style*. New York, NY: Random House.

Sapsford, R.J. (1978). "Life Sentence Prisoners: Psychological Changes During Sentence." *British Journal of Criminology*, 18:128-145.

Schroeder, A. (1976). *Shaking It Rough*. New York, NY: Doubleday.

Sellin, T. (1967). "Prison Homicides." In T. Sellin (ed.) *Capital Punishment*. New York, NY: Harper and Row.

Sherman, M.E. and G. Hawkins (1981). *Imprisonment in America: Choosing the Future*. Chicago, IL: University of Chicago Press.

Smith, J.F. (1973). "Prison Reform Through the Legislature." In E.O. Wright (ed.) *The Politics of Punishment: A Critical Analysis of Prisons in America*. New York, NY: Harper Colophon.

Stojkovic, S. (1984). "An Examination of Compliance Structures in a Prison Organization: A Study of the Types of Correctional Power." Paper presented at Annual Meeting of the Academy of Criminal Justice Sciences, March.

Straus, M.A., R.J. Gelles and S.K. Steinmetz (1980). *Behind Closed Doors: Violence in the American Family*. New York, NY: Doubleday/Anchor.

Subcommittee on Courts, Civil Liberties, and the Administration of Justice (1986). *Atlanta Federal Penitentiary*. Washington, DC: U.S. Government Printing Office.

Swigert, V.L. and R.A. Farrell (1977). "Normal Homicides and the Law." *American Sociological Review*, 42:16-32.

Sykes, G.M. (1958). *The Society of Captives: A Study of a Maximum Security Prison*. Princeton, NY: Princeton University Press.

Sylvester, S.F., J.H. Reed and D.O. Nelson (1977). *Prison Homicide*. New York, NY: Spectrum Publications.

Thomas, J. (1988). *Prisoner Litigation: The Paradox of the Jailhouse Lawyer*. Totowa, NJ: Allen and Littlefield.

Thompson, T. (1987). "Cubans, Guards Trapped in Cycle of Violence." *The Atlanta Journal*, April 19.

Toch, H. (1977). *Living in Prison: The Ecology of Survival*. New York, NY: The Free Press.

Toch, H. (1985). "Warehouses for People?" *Annals*, 478:58-72.

Toch, H. and K. Adams (1989). *Coping: Maladaptations in Prisons*. New Brunswick, NJ: Transaction Books.

Travis, L.F. III (1990). *Introduction to Criminal Justice*. Cincinnati, OH: Anderson Publishing Co.

U.S. Department of Justice (1989). Correctional Populations in the United States, 1987. Washington, DC: U.S. Government Printing Office.

Useem, B. and P. Kimball (1989). *States of Siege. U.S. Prison Riots, 1971-1986*. New York, NY: Oxford University Press.

Walker, L. (1979). *The Battered Woman*. New York, NY: Harper and Row.

Ward, D.A. and K.F. Schoen (1981). *Confinement in Maximum Security*. Lexington, MA: D.C. Heath.

Wheeler, S.B. (1961). "Socialization in Correctional Communities." *American Sociological Review*, 26:697-712.

Wilkinson, F.T. (1972). *The Realities of Crime and Punishment: A Prison Administrator's Testament*. Springfield, MO: Mycroft Press.

Wright, E. O. (1973). "Prison Reform and Radical Change." In E.O. Wright (ed.) *The Politics of Punishment: A Critical Analysis of Prisons in America*. New York, NY: Harper Colophon.

Yee, M.S. (1973). *The Melancholy History of Soledad Prison*. New York, NY: Harper's Magazine Press.

11

The Supreme Court and Prison Excessive Use of Force Cases: Does One Test Fit All?[†][††]

Rolando V. del Carmen

The use of force in prisons is necessary as a last resort to preserve order and instill discipline. Prison constituency and crowded conditions exacerbate tension and make the use of force by prison personnel inevitable, often in an effort to break inmate fights or to quell prison disturbances or riots. The question in prisons is not whether force can be used, but when and how.

The use of force causes concern among prison personnel partly because of possible civil lawsuits. There is hardly any state in the country in which cases have not been brought by prisoners, in federal or state courts, alleging excessive use of force by prison personnel. Courts have imposed damages. The question prison authorities often ask is: When does the use of force violate a prisoner's constitutional right as to warrant civil damages in a civil rights action? A case recently decided by the United States Supreme Court, *Hudson v. McMillian*,[1] provides some answers and therefore deserves focus and analysis.

The case originated in the Angola prison in Louisiana. In the early morning hours of October 30, 1983, inmate Keith Hudson and prison guard Jack McMillian got into an argument. Assisted by another prison guard, Marvin Woods, McMillian placed Hudson in handcuffs and shackles, took him out of his cell, and walked him toward the penitentiary's administrative lockdown area. En route, McMillian allegedly punched Hudson in the mouth, eyes, chest, and stomach, while Woods held Hudson in place and kicked and punched him from behind. Arthur Mezo, the supervisor on duty, saw the beatings but merely cautioned the officers "not to have too much

†Reprinted from *Federal Probation*, Vol. LVI, No. 2, 1992 by permission.
††The author would like to thank Michael Vaughn, a doctoral fellow at Sam Houston State University, for his legal research assistance in the writing of this chapter.

fun." As a result of the beating, the prisoner suffered minor bruises and swelling of the face, mouth, and lip. The beating also loosened the prisoner's teeth and cracked his partial dental plate.

Hudson brought action under title 42 U.S.C. Section 1983[2] against McMillian, Woods, and Mezo seeking damages for violating his constitutional rights. The federal magistrate found excessive use of force by the prison guards and condonation of their actions by the supervisor; the prisoner was awarded $800 in damages. The Fifth Circuit Court of Appeals reversed, holding that there was no violation of the Eighth Amendment prohibition against cruel and unusual punishment because there was no "significant injury," concluding that the injuries inflicted were "minor" and required no medical treatment.

The Supreme Court granted certiorari to decide a single issue: Does the use of excessive physical force by prison guards against a prisoner constitute cruel and unusual punishment even if the inmate does not suffer serious injury? The Court answered yes, saying that injury to the prisoner does not have to be "serious" or "significant" for the use of excessive force to become a constitutional liability: "whether the force was applied in a good faith effort to maintain or restore discipline, or maliciously and sadistically to cause harm."[3] The Court concluded that in this case the prison guards used force maliciously and sadistically to cause harm and therefore violated the prisoner's Eighth Amendment right.[4]

The question of what constitutes "cruel and unusual punishment" in a prison setting has been addressed by the Court in a number of cases with differing results. In *Estelle v. Gamble*,[5] the Court held that "deliberate indifference" to an inmate's medical needs constitutes cruel and unusual punishment. In *Rhodes v. Chapman*,[6] the Court said that double-celling at SOCF (Southern Ohio Correctional Facility) did not constitute cruel and unusual punishment because it was "unquestionably a top-flight, first-class facility," a far cry from the sometimes "deplorable" and "sordid" prison conditions that courts had declared unconstitutional. In *Whitley v. Albers*,[7] the Court held that the application of the "deliberate indifference" standard is inappropriate in prison disturbance cases, saying that "the question whether the measure taken inflicted unnecessary and wanton pain and suffering ultimately turns on whether force was applied in a good faith effort to maintain or restore discipline or maliciously and sadistically for the very purpose of causing harm."[8] In the more recent case of *Wilson v. Seiter*,[9] the Court held that a prisoner claiming that the conditions of confinement constitute cruel and unusual punishment must show a culpable state of mind on the part of prison officials for unconstitutionality to be proved. It added that the "deliberate indifference" standard applied to medical care cases also applies to cases involving conditions of confinement.[10]

The *Hudson* case is significant because for the first time the Court has held that "whenever prison officials stand accused of using excessive physical force in violation of the cruel and unusual punishment clause, the core judicial inquiry is that set out in *Whitley*; whether force was applied in a good faith effort to maintain or restore discipline, or maliciously and sadistically to cause harm."[11] *Hudson* states that the "malicious and sadistic" test will be used by the Court in all excessive use of force cases and not just in riot or prison disturbance situations, hence rejecting, in excessive use of force cases, the "deliberate indifference" test used in medical cases (*Estelle v. Gamble*) or conditions of confinement cases (*Wilson v. Seiter*).[12] The Court refused to adopt the two-pronged test used in other cases whereby violations of the Eighth Amendment are determined through a combined "subjective" (whether the officer acted with a culpable state of mind) and "objective" (whether the harm was serious as to establish a constitutional violation) test.[13] In excessive use of force cases, the Court has opted not to use the objective test, saying instead that "when prison officials maliciously and sadistically use force to cause harm, contemporary standards of decency are violated," regardless of whether or not significant injury is evident.[14] What is needed is a "malicious and sadistic" state of mind, hence preserving the subjective test.

Although the majority decision in *Hudson* repeatedly refers to the *Whitley* case, the core of the decision in fact relies on words used by the Second Circuit Court of Appeals in *Johnson v. Glick*.[15] In *Johnson*, the court said that "in determining whether the constitutional line has been crossed, a court must look to such factors as the need for the application of force, the relationship between the need and the amount of force that was used, the extent of injury inflicted, and *whether force was applied in a good faith effort to maintain or restore discipline or maliciously and sadistically for the very purpose of causing harm*.[16] (Emphasis added.) True to its persuasion in *Whitley*, the Court said in *Hudson* that whether the use of force be in a prison disturbance or in a lesser disruption, corrections officers need to keep a balance or restore discipline. This may require prison authorities to "act quickly and decisively," in turn necessitating that the prison administrators "be accorded wide-ranging deference in the adoption and execution of policies and practices that in their judgment are needed to preserve internal order and discipline and to maintain institutional security.[17]

Perhaps anticipating anxiety among prison guards who might fear that they can now be held liable for every use of force that results in any degree of injury, the Court stressed that not "every malevolent touch by a prison guard gives rise to a federal cause of action."[18] It quoted with approval a statement in *Johnson v. Glick*, where the court said that "not every push or shove, even if it may later seem unnecessary in the peace of a judge's chambers, violates a prisoner's constitutional rights."[19] Thus, the Court soothes apprehension among prison personnel with an assurance that not every injury under the *Hudson* test automatically leads to civil liability.

What, then, is the type of force in prison that does not violate a constitutional right? If "serious injury" is not the test, how is a prison guard to know whether a violation has in fact occurred? The Court answers this question, albeit ambiguously, by saying that the Eighth Amendment "excludes from constitutional recognition *de minimis* [trifle] uses of physical force, provided that such use of force is not of a sort that is 'repugnant to the conscience of mankind.'"[20] Stated conversely, even a *de minimis* use of physical force can lead to a violation if such is "repugnant to the conscience of mankind." What that phrase means is unclear except that the Court in *Hudson* rejected the Fifth Circuit's finding that the prisoner's claim was untenable because his injuries were "minor," saying instead that "the blows directed at Hudson, which caused bruises, swelling, loosened teeth, and a cracked dental plate, are not *de minimis* for Eighth Amendment purposes.[21] In the absence of clear guidelines (which may be impossible to formulate if they are to apply to most, if not all, excessive use of force cases), the determination of what constitutes a constitutional violation, except in extreme cases, will have to be resolved on a case-by-case basis.

The *Hudson* case was decided on a 7-2 vote, with two concurrences and two justices dissenting. In concurrence, Justice Stevens wrote that the less demanding standard of "unnecessary and wanton infliction of pain" should have been applied instead of the "malicious and sadistic" test.[22] Nonetheless, Stevens felt that what the prison guards did to the prisoner in this case resulted in the infliction of unnecessary and wanton pain. In another concurring opinion, Justice Blackmun said that he did not believe that the "malicious and sadistic" standard should be used in all allegations of excessive force, but that he was one with the Court in the opinion that the Eighth Amendment does not require a showing of "significant injury," which was the essence of the majority opinion.[23]

Justice Thomas penned a dissenting opinion, joined by Justice Scalia. In his first prison case since his appointment to the Court, Justice Thomas wrote the following lines which the news media quoted with an unrepressed "we told you so" tone. Said he:

> In my view, a use of force that causes only insignificant harm to a prisoner may be immoral, it may be tortious, it may be criminal, and it may even be remediable under other provisions of the Federal Constitution, but it is not "cruel and unusual" punishment.[24]

Taken in isolation those words sound callous and grossly insensitive to prisoners, leading columnist William Raspberry to write, "Come on, Clarence—conservative is one thing, but bizarre is another."[25] Without necessarily taking the cudgels for Justice Thomas, it must be said in his defense that his dissent, when read in full, does not support what appears to be an extremist view of prisoners' rights, or the lack of it. Towards the end of his dissent Justice Thomas says:

> Abusive behavior by prison guards is deplorable conduct that properly evokes outrage and contempt. But [that] does not mean that it is invariably unconstitutional. The Eighth Amendment is not, and should not be turned into, a National Code of Prison Regulation. To reject the notion that the infliction of concededly "minor" injuries can be considered either "cruel" or "unusual" punishment...is not to say that it amounts to acceptable conduct. Rather, it is to recognize that primary responsibility for preventing and punishing such conduct rests not with the Federal Constitution but with the laws and regulations of the various States.[26]

The above quotation from the dissent more accurately bespeaks the totality of Justice Thomas' view. To him, the remedy to the type of prisoners' rights violation that occurred in *Hudson* does not lie with the federal government but with the states, a view hardly original with Thomas. This view is in accord with the philosophies of judicial restraint and preservation of states' rights that were factors in Thomas' appointment by a conservative President to the High Court. Thomas' dissent is better understood in the context of his faithful adherence to the doctrine of *stare decisis* rather than to callous indifference to the plight of prisoners. In his words, the Court's "expansion of the Cruel and Unusual Punishment Clause beyond all bounds of history and precedent is...yet another manifestation of the pervasive view that the Federal Constitution must address all ills in our society."[27] This view is consistent with judicial restraint to which court conservatives are prone to subscribe.

The good news is that the *Hudson* decision has articulated a test for all excessive use of force cases in a prison setting; the bad news is that it fails to lay the issue to rest. The majority opinion categorically says that an injury caused by excessive physical force on a prisoner need not be "serious" to constitute cruel and unusual punishment, but it fails to provide a bright-line rule as to when and how that threshold is reached, except to say that under the facts of this case, such point was indeed reached. Neither does the decision address the issue of whether the acts committed by the prison guards may be unconstitutional as violative of other rights, such as the Fourteenth Amendment due process clause. The defendants in *Hudson* apparently conceded that "if available state remedies were not constitutionally adequate, petitioner would have a claim under the due process clause of the Fourteenth Amendment."[28] Justice Thomas, in his dissent, said: "I agree with respondents that this [referring to due process] is the appropriate, and appropriately limited, federal constitutional inquiry in this case."[29] Moreover, the decision fails to settle the issue of whether an Eighth Amendment violation occurs if the conduct by the officers was "isolated and unauthorized," as the State of Louisiana had claimed in *Hudson*.[30] The Court ducked that issue, saying that there was no need to decide that since the Court of Appeals left intact the magistrate's finding that the violence involved in this case was "not an isolated assault."[31] In litigation parlance, these issues were conveniently left by the Court "for another day."

Hudson v. McMillian is significant not only for having set, at least for now, the standard for violating the Eighth Amendment in excessive use of force cases in prisons, but also because it provides a window as to how the current Court might address some future prison cases. Although a great majority of prison cases decided by the Court during the last decade may be classified as anti-prisoner (defined as decisions that either strengthen the authority of prison officials or where prisoners' claims were denied), *Hudson* takes a route less traveled recently by the Court, making it less difficult for prisoners to obtain damages in section 1983 cases, hence reinforcing prisoners' rights. Does this signal a change of heart by the Court? Hardly. As the saying goes, "one swallow does not a summer make." Nonetheless, *Hudson* provides a glimmer of hope that, despite pervasive fears, the future may not be totally dismal for prisoners even under the present conservative Court.

Notes

1　60 LW 4151 (1992).

2　Title 42 U.S.C. Section 1983 provides: "Every person who, under color of any statute, ordinance, regulation, custom, or usage, of any State or Territory, subjects, or causes to be subjected, any citizen of the United States or other person within the jurisdiction thereof to the deprivation of any rights, privileges, or immunities, secured by the Constitution and laws, shall be liable to the party injured in an action at law, suite in equity, or other property proceeding for redress."

3　Supra Note 1, at 4153.

4　Id. at 4154.

5　429 U.S. 97 (1976).

6　452 U.S. 337 (1981).

7　475 U.S. 312 (1986).

8　Id. at 320-321.

9　59 LW 4671 (1991).

10　Id. at 14673.

11　Supra Note 1, at 4153.

12　Id. at 4153.

13　*Johnson v. Glick,* 481 F.2d 1028 (1973), at 1033.

14　Supra Note 1, at 4153.

15　Supra Note 13.

16　Id. at 1033.

17　Supra Note 1, at 4153.

18　Id. at 4153.

19　Id.

20　Id. at 4152

21　Id. at 4154.

22　Id.

23　Id. at 4155.

24　Id. at 4156.

25　*Houston Chronicle,* March 3, 1992, at 11A.

26　Supra Note 1, at 4158.

27　Id. at 4158.

28　Id. at 4159.

29　Id.

30　Id. at 4154.

31　Id.

12

Assaults on Prison Officers: Interactional Themes[†][††]

Stephen C. Light

The purpose of this study is to explore the interactional contexts surrounding officially reported assaults on prison officials. The development of a broader knowledge in this area is crucial for several reasons. First, to date there have been few scholarly examinations of this form of disrupted authority relation and no studies of the interactional themes within which they occur. We are beginning to understand more about the dynamics of collective disturbances in the prison setting (Martin, 1988) and about violent actions between prisoners (Wright, 1989), but little is yet known about individual inmates' challenges to the authority of their guards. In addition, a growing number of social-scientific studies have used the assaultive incident as one indicator of prison violence levels without examining closely the meaning of these events. I hope that careful exploratory analysis of these data will provide a foundation for understanding these incidents and that we may infer theoretical hypotheses that are amenable to further empirical evaluation.

An assumption of this study is that prison behavior occurs within complex interactions fueled by multiple motives and by situational definitions brought to these interactions by both guards and inmates (Owen, 1988). According to Gibbs (1981), "Violence does not emerge full-blown.... Any violent incident is the product of three interacting sets of variables: (1) The aggressor (personality, needs, concerns,

†Stephen Light. "Assaults on Prison Officers: Interactional Themes." *Justice Quarterly* 8(2):243-261, June 1991. Reprinted with permission of the Academy of Criminal Justice Sciences.
††Funding for this project was provided by National Institute of Justice Graduate Research Fellowship 84-IJCX-0036 and by a Faculty Research Fellowship Award from Old Dominion University. The author is grateful to Helen Eigenberg and Lucien Lombardo for helpful comments on earlier drafts, and to Jon Holloway for assistance with reliability analysis. The chapter also benefitted from suggestions by James Fyfe and three anonymous *Justice Quarterly* reviewers. A previous version of this chapter was presented at the 1989 annual meeting of the Academy of Criminal Justice Sciences, held in Washington, D.C.

perceptions, etc.), (2) the victim (personality, needs, concerns, perceptions, etc.), and (3) the situation (the human and physical environment in which the incident takes place)." According to Bowker (1980), most assaults on prison officers fall into one of two types: (1) patterned spontaneous attacks and (2) unexpected attacks. The former occur while prison personnel conduct routine tasks in risk-prone environments. Performance of potentially dangerous duties such as intervention in inmates' altercations may be expected to result in patterned spontaneous attacks more often than involvement in other, less highly charged interactions. Unexpected attacks, on the other hand, occur in an apparently random and unpredictable fashion. They cannot be avoided unless officers shun all contact with inmates, a coping strategy that is not always feasible.

Under what conditions do prisoners choose to employ direct physical confrontation in their relationships with prison officers? Most do not choose this option, of course: only 2 percent of the prisoners in this sample were reported to have assaulted an officer during the one-year study period. To be sure, alternative formal means of redressing perceived wrongs are available, including use of official inmate grievance procedures or initiation of a legal suit. Prisoners also may adopt informal means of social control such as sabotage, work slowdown, or refusal to follow orders. Assaultive behavior, on the other hand, has the advantage of being much more immediate and less impersonal, and therefore may be chosen over official means of obtaining satisfaction. It also may be preferred because, in contrast to other methods of dispute resolution, direct physical confrontation does not require the consent of the target. Instead "the injured party...decides unilaterally what redress of the grievance is appropriate and when and how it will be achieved" (Baumgartner, 1984:335).

In the analysis presented below, I develop a preliminary set of categories that begin to describe the interactional settings in which prisoners assault prison officers. Data are drawn from a large sample of official assault reports submitted by officers in a multi-unit state prison system.

Data and Methods

To clarify the dynamics of prisoners' assaults on correctional facility staff members, an ideal research design would consider the multiple perspectives of both aggressors and victims.[1] An effective alternative strategy that may be undertaken in the absence of detailed ethnographic accounts from participants on both sides entails the analysis of assaultive incidents as described in readily available official documents.

The archival data analyzed here are drawn from "Unusual Incident Reports" submitted to the central offices of the New York State Department of Correctional Services by staff members of the state's correctional facilities. The prison staff uses the incident report to inform the corrections department of "certain inmate behaviors that are potentially disruptive to the effective operation of the New York prisons" (New York State Department of Correctional Services, 1985). One such behavior is the assault on staff members, encompassing instances in which on-duty prison employees are struck intentionally by an inmate's body or by a thrown or wielded object. The initial decision to define an incident as "reportable" is made by the officer involved. A narrative account then is written by a supervisory officer, who submits a report of the incident to the Corrections Department's headquarters office. Although the assault report narrative is subject to the well-known biases inherent in official data (see Nettler, 1978), it serves as a useful indicator of the prevalence of certain broad types of assaultive interaction as seen through the eyes of official organizational representatives.[2]

The sample consists of the 694 incidents of assault by prisoners on officers that were reported to have occurred in 31 New York State prisons during calendar year 1983, the latest year for which complete data were available. Because the dynamics of female-only prisons often differ markedly from those of facilities for males (Giallombardo, 1966), assaults in female institutions were excluded from the analysis. New York City facilities constitute a separate authority and also were excluded.

As noted in Table 12.1, slightly more than 82 percent of the assault incidents took place in maximum security prisons, 15.4 percent occurred in medium security facilities, and 2.3 percent in minimum security prisons. In 96.7 percent of the incidents a single prisoner acted alone, and more than 88 percent of the prisoners in the sample were involved in only one assault on staff incident during the period of the study. The most commonly reported locations for the incidents were cell block or housing areas (49% of all incidents) and special housing units (23.9%). No other single location accounted for more than 5.2 percent of the total. Most of the incidents (76.6%) involved no weapon beyond the inmate's body, although in 10.6 percent of the cases dangerous weapons were used, including knives, blackjacks, and articles of metal or wood. Prisoners who assaulted an officer were generally younger than those who did not. The mean age of alleged assaulters was 27.3 years; the mean age of non-assaulters was 29.4 (p=.000). Data on most correctional officer characteristics unfortunately were not available.

Notably, many of the incidents were relatively trivial as to injurious outcome. More than one-half of all reported assaults on staff members (53.5%) resulted in no injury to the officer involved. Minor injury (e.g., scratch, slight bruise) was produced in 28.8 percent of assaults; 14.9 percent resulted in moderate injury (e.g., some loss of blood). Only 2.8 percent of the incidents resulted in serious injury to the affected officer (significant loss of blood, unconsciousness, stab wounds, injuries requiring emergency treatment). No assault-related deaths among officers occurred during the study period. For a detailed analysis of the severity of assaults in this sample, see Light (1990b).

After I examined in detail each document in the saturation sample of incident reports, I created abstracts of narratives and then used content analysis to identify thematic patterns. Twenty themes identified during initial analyses were reduced to

Table 12.1. Reported Assaults by Inmates on Prison Officers, 1983

Variable	%[a]	f
Assaults by Prison Security Level		
Maximum	82.3	571
Medium	15.4	107
Minimum	2.3	16
	100.0%	694
Number of Inmate Assailants per Incident		
1	96.7	670
2	2.9	20
3	.4	3
(missing)	—	1
	100.0%	694
Number of Incidents per Inmate		
(Assaulters Only)		
1	88.4	512
2	8.1	47
3	2.1	12
4	1.0	6
5	0.0	0
6	.2	1
7	.2	1
(missing)	—	10
	100.0%	589 inmates
Location of Incident		
Cell block/housing area	49.0	338
Special housing unit	23.9	165
Mess hall	5.2	36
Hospital	4.8	33
Yard	4.6	32
Administrative office	2.5	17
Inmate reception area	1.7	12
Gym/recreation area	1.6	11
Corridor	1.0	7
Shop	.9	6
Kitchen	.6	4
Classroom	.6	4
All others	3.6	25
(missing)	—	4
	100.0%	694
Weapon		
None or body	76.6	510
Metal/wood object	6.5	43
Food/water	6.0	40
Urine, feces, "unknown substance"	5.6	37
Knife/sharp object	3.0	20
Paper	1.4	9
Rock/blackjack	1.1	7
(missing)	—	28
	100.0%	694
Mean Inmate Age		
Prisoners involved in an assault	27.3 years	
Prisoners not involved	29.4 years	
Severity of Injury to Prison Officer		
No injury	53.5	364
Minor injury	28.8	196
Moderate injury	14.9	101
Serious injury	2.8	19
(missing)	—	14
	100.0%	694

[a] Percentages may not sum to 100 because of rounding.

14 after analysis revealed several to be inappropriate or redundant. The final set of themes includes the following: unexplained, officer's command, protest, inmates' fighting, search, movement, contraband, restraint, discipline, emotional instability, sexual, intoxication, medical, and "other" (see Table 12.2). Comparison of my coding decisions with those of an independent judge for a 10 percent sub-sample of the incidents revealed a .72 coefficient of intercoder reliability for theme categories.[3] Each thematic classification is discussed below in order of frequency.

Table 12.2. **Primary Assault Themes**

Theme	%[a]	N
Unexplained	25.8	179
Officer's Command	13.1	91
Protest	10.8	75
Search	10.7	74
Inmates' Fight	10.2	71
Movement	9.7	67
Contraband	7.2	50
Restraint	4.2	29
Discipline	3.7	26
Emotional Instability	2.0	14
Sexual	1.4	10
Alcohol/Drug Intoxication	.7	5
Medical	.3	2
Other	.1	1
	100.0%	694

[a] Percentages may not sum to 100 because of rounding.

The Themes

Unexplained

The largest category of incidents (25.8% of the total) consists of those classified as UNEXPLAINED. In their descriptions of these events, prison officers proposed no motives for the assaultive inmates' actions. Common here were officers' accounts of assaults occurring "for no apparent reason:"

> *Log # 30525*: While checking that inmate's cell door was locked on rounds, correctional officer received urine thrown in his face by inmate. Inmate then attempted to hit CO with broom and glass jar.

It is not surprising that the largest category of assaultive events is unexplained by the prison's keepers. In the daily clash between the unofficial inmate social structure and the official structure of the guards, prisoners of a total institution will attempt to conceal the motives behind many types of activity (Goffman, 1961). Prisoners also may express emotional energy by striking the first officer they encounter (Bowker, 1980). It is possible that many unexplained assaults are related to inmates' generalized concerns about autonomy: they may be committed in order to resist the authoritative regime of the prison's custodians. Goffman (1961) refers to adaptations of this type as "secondary adjustments." These incidents correspond closely to Bowker's (1980) "unexpected attacks," and undoubtedly result from many precipitating factors, not all of which may be readily discernible from these data.[4]

Disrupted guard-inmate interactions may culminate from a series of contributory factors acting over time (Toch, 1977). An inmate's assaultive act, although viewed by guards as meaningless in its immediate context, in fact may be readily interpretable in light of a series of related prior events.[5] In addition to assaulting an officer for instrumental purposes, prisoners may lash out in response to generalized emotional arousal. When expressively based assaults occur, it is likely that officers often will find themselves unable to connect the events with meaningful proximate causes and will feel unable to attribute motives to the actions. Therefore, they would be likely to place them into a residual category of events that occur "for no apparent reason."

Officer's Command

Verbal jousting sometimes comes to be characterized by increased tension and likelihood of violence. The issuance of a command may create a situation in which the powerless and dependent position of the prisoner is highlighted and reinforced, and in which the deprivation of autonomy develops increased social and psychological force. Issues concerning definitions of manhood and appropriate masculine role performance (Gibbs, 1981) or generalized concerns about self-esteem (Held, Levine & Swartz, 1979) also may come into play. The theme of OFFICER'S COMMAND was reflected in 13.1 percent of the incidents.

> Log # 30141: Inmate was standing on stairs leading to the gym and correctional officer told him to move. Inmate refused and correctional officer repeated his order. Inmate punched correctional officer on side of face.

Officers' orders to prisoners to enter or leave an area precipitated 51.1 percent of the command-related assaults on staff members, 12.5 percent followed requests for identification, 9.1 percent centered around appearance and/or sanitation issues, and an additional 8.0 percent involved other rules. Other commands producing resistance included orders to wait (6.8%), to surrender an object (4.5%), and to be quiet or calm (4.5%). Incident reports placed in the officer's command category contained no indication that the inmate perceived the order itself to be unjust or inconsistent. In deciding whether to place an incident into the OFFICER'S COMMAND or the PROTEST category, I attempted to discern the assaulter's apparent motive. If the assault narrative supported the impression that the order itself led primarily and immediately to the assault, I coded OFFICER'S COMMAND. On the other hand, if the inmate appeared to be protesting an officer's action or other situation (even if the action being protested was an officer's command), I coded PROTEST.

Protest

In 10.8 percent of the assault incidents, the inmates apparently perceived themselves to be the victims of unjust or inconsistent treatment at the hands of the security staff. These incidents reflect the theme of PROTEST, in which the inmate presumably is questioning the personal action of an individual guard rather than the overall authority of the organization or of its official representatives (see Toch, 1979:56). This point is consistent with research suggesting that just as prison staff members experience difficulty in the face of conflicting or ambiguous administrative role requirements (Cheek & Miller, 1982; Lombardo, 1981; Poole & Regoli, 1980), prisoners likewise come to rely on a predictable set of rules and enforcement patterns. When official policies shift radically, or when individual correctional officers diverge greatly in their manner of carrying out custodial duties, rule enforcement is likely to be perceived as capricious. Ironically, dissatisfaction and protest may result both when changes are intended to be positive (reforms) and when they are perceived to be punitive (McCleery, 1961).

In addition, certain goods and services take on the character of entitlements. Inmates may come to feel that these things are due them by right, and they become upset when access is abridged or denied (Goffman, 1961; Kratcoski, 1988; Sykes, 1958; Toch, 1977). These entitlements include food, shelter, clothing, access to a minimum level of medical attention, and possibly such intangibles as minimum levels of affection and recognition (Etzioni, 1968). When basic services are perceived to be withheld or conveyed inadequately, the aggrieved party may strike out as an affirmation of the possession of basic human rights.

> *Log # 39390*: Inmate requested escort to go to emergency sick call because of chest pains. Correctional officer left cell and called for escorting officers. Twenty minutes later they arrived.... As inmate passed original correctional officer he stated "What the f— took you so long, you m———— punk?" Inmate then hit correctional officer in the eye with his fist and continued striking him in the chest and stomach.

Prisoners also may protest when confronted with routine prison security procedures. Correctional officers in the New York sample encountered protests and resistance while performing such routine duties as refusing entrance to a mess hall after hours, denying permission for passage through a security grille, checking an inmate's identification card, and informing prisoners that visiting hours were over. A key factor in determining whether an officer's action deserves protest is the prisoner's perception of the officer's universalistic or particularistic situational motivations—that is, whether the officer is acting in accordance with a general norm or in reaction to personal feelings toward the individual prisoner (see Parsons, 1951). Unpleasant situations may be endured if other persons are affected similarly, but the perceived singling out of a particular prisoner is often viewed as harassment.

Search

More than 10 percent of the assaults involved the theme of SEARCH and were precipitated by an officer's attempted or actual examination of an inmate's person, cell, or property. These events are distinct from those searches that uncovered contraband and therefore were grouped together under CONTRABAND as a primary theme (see below). Of the assault incidents falling into the SEARCH category, 58.2 percent occurred during a completed or attempted frisk (cursory body search or patdown). If these incidents are added to the 14.9 percent involving a completed or attempted strip search, a total of 73.1 percent of the search incidents occurred during a search of the prisoner's body. The remaining 26.9 percent of the search incidents occurred during an actual or attempted search of the prisoner's cell. The prisoner is physically present during most cell searches in this sample because of a policy of the New York State Department of Correctional Services that has been in force since the 1970s: whenever possible, inmates should be present during a search of their cell or dormitory cubicle.

The search creates a situation in which inmates and guards must be in intimate physical proximity and in which the officer physically touches the inmate's body or property. Touching often carries a connotation of dominance; in the prison setting, with its caste divisions between officers and prisoners, an unwanted touch may convey a feeling of ritual pollution. A prison inmate may serve his interests by resisting a search if he is concealing prohibited items such as drugs or weapons, but the fact that contraband was not detected as a result of the searches in this category suggests that other processes related to resistance to authority may be at work in this set of interactions. The largest group of search incidents (28.4%) occurred in conjunction with the movement of inmates. This fact is not surprising because security practices often mandate searches before, during, and/or after inmates' movements.

> *Log # 30884*: CO was pursuing inmate who had fled from [the] area to avoid being frisked before entering mess hall, when inmate turned around and punched CO in the mouth.

Inmates' Fighting

INMATES' FIGHTING is the dominant theme in slightly more than 10 percent of the assaults. When a fight occurs between prisoners, one or more officers routinely will intervene in order to separate them. Often an officer is struck by one of the combatants as he or she responds. Prisoners' accounts often describe such actions as unintentional, but the purported accidental nature of violence directed at officers during inmates' altercations is questionable. Several accounts in fact suggest that some supposed inmate fights may be staged events that are undertaken in order to disguise covert objectives, as suggested by the following narrative:

> *Log # 31187*: Two correctional officers restrained two inmates, who were fighting, by holding them. One inmate broke away and started swinging at the other. The inmate who was being hit then struck his correctional officer over the head with a wooden chair. Inmate states chair was intended for other inmate, but correctional officer got in the way.

The scene created by a fight between prisoners occasionally offers uninvolved inmate bystanders the opportunity for an anonymous assault on an officer. The large number of persons present, the confusion of the moment, and the officer's focus on the combatant inmates combine to make it difficult to observe and apprehend the guilty party or parties.

> *Log # 32103*: While breaking up a fight between two inmates, CO received a severe cut on the right hand. Assailant or weapon could not be identified.

Movement

Inmates committed 9.7 percent of the total sample of assaults primarily during the MOVEMENT of inmates from one area of the prisons to another or during transfer between institutions. This category also includes otherwise unexplained events that took place during such movement.

> *Log # 29891*: While being escorted back to special housing unit cell from yard, inmate became verbally abusive. Without warning he turned and swung at sergeant, striking him on side of face, breaking his glasses, cutting him under the right eye and breaking his nose.

Factors precipitating such events are unclear on the basis of these data, but it is probable that movement-related incidents occur partly because of the increased number of opportunities for unrestricted activity during movement. For prisoners living in the special housing units, movement to showers or to exercise may represent one of the few circumstances in which they are physically close to officers. Before congregate movement occurs in other prison locations, cell or dormitory doors must be unlocked, and prisoners may mingle with other inmates and with prison employees. In addition, movement to a more secure area of the prison often occurs after an inmate has been involved in a rule infraction of some kind. The movement that follows such occurrences may provide an opportunity to protest, posture, or otherwise resolve the initial event socially and/or psychologically.

Contraband

CONTRABAND-related incidents occur when a correctional officer finds that an inmate possesses some item or substance that is prohibited by prison rules. Prisoner-officer relations are characterized by a continuous battle over the restriction of goods and services within the walls of the institution (Sykes, 1958); this situation encourages widespread adoption of a sub-rosa economic system of contraband resource distribution (Irwin, 1970). Prohibited items most often include drugs, weapons, and homemade alcoholic beverages, but also include unapproved cell furnishings or extra food items. Participation in the underground prison economy offers the inmate many advantages beyond access to scarce goods, including the strengthening of one's position in the unofficial status hierarchy and a concomitant increase in personal power and dominance. The occasion of detection therefore may give rise to incidents of resistance or efforts at concealment. Contraband was involved as a primary theme in 7.2 percent of the assaults on staff members.

> *Log # 31071*: Correctional officer smelled marijuana odor from cell and proceeded to search it with inmate present. Correctional officer found a marijuana "roach" and inmate lunged at correctional officer and slammed his hand against bars and threw roach off of tier.

More than 53 percent of the contraband-related assaults involved marijuana or alcohol; 14.9 percent resulted from the discovery of unapproved cell furnishings or other objects such as nail clippers or extra clothing. The discovery of a knife was involved in 8.5 percent of these assaults, while an additional 8.5 percent concerned contraband food items. The remaining 14.9 percent (N=7) includes such items as pornography, a glass painting, "fishing" line (for reeling in contraband from beyond arm's reach), a steel rod, and balloons used for hiding small items inside body cavities.

Restraint

RESTRAINT was the primary theme in 4.2 percent of the reported incidents (N=20). This category includes assaults precipitated by the application or removal of physical restraint devices such as handcuffs or ankle chains, or by officers' use of their bodies to subdue a recalcitrant prisoner. The largest category of restraint incidents involved the use of handcuffs (51.7%); other types of restraint included bodily force by an officer (31%), application of tear gas or tear dust (10.3%), and injection (7%). The application of restraint precipitated 56 percent of these incidents; 44 percent occurred during removal. A key to understanding these events lies in awareness of the circumstances under which restraint is applied. Physical restraint equipment commonly is used in cases in which an inmate is exhibiting violent behavior and/or is confined in a segregated housing unit for violent offenders. In addition, policies at many institutions call for the routine use of restraints in transporting prisoners in a vehicle, escorting them to or from a secure housing area, or supervising their attendance at a session of court.

Discipline

DISCIPLINE-related assaults occur while a staff member is disciplining an inmate or while an officer is presenting an inmate with information (usually unpleasant) about the outcome of a prison's disciplinary process. In common assaultive scenarios, an officer presents a notice of disciplinary proceedings to an inmate, who then assaults him, or an inmate attempts to attack one of the members of the panel during a disciplinary hearing.

> *Log # 32687*: As correctional officer served inmate with notice of [disciplinary] charges, inmate threw two cups of unknown liquid, striking officer and counselor.

In 42.3 percent (N=11) of the 26 discipline-related assaults, the context was an official prison disciplinary hearing. Another 42.3 percent (N=11) occurred when an officer informed a prisoner of the filing of disciplinary charges or of the outcome of a disciplinary process.

Emotional Instability

EMOTIONAL INSTABILITY was coded when the assault report specifically described the prisoner as having a history of mental illness or psychiatric treatment and when the reporting officer clearly stated this condition as contributing to the outburst. This category also describes those cases in which an inmate becomes severely distraught by unpleasant news (e.g., notice of divorce, death in the family). Placement in this category implies a lessened degree of self-control and reduced intentionality on the part of the assaultive prisoner. EMOTIONAL INSTABILITY accounts for 2 percent of the assaults.

> *Log # 29296*: As inmate was entering mess hall, he broke from line and struck correction officer with his fists. As he was being subdued by CO, inmate slashed him with a razor blade on left arm and side of face. (Report cites "apparent psychotic episode" as cause, and refers to inmate's "catatonic state").

Sexual and Remaining Categories

SEXUAL incidents include those in which the inmate uses his body or an object to touch the officer in an overtly sexual manner. Both male (N=1) and female (N=8) officers reported themselves to be victims of sexually related events, but relatively few of these incidents occurred (1.4% of the total sample). Of these, 88.9 percent (N=8) involved touching or fondling of the victim of the assault and 11.1 percent (N=1) involved poking or prodding with an object.

Each of the three remaining thematic categories accounts for less than 1 percent of the total sample of assault incidents. Although the small number of cases in these categories casts doubt on their utility as separate assault types, I include them here for the sake of interest and completeness. The two incidents categorized as MEDICAL occurred in the context of an illness or medical condition. In one such case an inmate became delirious after falling; in another, a seriously ill prisoner became violent during a hospital stay. ALCOHOL/DRUG INTOXICATION was coded in the five cases in which the reporting officer believed the inmate to be under the influence of alcohol or another drug. Finally, the residual OTHER category includes a single very interesting incident that did not lend itself to placement in the existing categories of the typology (see note 5).

Several cautions are in order in interpreting the above results. A primary issue concerns the discretionary processes by which official agents of social control in the prison choose to respond to certain incidents and not to others; this topic has received little research attention. In addition, certain alleged assaults may be attributed erroneously to inmates in order to cover for an officer's culpability (Toch, 1979:27). The distribution of reported assaults reflects both the true incidents of inmates' assault activity and the extent of reporting by guards. Finally, the thematic categories generated from content analysis of the assault data are ad hoc, and necessarily represent only crude and tentative measures of the contexts of assaultive disputes.

Discussion: Authority, Autonomy, and Social Control

The results of this study suggest that prisoners' assaults on staff members occur in a framework of opposed interests of prisoners and guards. Inmates are subject to the overt and subtle deprivations of prison life and therefore feel compelled to resist attempts to deprive them of the valued commodities of liberty, autonomy, goods and services, sexual relations, and security (Sykes, 1958). The deprivation of liberty may be perceived as an overarching consideration because, according to Toch (1977), "freedom" is perceived to be the most salient of seven environmental concerns noted by prisoners. The themes enumerated above suggest that routine interactions between officers and inmates may be disrupted when prisoners perceive that the norms surrounding them have been violated by an officer's action or lack thereof. In such situations the precarious legitimacy that officers possess in the eyes of inmates may evaporate. According to Toch:

> It is significant that ranking abuses of authority cited by today's inmates often revolve around "petty" or minor circumstances of their daily lives. Such restrictions are not necessarily seen by inmates as discrete incidents but they may be regarded as demonstrations of a propensity by authority for unwarranted interferences with inalienable rights (1977:99).

Correctional officers, on the other hand, must strive to conform to the occupational role requirements of their positions as official representatives of the prison administration and of the state. Accordingly, they are called upon to support and maintain the deprivations and pains of imprisonment. It is their duty to effect the "reproduction of social control" (Owen, 1988) on which prison order is based. Assaults often are triggered inadvertently by correctional officers even while they are performing their duty to uphold prison discipline and control. Many assaultive acts follow an order, a command, or an expectation communicated by an officer. Whether the order relates to a search, to a move to another area, or to general routine and discipline, prisoners constantly evaluate the legitimacy of the command in relation to powerful unofficial norms. Conduct by an officer that is perceived to be inconsistent with accepted practice or to be arbitrary, capricious, spiteful, unnecessary, or petty may be viewed as an occasion for resistance.

Herein lies a key to understanding the character of prison social relations and, more generally, the character of social relations between authority holders and subordinates in many similar social environments. In the prison, the contradictory nature of the officer's role requires that officers enforce social control measures while using discretion to satisfy powerful informal norms governing acceptable behavior by officers and inmates. The interests of officers and of prisoners are fundamentally opposed in the broadest sense. Ironically, however, they converge in any given interaction. It is in the best interests of both officers and prisoners to negotiate each situation with a minimum of disruption; both parties need to "make it through the day" (Owen, 1988). Officers and prisoners alike must tread this precarious path successfully by adhering to a set of informal norms that make "getting through the day" an easier and more predictable task.

When formal or informal norms are violated, assault on staff members may provide the opportunity to exercise sanctions against a correctional officer who is perceived to inhabit a deviant status. Likewise, officers may use the assault report to react to actual or perceived challenges to their personal (as opposed to legalistic or bureaucratic) authority. Social control, in other words, may be directed either upward against authority or downward against autonomy. It is noteworthy that in Lombardo's (1981) study, Auburn prison officers cited personal characteristics ("the way an officer handles himself") as their primary source of authority, thus suggesting that inmates' challenges to officers' directives are frequently viewed by guards as personal affronts. Such individualistic concerns may affect an officer's decision to discipline an inmate more strongly than whether the action is a breach of official institutional rules. Thus, although inmates' actions may be directed generally rather than specifically, officers often tend to define them as personal affronts (Bowker, 1980).

Regardless of the immediate cause of the episode, its culmination as an officially reported assault incident stems from the attitudes and behaviors of both prisoner and guard. The results obtained in this preliminary study reaffirm the importance of interactional social control processes in creating this form of behavior. It must be left to further research to delineate more clearly the influences of these attitudes and behaviors on the outcome of authority-based interactions, and to test the applicability of the above-cited themes to similar populations. Undoubtedly the most useful methodological design for such research will involve comparative examination of data from interviews conducted with both prisoner and officer participants in the same set of incidents. The degree of congruence between the narratives of prisoners and of guards will be highly instructive and will constitute a further step toward developing a middle-range theory of disrupted authority relations, applicable both inside the total institution and beyond its walls.

Notes

[1] An anonymous *Justice Quarterly* reviewer wisely raised the point that a research design calling for officers' and prisoners' clarification of reported incidents may well result in "numerous *Roshoman* stories in which it is difficult to determine whose account is the correct one." An alternative design, the reviewer suggests, would involve in-depth interviews that probe for officers' and prisoners' subjective accounts without linking them to written incident reports. I believe that the reviewer's point is well taken, and that the suggested approach would succeed in separating the research design from considerations of measurement error in official reports. On the other hand, I would prefer in this case to link participants' accounts to official assault reports because of the additional information provided, and not least for the potential public policy implications that may result from examining the validity and reliability of officially gathered data. By linking participants' accounts with official reports, a single research project might profitably address both the meaning of violent incidents and the important but little-studied issue of the quality of officially gathered prison violence data, which are used widely but often uncritically. For broader discussions of measurement error in prison data, see Hewitt, Poole and Regoli (1984), Light (1990a), and Schafer (1984).

[2] In recent years scholars have become aware of the potential for reliability and validity problems inherent in officially recorded data on prison rule infractions (Hewitt, 1984; Light, 1990a). Such difficulties are of less concern in this chapter, where officially gathered assault data are treated as interactional indicators (with both officer and inmate components) rather than as measures of the behavior of prisoners alone.

[3] Content analysis presents relatively little ambiguity when a given unit of analysis, such as a word or the number of lines of text, is simply being counted. Questions of reliability rightfully may arise, however, in instances such as this study, in which the coding process requires the researcher to recognize the occurrence of conceptual themes (Andren, 1981; Budd, Throp & Donohew, 1967).

After a training and orientation session conducted by the author, the reliability of the coding scheme was evaluated by a senior graduate student with considerable knowledge of criminal justice topics and social research methods but with no connection to the project. I computed a coefficient of reliability according to the formula suggested by Chadwick, Bahr and Albrecht (1984): This formula is simply the number of cases coded similarly by independent raters, divided by the total number of units coded. A commonly accepted standard for this measure, the authors report, is 60 percent agreement or greater. In a case-by-case comparison of approximately a 10 percent randomly selected subsample of the assault narratives (N=72), the second coder agreed with my original assignment of thematic categories 72 percent of the time (52 cases similarly coded, divided by 72 total items compared = 72% agreement).

[4] I have resisted the temptation to categorize further the incidents grouped together under the somewhat unsatisfactory designation "unexplained." In an analysis such as this, in which ad hoc categories are derived from a content analysis of official records, it is important to state when the data contain little information that may be used by the researcher to delineate the typology further. Of course, the fact that officers report no specific proximate causes for these events may be meaningful in itself. The UNEXPLAINED incidents are not attributable by officers to an immediately evident cause or causes, but I suspect that many are related to prisoners' generalized reactions to the perceived unpleasantness of the prison environment. This interpretation is supported by further analyses (not shown) of location, severity, and weapon used. UNEXPLAINED assaults exhibit the least severity of any of the themes. Therefore, many of them are relatively trivial as to injurious outcome. Nonetheless, they may be committed because they interfere with officers' duties or otherwise create hardships for official prison representatives. In addition, analysis of the location of assaults shows that a disproportionately high number of incidents occur in the special housing units (SHUs) of the prisons in the New York sample. Of these assaults, many involve no weapon or involve trivial "weapons" such as food, water, urine, feces, or paper. Therefore, UNEXPLAINED assaults, especially those taking place in SHUs, often may serve to accom-

plish the general harassment of officers by bored and disaffected charges. Some of the incident reports in this sample suggest that elements of play or gaming behavior also may be involved, as follows:

> *Log # 29615:* Two correctional officers entered inmate's cell because he was lying on the cell floor and appeared to be unconscious. Inmate then jumped at them, kicking and swinging his fist.

Alternatively, an inmate may assault an officer for strictly instrumental reasons, such as to receive a term in the relatively safe environment of the special housing unit (see Note 5). It is also possible that officers occasionally may use the assault report as a means of exerting social control over inmates. That is, some reported assaults on staff members may be officer-initiated. Almost no research has been conducted on this form of abuse of authority, but see Marquart (1986).

In sum, the large number of incidents in this sample that fall into the UNEXPLAINED category suggests that further research might focus profitably on alternative social definitions of the situation held by participants. Many of these incidents, although defined by official reports as assaults on staff, may relate more accurately to other definitions held by the prisoners and the officers involved.

5 The single incident appearing in the "OTHER" category of Table 12.2 clearly illustrates prisoners' use of the assault on staff for utilitarian ends. The narrative abstract for this incident reads as follows:

> *Log #31652:* Inmates were returning from supper meal. Inmate stepped out of line and hit sergeant in the eye with his fist and in the back several times. Inmate later said he did this because he wanted to get out of population fast, but didn't say why.

In this case, officers were able to make sense of the incident because the involved prisoner volunteered an explanation. I suspect that other incidents in this sample (especially some of the UNEXPLAINED category) in fact may be similar instances of the instrumental use of violence.

References

Andren, G. (1981). "Reliability and Content Analysis." In K.E. Rosengren (ed.) *Advances in Content Analysis* (pp. 43-67). Beverly Hills, CA: Sage Publications.

Baumgartner, M.P. (1984). "Social Control from Below." In D. Black (ed.) *Toward a General Theory of Social Control*, Volume 1 (pp. 303-345). Orlando, FL: Academic Press.

Bowker, L.H. (1980). *Prison Victimization.* New York, NY: Elsevier.

Budd, R.W., R.K. Throp and L. Donohew (1967). *Content Analysis of Communication.* New York, NY: Macmillan.

Chadwick, B.A., H. M. Bahr and S.L. Albrecht (1984). *Social Science Research Methods.* Englewood Cliffs, NJ: Prentice-Hall.

Cheek, F.E. and M.D. Miller (1982). *Prisoners of Life: A Study of Occupational Stress Among State Corrections' Officers.* Washington, DC: American Federation of State, County, and Municipal Employees (AFSCME).

Etzioni, A. (1968). "Basic Human Needs, Alienation, and Inauthenticity." *American Sociological Review*, 33, 870-885.

Giallombardo, R. (1966). *Society of Women: A Study of a Women's Prison.* New York, NY: Wiley.

Gibbs, J.J. (1981). "Violence in Prison: Its Extent, Nature, and Consequences." In R.R. Robert and V.J. Webb (eds.) *Critical Issues in Corrections* (pp. 110-149). St. Paul, MN: West Publishing.

Goffman, E. (1961). *Asylums.* Garden City, NY: Anchor Books.

Held, B.S., D. Levine and V.D. Swartz (1979). "Interpersonal Aspects of Dangerousness." *Criminal Justice and Behavior,* 6, 49-58.

Hewitt, J.D., E.D. Poole and R.M. Regoli (1984). "Self-Reported and Observed Rule-Breaking in Prison: A Look at Disciplinary Response." *Journal of Criminal Justice,* 12, 437-447.

Irwin, J. (1970). *The Felon.* Englewood Cliffs, NJ: Prentice-Hall.

Kratcoski, P. (1988). "The Implications of Research Explaining Prison Violence and Disruption." *Federal Probation,* 52, 27-32.

Light, S.C. (1990a). "Measurement Error in Official Statistics: Prison Rule Infraction Data." *Federal Probation,* 54, 63-68.

Light, S.C. (1990b). "The Severity of Assaults on Prison Officers: A Contextual Study." *Social Science Quarterly,* 71, 267-284.

Lombardo, L.X. (1981). *Guards Imprisoned: Correctional Officers at Work.* New York, NY: Elsevier.

Marquart, J.W. (1986). "Prison Guards and the Use of Physical Coercion as a Mechanism of Prisoner Control." *Criminology,* 24, 347-366.

Martin, R. (1988). "A Comparison of Prison Riots and an Evaluation of Causative Theories." Paper presented at the annual meeting of the Academy of Criminal Justice Sciences, San Francisco.

McCleery, R.H. (1961). "The Governmental Process and Informal Social Control." In D.R. Cressey (ed.) *The Prison: Studies in Institutional Organization and Change* (pp. 149-188). New York, NY: Holt, Rinehart & Winston.

Nettler, G. (1978). *Explaining Crime.* New York, NY: McGraw-Hill.

New York State Department of Correctional Services. (1985). *Unusual Incident Report 1985.* Albany, NY: New York State Department of Correctional Services, Division of Program Planning, Research and Evaluation.

Owen, B.A. (1988). *The Reproduction of Social Control: A Study of Prison Workers at San Quentin.* New York, NY: Praeger.

Parsons, T. (1951). *Toward a General Theory of Action.* Cambridge, MA: Harvard University Press.

Poole, E.D. and R.M. Regoli (1980). "Role Stress, Custody Orientation, and Disciplinary Actions." *Criminology,* 18, 215-226.

Schafer, N.E. (1984). "Prisoner Behavior, Staff Response: Using Prison Discipline Records." Presented at the annual meeting of the Academy of Criminal Justice Sciences, Chicago.

Sykes, G. (1958). *The Society of Captives.* Princeton, NJ: Princeton University Press.

Toch, H. (1977). *Living in Prison: The Ecology of Survival.* New York, NY: The Free Press.

Toch, H. (1979). *Peacekeeping: Police, Prisons, and Violence.* Lexington, MA: Lexington Books.

Wright, K.N. (1989). "Characteristics and Ecological Correlates of Violent and Victimized Inmates." Presented at the annual meeting of the Academy of Criminal Justice Sciences, Washington, DC.

Section III

Collective Violence
and Prison Riots

While war might be viewed as the failure of diplomacy, collective violence in prison periodically brings to the attention of the public and prison administrators the continuing failure of our prison system. The late 1920s and early 1930s, the 1950s, and late 1960s and early 1970s all saw riots occurring in many prisons throughout the nation. As we head deeper into the 1990s it is imperative that we come to a deeper understanding of the complex nature of collective prison violence. We must do so to avoid adding names to stand alongside Attica and New Mexico as symbols of correctional failure.

The readings in this section provide historical, descriptive, and analytical frameworks that ground the understanding of collective violence in both everyday experience and analytically rigorous frameworks. As with other sections of this collection, the contributions of inmates, staff, and administrators to the dynamic process of which riots are the result are explored. Read in conjunction with other sections of this collection they provide a comprehensive guide to understanding the complexities, experience, and meaning of violence behind prison walls.

225

13   American Prison Riots: 1774-1991[†]

Reid H. Montgomery, Jr.

The Problem of Prison Riots in America

The significance of prison riots is becoming increasingly recognized by correctional professionals and the public. Much of this recognition probably emanates from media coverage of the more sensational riots, conjuring images of burning prisons and mutilated bodies. While these extreme consequences may not be present as often as some reports imply, riots undeniably pose continuing and serious problems that have been woefully neglected. The enormity of the problems and the dimensions of their severity deserve close examination, rather than the casual and fleeting attention often provided.

An extensive study on national prison violence was undertaken in 1973 by a federally sponsored research team coordinated by the South Carolina Department of Corrections (1973). The research documented more than 200 riots between 1900 and 1970, with riots defined as incidents involving 15 or more inmates and resulting in property damage or personal injury.

This study suggested that the following variables or conditions are associated with prison riots:

> 1. There is a higher incidence of riots in maximum security prisons. Nearly 56 percent of the reported riots took place in maximum security prisons.

---

†Reprinted by permission of the author.

2. The larger a prison's planned capacity, the higher the incidence of riots. Of prisons reporting riots in this study, 82 percent were designed for more than 300 inmates. Castle (1991) recently reported that 1 in 50 persons in the United States is under the control of correctional authorities.

3. The older a prison is, the higher the incidence of riots. Many older buildings resemble warehouses rather than places to live and work.

4. As the amount of contact time between the warden and inmates decreases, the incidence of riots increases. Of those wardens who spent more than 25 hours per month in direct contact with inmates, the incidence of riots was generally 15 percent lower.

5. In prisons with more highly educated inmates and correctional officers, there is a slightly higher incidence of riots. Nearly 50 percent of the correctional officers in riot prisons had technical school or some college education, while only 40 percent of correctional officers in nonriot prisons had reached this educational level. Almost 6 percent more inmates in riot prisons had at least eleventh- or twelfth-grade educations than inmates in nonriot prisons.

6. In medium and minimum security prisons, absence of meaningful and productive job assignments increases the incidence of riots. In those institutions that provided meaningful and productive work assignments, there were approximately 10 percent fewer riots.

7. In prisons where inmates feel that active recreational programs are inadequate, there is a 10 percent higher incidence of riots.

8. In prisons with administrative/punitive segregation facilities there is a higher incidence of riots. The greater availability of administrative segregation suggests that the prisons tend to punish for wrong behavior more frequently than it rewards inmates for correct behavior (1973:32).

Montgomery and MacDougall (1984) conducted a follow-up study on American Prison riots from 1971-1983. This study used the same definition of prison riots as the South Carolina Department of Corrections study.

There was a total of 260 riots reported from 1971 to 1983 in the United States. Of the 35 states reporting disturbances, California (n=80), Florida (n=34), Virginia (n=18), Indiana (n=16), and Georgia (n=14) reported the greatest number. A breakdown of these riots by state is shown in Table 13.1.

The majority of prison riots occurred in July (13.5%), October (11.1%), and August (13.5%). March (4.4%) and February (5.6%) claimed the lowest percentages of riots.

Table 13.1. **Distribution of American Prison Riots by State,**
              January 1971 to December 1983

State		State	
Alabama	2	Nebraska	7
Alaska	0	Nevada	6
Arizona	0	New Hampshire	1
Arkansas	0	New Jersey	1
California	80	New Mexico	3
Colorado	3	New York	2
Connecticut	3	North Carolina	3
Florida	34	North Dakota	0
Georgia	14	Ohio	0
Hawaii	2	Oklahoma	3
Idaho	3	Oregon	1
Illinois	1	Pennsylvania	0
Indiana	16	Rhode Island	2
Iowa	5	South Carolina	1
Kansas	0	South Dakota	2
Kentucky	5	Tennessee	1
Louisiana	0	Texas	12
Maine	0	Utah	1
Maryland	2	Virginia	18
Michigan	2	Washington	10
Minnesota	5	West Virginia	2
Mississippi	0	Wisconsin	3
Missouri	0	Wyoming	3
Montana	1		

Total number of prison riots = 260.
Note: Information on prison riots was not obtained from Delaware, Massachusetts, or Vermont.

The majority of riots, 36 (13.8%), occurred in 1981 followed by 32 (12.3%) in 1983. Figure 13.1 gives a distribution of American prison riots by the year.

Figure 13.1. **Distribution of American Prison Riots by Year,**
            January 1971 to December 1983

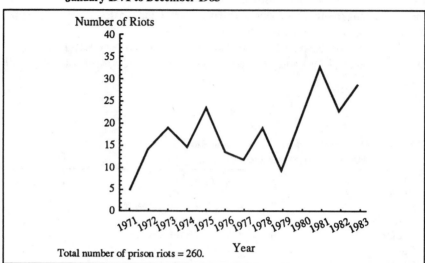

Total number of prison riots = 260.

Sixty riots (23.8%) involved 25 to 49 inmates, 39 (15.4%) involved 100 to 199 inmates, 36 (14.3%) involved 15 to 24 inmates and 34 (13.5%) involved 200 to 299 inmates. A total of 17 riots (6.7%) involved 400 to 499 inmates and one (.4%) involved 500 or more inmates. Figure 13.2 gives the distribution of prison riots by number of inmates.

Figure 13.2. **Distribution of American Prison Riots by Number of Inmates Involved,**
            January 1971 to December 1983

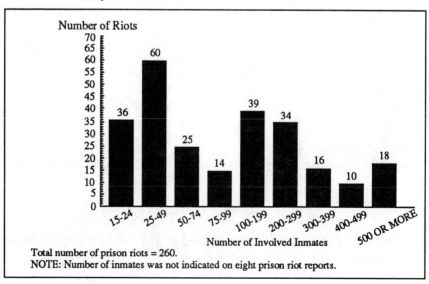

Total number of prison riots = 260.
NOTE: Number of inmates was not indicated on eight prison riot reports.

The Montgomery and MacDougall study (1984) discovered a wide variety of causes for the prison riots that occurred 1971-1983. The most reported cause was racial (34.2%). Table 13.2 shows the various causes reported.

Table 13.2. **Distribution of American Prison Riots by Reported Cause, January 1971 to December 1983**

Reported Causes	Frequency	Percent
1. Racial	88	34.241
2. Gang-related	4	1.556
3. Tension (or disagreement) between guard(s) and inmate(s)	1	0.389
4. Arson	3	1.167
5. Escape attempt	3	1.167
6. Reaction to prior incident	7	2.724
7. Living conditions (i.e., overcrowding, heat, food)	11	4.280
8. Inmates attacking staff	3	1.167
9. Alcohol-related	3	1.167
10. Power outage	5	1.946
11. Rumors	3	1.167
12. Staff attacking inmates	3	1.167
13. Demonstrations	19	7.393
14. Lockdowns or shakedowns	4	1.556
15. Protest over discipline	3	1.167
16. Insufficient classification	2	0.778
17. Dissatisfaction with rules or privileges	19	7.393
18. Disputes between inmates	4	1.556
19. Work stoppage or work-related	6	2.332
20. Inmates started disturbance by shouting, throwing objects, etc.	9	3.502
21. Revenge	2	0.778
22. Inmate unrest	2	0.778
23. Insufficient supervision or discipline	3	1.167
24. Other	15	5.837
25. No cause determined	1	0.389
26. Takeover attempt	3	1.167
27. Combination of two or more of the above including #7 and #17	11	4.280
28. Combination of two or more of the above including #1	4	1.556
29. Combination of two or more of the above	<u>16</u>	<u>6.226</u>
Total	257	100%

Total number of prison riots = 260.
Note: Cause of riot was not indicated on three prison riot reports.

In 226 (88%) of the 260 riots no hostages were involved. Table 13.3 shows the distribution of riots according to the number of hostages involved.

Table 13.3. **Distribution of American Prison Riots by Number of Hostages, January 1971 to December 1983**

Number of Hostages	Number of Riots
No hostages	226
One hostage	8
Two hostages	5
Three hostages	2
Four hostages	3
Five hostages	2
Six hostages	1
Seven hostages	1
Eleven hostages	1
Twelve hostages	2
Fourteen hostages	1
Eighteen hostages	1
Nineteen hostages	1
Twenty-two hostages	1
Thirty-two hostages	1
Fifty hostages	1
Total	257

Total number of prison riots = 260.
Note: Number of hostages was not indicated on three prison riot reports.

A total of 142 riots did not involve injuries. The study found 758 inmates were injured in the prison riots from 1971 to 1983. Table 13.4 shows the number of inmates injured and those who were killed. A total of 90 inmates were killed.

In all prison riots reported, a total of 81 staff members were injured. Seven staff members were killed or died as a result of the riot. Table 13.5 shows the distribution of injuries and deaths of staff members.

A total of 40 riots (16.6%) result in property damage ranging from $500 to $999. Twelve riots (3.3%) resulted in property damage over $1 million. Table 13.6 shows the distribution of property damage for the riots.

A total of 102 riots lasted between a few minutes and six hours. Ten riots endured between 24 and 36 hours and 11 riots lasted 48 hours or more. Table 13.7 shows the duration of prison riots.

Force or show of force was used to end 72.3 percent of the riots. Figure 13.3 illustrates how riots were ended.

Table 13.4. **Distribution of American Prison Riots by Number of Inmates Injured and Killed, January 1971 to December 1983**

Number of Riots	Number of Injured Inmates	Number of Killed Inmates
142	0	0
13	1	2
16	2	3
9	3	2
10	4	1
3	5	
7	6	2
2	7	
3	8	
4	9	
1	10	
2	11	
1	12	
3	14	
3	15	
3	16	2
1	17	
2	18	3
1	19	
1	20	
3	25	
1	26	
1	27	
1	28	8
1	30	
1	34	1
1	43	
1	50	
1	51	
1	62	
1	85	32
1	90	33
Total 241	748	89*

*On one prison riot report, number of injured inmates was not indicated, but one inmate was listed as "killed."

Total number of prison riots = 260.

Note: Number of injured inmates was not indicated on 15 prison riot reports. Number of killed inmates was not listed on nine prison riot reports.

Table 13.5. **Distribution of American Prison Riots by Number of Staff Members Injured and Killed, January 1971 to December 1983**

Number of Riots	Number of Staff Injured	Number of Staff Killed
180	0	0
20	1	1
11	2	2
10	2	3
7	4	
8	5	
2	6	1
3	7	
1	8	
2	9	
2	10	
1	12	
1	15	
Total 248	81	7

Total number of prison riots = 260.
Note: Number of injured staff members was not indicated on 12 prison riot reports.
Number of killed staff members was not indicated on 19 prison riot reports.

Table 13.6. **Distribution of American Prison Riots by Property Damage, January 1971 to December 1983**

Number of Riots	Property Damage
94	$0
40	Less than 500
2	500 to 999
16	1,000 to 4,999
7	5,000 to 9,999
6	10,000 to 14,999
0	15,000-19,999
3	20,000 to 24,999
7	25,000 to 49,999
9	50,000 to 99,999
13	100,000 to 499,999
3	500,000 to 999,999
8	1 million and over
33	Unspecified amount
Total 241	

Total number of prison riots = 260.
Note: Amount of property damage was not listed on 42 prison riot reports. However, 33 reports did mention damage and are listed as "unspecified amount" above.

Table 13.7. **Distribution of American Prison Riots by Duration of Riot, January 1971 to December 1983**

Number of Riots	Duration
26	Less than 1 hour
41	1 hr to 2 hrs 59 min
35	3 hrs to 5 hrs 59 min
19	6 hrs to 8 hrs 59 min
6	9 hrs to 11 hrs 59 min
1	12 hrs to 14 hrs 59 min
4	15 hrs to 17 hrs 59 min
1	18 hrs to 20 hrs 59 min
1	21 hrs to 23 hrs 59 min
10	24 hrs to 35 hrs 59 min
3	36 hrs to 47 hrs 59 min
<u>11</u>	48 hrs and above
Total 158	

Total number of prison riots = 260.
Note: Duration of riot was not indicated on 102 prison riot reports.

Figure 13.3. **Distribution of American Prison Riots by How Riot Was Ended, January 1971 to December 1983**

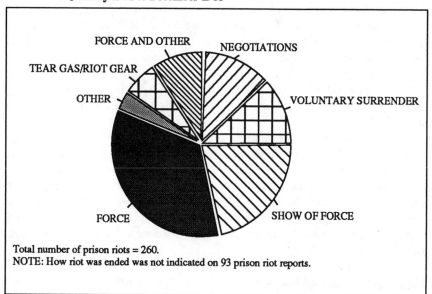

Total number of prison riots = 260.
NOTE: How riot was ended was not indicated on 93 prison riot reports.

Theories Explaining Riot Behavior

Fox (1972) theorizes that prison riots are spontaneous. He considers prisons as time bombs, detonated by spontaneous events. Fox explains his theory in five stages, four during the riot and one following the riot:

> First, there is a period of undirected violence like the exploding bomb. Second, inmate leaders tend to emerge and organize around them a group of ringleaders who determine inmate policy during the riot. Thirdly, a period of interaction with prison authority, whether by negotiation or by force, assists in identifying the alternatives available for the resolution of the riot. Fourthly, the surrender of the inmates, whether by negotiation or by force, phases out the violent event. Fifthly, and most important from the political viewpoint, the investigations and administrative changes restore order and confidence in the remaining power structure by making "constructive changes" to regain adminis- trative control and to rectify the undesirable situation that pro- duced a riot (Fox, 1971).

A prison riot occurred on July 28, 1991, at the Hawkins County Jail in Rogersville, Tennessee. The riot was reported across the United States by the Associated Press (*Albuquerque Journal*). This riot illustrates Fox's Time Bomb Theory of Riots.

The prisoners revolted during a dinner meal when milk rations ran out. Some of them went on a rampage and destroyed bunks, high security telephones and other jail equipment. The inmates gave up after five hours and no one was injured. The jail was designed for 42 inmates but 70 were housed there at the time of the riot.

The April Fool's Day prison riot took place on April 1, 1986, at the Kirkland Correctional Institution in Columbia, South Carolina. This riot is another example of Fox's Time Bomb Theory of Riots.

This riot started, according to Catoe (1986), when an inmate requested that a correctional officer bring him some Tylenol. This inmate was housed in Unit D of the Administrative Segregation Unit. This unit holds the most aggressive inmates.

Another inmate approached the correctional officer with a 16" long home- made knife when he returned. The inmate took the keys from the officer and unlocked 30 cell doors and released 32 violent inmates. The "freed" inmates, using a metal chair leg, broke the padlock on the fire exit door and moved into the recre- ational yard.

The inmates climbed over the Unit D recreation yard fence and broke open a large toolbox. Inside the box were crowbars, metal side grinders, bolt cutters, power saws, sledgehammers, and acetylene cutting equipment.

Armed with the tools, the inmates went to all general population dorms and freed another 700 inmates. A total of 22 employees were taken hostage and/or were trapped in buildings. Inmates began setting fires in the treatment building, education building, library and administrative offices in the dorm. Approximately $732,000 worth of fire damage occurred in this riot.

The riot ended when 35 members of the Reserve Emergency Platoon, armed with riot gear and shotguns loaded with birdshot, regained control of the institution. On May 13, 1986, the Richland County (SC) Grand Jury returned 36 indictments against 25 inmates for rioting, inciting to riot, and/or taking of hostages. A total of 11 inmates went on trial, and seven of them were convicted. Four were found not guilty of playing a role in the riot, and 21 others pleaded guilty (*The Columbia Record*, 1987).

Smith proposes a "conflict theory of riots." He believes that prison riots are a result of unresolved conflicts. Conflict exists, according to Smith, when one person wants another to exercise power in a specified manner but the other person, for whatever reasons, does not exercise that power. Accompanying the conflict is a conflict declaration, which is a verbal or written specification of how one person wants the other to exercise power. Four possible reactions to a conflict declaration (or possible riot), according to Smith, are the following:

> (1) the participants may bargain with each other; (2) one participant may withdraw from the conflict; (3) the participants may engage in physical combat; or (4) a third party may be called in to mediate the conflict (Smith, 1973).

Smeler (1973:36) takes a third approach to prison riots. His "theory of collective behavior" identified conditions (in sequence) that must be present to increase the probability of a riot. The six conditions or determinants of a riot are:

1. Structural conduciveness
2. Strain or tension
3. Growth or spread of a generalized belief
4. Precipitation factors
5. Mobilization and organization for action
6. Operation of mechanisms of social control.

The First Predictable Prison Riot

Dr. Geoffrey Alpert and Dr. Richard Hawkins (1989) report their views that prison riots at Oakdale, Louisiana and Atlanta, Georgia in 1987 were "predictable riots." This is based on their finding that on Friday, November 20, 1987, the U.S. State Department announced that federal inmates who were part of the Mariel boatlift of 1980 would be deported to Cuba.

Inmates at the Oakdale and Atlanta federal prisons rioted when they learned the news of the treaty with Cuba. These inmates, who rioted, were concerned about their return to Cuba. The riots ended with the help of Miami Auxiliary Bishop Agustin Roman. He acted as a negotiator with the Cuban detainees. The riots ended when the detainees were convinced that full and fair hearings would be provided for all inmates.

Strategies to Prevent Prison Riots

Recent studies have sought to measure and prioritize the factors felt or be most significant in causing riots by both inmates and staff. Further research has sought to document whether perceived problems are in fact resolved, or at least addressed, by decisionmakers.

The Collective Violence Research Project (1973:108) included nationwide surveys of inmates and correctional officers. A total of 904 inmates responded to the following question: "What do you feel is behind most riots in correctional institutions?" The responses are presented in Figure 13.4.

When asked the same question, correctional officers participating in the same study responded with similar, but not identical, concerns. A total of 704 correctional officers responded as shown in Figure 13.5.

Inmates and correctional officers place a different emphasis on factors contributing to prison riots. But a comparison of both sets of responses reveal shared perceptions on many related concerns and also pinpoints specific problem areas to be remedied.

The conclusion may be reached that both inmates and staff share many perceptions regarding factors and underlying riotous behavior (with some differences of emphasis) and that both groups are probably willing to make concessions or overcome these perceived ills. Yet, as social scientists and practitioners both can attest, unresolved requests and symbolic relief will not satisfy pressing concerns for an extended period of time or eliminate the sources of discontent. Ultimately, pressures for substantive relief reappear. These pressures, which are not amenable to resolution through improvements in communication or correctional management policies, emerge in nearly all correctional systems. When this situation occurs, even though the communication lines are open and shared perceptions of both inmates and staff are evident, solutions may be entirely dependent upon variables beyond the control of the correctional authority. For example, an outdated, poorly designed institution may have severe structural ills that can only be remedied through capital improvements and increased resources. In these situations, the only available avenue for reform may be through legislative action, or, more probably, litigation and judicial intervention.

Research into rioting reveals three important procedures that can assist in preventing riots: inmate grievance mechanisms to hear inmate complaints; the use of inmate councils to verbally communicate with prison officials; and the use of an attitudinal survey instrument for inmates to nonverbally communicate their concerns.

Figure 13.4. **Inmate Response**

Response	Percent
Guards	17
Racial Conflict	12
Lack of Communication	10
Administration	10
Frustrations	8
Conditions	8
Not Applicable	7
Unjust Treatment	5
Boredom	4
Prejudice/Favoritism	4
Aggressive Inmates	3
Inmate Power Struggle	3
Instigators	3
Food	2
Suppression	2
Parole System	2
Total	100

Figure 13.5. **Correctional Officers Response**

Response	Percent
Lack of Communication	14
Militants	12
Poor Conditions	11
Outside Influence	10
Boredom/Frustration	10
Racial Conflict	8
Food	6
Discipline	5
Incompetent Officers	4
Leniency Toward Inmates	4
Agitators	3
Overcrowded Conditions	3
Aggressive Leaders	3
Publicity/News Media	2
Program Limitation	2
Other	3
Total	100

Additionally, the incorporation of indicators of prison unrest into the training curriculum of correctional practitioners is deemed important.

A grievance mechanism according to the National Institute of Corrections (1982) is a device for resolving inmate grievances—usually through administrative means. A grievance usually involves a complaint about the substance or application of a written or unwritten policy or regulation; about the absence of a policy, regulation, or rule; or about any behavior or action directed toward an inmate. The grievance process may be handled by an ombudsman, who hears the complaints of inmates who feel aggrieved by the conditions of incarceration or the institution's management. According to the National Advisory Commission (1973), an ombudsman performs in a capacity similar to an inspector general and requires substantially the same degree of authority to stimulate changes, ameliorate problem situations, and render satisfactory responses to legitimate problems.

A second process that may be instituted to prevent prison riots is the use of inmate councils. Arrangements are typically made for representatives to discuss with other inmates their major concerns and anxieties. Inmates who have suggestions, problems, complaints, or grievances are able to communicate them to the inmate representative, who in turn relays the information to the inmate council. Ultimately, the major concerns reach the warden for resolution.

In addition, an attitudinal survey instrument may be used to measure inmate satisfaction. Research pinpoints 10 areas of major concern to inmates. They include: food, legal help, medical services, personal privacy, education, censorship, work, visitation, correctional officers, and administration. Such an instrument was administered to inmates in South Carolina at the beginning and end of a five-year period. The major findings were as follows:

1. The older the inmate, the greater his/her satisfaction in most areas.

2. The higher the institution's security classification, the greater
   the inmate dissatisfaction.

3. The longer the inmate's confinement, the greater the dissatisfaction (Montgomery, 1974).

Similarly devised instruments may be used to determine whether conditions are favorable for future prison riots or if conditions exist that merit administrative attention. An advantage of this instrument is that inmates are free to express their opinion without retribution from the administration, as anonymity is assured.

The "inmate inventory" utilizing a Likert scale of measurement, can be used to determine whether conditions exist for possible prison riots, or whether conditions exist that require inmate/administration amelioration. An advantage of this instrument is that an inmate is free to express his opinion without retribution from the administration. No identifying information is required in completing this inventory.

Rating Guide

A. When inmate marks a No. 5 blank, this indicates he is very dissatisfied with the stated item.

B. When inmate marks a No. 4 blank, this indicates he is somewhat dissatisfied with the stated item.

C. When inmate marks a No. 3 blank, this indicates he is neutral in his response to the stated item.

D. When inmate marks a No. 2 blank, this indicates he is somewhat satisfied with the stated item.

E. When inmate marks a No. 1 blank, this indicates he is very satisfied with the stated item.

Key to Inmate Inventory
(Specific Concepts)

I.

   1.

Meat

Enough : 1 : 2 : 3 : 4 : 5 : Not Enough

   2.

Forks, Spoons, Trays

Clean : 1 : 2 : 3 : 4 : 5 : Dirty

   3.

Taste of Food

Well Seasoned : 1 : 2 : 3 : 4 : 5 : Poorly Seasoned

II.

   1.

Lawyer

Available : 1 : 2 : 3 : 4 : 5 : Not Available

   2.

Law Books

Available : 1 : 2 : 3 : 4 : 5 : Not Available

   3.

Talks with Lawyers

Private : 1 : 2 : 3 : 4 : 5 : Not Private

III.

   1.

Doctors

Easy to See : 1 : 2 : 3 : 4 : 5 : Hard to See

   2.

Emergency Care

Fast : 1 : 2 : 3 : 4 : 5 : Slow

   3.

Medical Treatment

Adequate : 1 : 2 : 3 : 4 : 5 : Inadequate

IV.

1.

Ward

Safe : 1 : 2 : 3 : 4 : 5 : Dangerous

2.

Bed Linen

Clean : 1 : 2 : 3 : 4 : 5 : Dirty

3.

Sleeping Hours

Quiet : 1 : 2 : 3 : 4 : 5 : Noisy

V.

1.

Education

Good : 1 : 2 : 3 : 4 : 5 : Bad

2.

Exciting : 1 : 2 : 3 : 4 : 5 : Boring

3.

Enough : 1 : 2 : 3 : 4 : 5 : Not Enough

VI.

1.

Mail

Is Never : 1 : 2 : 3 : 4 : 5 : Is Always
Censored   Censored

2.

Adequate : 1 : 2 : 3 : 4 : 5 : Not Adequate
Postal Service   Postal Service

3.

My Mail is : 1 : 2 : 3 : 4 : 5 : My Mail is
Never Lost   Frequently Lost

VII.

1.

Work

Good : 1 : 2 : 3 : 4 : 5 : Bad

2.

Satisfying : 1 : 2 : 3 : 4 : 5 : Unsatisfying

3.

Meaningful : 1 : 2 : 3 : 4 : 5 : Meaningless

VIII.

1.

Visitation

Good : 1 : 2 : 3 : 4 : 5 : Bad

2.

Quiet : 1 : 2 : 3 : 4 : 5 : Noisy

3.

Well Organized : 1 : 2 : 3 : 4 : 5 : Poorly Organized

IX.

1.   *Most Correctional Officers*

Good : 1 : 2 : 3 : 4 : 5 : Bad

2.   Treat You As : 1 : 2 : 3 : 4 : 5 : Treat You As
                   A Person   An Inmate

3.   Always Keep : 1 : 2 : 3 : 4 : 5 : Never Keep
                  Their Word   Their Word

X.

1.   *Chance to See Warden*

Easy : 1 : 2 : 3 : 4 : 5 : Difficult

2.   *Treatment of Inmates by Institutional Administration*

Fair : 1 : 2 : 3 : 4 : 5 : Unfair

3.   *Prison Rules*

Clearly : 1 : 2 : 3 : 4 : 5 : Too General
Understood

(General Concepts)

I.

1.   *Food*

Good : 1 : 2 : 3 : 4 : 5 : Bad

2.   Hot : 1 : 2 : 3 : 4 : 5 : Cold

3.   Much : 1 : 2 : 3 : 4 : 5 : Little

II.

1.   *Legal Help*

Good : 1 : 2 : 3 : 4 : 5 : Bad

2.   Available : 1 : 2 : 3 : 4 : 5 : Not Available

3.   Needed : 1 : 2 : 3 : 4 : 5 : Not Needed

III.

1.   *Medical Services*

Good : 1 : 2 : 3 : 4 : 5 : Bad

2.   Fast : 1 : 2 : 3 : 4 : 5 : Slow

3.   Personnel Are : 1 : 2 : 3 : 4 : 5 : Personnel Are
                    Concerned   Unconcerned

IV.

1.   *Personal Privacy*

Good : 1 : 2 : 3 : 4 : 5 : Bad

2.   Available : 1 : 2 : 3 : 4 : 5 : Not Available

3.   Important : 1 : 2 : 3 : 4 : 5 : Not Important

V.

1.   *Education*

Qualified : 1 : 2 : 3 : 4 : 5 : Not Qualified

2.   *Institutional Library*

Adequate : 1 : 2 : 3 : 4 : 5 : Inadequate

3.   *Vocational Training*

Meaningful : 1 : 2 : 3 : 4 : 5 : Meaningless

VI.

1.   *Mail Service*

Fast : 1 : 2 : 3 : 4 : 5 : Slow

2.   Restricted : 1 : 2 : 3 : 4 : 5 : Unrestricted

3.   Always Sent : 1 : 2 : 3 : 4 : 5 : Never Sent

VII.

1.   *Pay*

High : 1 : 2 : 3 : 4 : 5 : Low

2.   Meaningful : 1 : 2 : 3 : 4 : 5 : Meaningless

3.   Helpful : 1 : 2 : 3 : 4 : 5 : Not Helpful

VIII.

1.   *Visiting Time*

Long Enough : 1 : 2 : 3 : 4 : 5 : Not Long Enough

2.   Visiting Room

Quiet : 1 : 2 : 3 : 4 : 5 : Noisy

3.   *Visit with Family*

Private : 1 : 2 : 3 : 4 : 5 : Not Private

```
IX.
   1.                    Most Correctional Officers
                  Consistent : 1 : 2 : 3 : 4 : 5 : Inconsistent

   2.                    Officers' Attitude Toward Inmates
                  Positive : 1 : 2 : 3 : 4 : 5 : Negative

   3.                    Treatment of Inmates by Officers
                  Fair : 1 : 2 : 3 : 4 : 5 : Unfair

X.
   1.                    Institutional Administration
                  Good : 1 : 2 : 3 : 4 : 5 : Bad

   2.                    Treat all : 1 : 2 : 3 : 4 : 5 : Play Favorites
                  Inmates Alike

   3.                    Responsive to : 1 : 2 : 3 : 4 : 5 : Not Responsive
                  Inmates' Needs                to Inmates' Needs
```

An inmate simply expressed his/her satisfaction or dissatisfaction with specific and general concepts. The "inmate inventory" can be administered by a warden to a random sample (e.g., 100 inmates) at an institution each month. If, for example, 90 percent of the inmates prove dissatisfied with medical treatment, the warden would have a definite need to investigate and correct the perceived problem area. The following instrument and rating guide, devised by one of the authors, has been tested and found successful.

Each measure serves to diffuse potentially volatile situations by channeling energies and attention in more rational and productive directions. Most importantly, these techniques are within the control of the correctional authority. By exercising them properly, some riots may be prevented, delayed, or at least contained, while the search for additional remedies continues. Current efforts are underway to incorporate riot research into the training curriculum to correctional professionals.

A course titled Containment of Prison Violence (1982:5), created by the National Institute of Corrections, trains correctional personnel to recognize signs of tension in their prisons. The following 12 general signs of tension among inmates are addressed:

1. Restlessness among inmates

2. Quiet or subdued actions of inmate groups

3. Avoidance of visual and/or verbal contact with staff

4. Increase in commissary purchases

5. Increase in the number of requests for assignment changes (both work and housing)

6. Unusual inmate gatherings

7. Increase in the number of incident reports

8. Appearance of inflammatory written material

9. Absence of inmates at popular functions

10. Increase in the number of complaints

11. Disturbances at other institutions

12. Assault upon an individual of another race or group.
    (National Institute of Corrections, 1982)

This style of training should become more prevalent as further research on riots is conducted. By operationalizing current theories and research results into job requirements and responsibilities, proper training assumes a vital role in correctional administration as an agent of both institutional stability and desired change.

A similar list of indicators of prison tension has been included in a recent publication of the American Correctional Association (1981) devoted to riots and disturbances. The indicators highlighted in this study were far more specific, numbering almost 30 behavior patterns. Again, they are intended to encompass and augment known precursors of institutional violence.

Changing Prison to Prevent Riots

The prison as we know it today is typically designed by architects prone toward duplicating the mistakes of the past. The architects according to MacDougall (1985), are influenced of course by the prison wardens, administrators, clients and politicians with traditional mind-sets. Architects in urban settings normally spend countless hours considering the mission or purpose of an envisioned structure along with the behavior of the occupants prior to finalizing the design. Considerations such as open space, privacy, colors, lighting, acoustics, aesthetics and landscaping are variables often weighed. For example, when university buildings are constructed it is fair to assume institutional purposes and the needs of those residing in its halls are reflected in the chosen design. This process, however, is not to be found in prison construction. When prisons are designed, the basic needs of privacy or a safe and therapeutic environment are forsaken. In fact, architects use yesterday's standards in modeling prisons and utilize outmoded features that inevitably neglect both occupant needs and institutional goals. As a result of such faulty planning, the monstrosities of the past are repeated, and the violence associated with such environments is magnified.

Of the many factors to be considered in correctional design, one that always surfaces as a contributor to institutional violence is that of insufficient prison space. Prisons are usually designed and built with extremely limited spacing, despite the fact that its residents are impacted by this environment every hour of the day. The tension that results from this close confinement certainly contributes to prison strife. Such an environment significantly differs from that of a community or city when instances of violence or strife occur. For instance, if a police officer or correctional officer arrives at a scene of mayhem, either may have to rely on force to quell the disturbance. But, after the dust has settled, the disputants in the city are able to retreat to their homes or separate areas with opportunities for avoiding further confrontations. In prisons, however, the combatants continuously interact and live in close proximity which engenders feelings of intense discomfort and hatred.

Another explosive factor in this formula for violence is the inmate personality. Most violence and riots take place in maximum security institutions. The populations of these prisons are inordinately composed of individuals who have experienced violence both as victims and perpetrators. Recent studies indicate that lengthier sentences and higher levels of serious criminal behaviors are creating a "society of lifers," whose institutional behaviors are becoming more and more difficult to manage. The potential of explosive violence resulting from this trend is increasingly recognized.

Boredom and the absence of meaningful employment, educational, and vocational opportunities are also contributing factors to prison violence and riots. American prisons are unable to achieve high levels of meaningful employment for their inmates. Programs aimed at preventing violence by providing beneficial and productive programs have proven difficult to institute by financially strapped administrators. For instance, it has been easy to purchase firearms or to rewire an electric chair, yet extremely difficult to fund programs aimed at changing personalities and behaviors. Building inmate self-esteem or raising educational aspirations have likewise received little or no attention. The consequence of these priorities has been the abandonment by the inmate of one of the most important control functions of an institution—HOPE. Thus, antiquated prisons packed with populations of violent individuals lacking in productive activities or programs and devoid of hope pose serious threats to institutional safety and tranquility.

Is there a way to manage American prisons with these limitations and still reduce the potential for violence? While the solutions and alternatives are not always obvious, the answer is an unequivocal, "yes." Such improvements will require major changes in the management and administration of correctional institutions, and necessitate an improved understanding of correctional dilemmas, along with the support of the community as a whole. A brief synopsis of some of the anticipated changes required to lessen institutional violence will be presented.

Correctional officials and employees who can identify, understand, and resolve problems that instigate violent behavior are critical. The fear of violence and riots can also dominate the thinking of a warden to the point where he or she assists in their occurrence. The warden whose total effort is directed toward outmoded security measures for yesterday's crisis is in fact feeding the fire of violence. There have been documented accounts of some annual mini-riots stemming from the fact that the prisoners and administrators have come to expect them as regular annual events. Dedicated workers should be able to reduce the risk of such events through proper and insightful planning, and the implementation of recognized preventive measures. Administrators must realize that the supervisory techniques successfully employed in prison industries may be utilized in other areas. They typically involve focusing attention upon the individual, properly structuring incentives toward desired goals, and the achievement of climates conducive to desirable behaviors. It may be recognized that serious personnel problems will continue to exist until employees have the requisite supervisory skills required of their positions. The recruitment, selection, and promotion of qualified professionals into positions of authority are essential for coping with increasingly violent and disruptive behaviors.

Change is also an important factor that must be understood by administrators in managing their prisons. The casual and hasty promulgation and acceptance of rule changes may cause ripples of discontent that soon increase in magnitude. Each time a new rule or policy change emerges, employees and inmates are threatened by perceptions of how their lives may be impacted. The thinking warden uses the planning process to document the need for changes and to ensure those affected that the consequences will not be adverse to their interests. Changes should be announced in advance so that potential obstacles may be identified and appropriate adjustments made.

Qualities of leadership cannot be overestimated in managing prisons. People will follow a leader who has consistent policies and follows them without bias, and is willing to bend or depart from rigid enforcement when an exception or compassionate departure is in order. In far too many institutions, those subjected to regulations feel that they may not be treated the same as the neighboring cell mate, or in a manner reasonable under the circumstances. Effective leadership can avoid such pitfalls.

Administrators must also focus their attention upon the primary client of the correctional system—the inmate. Often the administrative office structures an organizational chart of his/her employees that only reflects paid employees and not the inmates who are, in actuality, the primary actors within the system. Administrative planning must therefore consider the inmate's needs and perspectives if prison operations are to prove successful.

Communication is another concern that is frequently mentioned in corrections, but rarely understood or systematically developed within correctional operations. All too often the various segments of the organization fail to trust or talk openly with each other. This fragmentation and distrust frequently solidifies, fed by the recalcitrance of competing officers, middle managers, inmate groups, and others. Wardens must seek to avoid such stalemates by refusing to remain isolated in the front office and by actively managing, measuring, and leading the institution. A prison administrator who communicates with his entire organization and regularly deals with surfacing problems is likely to avoid prison disturbances through early detection and diffusion practices.

A topic related to improved organizational communications is that of participatory management. Within every institution, inmates and employees have a need to feel that they have some voice in institutional management. People who are allowed to participate in management decisions will take more active roles within the organization. Individuals who do not feel a part of the organization will tend to criticize and work against such systems. By effectively delegating and sharing responsibilities, workers will learn that success in institutional control will be enhanced. Often the best ideas for improvement emanate from the individuals closest to the problems. Corrections administrators must seek and adapt the proven management techniques of private industry, such as "work simplification" (utilized by Texas Instruments and Ford Motor Company) to bring an organization together.

Positive motivation is an additional concern to organizations in need of improvement. Most correctional systems are viewed by society as failures, and such perceptions can easily permeate the organizations themselves. Wardens too frequently permit the negative forces in their organization to dominate its operation and direction. The effective warden will develop programs that promote positive attitudes regarding the institution, leaving the few disgruntled members without a following. It should be remembered that prison disturbances require more than just a few followers or participants to develop into full-fledged riots.

Finally, some settlement upon a reasonable, rational goal in corrections by politicians, professionals and the public is to be encouraged if further progress toward reducing violence is desired. A working consensus on the mission to be served by prisons would obviously facilitate their operation and management. Recognizing that punishment is indeed the crux of current imprisonment policies, further attention must be devoted to the realization that past prison practices have frequently made inmates and releasees even more violent. Must correctional staff and society as a whole continue to suffer these ills? Does punishment really require the deprivation of an individual's manhood, self-worth, or even his life?

In answering the tough questions of modern prison reform, the issue of prison violence remains central. The prison of tomorrow will likely continue to seek punishment through confinement. Still, changes promoting the safety of all who reside or work within the walls of these institutions must be instituted, and the benefits will eventually extend to society as well. Among the obvious benefits should be a regulation of the senseless deaths of inmates and prison employees alike.

Futuristic Concepts

There are even futuristic concepts in terms of preventing prison riots. Ellis MacDougall (1986) suggests "...huge prisons could be built on the floor of the ocean, away from the general population and with little opportunity for prisoners to escape." It is doubtful many inmates would want to riot in this type of environment.

Robots used in prison security are another futuristic concept. Unauthorized intruders would be tracked down with infrared and ultrasonic sensors. An "ammonia sniffer" would detect the odor given off by inmates. Robots equipped with television cameras would immediately alert prison authorities to riot outbreaks. Stephens (1990) points out that electronic scanning is already possible from a van, a helicopter, an airplane, or a satellite.

Innovative thinking will be necessary to prevent future prison riots. This process is required because of the increasing rates (Epstein, 1992) of incarceration. The population of United States' jails and prisons has doubled to 1.2 million since 1980. If the United States is moving ahead as the world's leader in locking people up, then we can expect more prison riots in the future.

References

Alpert, G.P. and R. Hawkins (1989). *American Prison Systems*. Englewood Cliffs, NJ: Prentice-Hall.

American Correctional Association Committee on Riots and Disturbances. (1981). *Riots and Disturbances in Correctional Institutions*. College Park, MD: American Correctional Association.

Castle, M.N. (1991). "Alternative Sentencing: Selling it to the Public." *National Institute of Justice*. Washington, DC: U.S. Department of Justice.

Catoe, W.D. and J.L. Harvey (1986). *A Review of the Kirkland Correctional Institution Disturbance on April 1, 1986*. Columbia, SC: South Carolina Department of Corrections.

Epstein, A. (1982). "U.S. Jails Overflowing, But Crime Rate Steady." *The Columbia Recorder*. Washington Bureau News Story.

Fox, V. (1971). "Why Prisoners Riot." *Federal Probation*, 35, 9-14.

Fox, V. (1972). "Prison Riots in a Democratic Society." *Police*, 16, 33-41.

MacDougall, E. (1985). Foreword. *Prison Violence in America*. First Edition. Cincinnati, OH: Anderson Publishing Co.

MacDougall, E. and R. Montgomery (1986). "Curing Criminals." *The Futurist*, pp. 36-37.

Mahan, S. (1985). "An 'Orgy of Brutality' at Attica and the 'Killing Ground' at Santa Fe: A Comparison of Prison Riots." *Prison Violence in America*. First Edition. Cincinnati, OH: Anderson Publishing Co.

"Milk Shortage Sparks Prison Rampage." (1991). *Albuquerque Journal*, July 28, p. A13.

Montgomery, R. (1974). *A Measurement of Inmate Satisfaction/Dissatisfaction in Selected South Carolina Correctional Institutions*. Ph.D. dissertation, University of South Carolina.

Montgomery, R. and E. MacDougall (1984). *American Prison Riots 1971-1983*. (Monograph). Columbia, SC: University of South Carolina (Graphics by Ms. Brenda Moore).

Morris, R. (1983). *The Devil's Butcher Shop: The New Mexico Prison Uprising*. New York, NY: Franklin Watts Publishing Company.

National Advisory Commission of Criminal Justice Standards and Goals, U.S. Department of Justice (1973). *Corrections*, Washington, DC: U.S. Government Printing Office.

National Institute of Corrections, U.S. Department of Justice (1982). *Containment of Prison Violence*. Washington, DC: U.S. Government Printing Office.

"Prison Riot Prosecution Complete." (1987). *The Columbia Record Newspaper* (January).

Smeler, N. (1973). "The Theory of Collective Behavior." *Collective Violence in Correctional Institutions: A Search for Causes*. Columbia, SC: State Printing Company.

Smith, A. (1973). "The Conflict Theory of Riots." In South Carolina Department of Corrections (Collective Violence Research Project), *Collective Violence in Correctional Institutions: A Search for Causes*. Columbia, SC: State Printing Company.

Stephens, G. (1990). "High-Tech Crime." *The Futurist*, pp. 20-25.

Useem, B. and P. Kimball (1989). *States of Siege (U.S. Prison Riots, 1971-1986)*. New York, NY: Oxford University Press.

14

An "Orgy of Brutality" at Attica and the "Killing Ground" at Santa Fe: A Comparison of Prison Riots[†][††]

Sue Mahan

The first prison riot occurred in the United States in 1774 before our country had even declared its independence. Prison violence has erupted with some frequency ever since. During the past decade, two of the bloodiest and most violent riots in American prison history occurred in September 1971, at the Attica State Correctional Facility in New York; and in February 1980, at the Penitentiary of New Mexico in Santa Fe. Investigative reports conducted by each of the respective states uncovered striking similarities between the two uprisings, and that common elements existed at all levels in the prison systems.

Collective Violence in Correctional Settings

Despite the frequency with which prisons in the United States have exploded into riots, there is little in the way of accumulated knowledge about predicting or preventing the violence. Due to their spontaneous and dangerous nature, observation and experimental research about them has been necessarily limited. There has been more study of prison violence in a general sense, including homosexual rape and "garden variety" assaults (Cohen et al., 1976; Goldstein, 1975). Much less is known about actual riots, by which is meant a seizure of control over part or all of the prison and presentation of demands that are said to represent a large group of prisoners.

---

†Reprinted by permission of the author.
††The title of this chapter and material about Attica came from the following: The Select Committee on Crime (1971); The New York State Special Commission on Attica (1972); and Wicker (1975). The title and material about Santa Fe came from the following: *The Albuquerque Journal and Tribune* (1980); Serrill and Katel (1980); Attorney General, New Mexico (1980).

Thus far, no well-defined stages for prison riots have been established to explain how they develop. Although Fox and others (Killinger et al., 1979:158; Desroches, 1974) have listed patterns typical of prison riots, they are quite general and do not lead to prediction. The three predisposing, long-term causes of riots have also been explained only in a general way: physical and emotional deprivations, lack of public attention to prisoners' needs, and conflict over administration (Wilsnack, 1976:69).

Actual "triggering" of precipitating causes have been explained simply as having a sense of "urgency" and calling forth an explosive, spontaneous eruption (Killinger et al., 1979:158). Although the need for independent inquiries to study the nature of riots and to examine the evidence about them has been frequently mentioned (Zellick, 1978), the commissions appointed to study actual riots are usually political in nature and official reports about them suffer from this bias.

In some investigations about prison violence, corrections officials have been called to account. It has been shown that prison administrations play a large part in making violence is more likely by their management (Morris & Hawkins, 1974). Studies show violence more likely in settings of chronic, long-term crowding and idleness, with frequent changes in rules and personnel (Bidna, 1975). Tighter, repressive security also has been shown to contribute to higher prison fatality rates (McCain & Paulus, 1980).

On the other hand, prison management that emphasizes participation and accountability of prisoners and staff, that takes prisoners' complaints and nonviolent resistance seriously, and that stresses security through the use of defensible space throughout the entire facility, has managed to lower the rates of violence (Wilsnack, 1976:72). In addition, the involvement of community resources and other systems of various kinds in the corrections process is believed to make violence less likely (Douglas, 1969).

Explanations of riots cannot be directed only at the official level. Studies of riots must investigate the setting, the situation, the environment of the violence, but they must also be directed toward the individuals involved. Much of the violence that is found in prisons is a reflection of street violence common enough in other social settings besides prisons. It is the collectivized nature of the violence that explodes in riots which makes them so frightening and difficult to explain and control.

Many of the reports about riots identify the correctional officers as the key figures (Gould, 1974; Stotland, 1976). Frequently, security lapses, mistakes, and errors in judgment on the part of line officers are said to make riots possible. Guards are called the "weak links" when uprisings are not contained and full-scale riots develop (Crough, 1980).

By minimizing hostile confrontations between prisoners and themselves, guards can also lower the incidence of violence. Prison guards have been found to view their world of work in terms of "we/they," and to promote custody and security over treatment. It is also clear that corrections officers are likely to be stigmatized by what is frequently looked on as "dirty work," and often find themselves locked in by bureaucratic policy, just as are the prisoners (Jacobs & Retsky, 1977:49-65). Rarely in riot studies have hostages been considered or their roles as pawns uncovered (Crelinsten & Szabo, 1979).

A great deal of what has been written about researching riots is devoted to prisoners and their personalities. Prison violence is more likely for young prisoners with a lot of time to serve and nothing left to lose (Patrick et al., 1979). Prison violence is more likely when the convict culture has been displaced due to administrative policy. Without the stability of relationships which the convict code promotes, struggles for power are likely sources for the friction which sparks eruptions of violence.

It is unlikely that one single, uniting motive impels those who participate in riots. However, the need to prove manhood and to demonstrate masculinity after repeated threats to self-esteem is frequently mentioned as an underlying motive in riots (Toch, 1976:54). In addition, inability of prisoners to control privacy and space induces stress (Clements, 1979). Reactions to the stress of crowding may include suspicion, isolation, physical disease, and intense violence.

The results of such studies of collective violence in correctional settings include clear proposals for reform (Carlson, 1976:123). In fact, community alternatives to penal institutions that breed criminality and violence have been proposed repeatedly for over 100 years (Travis, Schwartz & Clear, 1992). Knowledge of the destructive nature of the very structure of the prison continues to accumulate (Zimbardo, 1971), and structural changes that would limit violence and curtail the destructive potential of prisons have been rare indeed (Irwin, 1980).

Comparison of Two Notorious Riots

Prison riots are dramatic examples of the potential for destruction present in the structural arrangements of prisons. Two notorious prison riots make fruitful subjects for study of the real, but seldom considered, structural and social arrangements found in prisons. From studying these riots, it is possible to determine common processes and similar arrangements that were integral to the upheavals that took place.

Public attention was captured by the grisly events at Attica and Santa Fe, and for a short time at least, media coverage was focused on the plight of prisoners. Forty-three men died in the riot at Attica, making it the most deadly riot in United States history. The riot at the New Mexico State Penitentiary resulted in 33 deaths. Yet it was far more costly than Attica in terms of millions of dollars in destruction to facilities. The directly attributable cost of the event reached almost exactly $1 million an hour; the riot lasted 36 hours.

Differences in historical situations during 1971, the year of the Attica riot, and 1980, when the Santa Fe event took place, have been noted. Dramatic differences in the ways the riots took place have come to obscure many striking similarities that played an important part in these revolts. The common elements in the two riots introduce important considerations for change. These are not superficial changes, though. A redirection of the penal system is called for. If prison riots continue to increase in intensity and frequency, the need to consider these common elements, and the changes called for, grows desperate.

Differences Between the Riots

Reports about the riots at Santa Fe and Attica show important similarities between the two events. But first the differences. At Santa Fe, the deaths were all murders of prisoners by other prisoners. This contrasts with Attica, where four deaths were caused by prisoners and 39 others were killed by state officers. The Attica prisoners were mostly Black; the majority of prisoners at Santa Fe were Chicano.*

Another major difference was the type of leadership that arose among prisoners. At Attica, an overarching leadership group was formed, but decisions were made by the entire group of rioters. At Santa Fe, there was no overarching leadership; prisoners formed bands and cliques and decisions were made on a personal basis.

The rioters at Attica were involved in a type of political consciousness that was also different from that found among inmates at Santa Fe. The Black Muslims were an important force at Attica. They are credited with keeping order and control during the long, stressful days of the takeover. Identification with Black political movements on the outside also helped to unite prisoners inside Attica.

The situation at Santa Fe nine years later showed conditions that were considerably different. Outside loyalties and identifications for prisoners were limited to neighborhood ties. Inside the prison, prisoners banded together in groups of "homeboys" who came together because of similar experiences and backgrounds, not political ideals. There was also no parallel to the Black Muslim influence at Santa Fe, although the Roman Catholic tradition was strong. The chapel was one of the few areas of the prison left undamaged after the smoke from the riot cleared. The Catholic Bishop in Santa Fe took this as a sign that the men had not lost faith. But the rest of the mayhem and devastation at Santa Fe demonstrates that their faith had little influence on keeping order and control.

Other differences between the riots are more directly related. The record shows that during the riot both prisoners and state officials at Santa Fe were considering the events that had taken place at Attica nine years before, and their actions were in part a result of their understanding of what happened there.

At Attica, Governor Rockefeller was strongly criticized because he refused to become personally involved in the events connected with the riot. At Santa Fe, Governor King was openly active in handling the affair.

In Attica, an observer's committee was involved in the negotiations. There was confusion about authority, conflicting priorities, communications breakdowns,

---

*At Santa Fe, the population of prisoners consisted of approximately 58 percent Chicano, 30 percent White, 10 percent Black, and 1.5 percent American Indian. At Attica, the breakdown was 55 percent Black, 36 percent White, 8.5 percent Puerto Rican, and 5 percent American Indian.

and open disputes among committee members. Negotiations at Santa Fe were handled directly by corrections officials.

The prisoners at Attica insisted on open negotiations in front of the entire group. They argued for a set of demands which represented all those held there. No meaningful change came about as a result of these negotiations, and 39 lives were lost in spite of them. During the Santa Fe riot, prisoner's negotiations were mostly in their own self-interest. Those involved changed from one meeting to the next as prisoners traded the lives of hostages for personal benefits. Prisoners' concerted efforts at Santa Fe were instead directed toward destroying the prison itself.

Sympathetic demonstrators also had the events of Attica in mind while they kept a vigil outside the prison at Santa Fe. There were large signs as a testament to the fear of a state massacre reading: "Remember, No More Attica." It is clear that the lessons that were learned from the massacre at Attica were limited. Though the riot in 1971 was studied in minute detail and from multiple perspectives, nine years later, another riot with the same awesome power and potential for destruction was not prevented by what was learned at Attica. Structural arrangements remained the same.

Similarities in the Riots

The feelings expressed by prisoners at Attica and at Santa Fe were remarkably similar. At Attica, one of the leaders brought a great stir from the rest of the rioters when he announced to the group: "We don't want to rule; we want to live. But if we cannot live like people, let us at least try to die like men." At Santa Fe, a prisoner's radio broadcast being monitored was reported: "I'm up to my neck in this. If I'm going to die, I'm going to die like a man."

Explanations of the riots have centered around fiscal and budgetary matters, particularly overcrowding, which was critical in the riots that ensued at Santa Fe and Attica. Poor food and lack of adequate facilities for mental or physical health contribute to prison riots. However, the basic problems are structural. Overcrowding and inadequate facilities were symptomatic of them. From reports about what transpired at Attica and Santa Fe, quotes from public officials and prisoners emphasize the deep-seated conflicts that are acted out in hostage-taking and riots.

> William Ciuros, Correctional Officer at Attica: "We are dealing with the misfits of society."

> Warden Mancusi, Attica: "You are dealing with a highly selected individual who has been a failure from all of society."

> Perry Ford, Inmate at Attica. "I have been beaten in institutions all my life" [Select Committee on Crime, 1971].

> Authorities have taken a hands off attitude (at Santa Fe), "The prisoners are only hurting themselves." Inmate radio spokesman, Santa Fe (although scores of dead were already reported): "You make one funny move into the prison and we're going to start killing people...if you don't meet our demands, it's not going to be just inmates we're going to kill...I'm serious. My brother is serious. We have to live in here. Treat us like human beings" [*Albuquerque Journal and Tribune*, 1980].

Life inside prisons on a day-to-day basis is not unlike wartime situations where a truce has been called. Riots are the inevitable battles that ensue when two opposing sides confront one another regularly (Fox, 1973).

Prisoners proved themselves to be desperate to have their complaints made public in both riots. There was a great interest in media coverage of the events and in having prison problems brought to public attention by the press. Prisoners in both riots asked for media coverage as their first negotiated demand.

Among their complaints, prisoners made frequent mention of harassment and ill treatment at the hands of corrections officers before the riots. In both prisons, these complaints were subsequently borne out when later investigations uncovered documented cases of brutality and harsh and inhuman disciplinary procedures against prisoners.

After the retaking of Attica, witnesses reported extreme cases of brutality and torture of men falsely accused of being "ringleaders." Other concerted harassment and injury was documented, such as prisoners forced through gauntlets and beaten with sticks and clubs. There are no reports of disciplinary actions against those officers involved.

Rumors of brutality followed the riot at Santa Fe as well. Investigations uncovered the routine use of strip cells for discipline, and that in extreme cases, body casts were applied to restrain emotionally disturbed prisoners. Numerous inquiries eventually linked the deputy warden himself to cases of harassment and cruelty. He was eventually removed from his post at the prison and given a management position for the state corrections system.

The situation for inmates at both prisons was hopelessly similar, especially overcrowding. According to records, the capacity of Santa Fe was set at 900, but there were 1,136 prisoners held there at the beginning of the riot. The capacity of Attica was 1,200, but approximately 2,225 were being held there when the riot broke out.

Overcrowding, when added to other conditions present at Attica and Santa Fe, led to particularly volatile situations. In both cases, the prisoners were young. As a group, their average age was under 28. In 1971 and in 1980, prisoners were called more troublesome, more impatient, and more prone to violence than prisoners incarcerated a decade before. Due to changes in sentencing laws prior to both riots, prisoners were serving longer sentences than those who had been sentenced for the same crimes prior to the change in the law. Along with great disparity of sentences, there was little diversification or separation of prisoners. Without a variety of facilities for various kinds of prisoners, controls and security for all prisons were much more restrictive than was necessary for most of them.

Neither Attica nor Santa Fe included adequate provisions for the classification and handling of diverse prisoners. At the time of the riot, 90 percent of the prisoners incarcerated in the New York state system of corrections were in maximum security. There were only educational programs for 300 of the more than 2,000 prisoners held at Attica, although approximately 1,720 (86%) of those held there had no high school diploma.

In New Mexico nine years later, the situation at the time of the riot was remarkably similar. Opportunities for education and training were available to only a few. At the same time, men serving 60-day, presentence evaluation terms were housed in the same dormitories with those sentenced for life.

In both prisons, the majority of prisoners were idle for most of the time. The average prisoner at Attica served 16 to 23 hours per day in his cell. At Santa Fe, more than one-third of the prisoners were idle all day; many more were occupied for only a few hours a day. Doing time for most of the men held at Santa Fe and Attica meant doing nothing at all.

In both prisons, there were few meaningful activities for the prisoners. There were few constructive ways in which prisoners could earn the respect or cooperation of their fellows. Leadership positions became dependent on violence rather than granting favors or access to resources. Without ways of gaining status that were constructive or positively rewarding, status at Attica and Santa Fe became a matter of violence, and cooperation was often coerced using fear. In such settings, antagonisms exist on two levels, prisoner to officer and prisoner to prisoner.

Murders of prisoners by prisoners during the two riots may be seen as retaliations, reprisals, and warnings for traitors to the war effort. The riot at Santa Fe became a killing ground for those involved in power struggles seeking status through violence. There were three such reprisal killings at Attica, but details about them are scarce. It was reported that the three prisoners were killed as traitors. Rumors about the deaths included the same extremes of vengeance that characterized the murders of prisoners at Santa Fe.

Rumors and warnings of riots persisted in both prisons for months prior to the actual explosion. At Attica, a day of silence during August presaged the revolt in September. At Santa Fe, the escape of 11 convicts in December demonstrated prisoner solidarity and frustration that erupted in mass action in February.

Corrections officers at Attica had noticed an increase in tensions among prisoners housed in Cell Block D for some time prior to their beginning the riot. Dormitory E-2 at Santa Fe was also known by officers be beset with tension and difficult to manage. In fact, E-2 was the location of the initial incident which began the riot. In spite of the tensions and friction building up in these areas, precautions taken by officers actually sparked the riots. At Attica, prisoners refused to return to their cells when officers ordered them to go there for disciplinary reasons. This conflict triggered the riot. At Santa Fe, extra officers were called on to assist in closing down dormitory E-2 for the night. One of these officers left a door open, and waiting prisoners took advantage of the opportunity to begin the takeover.

At both Attica and Santa Fe, the lack of training and preparation of the guards for their positions was made a major issue in the charges following the riots. In both prisons, the officers were untrained in handling prison violence and were seldom trained in any way, other than "on the job," for all aspects of their work.

In both cases there was a lack of emergency preparation on the part of corrections officials. At Attica, lack of a well-communicated plan to take back the institution led to 39 deaths. The fear and confusion of the officers involved and their emotional arousal turned the assault on the prison into an orgy of brutality. Corrections officials at Santa Fe also demonstrated lack of preparation for the riot. Because of security lapses, prisoners were able to gain control of the entire facility in less than one-half hour. Officials might have regained the prison right away except that they did not have a complete set of keys for the exits.

When major prison riots occur, interested parties often look for the precipitating cause which made it possible for the riot to spread and swell and gain momentum. Precipitating or "triggering" causes for the two riots were also similar. At Attica, a defective weld gave way under the pressures of prisoners forcing themselves against an iron gate. This opened the way into "Times Square" and access into all the cell blocks of the prison. At Santa Fe, the iron mesh enclosing the "Control Center" had been recently replaced by security glass. The $1^3/_{16}$" glass broke easily when prisoners pounded on it with a fire extinguisher, allowing access to the locking devices of the prison. It is difficult to assess the real importance of such precipitating factors. What is clear is the dangerous folly of depending on mechanisms for security rather than maintaining an alert, well-trained staff, or giving attention to the concerns of those prisoners who are to be held secure.

Administrators of the state department of corrections in New York and New Mexico were involved in the development of unstable and inconsistent policy for the prisons. Struggles for power between various levels of the bureaucratic state systems led to discrepancies and rising and lowering expectations on the part of the prisoners held in the prisons of the two states.

Inconsistent approaches to corrections were combined with changes in personnel in the two state systems just prior to both riots. Changes in administration of the system of corrections in New York and the appointment of a new commissioner led to the promise of reform in January of 1971. By September, seven months later, prisoners were convinced the new commissioner was a "cop out" and that real change was blocked by the warden. In the New Mexico system, the Secretary of Corrections resigned in late 1979 and a new appointee had not yet taken office at the time of the riot. At the prison, a new warden had also served only seven months prior to the riot. After the trial period, expectations for the new warden had fallen. He was believed to have sold out to the entrenched prison management clique known as the "Santa Fe Five." In both prisons, there was a conflict over the security goals of the corrections officers and the reform goals of the incoming administration, with security goals winning the most emphasis in the running of the prison.

At the level of involvement of state government in the two corrections systems, lack of concern and political expediency were stamped on the state corrections system in New York and New Mexico. In both states, legislators had demonstrated their insensitivity to criminal justice needs by their failure to legislate adequate money. In addition, changes in sentencing laws in both New York and New Mexico contributed to wide disparity of sentences, discontent, and feelings of betrayal on the part of the prisoners. The most important grievance listed by prisoners in both Attica and Santa Fe had to do with the courts and the parole board. Resentment and frustration leading to hostility and anger at obvious, arbitrary discretion and disparity in the treatment of prisoners was an overriding concern at the time of both riots.

Similarities between the structural situations at Attica and Santa Fe exist on five important levels:

1. Prisoners felt they were not being treated as human beings.

2. Line officers were unprepared; plans and regulations at the prisons were developed without their input.

3. Administrators lacked consistency. There was no stability in developing policy and goals for the system.

4. Legislators were insensitive to the needs of the penal system and the impact of statutes on the lives of officers and prisoners.

5. The public was unconcerned about the system of corrections in their states, and media attention was focused on the prison only when a drastic event took place.

These common elements in the two prison riots are indicative of the structural changes that are necessary if prevention of future devastating prison riots is to be realized.

At the level of the individual prisoner, he cannot be expected to act in a just and lawful way in a system where he is the recipient of brutality and unlawful treatment. Nor will he be likely to develop a sense of self-worth or the impetus for positive social action in a system where he is automatically presumed a failure and a misfit by his status.

At the next level, that of the guard or line officer, these individuals cannot be expected to maintain security for a system they do not understand and about which they have no say. Guards must be trained to promote their common interest, along with inmates, in working together to promote harmony for all.

Corrections officials cannot be expected to take an active part in riot prevention if political interests and conflict over bureaucratic power distracts them from their responsibilities for the prisoners and staff. Administrative consistency and fairness are essential for preventing riots, but they cannot coexist in a system where expediency and disagreement are the hallmarks of administrative policy.

On the level of state government, lawmakers who are politicians point out the lack of constituency of prisoners and prison officials. Although funding for prisons may be an unpopular issue, the costs of riots are often far greater than the cost of restructuring the system. Indeed, it is impossible to fully calculate the amount of damage done by this type of violence. In addition, irresponsible laws that result in overcrowding, and disparity in the treatment of prisoners both add to the likelihood of riots. Legislators must be held responsible for the part played in riots by their action, or lack of it, along with officials, guards, and prisoners.

The final level of responsibility for prison riots rests with the public. Prisoners at Attica and Santa Fe were driven to desperate lengths in order to achieve recognition and the sense of being relevant to society. Prisoners can be expected to use such drastic measures unless they have access to structural means of achieving recognition and relevance. Public attention to prisoners and interest in prisons is an important and crucial element in preventing future Atticas and Santa Fes throughout the United States.

During both riots, prisoners came to believe the only way to prove their humanity was by dying. At Attica: "Let us at least try to die like men." At Santa Fe: "If I'm going to die, I'm going to die like a man." They saw nothing short of death that would regain their individuality and give them an identity. Prison reform to prevent riots must be directed toward this basic level, as well as toward staff changes, administrative changes, legislative changes, and changes in public attention. The highest priority in prison reform must be given to changing those structures in prison which so alienate and isolate prisoners that they cease to be considered as humans. "We have to live here. Treat us like human beings."

References

Albuquerque Journal and Tribune [New Mexico] (1980). Feb. 3 - June 15.

Attorney General of New Mexico. (1980). Report of the Attorney General on the February 2 and 3, 1980 Riot at the Penitentiary of New Mexico. Santa Fe, NM: Office of the Attorney General of New Mexico.

Bidna, H. (1975). "Effects of Increased Security on Prison Violence." *Journal of Criminal Justice*, 3, (1):33-46.

Carlson, R. (1976). *The Dilemmas of Corrections*. Lexington, MA: D.C. Heath.

Cohen, A., G. Cole and R. Bailey (1976). *Prison Violence*. Lexington, MA: D.C. Heath.

Crelinsten R. and D. Szabo (1979). *Hostage Taking*. Lexington, MA: D.C. Heath.

Crouch, B. (1980). *Keepers: Prison Guards and Contemporary Corrections.* Springfield, IL: Charles C Thomas.

Desroches, F. (1974). "Patterns in Prison Riots." *Canadian Journal of Criminology and Corrections,* 5, (2):332-351.

Douglas, S. (1969). "Prison Riot: Assaulters vs. Defenders." *Archives of General Psychiatry,* 21, (3):359-362.

Fox, V. (1973). "Why Prisoners Riot." In G. Killinger and P. Cromwell (eds.) *Penology: The Evolution of Corrections in America* (pp. 319-330). St. Paul, MN: West Publishing Co.

Goldstein, J. (1975). *Aggression and Crimes of Violence.* New York, NY: Oxford University Press.

Gould, R. (1974). "The Officer Inmate Relationship: Its Role in the Attica Rebellion." *Bulletin of the American Academy of Psychiatry and the Law,* 2, (1):34-35.

Irwin, J. (1979). "The Convict World." In G. Killinger et al. (eds.) *Penology: The Evolution of Corrections in America.* Second Edition (pp. 126-138). St. Paul, MN: West Publishing.

Irwin, J. (1980). *Prisons in Turmoil.* Boston, MA: Little, Brown.

Jacobs, J. and H. Retsky (1977). "Prison Guard." In R. Leger and J. Stratton (eds.) *The Sociology of Corrections* (pp. 49-64). New York, NY: John Wiley.

Killinger, G., P. Cromwell and J. Wood (1979). *Penology: The Evolution of Corrections in America.* Second Edition. St. Paul, MN: West Publishing Co.

McCain, G. and P. Paulus (1980). *Effect of Prison Crowding on Inmate Behavior.* Washington, DC: LESS, U.S. Department of Justice.

Morris, N. and G. Hawkins (1974). "Attica Revisited: The Prospect for Prison Reform." *Psychiatric Annals,* 4 (3):21-42.

New York State Special Commission on Attica. (1972). *Attica.* New York, NY: Bantam Books.

Patrick, J., J. Mabli, C. Holley and J. Walls (1979). "Age and Prison Violence." *Criminal Justice and Behavior,* 6, (2):175-186.

Select Committee on Crime. (1979). *Prisons in Turmoil.* Washington, DC: 92nd Congress, Nov. 29-Dec. 3.

Serill, M. and P. Katel (1980). "New Mexico: The Anatomy of a Riot." *Corrections Magazine,* 6, (2):6-24.

Stotland, E. (1976). "Self-Esteem and Violence by Guards and State Troopers at Attica." *Criminal Justice and Behavior,* 3, (1):85-96.

Toch, H. (1976). "A Psychological View of Prison." In A. Cohen et al. (eds.) *Prison Violence* (pp. 43-60). Lexington, MA: D.C. Heath.

Travis, L., III, M. Schwartz and T. Clear (1992). *Corrections: An Issues Approach.* Third Edition. Cincinnati, OH: Anderson Publishing Co.

Wicker, T. (1975). *A Time to Die.* New York, NY: Quadrangle/New York Times Books.

Wilsnack, R. (1976). "Explaining Collective Violence in Prisons." In A. Cohen et al. (eds.) *Prison Violence* (pp. 61-74). Lexington, MA: D.C. Heath.

Zellick, G. (1978). "The Hull Prison Riot." *British Journal of Criminology*, 18, (1):75-78.

Zimbardo, P. (1972). "Pathology of Imprisonment." In M. Schwartz et al. (eds.) *Corrections: An Issues Approach* (pp. 84-86). Cincinnati, OH: Anderson Publishing Co.

15

Judicial Reform and Prisoner Control: The Impact of *Ruiz v. Estelle* on a Texas Penitentiary[†][††]

James W. Marquart & Ben M. Crouch

In the 1960s, a "due-process revolution" occurred in which the judiciary addressed and attempted to remedy aspects of many of this society's institutional ills. Almost since the start of this revolution jails and prisons have been an important focus of judicial attention. In general, the courts have expanded the constitutional rights of prisoners at the expense of the so-called "hands-off" doctrine (Calhoun, 1977; Jacobs, 1980). That is, the courts have rejected the traditional view that prisoners were socially "dead" and managed at the discretion of the prison staff. Courts for the past 15 years have responded sympathetically to prisoners' grievances and have issued as well as administered many rulings forcing prison organizations to modify or cease numerous institutional policies and procedures. To illustrate, as of December 1983, 30 state prison systems were operating under court order or consent decrees designed to alleviate prison overcrowding (U.S. Department of Justice, 1984). This change in court posture has made possible the fuller integration of the penitentiary within the central institutional and value systems of the society (Shils, 1975:93; Jacobs, 1977).

Despite the proliferation of "prisoner rights" cases, there exists relatively little empirical research on the impact of judicially mandated reforms on prison structures and operations. The sociology of confinement literature typically describes court-ordered reforms as part of or ancillary to changes wrought by shifts in prison

†Reprinted from *Law and Society Review*, Vol. 19:4. Reprinted by permission of the Law and Society Association.
††This is a revised version of a paper delivered at the annual meeting of the Southern Sociological Society, Charlotte, April 1985. Support for this research was provided by the National Science Foundation Program in Law and Social Science (SES-8410925). The assistance of two anonymous referees and Julian B. Roebuck, Frank Cullen, Bruce Jackson, and David Demo in reading earlier drafts is gratefully acknowledged. We are also especially grateful to Richard O. Lempert for his critical comments and editorial suggestions.

administration (Carroll, 1974; Jacobs, 1977; Colvin, 1982), goals (Carroll, 1974; Stastny & Tyrauner, 1982), or inmate populations (Irwin, 1980; Crouch, 1980). When researchers have directly examined court-ordered reforms (e.g., Kimball & Newman, 1968; *UCLA Law Review*, 1973; Champagne & Haas, 1976; Turner, 1979), their analyses have been narrowly focused and do not assess the long-term effects of intervention on the prison community. Because systematic empirical research is lacking, we have only some general ideas about what happens in prisons when courts intervene and alter an established order. Jacobs (1980) summarizes those general ideas in a recent article and notes that court-ordered reforms often lead to a demoralized staff, a new generation of prison administrators, a bureaucratic prison organization, a redistribution of power within the prison, and a politicized and often factionalized inmate society.

The most general observation made about the consequences of judicial intervention has been that prisons have become increasingly bureaucratized (Jacobs, 1977; Turner, 1979). Authority in prisons is no longer unrestricted but based instead on formal procedures and policies. The days of the autonomous "big house" warden are history. Bureaucratization has also affected prisoner control. The harsh disciplinary measures of the past have been replaced with a legalistic due-process model, similar, in some respects, to hearing procedures in non-prison settings. We do not know, however, how the bureaucratization of prisons and prisoner control that judicial intervention has engendered has affected day-to-day life within the prison community. We need to know what transpires within prisons after court-ordered reforms have been implemented by the administrators. In particular, we need to know more about the consequences of court-ordered reforms for prison control systems and for relationships among the parties—inmates, guards, and administrators—on whom control ultimately depends.

This chapter is a case study and institutional analysis that examines the impact of legal intervention on a Texas penitentiary—the Eastham Unit. This study, unlike many legal impact studies, is not primarily concerned with the "gap" question—whether compliance has been achieved. Rather, it analyzes the institutional implications of a judicial remedy that has been implemented in good faith. The case in question is *Ruiz v. Estelle* (1980), a massive class action suit against the Texas Department of Corrections (TDC) in which a federal district judge ordered TDC to make wholesale organizational changes (e.g., in health care, overcrowding, inmate housing). Our focus is on a central feature of *Ruiz* that ordered TDC and Eastham to abandon certain official and unofficial methods of prisoner control. Our objective is to analyze the prisoner control structure at Eastham prior to this case, the specific changes that were ordered, and how these changes affected the prison community. In the last section, we contrast several organizational elements of the old order with the emerging bureaucratic-legal order and discuss the implications of this shift in structure and philosophy for daily control. In effect, this analysis examines a penitentiary before, during, and after the implementation of a legal reform.

Setting and Method Study

The research site was the Eastham Unit of the Texas penal system. Eastham is a large, maximum security institution located on 14,000 acres of farmland, which housed, in 1981, nearly 3,000 inmates (47% black, 36% white, 17% Hispanic). Inmates assigned to this prison were classified by the Texas Department of Corrections as recidivists over the age of 25, all of whom had been in prison (excluding juvenile institutions) three or more times. Eastham has a reputation for tight disciplinary control, and so receives a large number of inmate troublemakers from other TDC prisons. Structurally, the prison has 18 inside cell blocks (or tanks) and 12 dormitories that branch out from a single central hall—a telephone pole design. The Hall is the main thoroughfare of the prison and is almost one-quarter of a mile long, measuring 16 feet wide by 12 feet high.

The data for this chapter were collected in two phases through participant observation, interviews with guards and inmates, searching documents and inmate records, and informal conversations resulting from the participant observation. In phase one, the first author entered the penitentiary as a guard and collected dissertation data on social control and order for 19 months (June 1981 through January 1983). He worked throughout the institution (e.g., cell blocks, shops, dormitories) and observed firsthand how the guards cultivated "rats" and meted out official and unofficial punishments. In addition, he cultivated 20 key informants among the guards and inmate elites, with whom he discussed control and order as a daily phenomenon. The first author's close relationship with these informants and their "expert" knowledge about prison life and prisoner control were essential to the research (see Jacobs, 1974b; Marquart, 1984). Most importantly, his presence allowed observation and documentation of the control structure before, during, and for a short period after the reform measures were implemented.

In the second phase of research, the authors returned to Eastham and collected data from late September 1984 until January 3, 1985. Data collection procedures involved intensive observation and open-ended structured interviews (tape-recorded) with a cross section of 30 officers and 60 inmates. The inmate interviews addressed such issues as race relations, gang behavior, violence, relations with guards, and prison rackets. The officer interviews focused on such topics as morale, violence, gang behavior, unionism, and relations with inmates. While formal and taped interviews were conducted, the researchers also obtained valuable insights from daily observations of and informal conversations with guards on and off duty throughout the prison as well as from inmates at work, recreation, meals, and in their cells. Furthermore, we closely interacted with 17 key informants—10 inmates and 7 officers—who provided a constant source of support and information. Available official documents (e.g., memos, inmate records, solitary confinement log books) were used to substantiate and corroborate the interview and observational data.

The Change Agent: *Ruiz v. Estelle*

In December 1980 Judge William W. Justice (Eastern District of Texas) delivered a sweeping decree against the Texas Department of Corrections in *Ruiz v. Estelle*. That decree, a year in the writing following a trial of many months, was the culmination of a suit originally filed with the court in 1972. The order recited numerous constitutional violations, focusing on several issues. First, TDC was deemed overcrowded. Prison officials were ordered to cease quadruple and triple celling.[1] To deal with the overcrowding problems, TDC erected tents, expanded furloughs, and in May 1982 even ceased accepting new prisoners for approximately 10 days. Moreover, a "safety valve" population control plan passed by the legislature in 1983 and a liberalized "good time" policy have been used to expand parole releases. Nevertheless, overcrowding continues. A second issue was TDC's security practices. The judge ordered the prison administrators to sharply reduce and restrict the use of force by prison personnel. He also demanded the removal and reassignment of special inmates known as "building tenders" since the evidence clearly indicated that these inmates were controlling other inmates. To further increase security, the decree called for TDC to hire more guards and to develop a much more extensive inmate classification plan. Thirdly, the judge found health care practices, procedures, and personnel in need of drastic upgrading. A fourth shortcoming involved inmate disciplinary practices. Problems included vague rules (e.g., "agitation," "laziness"), the arbitrary use of administrative segregation, and a failure to maintain proper disciplinary hearing records. Fifth, the court found many problems with fire and safety standards in TDC. Finally, TDC was found to have unconstitutionally denied inmates access to courts, counsel, and public officials.

To implement this sweeping decree, Judge Justice appointed Vincent Nathan to serve as special master. Because TDC encompassed 23 units in 1981 (it now has 27), a group of monitors was hired to visit the prisons regularly and gauge compliance. The nature and extent of noncompliance with each aspect of the decree are contained in a series of lengthy monitors' reports and have served as the basis for ongoing negotiation and policy changes by the prison system.

Since our concern in this chapter is with the official and unofficial means of prisoner control that were ruled unconstitutional by the court, we limit our analysis to those parts of the court order (e.g., removal of building tenders and changes in security practices and personnel) relevant to that concern. To appreciate the effects of the order, we must first understand how Eastham was organized and how it operated prior to the court's intervention.

Prisoner Control Under the Old Order

The control of older, hard-core criminals presents special problems in any prison. At Eastham, the staff maintained tight discipline and control through a complex system of official rewards and punishments administered by an elite group of prison officers. Basically, this control system rewarded those inmates who had good prison records with such privileges as good time, furloughs, dormitory living instead of a cell, and jobs other than field work. On the other hand, the staff severely punished those inmates who challenged the staff's definition of the situation. The most unusual and important element in controlling the prisoners in the old order centered on the staff's open and formal reliance upon a select group of elite inmates to extend their authority and maintain discipline. It was this latter system of prisoner control, called the "building tender (BT) system,"[2] that the court ordered TDC to abolish.

The Building Tender/Turnkey System

The staff employed a strategy of coopting the dominant or elite inmates with special privileges (e.g., separate bathing and recreational periods, better-laundered uniforms, open cells, clubs or knives, "friends" for cell partners, craft cards) in return to aid in controlling the ordinary inmates in the living areas, especially the cell blocks. The use of select inmates to control other inmates is ubiquitous and has been documented in such various prison settings as the Soviet Union (Solzhenitsyn, 1974; 1975), India (Adam, n.d.), Australia (Shaw, 1966), and French Guiana (Charriere, 1970), as well as in Nazi concentration camps (Bettleheim, 1943; Kogon, 1958) and the management of slaves (Blassingame, 1972). The most notable as well as notorious use of pro-staff-oriented inmates (convict guards) has occurred in the Mississippi, Arkansas, and Louisiana prison systems (see McWhorter, 1981; Murton & Hyams, 1969; Mouledous, 1962). In these prisons, selected inmates were issued pistols and carbines to guard the other inmates. However, these elite inmates, unlike the inmate agents at Eastham, were housed in separate living quarters.

Structure and Work Role. The BT system at Eastham involved three levels of inmates. At the top of the hierarchy were the "head" building tenders. In 1981, each of the 18 blocks had one building tender who was assigned by the staff as the "head" BT and was responsible for all inmate behavior in "his" particular block. Indeed, "ownership" of a block by a head BT was well recognized: inmates and officers alike referred informally but meaningfully to, for example, "Jackson's tank" or "Brown's tank." Essentially, the head BT was the block's representative to the ranking officers. For example, if a knife or any other form of contraband was detected in "his" living area, it was the head BT's official job to inform the staff of the weapon's whereabouts and who had made it, as well as to tell the staff about the knife-maker's character. In addition, these BTs would help the staff search the suspected inmate's cell to ferret out the weapon. Because of their position, prestige, and role, head BTs were the most powerful inmates in the prisoner society. They acted as overseers and frequently mediated and settled disputes and altercations among the ordinary inmates. This role frequently called for the threat of or use of force. They stood outside ordinary prisoner interaction but by virtue of their position and presence kept all other inmates under constant surveillance.

At the second level of the system were the rank-and-file building tenders. In every cell block or dormitory, there were generally between three and five inmates assigned as building tenders, for a total of nearly 150 BTs within the institution. These inmates "worked the tank," and their official role was to maintain control in the living areas by tabulating the daily counts, delivering messages to other inmates for the staff, getting the other inmates up for work, cleaning, and reporting any serious misbehavior by inmates to the head BT who, in turn, told the staff. Another important duty of the BTs was the socialization of new inmates into the system. When new inmates arrived at a living area, BTs informed them of the "rules," which means "keep the noise down, go to work when you are supposed to, mind your own business, and tell us [the BTs] when you have a problem." In addition to these tasks, the BTs broke up fights, gave orders to other inmates, and protected the officers in charge of the cell blocks from attacks by the inmates.

The BTs also unofficially meted out discipline to erring inmates. For example, if an inmate had to be told several times to be quiet in the dayroom (the living area's TV and recreation room), stole another inmate's property, or threatened another inmate, he was apt to receive some form of physical punishment. If this initial encounter did not correct the problem, the BTs, with tacit staff approval, would severely beat the inmate (sometimes with homemade clubs) and have him moved to another cell block. This process, called "whipping him off the tank" or "counseling," was not uncommon, and some inmates were moved frequently throughout the prison. Although the BTs were "on call" 24 hours a day, the head BT assigned the other BTs to shifts (morning, evening, and night) to provide the manpower needed to manage the block. The living areas were their turf, and the staff basically left the management of these areas in their hands.

The third level of the building tender system consisted of inmates referred to as runners, strikers, or hitmen. Runners were not assigned to work in the blocks by the staff; rather, these inmates were selected by the BTs for their loyalty and willingness to act as informants. They also worked at regular jobs throughout the prison. Runners performed the janitorial work of the block, sweeping and dispensing supplies to the cells. They also served as conduits of information for the BTs since they had more contact with the ordinary inmates than BTs and picked up important information. More importantly, runners served as the physical backups for the BTs. If a fight or brawl broke out, the runners assisted the BTs in quelling the disturbance. As a reward for their services, runners enjoyed more mobility and privileges within the block than the other inmates (but less than the BTs). The BT crew in each tank recruited their runners, and selection was based primarily on the inmate's ability to work and willingness to inform. Moreover, many runners were friends of or known by the BTs in the free world; some runners were also the homosexual partners of their BT bosses. Some tanks had three or four runners, while others had seven, eight, or even nine. The number of runners totaled somewhere in the vicinity of 175 to 200 inmates.

The final aspect of the building tender system consisted of inmates referred to as turnkeys, who numbered 17 in 1981. As mentioned earlier, the prison contained a large corridor known as the Hall. Within the Hall were seven large, metal-barred doors, or riot barricades. Turnkeys worked in six-hour shifts, carrying on long leather straps the keys that locked and unlocked the barricades. They shut and locked these doors during fights or disturbances to prevent them from escalating or moving throughout the Hall. In addition to operating the barricades, turnkeys routinely broke up fights, assisted the BTs, and protected the prison guards from the ordinary inmate. These doorkeepers also passed along information to the BTs about anything they heard while "working a gate." More importantly, turnkeys assisted the cell block guards by locking and unlocking the cell block doors, relaying messages, counting, and keeping the Hall free of inmate traffic. In fact, the block guards and turnkeys worked elbow to elbow and assisted one another so much that only their respective uniforms separated them. When off duty, the turnkeys, who lived in the blocks, assisted the BTs in the everyday management of the block. In terms of power and privileges, turnkeys were on the same level as the regular BTs.

The building tender system functioned officially as an information network. Structurally, the staff was at the perimeter of the inmate society, but the building tender system helped the staff penetrate, divide, and control the ordinary inmates. BTs and turnkeys in turn had snitched working for them not only in the living areas but throughout the entire institution. Thus, the staff secured information that enabled them to exert enormous power over the inmates' daily activities. As mentioned earlier, the BTs and turnkeys were handsomely rewarded for their behavior and enjoyed power and status far exceeding that of ordinary inmates and lower ranking guards. Unofficially, these inmates maintained order in the blocks through fear, and they physically punished inmates who broke the rules.

Selection of BTs and Turnkeys. These inmate "managers" of the living areas performed a dangerous job for the staff. Vastly outnumbered, BTs and turnkeys ruled with little opposition from the ordinary inmates. In reality, most of the ordinary inmates justifiably feared their "overseers" because of their status and physical prowess. The BTs and turnkeys were selected through an official appointment procedure to perform a "formal" job within the living areas. The selection procedure began with the staff at Eastham (and the other TDC prisons), who recommended certain inmates as BTs/turnkeys to the Classification Committee (a panel of four TDC officials, all with prison security backgrounds). This committee then reviewed each inmate's record and made the final selections. Recommendations to the Classification Committee from the staff were not always honored, and fewer than one-half of those recommended were selected for BT/turnkey jobs. One supervisor who was an active participant in the recruitment process at Eastham expressed his preference, which was typical:

> I've got a personal bias. I happen to like murderers and armed robbers. They have a great deal of esteem in the inmate social system, so it's not likely that they'll have as much problem as some other inmate because of their esteem, and they tend to be a more

aggressive and a more dynamic kind of individual. A lot of
inmates steer clear of them and avoid problems just because of
the reputation they have and their aggressiveness. They tend to
be aggressive, you know, not passive.

The majority of the individuals selected for BT and turnkey positions were
the physically and mentally superior inmates who appeared to be natural leaders.
Generally, BTs and turnkeys were more violent and criminally sophisticated than
the regular inmates. For example, of the 18 head BTs at Eastham, eight were in prison
for armed robbery, five for murder (one was an enforcer and contract-style killer),
one for attempted murder, one for rape, one for drug trafficking, and two for burglary. Their average age was 39 and their average prison sentence was 32 years. Of
the 17 turnkeys, there were three murderers, three armed robbers, six burglars, two
drug traffickers, one rapist, one car thief, and one person in for aggravated assault.
Their average age was 31 and their average sentence 22 years. In contrast, the
average TDC inmate in 1981 had a 21-year sentence, with a modal age category between
22 and 27. These data clearly show that the BTs and turnkeys were older than most
inmates and more likely to be violent recidivists. This is consistent with the patterns
noted by others who have described inmate leaders (e.g., Clemmer, 1940; Schrag,
1954).

Race. Most of the regular BTs/turnkeys came from the black and white inmate
populations. Only a handful of Hispanic inmates were ever recruited for these positions. The staff distrusted most Hispanic inmates, perceiving them as dangerous, clan-
nish, and above all "sneaky." Hispanic inmates, primarily for cultural reasons, were
tight-lipped and generally avoided any voluntary interaction with the staff or other
inmates. They feared being labeled as pro-staff because physical reprisals from
other Hispanics for snitching were common inside as well as outside the prison world.
Moreover, Hispanic inmates were generally not as imposing physically as inmates
of other races.

Although black and white inmates both served as BTs, power was not equally
distributed between the races. The predominantly rural, white, ranking guards kept
the "real" power in the hands of the white BTs. That is, of the 18 head BTs, there
were 14 whites, three blacks, and one Hispanic. The ranking staff members were
prejudiced and "trusted" the white BTs more than members of the other two races.
In short, with the help of the staff, a "white con" power structure similar to a caste
system dominated the inmate society in the same way the "old con" power structure ruled Stateville (Joliet, Illinois) in the 1930s through the 1950s (see Jacobs, 1977).

The Staff and Unofficial Control

The staff at Eastham did not leave control of the prison totally in the hands of
their inmate agents. In addition, the guards actively enforced "unofficial" order
through intimidation and the routine use of physical force. Rules were quickly and

severely enforced, providing inmates with clear-cut information about where they stood, what they could and could not do, and who was boss (cf. McCleery, 1960). The unification of symbiotic relationships of these two groups—that is, guards as inside outsiders and inmate agents as elite outside insiders—precluded revolt at practically every level.

Intimidation. Inmates who challenged a guard's authority (e.g., by insubordination, cursing at him, or "giving him a hard time") were yelled at by guards or supervisors (sergeants, lieutenants, and captains). Racial epithets, name calling, derogation, threats of force, and other scare tactics were common. These methods, though physically harmless, ridiculed, frightened, or destroyed the "face" of the offending inmate. The following remarks by one ranking officer are an example. "You stupid nigger, if you ever lie to me or to any other officer about what you're doing, I'll knock your teeth in." On another occasion, a supervisor made this typical threat: "Say big boy, you're some kind of motherfucker, aren't you? I oughta just go ahead and whip your ass here and now."

Verbal remarks such as these were routine. In some cases, inmates were threatened with extreme physical force (e.g., "you'll leave here [the prison] in an ambulance") or even death ("nobody cares if a convict dies in here; we'll beat you to death"). Such threats of physical force were scare tactics meant to deter inmates from future transgressions.

Physical Force. Coercive force is an important means of controlling people in any situation or setting. At Eastham, the unofficial use of physical force was a common method of prisoner control. Inmates were roughed up daily as a matter of course. Within a two-month period, the first author *observed* over 30 separate instances of guards using physical force against inmates. Key informants told the researcher that this number of instances was not surprising. Indeed, as Marquart (1985) notes, fighting inmates was an important value in the guard subculture. Guards who demonstrated their willingness to fight inmates who challenged their authority were often rewarded by their supervisors with promotions, improved duty assignments, and prestigious labels such as "having nuts" or being a "good" officer. The willingness to use force was a rite of passage for new officers, and those who failed this test were relegated to unpleasant jobs such as cell block and gun tower duty. Those who refused to fight were rarely promoted, and many of these "deviant" officers eventually quit or transferred to other TDC prisons.

Generally, the physical force employed by ranking officers was of two kinds. First, some inmates received "tune-ups" or "attitude adjustments." These inmates were usually slapped across the face or head, kicked in the buttocks, or even punched in the stomach. The intent of a "tune-up" was to terrorize the inmate without doing physical damage. More serious, but still a "tune-up," was the "ass whipping" in which the guards employed their fists, boots, blackjacks, riot batons, or aluminum flashlights. These were meant to hurt the inmate without causing severe physical damage. Like simple "tune-ups," "ass whippings" were a common and almost daily form of unofficial control. Both were "hidden" in that they were conducted in private settings free from inmate witnesses.

The second form of force was beatings. Beatings occurred infrequently and were reserved for inmates who violated certain "sacred" rules by, for instance, attacking an officer verbally or physically, inflicting physical harm on other inmates, destroying prison property, or attempting to lead work strikes, to escape, or to foment rebellion against the rules or officers. Inmates who broke these rules were defined as "resisting" the system and were severely injured—often suffering concussions, loss of consciousness, cuts, and broken bones. Although beatings were rare, many were conducted in front of other inmates (always in the name of "self-defense") and served to make examples of those inmates who dared to break important norms.

The threat and use of force were everyday realities under the old order, and the guards routinely used force to subdue "unruly" inmates (see *Ninth Monitor's Report*, 1983). Although rewards and privileges served as important official means of control, the prison order was ultimately maintained through the "unofficial" use of fear and terror. The staff ruled the penitentiary with an iron hand and defined most situations for the inmates. Those inmates who presented a serious challenge (e.g., threatening or attacking officers, fomenting work strikes) to the system were harassed, placed in solitary confinement, and sometimes beaten into submission. To the outsider, it might seem that this control structure would create enormous tension and foster mass revolt, but, as we have seen, the small number of guards did not face the inmates alone. The BTs and turnkeys with whom the guards shared power served as a first line of control and functioned as a buffer group between the staff and ordinary inmates.

This type of prisoner control can be referred to as internal because of the important official role given to insiders. It was proactive in nature since the elite inmates knew when trouble was likely to arise and could move to forestall it. BTs and turnkeys functioned as the communication link between the officials and ordinary inmates. The BTs dealt with most of the inmate problems within the living areas and thereby insulated the staff from the multitude of petty squabbles arising in the course of prison life. Riots and mob action were obviated by this relentless BT surveillance and control. Problem situations were passed upwards to the guards. In this old order, the staff, BTs, and turnkeys maintained an alliance that ensured social order, peace, the status quo, and stability. But the institutional arrangement that made for such a "well-working" prison fostered an atomistic inmate community fraught with fear and paranoia.

Eastham in Transition

Although there were some efforts to ease overcrowding and to reform prison operations such as medical services, the dominant posture of TDC in 1981 and most of 1982, at all levels, was to resist the court order both through legal action and by noncompliance. Prison officials rejected the intrusion of the court as a matter of principle and particularly feared the consequences of relinquishing such traditional control measures as the BT system. Initially, TDC fought the BT issue. However, additional court hearings in February 1982 made public numerous examples of BT/turnkey perversion and brutality.[3] In late May 1982, attorneys for the state signed a consent decree agreeing to dismantle the decades-old inmate-guard system by January 1, 1983.

Compliance

To comply with the decree, the staff in September 1982 reassigned the majority of the BTs to ordinary jobs (e.g., laundry, gym, showers) and stripped them of all their former power, status, and duties. Even BTs reassigned as orderlies or janitors in the living areas were not permitted to perform any of their old BT duties. Court-appointed investigators, called monitors, oversaw the selection of orderlies and kept close tabs on their behavior. These outside agents periodically visited Eastham and asked their own inmate informants to make written statements about any orderly's misbehavior. Consequently, several inmate orderlies lost their jobs for fighting with and giving orders to the ordinary inmates; they were replaced by less quarrelsome ordinary inmates.

To reduce the chances of violence against the former BTs, the staff moved many of them into several blocks and dormitories for mutual protection. While some former BTs were indeed fearful, most did not fear retaliation. As one former BT stated:

> Man, I've been doing this [prison] for a long time and I know how to survive. I know how to do it. I'm not going to stab nobody, I'm going to cut his fucking head off. I'm doing 70 years and it doesn't make a bit of difference and I'm not going to put up with any of that shit.

These inmates all spoke of their willingness to use force, even deadly force, in the event of attacks from the ordinary inmates. The ordinary inmates were well aware of the BTs' reputations and propensity for violence. They did not seek revenge. In short, the ordinary inmates were glad to be "free" from the BT system and stayed away from the BTs, whom they still feared. As a general rule, when an inmate exemplifies his courage and willingness to fight and stand up for his rights under adverse conditions, he is left alone. Turnkeys were formally removed from their jobs and reassigned elsewhere during the last week of December 1982. These inmates were moved in with their BT counterparts and did not experience any retaliation from the ordinary inmates.

In addition to removing the BTs and turnkeys, TDC was ordered to hire more officers to replace the former inmate guards. Eastham received 141 new recruits during November and December 1982. The guard force was almost doubled. Guards were assigned to the barricades and had to learn from the former turnkeys how to operate them (e.g., how to lock and unlock the doors, what to do when fights broke out). More importantly, a guard was assigned to every block and dormitory. For the first time in Eastham's history (since 1917), guards had assignments within the living areas. Also for the first time, the guards maintained the security counts.[4]

Compliance with the court order also required the TDC to quit using physical force as an unofficial means of punishment and social control. At Eastham, in early 1983, ranking guards were instructed to "keep their hands in their pockets" and refrain from "tuning up" inmates. In fact, guards were told that anyone using unnecessary force—more force than was needed to subdue an unruly inmate—would be fired. The staff at first believed this rule would be "overlooked" and that the TDC administration would continue to support a guard's use of force against an inmate. But in this they were disappointed. In March 1983, a ranking guard was fired and two others were placed on six months' probation for beating up an inmate. Another incident in April 1983 led to the demotions and transfers of three other ranking guards. These incidents were investigated by TDC's Internal Affairs, which was organized in November 1982 to investigate and monitor all inmate complaints about guards' use of force. The termination and demotions had their intended effect, for they spelled the end of the guards' unofficial use of force (see *Houston Chronicle*, January 28, 1984). This series of events sent a message to the guards and inmates at Eastham (as well as throughout the TDC) that noncompliance with the court order would be dealt with harshly.

In sum, within six months the staff (aided by the BTs) changed the prisoner control system by abolishing the decades-old building tender/turnkey system without incident. Although the guards initially attempted to resist complying with the decree's restrictions on the use of force, a firing and several demotions broke their will to resist. These changes in response to the reform effort were substantial, and they set in motion a series of further changes that fundamentally altered the guard and inmate societies.

The New Order

Once the BTs/turnkeys were removed from their jobs and the guards finally quit using unofficial force, the highly ordered prison social structure began to show signs of strain. The balance of power and hierarchical structure within the prisoner society were leveled, and the traditional rules governing inmate behavior, especially in the living areas, were discarded. That is, the ordinary inmates no longer had to act according to the BTs' rules or fear physical reprisals from BTs. The guards' use of physical force as a means of punishment was abolished, and a new system of prisoner discipline/control was established that emphasized due process, fairness, and prisoners' rights. The implementation of these reforms resulted in three major changes within the prison community.

Changes in Interpersonal Relations Between the Guards and Inmates

The initial and most obvious impact of the *Ruiz* ruling has been on the relations between the keepers and the kept. Formerly, inmates were controlled through relentless surveillance and by a totalitarian system that created a docile and passive ordinary inmate population. In all interactions and encounters, the guards and their agents defined the situation for the ordinary inmates. The penitentiary's social structure was, in effect, a caste system, whereby those in the lowest stratum (the ordinary inmates) were dictated to, exploited, and kept in submission.

Now, however, with the abolition of the BT/turnkey system and the disappearance of "tune-ups" and "beatings," a new relationship between keepers and kept has emerged. It is characterized by ambiguity, belligerence, confrontation, enmity, and the prisoners' overt resentment of the staff's authority (see, e.g., Carroll, 1974). Inmates today no longer accept "things as they are." They argue with the guards and constantly challenge their authority. Moreover, the guards now find themselves in the position of having to explain and justify the rules to the inmates. The guards no longer totally define situations for the inmates.

Disciplinary reports show the contrast between the new (1983 and 1984) and old (1981 and 1982) orders.[5] We see from Table 15.1 that reported inmate threats towards and attacks on the guards increased by 500 percent and more over two years. The data do not precisely mirror behavior since some challenges to authority that would have been dealt with by unofficial coercion under the older order had to be reported or ignored under the new one. Nevertheless, it is clear from these data, as well as from interviews and observations, that the behavior of inmates towards the staff became increasingly hostile and confrontational. Simple orders to inmates

Table 15.1. **Selected Disciplinary Cases Resulting in Solitary Confinement: Direct Challenges to Authority from 1981 to 1984***

	1981	1982	1983	1984
1. Striking an Officer	4	21	38	129
	(1.3)	(6.5)	(12.0)	(49.4)
2. Attempting to Strike an Officer	7	9	18	21
	(2.3)	(2.7)	(5.7)	(8.0)
3. Threatening an Officer	4	5	38	109
	(1.3)	(1.5)	(12.0)	(41.8)
4. Refusing or Failing to Obey an Order	90	65	72	213
	(30.6)	(20.1)	(22.8)	(81.7)
5. Use of Indecent/Vulgar Language	11	14	89	94
(Cursing an Officer)	(3.7)	(4.3)	(28.2)	(36.0)
TOTAL	116	114	225	566
Population Levels	2,938	3,224	3,150	2,607

*Numbers in parentheses indicate the rate per 1,000 inmates. The population figures are based on the average monthly population at Eastham.

(e.g., "tuck in your shirt," "get a haircut," "turn your radio down") were often followed by protracted arguments, noncompliance, and such blistering verbal attacks from inmates as "fuck all you whores, you can't tell me what to do anymore," "get a haircut yourself, bitch," "quit harassing me, you old country punk," or "get your bitchy ass out of my face, this is my radio not yours." Not surprisingly, the number of cases for using indecent and vulgar language also steadily rose from 1981 to 1984. Indeed, the experience of verbal abuse became so commonplace that many officers overlooked this rule violation. On one occasion for example, one author observed an officer ask an inmate why he was leaving his area. The inmate walked past the officer and gruffly responded, "I'm going to work, so what the hell are you fucking with me for? If you got any other questions, call the kitchen." The officer turned around and walked away.

There are several reasons for this drastic change in interpersonal relations between guards and prisoners. First, there are simply more guards, which translates into more targets for assaults, verbal abuse, and disciplinary reports. Second, the guards are restricted from physically punishing "agitators," so fear of immediate physical reprisals by the guards has been eliminated. Third, the guards no longer have their inmate-agents to protect them from physical and verbal abuse or challenges to their authority by the ordinary inmates. By and large, the inmates feared the BTs more than the security staff. Purging the BT system eliminated this buffer group between the guards and ordinary inmates. Today the guards are "alone" in dealing with the prisoners, and the inmates no longer fear physical retaliation from the officials.

In addition to, and perhaps as important as, these changes in the control structure, the social distance between the guards and prisoners has diminished. The "inmates-as-nonpersons" who once inhabited our prisons have become citizens with civil rights (see Jacobs, 1980). In the past, inmates at Eastham, subjected to derogation and physical force and ignored by extramural society, saw little to gain from challenging the system. Recent court reforms, however, have introduced the rule of law into the disciplinary process. Inmates now have many due-process privileges. They can present documentary evidence, call witnesses, secure representation or counsel, and even cross-examine the reporting guard. They are in an adversarial position *vis à vis* their guards, which at least in some procedural senses entails a kind of equality. Moreover, the inmates' moral status has been improved because the guards can no longer flagrantly abuse them without fear of retaliation—verbal, physical, and/or legal. Although the guards ultimately control the prison, they must now negotiate, compromise, or overlook many difficulties with inmates within the everyday control system (see, e.g., Sykes, 1958; Thomas, 1984).

The second major change concerns a restructuring of the inmate social system. The purging of the BT/turnkey system and the elimination of the old caste system created a power vacuum. The demise of the old informal or unofficial rules, controls, and status differentials led to uncertainty and ambiguity. In such situations, as Jacobs (1977) and Irwin (1980) suggest, realignments of power in prison often mean the heightened possibility of violence.

The Rise of Inmate-Inmate Violence. Prior to *Ruiz* and the compliance that followed, inmate-inmate violence at Eastham was relatively low considering the types of inmate incarcerated there and the average daily inmate population. Table 15.2 illustrates the trends in inmate-inmate violence at Eastham. The data in this table clearly document a rise in serious violence between inmates. The most remarkable point here is that the incidence of violence increased while the prison population decreased by over 300 inmates.

Table 15.2. Selected Inmate-Inmate Offenses Resulting in Solitary Confinement:
Weapons Offenses 1981-1984*

	1981	1982	1983	1984
1. Fighting with a Weapon	25	31	46	31
	(8.5)	(9.6)	(14.6)	(11.8)
2. Striking an Inmate with a Weapon	21	25	40	57
	(7.1)	(7.7)	(12.6)	(21.8)
3. Possession of a Weapon	40	25	59	134
	(13.6)	(7.7)	(18.7)	(51.4)
4. Homicide	0	1	0	3
	(0)	(.3)	(0)	(1.1)
TOTAL	86	82	145	225
Population Levels	2,938	3,224	3,150	2,607

*Numbers in parentheses indicate the rate per 1,000 inmates. The population figures are based on the average monthly population at Eastham.

Prison overcrowding raises constitutional problems, but it is extremely difficult for a judge to decide when population levels constitute cruel and unusual punishment barred by due process or the Eighth Amendment. To make this decision, judges attempt to link population levels with various major forms of institutional violence (i.e., assaults, homicides, suicides). Cox et al. (1984) maintain that high degrees of overcrowding (especially in large institutions) have a variety of negative psychological and physical side effects, including higher death and disciplinary infraction rates. However, Ekland-Olson (1985:32) tested the overcrowding-tension-violence model and concluded, among other things, that "There is no supportable evidence that institutional size or spatial density is related to natural death, homicide, suicide or psychiatric commitment rates in prison.... There is evidence to support the idea that crowding is not uniformly related to all forms of prison violence." While the Eastham data do not allow us to choose between these views, they are consistent with Ekland-Olson's position and suggest that there is no simple relationship between crowding and violence. They also suggest that the social organization of a prison is a more important predictor of violence than crowding per se.

When the BTs were in power, one of their unofficial roles was to settle disputes, disagreements, and petty squabbles among the inmates in the living areas. Inmates came to the BTs not only for counsel but to avoid discussing a problem with the guards. The disputes often involved feuding cell partners, love affairs, petty stealing, or unpaid debts. The BTs usually looked into the matter and made a decision, thereby playing an arbitrator role. Sometimes the quarrelers were allowed to "fight it out" under the supervision of the BTs and without the staff's knowledge. Inmates rarely took these matters into their own hands by attacking another inmate in a living or work area. To do so would invite a serious and usually injurious confrontation with the BTs. Fist fights were the primary means for settling personal disputes or grudges. Weapons were rarely used because the BTs' information network was so extensive that it was difficult for an inmate to keep a weapon for any length of time. Furthermore, any inmate who attacked another inmate with a weapon was usually severely beaten by the BTs and/or the guard staff. Although the BTs ruled through fear and terror, their presence helped restrain serious violence among the inmates.

To avoid the labels of punk, rat, or being weak, inmates involved in personal disputes shy away from telling guards about their problems. With the BTs gone, this leaves the inmates on their "own" to settle their differences. The inmates' sense of justice—a revenge and machismo-oriented system with characteristics of blood feuds— is given full sway (see Ekland-Olson, 1985). The system means that inmates are virtually "cornered" and forced to use serious violence as a problem-solving mechanism. Physical threats, sexual come-ons, stealing, and unpaid debts are perceived as similarly disrespectful and as threats to one's "manhood." For example, not paying a gambling debt is a form of disrespect, and in a maximum security prison being "disrespectful" can lead to physical confrontations. Not *collecting* a gambling debt or *submitting* in the face of threats is also seen as weak or unmanly behavior. Inmates who are labeled weak are often preyed upon by inmates anxious to maintain or establish their reputations as "strong."

Fist fights, the "traditional" dispute-settling mechanism in the old order, are no longer an effective means of settling a problem. One inmate, whose response was typical, described the transition from fist fights to serious violence:

> Used to, you could fight on the tank [block] or in the field. You know, they'd [BTs and/or staff] let you settle it right then and there. After a fight, they'd make you shake hands. Yeah, grown men shaking hands after a fight. But it was over, you didn't have to worry about the dude creeping [sneak attack] on you. Now, oh man, there's more knifings and less fist fights. If somebody has trouble, they're gonna try to stick the other guy. Whoever beats the other to the draw wins. See, their attitude has changed. They don't believe in fist fights anymore, it's kidstuff to them. If you got a problem with a dude today, you better stick him. It wasn't like that when I was here in the 60s and 70s.

To the inmates, using a weapon proves more effective because if a "tormentor" is seriously wounded, he will be transferred to another prison hospital and, when recovered, to another Texas prison. Furthermore, an inmate who uses serious violence for self-protection obtains a reputation for being "crazy" or dangerous, which reduces the possibility of other personal disputes.

To many inmates, killing or seriously wounding a tormentor in response to a threat is justifiable behavior. At Eastham, violent self-help has become a social necessity as well as a method of revenge. Rather than lose face in the eyes of one's peers and risk being labeled weak, which is an open invitation to further victimization, many inmates see assaultive behavior as a legitimate way to protect their "manhood" and self-respect. This is a dangerous situation for all and especially for genuinely "weak" inmates who feel trapped and may use extreme violence as a last resort.

The Emergence of Inmate Gangs. As personal violence escalated, inmate gangs developed—partly as a response to the violence but chiefly to fill the void left by the BTs. Prior to 1982, only one inmate gang, the Texas Syndicate, or TS, existed at Eastham. This group, which evolved in California prisons (see Davidson, 1974), consisted of Hispanic inmates primarily from San Antonio and El Paso. It was estimated to have had about 50 full-fledged members and is reputed to have carried out "hits" or contracts on other prisoners at other TDC prisons.

Since 1983, a number of cliques or gangs have appeared at Eastham. Several white groups (Aryan Brotherhood or AB, Aryan Nations or AN, Texas Mafia or TM) and several black groups (Mandingo Warriors, Interaction Organization, Seeds of Idi Amin) have gained a foothold within the inmate society. All of these groups have a leadership structure and recruitment procedures, such as "kill to get in and die to get out" for the AB. Like the TS, these are system-wide organizations. Top ranking guards at Eastham estimate the number of prisoners who are members at between 8 and 10 percent of the prison population. Of the various groups, the TS and AB are the largest and best organized groups at Eastham.

The presence of the gangs was not really felt or perceived as a security problem until late 1984. Prior to this time, the staff had identified and kept tabs on the gang leaders as well as on recruiting trends. The staff also uncovered several "hits," but violence did not erupt. Then, in November 1984, two ABs stabbed two other ABs; one victim was the AB leader. Early December saw four TS members stab another TS in a cell block. Shortly thereafter, several members of the Texas Mafia murdered another TM in an administrative segregation block, a high security area housing inmates with violent prison records, known gang leaders, and many gang members. In the final incident a TS leader at Eastham murdered a fellow TS member, in the same segregation block as the previous murder, on January 1, 1985. Thus, gang-related violence has emerged at the prison but within the gangs themselves. In short, the gangs are locked in internal power struggles.

The rise of inmate-inmate violence has created a "crisis" in self-protection. Some inmates have sought safety in gangs, as we have seen. The staff is perceived—with justification—as unable to maintain control. Interviews with inmates reveal that gang membership offers identity, a sense of belonging, and a support system for the member. Revenge is also a powerful drawing card (cf. Jacobs, 1974a). Gang members know that if they are threatened, assaulted, or stolen from, they will have assistance in retaliating against the offender. On the other hand, nonmembers who fear for their personal safety feel they must rely on themselves. These inmates have felt it increasingly important to obtain weapons (see Table 15.2). In short, violence has almost become an expectation, both as a threat and as a means of survival.

Reactions of the Guards

The reforms have upset the very foundations of the guard subculture and work role. Their work world is no longer smooth, well-ordered, predictable, or rewarding. Loyalty to superiors, especially the warden, the job, and/or organization— once the hallmark of the guard staff at Eastham—is quickly fading. The officers are disgruntled and embittered over the reform measures that have "turned the place over to the convicts."

Fear of the Inmates. Part of the *Ruiz* ruling ordered TDC to hire hundreds of guards to replace the BTs. Eastham received 150 new guards between November 1982 and January 1983. For the first time guards were assigned to work in the living areas. It was hoped this increase in uniformed personnel would increase order and control within the institution. Contrary to expectations, the increase in inexperienced personnel and the closer guard-inmate relationships resulted in more violence and less prisoner control. As indicated earlier, assaults on the staff skyrocketed between 1981 (4) and 1984 (129). Additionally, one officer was taken hostage and three guards were stabbed by inmates at Eastham in 1984.

Fear of the inmates is greatest among the rank-and-file guards, most of whom are assigned to cell block duty and have close contact with the inmates. These personnel bear the brunt of the verbal abuse, assaults, and intimidation that have increased since the new system was implemented. The new guards are hesitant to enforce order, and this is evidenced in the officers' less authoritative posture towards the inmates. One guard put it this way: "Look, these guys [prisoners] are crazy, you know, fools so you gotta back off and let them do their thing now. It's too dangerous around here to enforce all these rules." Previously, guards were not subjected to verbal abuse, threats, and derogation. Compliance was effected through fear and physical force. Today, the guards cannot physically punish "troublemakers" and must informally bargain with the inmates for control. Many officers have stated that they try to enforce the rules but to no avail, since their supervisors overlook most petty rule violations to avoid clogging the prisons' disciplinary court docket.[6]

The traditional authoritarian guarding style at Eastham has been replaced with a tolerant, permissive, or "let's get along" pattern of interaction. Furthermore, the guards, especially new officers,[7] fear retaliation from inmates and officials to the point of not enforcing the rules at all. The attitude currently prevailing among the guards is summed up by the following guard's statement: "I don't give a damn about what they do, as long as they leave me alone. I'm here to do my eight hours and collect a paycheck, and that's it."

"We've Lost Control." The rise in inmate-inmate violence, the emergence of violent gangs, the loss of traditional control methods, the combative nature of guard-inmate interactions, the derogation of guards, and the influx of inexperienced guards have contributed to a "crisis in control" for the guards (Alpert et al., 1985). Many of the guards, especially the veterans, perceive the changes wrought in the wake of *Ruiz* as unjustified and undermining their authority. They feel they can no longer maintain control and order within the penitentiary. This is not because they have not tried the new disciplinary system. Indeed, as we see in Table 15.3, the total number of solitary confinement cases has skyrocketed since 1981.

Table 15.3. **Inmates Sentenced to Solitary Confinement from 1981 to 1984***

	1981	1982	1983	1984
All Offenses	487	404	889	1,182
	(165.7)	(125.3)	(282.2)	(453.0)
Population Levels	2,938	3,224	3,150	2,607

*Numbers in parentheses indicate the rate per 1,000 inmates. The population figures are based on the average monthly population at Eastham.

These data reveal that the rate of serious disciplinary infractions (violence and challenges to guards' authority) rapidly increased after the reforms in 1983 despite a decrease in the inmate population. The rapid increase in rule violations has demoralized the guard staff to the point of frustration and resignation. Interviews with guards and inmates revealed that most inmates are no longer afraid of being "written up," losing good time, and spending time in solitary confinement.[8]

The traditional means of dealing with "unruly" prisoners have been abolished and replaced with more official, due-process methods. Standards and guidelines for the guards' use of force have been implemented. Whenever a guard uses force to control an inmate for whatever reason (e.g., breaking up fights, taking an inmate into custody), the officer must submit a written report detailing all phases of the incident. When a use of force involves a scuffle, all parties are brought to the prison's hospital to photograph any injuries or abrasions. Forced cell moves are also videotaped. Documentation and accountability are musts for the guard force today. Furthermore, whenever physical force is used against inmates, Internal Affairs investigates the incident. Their investigation of a guard taken hostage on October 15, 1984, involved interviews with 38 prison officials and 21 inmates. Twenty-four polygraph tests were also administered (*Houston Chronicle*, February 14, 1984). This investigation revealed that unnecessary force was used to quell the disturbance. Eleven guards and two wardens were reprimanded, and two guards were demoted and transferred to other prisons. Thus, the disciplinary process itself frustrates the line officers—so much so that they often "look the other way" or simply fail to "see" most inmate rule violations. Moreover, the implementation of the new disciplinary process has strained the once cohesive relations between the guards and their superior officers. Not only do the latter sometimes fail to back up the guards' disciplinary initiatives because of the pressures of crowded dockets, but they may also initiate investigations that result in guards being sanctioned.

Some Conclusions on Court Reforms and Prisoner Control

The *Ruiz* ruling sounded the death knell for the old prison order in Texas. Legal maneuverings and a new prison administration have given increasing substance to the new order that *Ruiz* initiated. Table 15.4 summarizes the distinctions between the old, or inmate-dependent, order and the new, bureaucratic-legal order. We have included only those elements of each order that are directly relevant to prisoner control.

Table 15.4. **A Summary Depiction of Eastham Before and After *Ruiz***

	Inmate-Dependent Pre-*Ruiz* Era	Bureaucratic-Legal Order Post-*Ruiz* Era
1. Decision-making Power	Decentralized—warden establishes many policies and procedures at the prison. Prison administrators enjoy a high degree of autonomy.	Centralized—warden carries out directives established in central TDC office. Less unit flexibility; prison officials allowed little autonomy.
2. Staff/Inmate Relations	Based on paternalism, coercion, dominance, and fear. Majority of the inmates are viewed and treated as nonpersons. Guards define the situation for the inmates.	Based on combative relations wherein guards have less discretion and inmates challenge the staff's authority. Guards fear the inmates.
3. Prisoner Control Apparatus	Internal-proactive control system based on information. Guards penetrate the inmate society through a system of surrogate guards. Organized violence, riots, mob action, and general dissent are obviated. Punishment is swift, severe, and often corporal. Control is an end in itself.	External-reactive control system in which the guard staff operates on the perimeter of the inmate society. Loss of information prevents staff from penetrating inmate society; thus they must contain violence. Punishment is based on hearings and due-process considerations. Control mechanisms are means-oriented.
4. Inmate Society	Fractured and atomistic due to the presence of BTs—official snitches.	Racially oriented with the emergence of violent cliques and gangs.

We do not mean to suggest by our headings that prior to the court ruling Eastham was not bureaucratically organized. Indeed, all of the trappings (e.g., rules, records, accountability) were present. Under the old order, however, those trappings rarely penetrated the daily operations of the prison. Eastham officials enjoyed considerable autonomy from the central prison administration. Guards, particularly those in the mid-ranks, exercised much discretion in their dealings with inmates. The inmate-dependent order openly recognized the importance of informal relations between officers and inmates and the manipulation by staff of a *sub rosa* reward system. The old regime fostered particularistic relations (the "major's boy," BTs, and other institutional snitches), which were important to control and kept the inmate community fractured and atomistic. The elite inmates were a reliable source of information about inmate activities that could threaten order. Finally, the control mechanisms consistent with this regime were ends-oriented. That is, order and the dominance of staff over the inmates were maintained by pragmatic means selected over time to achieve these ends. Where force and other sanctions were used by BTs and guards, they were employed immediately following a transgression. This strategy engendered fear among both the offenders and those who observed the punishment.

The transition towards a bureaucratic-legal order at Eastham permits less autonomy. To increase central office control over TDC's many prisons, the new TDC administration (under Raymond Procunier) established, in 1984, regional directors to supervise more closely the wardens of individual units. As elsewhere, new policies to carry out court-ordered reforms have also reduced the discretion of all unit officials (Glazer, 1978). Written directives regarding disciplinary or supervisory procedures emphasize legal standards more than the traditional, cultural values that once defined prison objectives. The precedence of legal standards is especially evident in the "use of force" policy. Each time some physical means of control is used, a "use of force" report (a series of statements and photographs) must be completed and filed with the central office. Whenever a physical confrontation is anticipated (e.g., forced cell moves), the action is videotaped. The watchword is documentation. The bureaucratic-legal order also discourages informal relations between officers and inmates. Yet fewer staff-inmate links limit organizational intelligence and thus the ability to anticipate trouble. Officers regularly complain that "We don't know what's going on back there [in the tanks]." At the same time, prison relations are universalistic; all inmates are to be treated alike, and unless they are officially found to have violated some prison rule, they are due equal benefits and freedom regardless of demeanor or attitude. Lastly, control mechanisms are more means-oriented. The focus is as much on how the control is effected as it is on whether or to what extent it is effective. The legality of the means appears to many staff members to take precedence over the deterrent effect of the control effort. One consequence of this focus is a disciplinary procedure that effectively distances the punishment from the offense in both time and place. Thus, the staff's authority rests not on threat of force or other informal means of domination but on explicit rules.

Although court intervention has made Eastham's operations more consistent with constitutional requirements of fairness and due process, the fact remains that life for the inmates and guards at Eastham is far less orderly than it was before. Authority has eroded, and the cell blocks and halls are clearly more dangerous. Our observations and the data presented in Tables 15.1 through 15.3 suggest that the push toward the bureaucratic-legal order, at least in the first few years after the decree, lessened control to the point that many are increasingly at risk behind the walls.

The court-prompted reforms have created for prison officials a dilemma analogous to that experienced by police (Skolnick, 1966). Guards, like police, must balance two fundamental values: order and rule by law. Clearly, order can be maintained in a totalitarian, lawless manner. In a democratic society, order must be maintained under rules of law. Having been mandated to maintain control by constitutional means, Eastham prison officials face a problem that pervades our criminal justice system today. Specifically, as Jacobs and Zimmer (1983:158) note: "[T]he great challenge for corrections is to develop an administrative style that can maintain control in the context of the legal and humane reforms of the last decade."

Officials at Eastham certainly feel this challenge. They feel pressure to comply with the court and the central office directives designed to operationalize that compliance. Yet the unanticipated consequences of today's reforms have jeopardized the staff's ability to maintain and enforce order. While prisoners in many institutions now have enhanced civil rights and are protected by many of the same constitutional safeguards as people in the free society, they live in a lawless society at the mercy of aggressive inmates and cliques. The dilemma apparently facing society and prison administrators revolves around the issues of rights versus control. Should prisons be managed through an authoritarian structure based on strict regimentation, fear, few civil rights, and controlled exploitation, in which inmates and guards are relatively safe? Or should prisons be managed within a bureaucratic-due-process structure espousing fairness, humane treatment, and civil rights, in which inmate and guard safety is problematic—and where uncontrolled exploitation is likely? One would like to believe that the civil rights, and personal safety goals within prison settings are not incompatible, but we may ultimately have to confront the fact that to some extent they are. At the very least, the experience at Eastham suggests that reforms, especially in maximum security prisons, should be: (1) phased in gradually rather than established by rigid timetables, (2) implemented with a fundamental appreciation of the entire network of relationships and behaviors involved, and (3) undertaken with a healthy sensitivity to the unanticipated negative consequences that have often surrounded attempts to "do good" (Glazer, 1978; Rothman, 1980).

Notes

[1] The order also called for an end to double celling, but this element was later vacated by the Fifth Circuit Court of Appeals.

[2] For a more detailed analysis of the BT system, see Marquart and Crouch (1984).

3 The news media extensively covered these hearings, and press releases provided grisly examples of BT/turnkey brutality and perversions (see the numerous *Houston Post and Houston Chronicle* articles between February 16, 1982, and July 1, 1982).

4 The former BTs had to show the guards how to keep the living area counts. Thus, the staff adopted a system of counting that the BTs had developed.

5 The data presented in the three tables reflect disciplinary infractions resulting in solitary confinement. We recognize the limitations here and know our data are quite conservative. The TDC's recordkeeping on all disciplinary cases (minor and major) was nonsystematic, and we had to rely on Eastham's disciplinary log books. However, our interviews and observations are consistent with the rise in violent and other behavior reflected in the tables.

6 This is like the situation in many large cities, where police and prosecutors have relationships of accommodation with minor criminals. Some crimes must be prosecuted, whatever the cost to the system. Other crimes are not worth the trouble, so agents of justice ignore them or find ways to handle them simply.

7 Interviews with ranking guards indicated that the rise of inmate-guard and inmate-inmate violence has contributed to the turnover of new guards. Of the 246 guards assigned inside the building, 125, or 51 percent, have less than one year of experience, and these numbers include ranking guards.

8 A guard's threat to seek solitary confinement has also become less intimidating since *Ruiz* because of the due-process protections imposed and limitations on the good time that can be forfeited. Also, the guard who seeks solitary confinement for an inmate knows he is triggering a hearing in which his own actions may be questioned. The increase in solitary confinement cases should be read in light of these disincentives.

References

Adam, H.L. (no date). *Oriental Crime*. Clifford's Inn, London: T. Werner Laurie.

Alpert, C., B.M. Crouch and C.R. Huff (forthcoming) "Prison Reform by Judicial Decree: The Unintended Consequences of *Ruiz v. Estelle*." *The Justice System Journal*.

Bettleheim, B. (1943). "Individual and Mass Behavior in Extreme Situations." *Journal of Abnormal and Social Psychology*, 38, 417.

Blassingame, J.W. (1979). *The Slave Community*. New York, NY: Oxford University Press.

Calhoun, E. (1978). "The Supreme Court and the Institutional Rights of Prisoners: A Reappraisal." *Hastings Constitutional Law Quarterly*, 4, 219.

Carroll, L. (1974). *Hacks, Blacks, and Cons*. Lexington, MA: Lexington Books.

Champagne, A. and K.C. Hass (1976). "Impact of *Johnson v. Avery* on Prison Administration." *Tennessee Law Review*, 43, 275.

Charriere, H. (1970). *Papillon*. New York, NY: Basic Books.

Clemmer, D.C. (1940). *The Prison Community*. Boston, MA: Christopher Publishing House.

Colvin, M. (1982). "The 1980 New Mexico Prison Riot." *Social Problems*, 29, 449.

Cox, V.C., P.B. Paulus and G. McCain (1984). "Prison Crowding Research: The Relevance for Prison Housing Standards and a General Approach Regarding Crowding Phenomena." *American Psychologist*, 39, 1148.

Crouch, B.M. (1980). "The Guard in a Changing Prison World." In B.M. Crouch (ed.) *The Keepers: Prison Guards and Contemporary Corrections*. Springfield, IL: Charles C Thomas.

Davidson, R.T. (1974). *Chicano Prisoners: Key to San Quentin*. New York, NY: Holt, Rinehart, and Winston.

Ekland-Olson, S. (1985). "Judicial Decisions and the Social Order of Prison Violence: Evidence from the Post-*Ruiz* Years in Texas." Unpublished manuscript.

Glazer, N. (1978). "Should Judges Administer Social Services?" *Public Interest*, 50, 64.

Irwin, J. (1980). *Prisons in Turmoil*. Boston, MA: Little, Brown and Company.

Jacobs, J.B. (1974a). "Street Gangs, Behind Bars." *Social Problems*, 21, 395.

Jacobs, J.B. (1974b). "Participant Observations in Prison." *Urban Life and Culture*, 3, 221.

Jacobs, J.B. (1977). *Stateville: The Penitentiary in Mass Society*. Chicago, IL: University of Chicago Press.

Jacobs, J.B. (1980). "The Prisoner's Rights Movement and Its Impact, 1960-1980. *Crime and Justice: Annual Review of Research*, 2, 429.

Jacobs, J.B. and L. Zimmer (1983). "Collective Bargaining and Labor Unrest." In J. Jacobs (ed.) *New Perspective in Prisons and Imprisonment*. Ithaca, NY: Cornell University Press.

Kimball, E.L. and D.J. Newman (1968). Judicial Intervention in Correctional Decisions: Threat and Response. *Crime and Delinquency*, 14, 1.

Kogon, E. (1958). *The Theory and Practice of Hell*. New York, NY: Berkley Publishing.

Marquart, J.W. (1984). "Outsiders as Insiders: Participant Observation in the Role of a Prison Guard." Unpublished manuscript.

Marquart, J.W. (1985). "Prison Guards and the Use of Physical Coercion as a Mechanism of Prisoner Control." Unpublished manuscript.

Marquart, J.W. and B.M. Crouch (1984). "Coopting the Kept: Using Inmates for Social Control in a Southern Prison." *Justice Quarterly*, 1, 491.

McCleery, R.H. (1960). "Communication Patterns as Bases of Systems of Authority and Power." In R.A. Cloward et al., *Theoretical Studies in Social Organization of the Prison*. New York, NY: Social Science Research Council.

McWhorter, W.L. (1981). *Inmate Society: Legs, Halfpants and Gunmen: A Study of Inmate Guards*. Saratoga, CA: Century Twenty-One Publishing.

Mouledous, J.C. (1962). "Sociological Perspectives on a Prison Social System." Unpublished master's thesis, Department of Sociology, Louisiana State University.

Murton, T. and J. Hyams (1969). *Accomplices to the Crime: The Arkansas Prison Scandal*. New York, NY: Grove Press.

Ninth Monitor's Report of Factual Observations to the Special Master (1983).

Rothman, D. (1980). *Conscience and Convenience*. Boston, MA: Little, Brown.

Schrag, C. (1954). "Leadership Among Prison Inmates." *American Sociological Review*, 19, 37.

Shaw, A.G.L. (1966). *Convicts and the Colonies*. London: Faber and Faber.

Shils, E.A. (1975). *Center and Periphery: Essays in Macrosociology*. Chicago, IL: The University of Chicago Press.

Skolnick, J.H. (1966). *Justice Without Trial*. New York, NY: John Wiley and Sons.

Solzhenitsyn, A.I. (1974). *The Gulag Archipelago*. New York, NY: Harper and Row.

Solzhenitsyn, A.I. (1975). *The Gulag Archipelago II*. New York, NY: Harper and Row.

Stastny, C. and G. Tyrauner (1982). *Who Rules the Joint?* Lexington, MA: Lexington Books.

Sykes, G.M. (1958). *The Society of Captives*. Princeton, NJ: Princeton University Press.

Thomas, J. (1984). "Some Aspects of Negotiated Order, Loose Coupling and Mesostructure in Maximum Security Prisons." *Symbolic Interaction*, 4, 213.

Turner, W.B. (1979). "When Prisoners Sue: A Study of Prisoner Section 1983 Suits in the Federal Courts." *Harvard Law Review*, 92, 610.

UCLA Law Review (1973). "Note, Judicial Intervention in Corrections: The California Experience—An Empirical Study." *UCLA Law Review*, 20, 452.

U.S. Department of Justice (1984). "Prisoners in 1983." *Bureau of Justice Statistics Bulletin*. Washington, DC: U.S. Government Printing Office.

16

Stress, Change, and Collective Violence in Prison[†]

Lucien X. Lombardo

Prison riots have traditionally been explored as if they were singular events—aberrations in the life of prison communities. In studying riots researchers have generally pulled back from the dynamics of day-to-day prison life, focusing instead on the relationship between prison conditions and collective violence. Here, instead, I attempt to relate collective violence to the stresses experienced and coped with by those living and working in prison. I explore the normal conditions of prison life for clues to the development of collective violence. In short, this chapter is an attempt to think about prison collective violence from an integrative perspective that recently published studies concerning the dynamics of prison life make possible for the first time.

Sociological studies of prison riots implicitly assume both the *collective* and *violent* nature of prison disturbances without seeking to explain how either of the crucial defining characteristics develops (Garson, 1972a; Desroches, 1974; Wilsnack, 1976). Inmates and prison staff are assumed to be mutually hostile *groups*, and the violence of a riot is simply a more overt expression of underlying inmate-staff hostility. In this context, riots erupt when the staff loses its ability to exercise power and control over inmates living under conditions of deprivation. When controls break down, inmate frustration finds its outlet in violence.

Wilsnack (1976) illustrates this position in developing a theoretical interpretation of riots that integrates survey findings with previous studies:

> For a riot to erupt there must be not only deprived and powerless
> *inmates* and attention from influential outsiders, but also an uncer-

†Reprinted by permission of Waveland Press, Inc.

tain and unstable administration. If the stability reduces the effectiveness of *staff* control, it may provide a rare opportunity for
inmates to seize enough power and time to get their message out
and to make the right people take it seriously [emphasis added].

Implicit in this formulation of riots is a "frustration aggression" explanation for
the inmates' violent behavior. The motivation for rioting is found in the deprivations
and powerlessness of inmates (interference with goal-response). The instability
and uncertainty of staff allow these long-standing frustrations to surface (reduction
of inhibition to aggression). These frustrations are then expressed as aggressive
violence directed at the prison administration (an act with the goal-response of
injury to an organism; Dollard et al., 1970).

This approach leaves essential questions unanswered. For example, why do staff
who have run prisons without riots (for years, in most cases) become ineffective?
Why do inmates who are constantly deprived and powerless (Sykes, 1958) now react
to these conditions with violence? Why are inmates who are normally able to "cor-
rupt guard authority" (Sykes, 1958) not able to continue doing so? Through what
processes do outsiders (politicians, the media) contribute to the eruption of violence?
We must explore the process by which individual inmates are moved to join in
collective action and the reasons that collective action takes the particular violent
forms that it does. These are the issues that are discussed below.

The starting point for this discussion is *stress*, as it is experienced and coped with
by individual inmates and individual staff. Next, we explore how the mutual interactions of these two groups of stressed individuals shift to collective reactions, setting the stage for violence from and among the inmates and violent retaliation from
the prison authorities (Toch, 1977a).

Preconditions and Process in Prison Collective Violence

Analyzing data from prisons that have had riots, those that exhibited non-riot
resistance, and those that had no riots, Wilsnack (1976) identifies three types of "preconditions" associated with riots: (1) inmate deprivation and social disorganization,
(2) administrative conflicts and instability, and (3) pressure and publicity from outside the walls. If we examine each of these preconditions as "stressors" found in the
prison environment from the perspectives of inmates and guards who inhabit and
work in prisons, some light may be shed on the process by which preconditions become
transformed into collective violence.

Before we do this, however, it is important to distinguish among the factors. Some
of what Wilsnack calls "preconditions" may well be thought of as parts of a *process*
that eventually leads to a riot. Others may relate to the "context"—that is, the particular conditions of deprivation—in which this process takes place.

Such objective conditions as overcrowding, idleness, tight security, and heterogeneous populations that mix inmates varying in age, criminal experience, and race (Wilsnack, 1976) provide individual inmates and guards with motivations and opportunities to develop strategies for coping. The success or failure of these strategies is judged by the individual who employs them. In addition, the relative salience of each condition varies for the individual inmate or guard, and not according to evaluations by observers (Toch, 1977a).

Other factors associated with prison disturbances, however, seem to be involved more clearly in the "process of prison riots"—that is, the process of coping with "objective conditions" in such a way as to promote collective violent action. These *process factors* include increased inmate assaults, assaults on staff, poor communication, publicity about prison conditions, and absences and/or changes in key prison staff (Wilsnack, 1976).

These process factors are not only problems in themselves, but also contribute to the intensity with which inmates and staff experience the "objective conditions" of confinement. These factors tend to be adjustments of some inmates and staff that upset whatever adjustments other inmates and staff have made. Though "objective conditions" can be measured in some ways, they are *subjectively* interpreted partly in terms of the behavior of fellow inmates (Toch, 1977a) and guards (Lombardo, 1989). It is in the alteration of these subjective worlds that process factors may make their contributions to the development of collective violence.

Objective Preconditions: Inmate Perspectives

Such objective prison conditions as overcrowding, heterogeneous inmate populations, idleness, and tight security restrictions contribute to the creation of stressful prison environments (Toch, 1977a) and to prison disturbances (Wilsnack, 1976). If such conditions always produce stress, however, why do they not always produce collective violence as a response? Part of the answer may be found in the differential salience of these conditions and in mechanisms individual inmates find to cope successfully or unsuccessfully with the stress these conditions produce.

Toch demonstrates that the crowding of prison life exacerbates an inmate concern for privacy and the invasion of personal space by the noise, smells, and behavior of others. Inmates concerned with privacy wish to remove themselves from overstimulating environments. Some attempt to isolate themselves from sources of irritation (Toch, 1977a). Others attempt to enclose themselves in social groups composed of similar privacy-oriented inmates (Toch, 1977a). Even under normal conditions, however, such isolation and privacy affiliation are difficult to achieve. There are always inmates whose concern for "activity" and being free from the boredom and understimulation of prison life leads them to create the very conditions those concerned with privacy seek to avoid.

It is in this social matrix that the objective conditions frequently associated with prison collective violence have their impact. Overcrowding increases the stress produced by an overstimulating environment and makes the possibility of obtaining privacy much less likely. Heterogeneous inmate populations (especially those mixing younger and older inmates) increase the probabilities that all groups will find it more difficult to cope successfully with their environment (Toch, 1977a).

Given the scarce resources of most prisons, overcrowding is also related to a decline in opportunities for inmates concerned with activity to keep themselves involved in tasks that provide ego involvement, self-actualization, or simply the release of pent-up energy (Toch, 1977a). When available slots in prison programs disappear and waiting lists become longer, idleness increases. Idle inmates are more likely to be faced with the disturbing and painful effects of their environment; this results in a heightening of the inmates' experience of stress.

Tight security is also capable of having positive and negative effects on different segments of heterogeneous inmate populations. For inmates who are concerned with safety and structure, tight security offers protection from physical assault by other inmates. It also provides certainty and predictability, reducing stress for inmates concerned with these issues. For others, however, tight security means a loss of freedom and a lessened ability to control one's own life. Under such conditions, inmates are more likely to express concerns about the abuse of authority and officer harassment and to make more frequent demands for respect. When tight security measures are not satisfactorily explained to inmates, these concerns may surface as "censorious" behavior (Mathiesen, 1965), with inmates criticizing staff unfairness, partiality, and unreasonableness (Lombardo, 1989).

From the inmates' perspective, each of the objective factors associated with collective violence (overcrowding, idleness, and tight security) is made more salient by the impact of a heterogeneous inmate population. In diverse groups there is an increased likelihood that individual inmates' attempts to find places within the prison where their environment and individual needs are at least compatible (Toch, 1977a) will be doomed to failure and frustration. Though coping strategies have a modest chance of success under normal conditions, a "critical mixture" of abnormal conditions brings new sources of stress to the surface as formerly satisfying living strategies begin to fail.

Objective Preconditions: Guard Perspectives

As they pursue their daily tasks, individual guards also spend time and energy creating work environments that are compatible with their individual needs. Some seek situations in which they can overcome boredom by keeping active (cell blocks, work details). Others seek positions where they can maintain a relative degree of privacy and isolation from what they perceive as the overstimulation of interactions with prisoners and/or administrators (wall posts, administration building assignments). Still others seek assignments where they can exert control, experience autonomy, and make decisions (Lombardo, 1989).

In addition to meeting their individual concerns, guards must also cope with the stresses produced by their prison environment; they must seek to reduce pressures and to enhance satisfactions. In this connection, relations with individual inmates take on special significance. Helping inmates cope with their institutional and personal needs is also a way for some guards to cope with their perceived powerlessness. Helping inmates gives guards a sense of control and purpose in a social environment that defines helping behaviors as not acceptable. Exercising discretion in enforcing rules and seeking to establish a "legitimate" basis for inmate cooperation and personal authority provides the guard with an opportunity to achieve recognition from inmates for being fair and enhances guard feelings of self-esteem and self-respect (Lombardo, 1989). Good relations with inmates also provide guards with communication networks that otherwise may be lacking (Lombardo, 1989).

The "objective conditions" of overcrowding, idleness, tight security, and heterogeneous inmate populations adversely affect the prison guards' ability to maintain their work environment as directly as these conditions affect the inmates' ability to structure their living environment. The time, energy, and attention of the guard are scarce resources—resources upon which overcrowding makes great demands. Under normal conditions guards are often able to help inmates cope with their privacy and safety concerns. However, an increase in inmates per officer not only increases the *number of demands* for assistance, it also *diminishes the opportunities* to help by reducing the number and variety of work or housing locations capable of satisfying inmate concerns. With fewer options, officers face more frustrated inmates. In addition, they lose opportunities to make positive contributions, thus reducing their own levels of satisfaction.

Tight security and strict rule-enforcement policies have an adverse effect on guards as well as on inmates concerned with autonomy and freedom. Where guards previously exercised discretion and interpreted individual rule enforcement interactions in light of the characteristics of the situation and the inmate involved (Lombardo, 1989), they now must respond "by the book." Any personal legitimacy a guard may have established now erodes. The guard is forced to rely on legalistic responses, which are more likely to evoke hostile reactions from inmates. In addition, tight security means that guards lose the degree of autonomy and control that previously satisfied their own personal needs.

As a general work strategy prison guards frequently adapt directives from prison administrators to the realities of their work situations. In doing so guards maintain an operational smoothness that provides predictability and structure. As overcrowding, tight security, idleness, and heterogeneous inmate populations develop, the guards' ability to make situational adjustments becomes severely circumscribed. As directives limit the guards' ability to control their environment, they must abandon their previous adjustment strategies, and this allows new problems to surface.

Officers reacting in non-preferred ways to changing conditions and perceived administrative interference do so even though they may know that this increases inmate stress. As officers change "styles," inmates predictably lose some of the indirect autonomy they experienced from officer assistance. Inmates also lose structure as officers vary their previously predictable responses. Where officers were previously able to alleviate stress, they must now contribute to it, causing inmates to seek new avenues of adjustment. This appears to have been a critical factor in promoting the infamous Attica uprising, which followed a decrease in predictability and structure of supervision:

> Inmates not only faced inexperienced officers but might face new ones every day. The inmates could never learn what was expected of them from one day to the next, and the officers could never learn whether an inmate's uncooperative behavior resulted from belligerence, indifference, illness, or some other medical or personal problem. Inmates no longer could adjust to the officer who commanded them, but had to readjust to a succession of officers who changed from day to day. Officers, too, were adversely affected by this change. Likely to work with different groups of inmates each day, the officers had no incentive to establish rapport or respect with a group of inmates whom they might not see again for days or weeks. There was neither opportunity nor desire to develop any mutual understanding [New York State Special Commission on Attica, 1972:127].

Stress and the Process of Collective Violence: From Individual to Collective Behavior

In the early 1970s Jayewardene et al. (1976) surveyed Canadian correctional staff members concerning their perceptions of the "process leading inevitably and inexorably to a major prison disturbance." The staff members noted changes in the normal behaviors of inmates seeking to make adjustment to new conditions: There were increases in rumors, in transfer requests, and in inmates reporting to sick call. In addition, inmates sought new job assignments or began to engage in recreational activities where they previously had not (Jayewardene et al., 1976). Talkative inmates became reticent and inmate responses to supervision (censorious behavior included) became signs of defiance. Inmates who were generally unpopular and isolated became talkative and sought out staff when "trouble" was brewing (Jayewardene et al., 1976).

What these staff members were observing is the process by which inmates seek new niches when their old ones begin to be destroyed by change. Inmates were still reacting as individuals, but the groundwork for the development of a collective response to stress was being constructed.

In discussing the processes of communication in social groups, Festinger (1968) describes situations in which individuals depend on "social reality" to determine the validity of their attitudes, opinion, and beliefs when they are unable to depend on experiences of "physical reality" to test these beliefs. In prison environments that are undergoing change, the certainty, predictability, and structure provided by environmental niches and other coping options represent the "physical reality." Niches provide opportunities for individual inmates to meet their needs in terms of perceived attributes of special prison environments, and without direct reference either to other inmates or to their "status as inmates." The meaning they derive from their experiences is tested against the reality that they as individuals experience to be true. Basing their attitudes, opinions, and beliefs on this "physical reality," the "social reality" of what an inmate is supposed to experience is largely irrelevant.

However, as niches begin to erode under the pressure of overcrowding, idleness, tight security, and heterogeneous inmate populations, inmates' ability to determine their own reality begins to slip away. Increased communication among themselves (Jayewardene et al., 1976) becomes a method by which inmates get a fix on the "social reality" of the prison environment. This communication marks the beginning of inmates moving forward and recognizing themselves as a "collective" and a group (Janis, 1968).

During conditions of change, correctional officers are also vulnerable to this process. The existence of an officer reference group capable of influencing the attitudes and behaviors of individual correctional officers is something that cannot safely be assumed. Rather than a cohesive group with widely accepted norms and sanctions, the officers may be better described as a highly fragmented collection of individuals. To be sure, their work requires a degree of interdependence, but officers express a high degree of independence in attitude, opinion, and beliefs. Rather than maintaining close personal relationships with their comrades, officers tend to go their own way, seeking to avoid personal contact and communication with each other outside of the institution. Inside the institution, officers create their own "niches" (Lombardo, 1989).

In Festinger's (1968) terms, these officers interpret prison conditions on the basis of a "physical reality." However, as objective prison conditions begin to change, and as absences and/or changes in key staff, poor communication, and publicity about prison conditions (Wilsnack, 1976) begin to impinge on the guard's world, the reliability of this "physical reality" diminishes. Relationships with inmates begin to take on an increasingly "formal" character. And as inmates increase "censorious" responses to guard formality, hostility and mutual suspicion increase. Inmates now behave in ways more likely to be interpreted by guards as challenges to their authority and to their position as guards (Jayewardene et al., 1976; Lombardo, 1989). By sharing these experiences, guards begin to develop a "social reality" of themselves and inmates at variance with their normal subjective experiences, but confirmed by the experiences of others.

The stage is set for confrontation. Individuals who *live* in the prison are becoming "inmates," and those who *work* in the prisons are becoming "guards," in their own eyes and in the eyes of others. Role-playing behavior based on a new socially determined reality begins to replace coping behavior based on individually determined physical reality. Guards and inmates now begin to behave in collective and symbolic ways, each interpreting and reacting to the behavior of the other in terms of the stereotypical images their new "social reality" has created.[1]

Wilsnack (1976) finds increased numbers of inter-inmate assaults and assaults on prison staff associated with prisons that experienced riots. Such confrontations can plausibly contribute to the development of a collective response by providing the conditions necessary for what Janis (1968) refers to as the "contagion effect." This phenomenon describes the spread of excitement or violence and the development of group identification when the group is faced with an external threat. The conditions for contagion, as identified by Redl and Wineman,[2] are:

   (a) an initiator who must openly "act out" in such a way that he obviously gratifies an impulse that the rest of the members have been inhibiting;

   (b) the initiator must display a lack of anxiety or guilt; and

   (c) the other members who perceive the initiator's actions must have been undergoing for some time an intense conflict with respect to performing the forbidden act (Janis, 1968:87).

Though increasing numbers of violent confrontations between inmates and/or between inmates and guards may in themselves represent last-ditch responses to stress, they are also sources of stress, stimuli for contagion, and occasions for group identification.

Lockwood sees violence as a transition stage in the movement from individual to collective responses to stress. He notes that:

> there is a point in the process leading up to outbreaks of [collective] violence where emotion and mass enthusiasm overbalance individual inmate thinking. Small cliques go over as a group to the side of the protestors. The importance of group action is reinforced by the staff techniques of transferring or segregating those who protest. At this particular stage, a man chooses between group loyalty and personal security. If he chooses group loyalty—then the process begins to take place as a group phenomenon [Lockwood, personal communication].

In reviewing antecedents of prison riots, I have thus far traced the erosion of preliminary responses to stressful conditions and the consequent inability of both inmates and guards to develop new solutions to compounded stress. The interpersonal character of these failures leads to the development of social definitions of the problem, mutual hostility of inmates and staff, stereotypical behaviors, and, ultimately, to violence.

Stress and Collective Violence in Prison

While the collective nature of prison riot behavior might be understood in terms of a shift from individual to group solutions to stress and from "physical" to "social" definitions of stress and coping, the violent content may be, at least in part, an extension of a "subculture" of violence that permeates prisons. Violence and a concern for safety remain parts of a prisons' subjective reality no matter how infrequently incidents of violence actually occur. With regard to the objective and subjective reality of prison sexual violence and its impact on victims, Lockwood (1980) observes:

> The impact of victimization is not necessarily related to the level of force deployed in an incident or to the "objective" danger of the environment. To an extent the impact of target experience is based on the perception of danger and the expectation of physical harm rather than actual danger and physical harm. Environments themselves viewed as threatening, can be responsible for victim trauma.

Where violence is perceived as a way of life, it is expected that violence will be used to settle disputes. Guards refer to the assumed fact of violence, not its probability, as one of their primary concerns (Lombardo, 1989). Jack Abbott, a long-term resident of prisons with expertise in the practice of violence, claims that in prisons:

> *everyone* is afraid. It is not an emotional or psychological fear. It is a practical matter. If you don't threaten someone at the very least, someone will threaten you. When you walk across the yard or down the tier to your cell, you stand out like a sore thumb if you do not appear either callously unconcerned or cold and ready to kill. Many times you have to "prey" on someone, or you will be "preyed" on yourself. After so many years, *you are not bluffing*. No one is [Abbott, 1981:121-122; emphasis in original].

This violent content of prison life is not always available for collective deployment. For this to occur, restraints inhibiting overt expressions of violence must be reduced and justifications for the use of collective violence must be put into place.

One of the most powerful restraints inhibiting outbursts of collective violence in prison is the "status quo," comprising stable conditions (no matter how depriving) within which individuals develop lifestyles that satisfy their felt needs, even where survival is the only need that can be satisfied (Bettelheim, 1943). Stability increases vested interest in the status quo, and prevents depriving conditions from being viewed as arbitrary. Changes in the status quo can draw attention to the perceived *illegitimacy* of the conditions, even where conditions have improved in an objective sense (Fogelson, 1971). Pastore (1952) and Berkowitz (1981) have demonstrated that frustrations perceived as arbitrary or illegitimate promote more aggressive reactions than frustrations perceived as lawful or legitimate.

Staff behavior or institutional policy that alters accepted patterns of adaptation can be perceived as arbitrary and illegitimate by both inmates and staff. When reasonable explanations for staff behavior are not offered to inmates and when previously offered explanations for inmate rule violations are not accepted, the perceived arbitrariness and illegitimacy of staff control is increased. To the extent that staff are not involved in making decisions about their work routines, the legitimacy of administrative changes is not obvious to them. Unfavorable publicity focusing on conditions inside the prison (Wilsnack, 1976) strengthens the belief of guards and inmates that existing conditions need not be maintained.

Other restraints inhibiting a violent response to stressful conditions include a concern for personal safety given the perceived overwhelming opposition of the authorities, the fear of arrest (and an extended term of imprisonment), and a commitment to orderly social change and achieving improved conditions through established procedures (Fogelson, 1971). Under normal conditions these restraints operate in the prison setting, but as conditions change, they are subject to erosion. With increasing threats to personal safety evidenced by the prevalence of inter-inmate assaults and the failure of prison administrators to reduce the threat, the potency of administrative control is thrown into serious question. Though inmates know that violent revolt will undoubtedly be crushed, by force if necessary, one of the restraints deterring the outbreak of such violence is severely weakened.

Similar changes weaken the fear of keep-lock and disciplinary procedures. Under normal conditions, a disciplinary penalty of one day or one week may be experienced as a punishment, by some inmates at least. The loss of interpersonal contacts and of social and economic benefits from the maintenance of social relations can cause at least annoyance—especially when one's territory may be taken over by another and when loss of a privileged work assignment may deprive the inmate of a niche. Under conditions of change, instability, turmoil, and danger, a keep-lock may come to mean nothing. Finally, where formal grievance mechanisms do not exist, the chances for achieving orderly change through informal bargaining and administrative responses to crisis situations may have run out. Even where there are formal grievance channels, failure to resolve salient issues satisfactorily often leads to feelings of impotence. Established procedures are redefined as a sham designed and used by administrators to prevent real change.

Justifications for the Use of Violence in Prison Riots

With the state of flux created by the erosion of established patterns of behavior, the development of mutually stereotypical definitions by staff and inmates, and the loosening of restraints that curb riot tendencies, what is needed to unleash collective violence is a set of justifications for its use. Such justifications may be found in the social processes involved in individuals' reactions to stress and in the process of conversion from individual to collective response.

In analyzing situations in which individuals take action for what they personally believe is wrong (the infliction of violence on others) but which they pursue in spite of the disapproved effects, Duster (1971) identifies six conditions that contribute to defining the situation as one permitting such contradictory behaviors. Focusing on incidents from the Vietnam War and police involvement with the Black Panthers in the 1960s, Duster refers to these as "conditions for guilt-free massacre," a set of rationalizations with which individuals can shield themselves from responsibility for their actions. These conditions include: (1) the denial of the humanity of the victims; (2) organizational grounds for action that supersede individual grounds for action; (3) loyalty to the organization that supersedes every other consideration; (4) the fact that an organization uses secrecy and isolation as a cover for its actions; (5) the existence of a target population; and (6) the motivation to engage in violence (Duster, 1971).

Denial of Humanity. Though guards may normally see inmates as people and clients for services (Lombardo, 1989) and inmates may perceive guards as solutions to rather than creators of problems (Toch, 1977a; Lockwood, 1980), when stressful conditions remain unresolved such perceptions are likely to change and the underlying "social definitions" of criminal and guard as less than human are likely to emerge. At Auburn such less-or-more-than human stereotypes (as subhuman or superhuman) dominated correctional officers' pre-employment images (Lombardo, 1989). Guards have a second group that may be seen as "less than human," the correctional administrators. It is easy for guards to look upon administrators as an outgroup. Lack of meaningful contact turns administrators into "callous, calculating manipulators" constantly attempting to interfere in the officers' work environment, usually to the officers' detriment. Officers feel that they are "treated like children" or "like numbers." Feeling dehumanized facilitates their adoption of a rejecting stance toward the administration.

Organizational Goals Supersede Individual Goals. For inmates under pre-riot stress, conditions within the prison and within the criminal justice system turn from individually experienced stress to shared grievances that call for consensus-based "demands." Though aggrieving conditions may have existed for years preceding violence, the breakdown of normal patterns of prison behavior encourages inmates to view these conditions from a shared, jaundiced, impatient perspective.

For the guard, organizational goals such as rehabilitation, incapacitation, and punishment often have little meaning in the normal work situation. Guards perform their duties in ways that fulfill more immediate personal goals: They try to keep active, find some meaning in their work, or just stay out of trouble (Lombardo, 1989). When the status quo becomes upset and organizational goals (expressed through administrative directives) begin to impinge on guards' routines, they may choose one of several available goals and substitute it for their own. The behavior of one officer pursuing an organizational goal may contribute little.to disruption of routine. However, many officers working at cross-purposes with each other and with institutional goals may magnify the extent of "institutional breakdown."

Loyalty to the Organization Supersedes Every Other Consideration. Under normal conditions inmate loyalty to peers is minimized by the competition for goods, status, and power. Such divisions serve as social control mechanisms supplementing and sometimes substituting for weak formal mechanisms of control (Cloward, 1977). In developing a collective response, however, loyalties to self or clique become secondary to loyalties to "inmates" as a group, which implies a closing of ranks against the institutional administration and correctional staff.

While officers have little reason to display or express loyalties toward other officers (Lombardo, 1989), a combination of perceived threats from inmates (increases in censoriousness and violence), the administration (changes in work routines), and the media (criticisms in the press) leads officers to close ranks. Where officers feel challenged, seemingly on all fronts, loyalty to the guard fraternity can become an overriding concern.

Organizational Secrecy and Isolation to Cover Its Actions. The perceptions that correctional agencies employ secrecy and seek to maintain isolation are prevalent not only among critics of correctional institutions but also among inmates and correctional officers. When unusual incidents (killings, drug investigations, fires) occur, all groups express dissatisfaction with the explanations offered by administrators. The administration is perceived as acting "as if it had something to hide."

This factor is particularly relevant in understanding guard violence in the aftermath and retaking of prisons. Duster (1971) comments that in military and police organizations "public control and scrutiny are to be avoided at all costs on the grounds of inexpertise ('the general knows best') and of subversion ('enemies of the people are among the people')." According to the Attica Commission, officers at Attica held similar opinions concerning court interventions into the correctional process:

> Guards almost universally felt that courts were interfering in matters in which they had no competence. Judges, they felt, knew nothing about prisons or prisoners and could not come to an intelligent decision concerning either (New York State Special Commission on Attica, 1972:125).

The role of the media and reformers (Wilsnack, 1976) in threatening to "expose" abuses magnifies the salience of secrecy and isolation.

A Target Population with Inferior Fire Power. Though inmates know that the ulti-mate result of any violent collective disturbance will be repression, they also know that their own overwhelming numbers and physical power (guards are usually not armed, while inmates, especially during times of unrest, are frequently armed with homemade weapons) makes the target population (guards and prison administrators) particularly vulnerable. For guards, their target population preceding the riot may be the prison administration. The administrators have no power except that exercised through guards. If guards desert administrators and allow violence to erupt, admin-istrators are left to fight the battle alone. The turnover in prison administrators fol-lowing outbreaks of violence demonstrates that guards have the ability to massacre by inaction.

Following riots, in retaking the prison and the aftermath, officer violence focuses on inmates as a powerless target population. With inmates locked in their cells, cell-to-cell searches following riots are often occasions for wanton property destruction and even for widespread physical abuse of inmates.

A Motivation to Engage in Violence. For inmates using violence to take over a prison, or for guards using violence to retake the prison, the motivation is fre-quently expressed in catch phrases. "It's in the national interest" justifies military actions, and "It's in the line of duty" serves as a motivation for normally inappro-priate police behavior. Prisoners have to "show we're men" and guards and prison administrators have to "get this place back" and "restore order and regain author-ity." Such phrases serve to focus and justify violent behavior.

Summary

The subculture of prison violence, coupled with the loosening of restraints against violence and the development of a collective response to stress, provide both inmates and guards with the motivations and justifications for their own brand of collective violence in prison settings. When viewed in the context of the ongoing life of prison communities, prison collective violence can serve a large variety of needs for different individuals. But once individuals develop a "collective sense" and violence is set into motion, such individual motivations appear to be superseded by the drama of the event, though individual concerns must still be considered if we are to understand the motives of participants adequately.

Toch's (1969) comments on the beginning of the Watts riot of 1965 provide a concise summary of these observations:

> Once collective violence has been initiated, it acquires a momen-tum of its own; even if people did not suffer from grievances riots would attract and recruit participants. They would do so because they appeal to boredom, anger, frustration, desire for adventure; because they provide a ready-made opportunity to discharge feeling; because they furnish festive activity with the sanction of peers and under the aegis of principle.

As violent crowds form, by-standers are invited to join; if not, they find it natural to fill the gaps within the ranks. Streets become an arena for heroism, a proving ground for bravery. A stage for protest. Boys can achieve manhood heaving rocks or defying police officers; men can acquire purpose through riot-connected projects. At some points nonviolence requires special explanation and requires special motives. Violence becomes, temporarily, a way of life.

Notes

[1] One of the most graphic (though least consequential) examples of the confrontational potential that lies beneath the surface of this combination of prison/staff "role behavior" (as opposed to the individual behavior of the persons occupying the roles) occurred during the "simulated prison" experiment conducted at Stanford University in 1971 (Haney et al., 1977). One interpretation for the "prison rebellion" at Stanford is that it was a reaction to the harsh conditions imposed on the students who participated. However, the short time involved and the minimally harsh conditions make this rebellion seem more like the "thing to do." That is, it became assumed that "prisoners" are expected to rebel, and that prisoners are expected to use violence to respond to prison staff. It is possible that the "scripts" the Stanford subjects were following were derived from their expectations and assumptions concerning the behaviors of guards and inmates, rather than from their personal reactions to their immediate situation. They developed a group identity as they reinforced each other in their beliefs about the reality of their confinement. Instead of individuals testing and evaluating their own experiences, these student-inmates and student-guards accepted the "social definition" of their situation and acted out the expected rebellion.

[2] See Redl (1966:155-213) for a thorough discussion of this process.

References

Abbott, J. (1981). *In the Belly of the Beast*. New York, NY: Random House.

Berkowitz, L. (1981). "On the Difference Between Internal and External Reactions to Legitimate and Illegitimate Frustrations: A Demonstration." *Aggressive Behavior, 7*, 83-96.

Bettelheim, B. (1943). "Individual and Mass Behavior in Extreme Situations." *Journal of Abnormal and Social Psychology*, 38, 417-452.

Cloward R.A. (1977). "Social Control in the Prison." In R.G. Leger and J.R. Stratton (eds.) *The Sociology of Corrections*. New York, NY: John Wiley.

Desroches, F. (1974). "Patterns in Prison Riots." *Canadian Journal of Criminology and Penology*, 16, 332-351.

Dollard, J., L. Doob, N. Miller, O.H. Maurer and R. Sears (1970). In E. Magargee and J.E. Hokanson (eds.) *The Dynamics of Aggression*. New York, NY: Harper & Row.

Duster, T. (1971). "Conditions for Guilt-Free Massacre." In N. Sanford and C. Comstock (eds.) *Sanctions for Evil*. Boston, MA: Beacon.

Festinger, L. (1968). "Informal Social Communication." In D. Cartwright and A. Zander (eds.) *Group Dynamics*. New York, NY: Harper & Row.

Fogelson, R.M. (1971). *Violence as Protest: A Study of Riots and Ghettos*. Garden City, NY: Doubleday.

Garson, G.D. (1972a). "The Disruption of Prison Administration: An Investigation of Alternative Theories of the Relationship Among Administrators, Reformers and Involuntary Social Services Clients." *Law and Society Review*, May, pp. 531-561.

Garson, G.D. (1972b). "Force Versus Restraint in Prison Riots." *Crime and Delinquency*, 18(4), 411-421.

Haney, C., C. Banks and P. Zimbardo (1977). "Interpersonal Dynamics in a Simulated Prison." In R.G. Leger and J.R. Stratton (eds.) *The Sociology of Corrections*. New York, NY: John Wiley.

Janis, I. (1968). "Group Identification Under Conditions of External Danger." In D. Cartwright and A. Zander (eds.) *Group Dynamics*. New York, NY: Harper & Row.

Jayewardene, C.H.S., H.B. McKay and B.E.A. McKay (1976). "In Search of a Sixth Sense: Predictors of Disruptive Behavior in Correctional Institutions." *Crime and/et Justice*, 4(1), 32-39.

Lockwood, D. (1980). *Prison Sexual Violence*. New York, NY: Elsevier.

Lombardo, L.X. (1989). *Guards Imprisoned: Correctional Officers at Work*. Second Edition. Cincinnati, OH: Anderson Publishing Co.

Mathiesen, T. (1965). *Defences of the Weak*. London, England: Tavistock.

Newman, G. (1979). *Understanding Violence*. New York, NY: J.B. Lippincott.

New York State Special Commission on Attica. (1972). *Attica*. New York, NY: Bantam Books.

Pastore, N. (1952). "The Role of Arbitrariness in the Frustration-Aggression Hypothesis." *Journal of Abnormal and Social Psychology*, 47, 728-731.

Redl, F. (1966). *When We Deal with Children*. New York, NY: The Free Press.

Sykes, G. (1958). *The Society of Captives: A Study of a Maximum Security Prison*. Princeton, NJ: Princeton University Press.

Toch, H. (1969). *Violent Men: An Inquiry into the Psychology of Violence*. Chicago, IL: Aldine.

Toch, H. (1977a). *Living in Prison: The Ecology of Survival*. New York, NY: The Free Press.

Toch, H. (1977b). *Police, Prisons, and the Problem of Violence*. Washington, DC: U.S. Government Printing Office.

Wade, A.L. (1967). "Social Processes in the Act of Juvenile Vandalism." In M.B. Clinard and R. Quinney (eds.) *Criminal Behavior Systems: A Typology*. New York, NY: Holt, Rinehart & Winston.

Wilsnack, R.W. (1976). "Explaining Collective Violence in Prisons: Problems and Possibilities. In A. Cohen, G. Cole and R. Bailey (eds.) *Prison Violence*. Lexington, MA: D.C. Heath.

17

A Typology of the Causes of Prison Riots and an Analytical Extension to the 1986 West Virginia Riot[†][††]

Randy Martin & Sherwood Zimmerman

On January 1, 1986, inmates at the West Virginia State Penitentiary seized one wing of the prison and held it for approximately three days. During this takeover, 15 guards and one food service worker were taken hostage. This riot resulted in neither the carnage nor the severe destruction of property that occurred at Attica in 1971 or in Santa Fe in 1980. It did, however, prompt the question that everyone asks (or attempts to answer) after such a disturbance: What caused this riot? In the aftermath of riots, this question is asked repeatedly by the public, by political leaders, by the media, by correctional administrators, and by institutional staff members and their unions. As in the official investigation of the West Virginia riot, however, the answers never seem to be fully satisfactory.

We start our analysis by examining the methodological problems associated with conducting rigorous social, scientific inquiries into prison riots. We develop a typology that structures the more prominent models that have been advanced to "explain" the occurrence of riots. This typology is the basis for our assessment of the utility of these models as etiological explanations. Next we analyze the account of the 1986 takeover of the West Virginia State Penitentiary, using an integrated conceptual structure that draws on several of the current models of prison riots. Finally, we compare and contrast our analysis of the West Virginia riot with the available information

†Randy Martin and Sherwood Zimmerman. "A Typology of the Causes of Prison Riots and an Analytical Extension to the 1986 West Virginia Riot." *Justice Quarterly* 7(4):711-737, December 10, 1990. Reprinted with permission of the Academy of Criminal Justice Sciences.
††While accepting full responsibility for the content of this chapter, we want to acknowledge our colleague Jake Gibbs for his excellent counsel while we were preparing the manuscript. We also want to thank our three anonymous *Justice Quarterly* reviewers. The participation of all these individuals energized and greatly improved our work.

about selected other collective disturbances. The purpose of these comparisons is to highlight strengths and weaknesses of the explanatory models and to extend the findings of the analysis.

Methods for Analyzing Prison Riots

More than 300 prison riots have occurred in this country since the first was reported in 1774, and 90 percent of these have taken place since 1952. Beginning with Sykes's (1958) classic work, there has been a sustained inquiry into the causes and consequences of modern prison riots. Given the body of literature this inquiry has generated, and the documented increases in the magnitude of violence and destruction in such disturbances (Barak-Glantz, 1985; Desroches, 1974; Dillingham & Montgomery, 1985; Flynn, 1980; Mahan, 1985), one might think that sufficient knowledge would have been accumulated to support some reasonably definitive explanation. Yet, as Dillingham and Montgomery (1985) point out, there is relatively little reliable and valid information about why riots occur, and our ability to predict (and thereby prevent) prison riots is at best rudimentary.

There are two important constraints on the ability to understand the dynamics of prison riots. One limit is the inadequacy of the information that is typically available. A primary reason for the limited amount and quality of information is the retrospective nature of the methods that must be used to collect data. These methods are retrospective because invariably they rely on the residue of events as reconstructed by riot participants.[1] Their purpose is to provide insights into the events leading up to and taking place during a riot, and there is great variability in how effectively this purpose is achieved. Many of these post-riot autopsies are superficial, and consequently they generate little information about the actual causes of the riot. The prevalence of such superficial analysis suggests to the uncharitable that there may be institutional reasons for not wanting accurate information about why a riot actually occurred (for a discussion of this issue, see Fox, 1972). One result of so many ineffective analyses is that our knowledge base about prison riots is still deficient; this deficiency in turn contributes to our lack of understanding about prison riots as a class of events.

The second important constraint is that even when an effective post-riot analysis is conducted, the information produced is often of limited value for generalizing the phenomenon of prison riots. Prison riots are low-frequency, high-salience events, and although they have important operational, political, and moral consequences, their infrequency makes them highly idiosyncratic. The "spontaneity and danger" that characterize riots also limit the possibilities for direct observational analysis and for experimental research (Mahan, 1985). These factors combine to impede the identification and rigorous measurement of the causal forces preceding a riot. Consequently it is difficult to create and adequately test generalizable explanations of the causes and courses of riots.

In addition, a great number of factors often precede prison riots, and any adequate multivariate explanation would have to include many of these factors. One problem associated with using these factors is that many are extremely difficult to measure with sufficient reliability and validity to support confirmatory analyses of explanatory models. A second problem is that because there are more factors than riots, it is difficult to construct, and therefore virtually impossible to test, quantitative explanatory models. Knowledge about prison riots is relatively limited, and probably will continue to grow slowly and intermittently given these pervasive problems.

Despite the dearth of what Flynn (1980) calls "empirically verified information on exact causes of riots," several conceptual models have been developed in attempts to explain these endemic prison disturbances. These models range from structural paradigms to random-event "explanations." None provide a necessary and sufficient explanation of why prison riots occur, although together they may identify many of the environmental conditions and institutional relationships that are clearly relevant to a coherent general model. The discussion that follows classifies and examines the current conceptual models of why prison riots occur.

A Typology of Conceptual Models of Prison Riots

Before discussing the current range of "explanatory" models of prison riots, the concept of a prison riot must be defined. Although there is no universally accepted definition, some common definitional ground does exist. In 1986 Conant offered a motivation-oriented definition referring to a riot as a "spontaneous outburst of group violence characterized by excitement mixed with rage...usually directed against alleged perpetrators of injustice or gross misuses of political power" (1968). More recent definitions have focused on specific behavioral components, characterizing riots as incidents that involve the seizure of control over part or all of the prison through violence or force, the destruction of property, and the presentation of demands by a group of inmates (Dillingham & Montgomery, 1985; Flynn, 1980; Mahan, 1985).

In his seminal study of prisons, Gresham Sykes (1958) provided the first analysis of modern prison riots. He viewed prisons as having a seriously constrained capacity for adapting to perturbations in institutional routines. This difficulty in accommodating change occurs because these institutions are capable of receiving only minimally effective positive feedback, to use the terminology of systems theory. The lack of feedback results in the use of custodial "solutions" to problems. Such "solutions" are effective in the short run, but the underlying difficulties remain. The application of custodial power in managing an incident also results in increased tension between inmates and staff, creating an environment in which further incidents are likely. This situation, according to Sykes, results in progressive departures from a state of equilibrium and, over time, in an increasingly pressurized institutional environment. Some random incident (the spark) then occurs, which escalates out of control in an environment that is preconditioned to collective violence (the tinder), and a prison riot occurs (the conflagration).

Many of the insights produced by Sykes's model remain valid and valuable. This model is limited, however, because the framework of the riot-generation process contains little substantive content. Indeed, the attempt to identify the substantive factors involved in producing prison riots or otherwise to elaborate Sykes's model has been the focus of most subsequent riot studies.

Building on Sykes's framework, the discussion that follows classifies current explanations for prison riots into a typology of six conceptual models: environmental conditions, spontaneity, conflict, collective behavior/social control, power vacuum, and rising expectations. This discussion is summarized in Table 17.1.

Table 17.1. **Conceptual Models of Prison Riots: A Typology**

CONCEPTUAL MODEL	
	Environmental Conditions
Sykes (1958)	Focus is on distal causes or "preconditions":
Official Reports	-ACA identifies four categories of "causes."
(e.g., ACA 1981)	-The explanation for a riot involves the manner in which environmental conditions collectively created "a bomb that is waiting to explode."
	-Necessary but not sufficient conditions for riots.
	-Little attention is given to the problems and choices faced by subcultural groups.
	-Little attention is given to the dynamic aspects of prison environments.
	-Explanations do not focus on the interactions among the subcultural groups involved (administration, COs, inmates).
	Spontaneity
Sykes (1958)	Focus is on proximate cause of an individual disturbance:
Conant (1968)	
Fox (1971, 1972)	-Environmental conditions become preconditions, creating a climate in which a riot can occur from some "spontaneous event" (precipitating cause).
Mahan (1985)	
	-Special attention is given to an incident or a string of incidents that trigger a riot.
	-Little attention is given to the problems and choices faced by subcultural groups.
	-Little attention is given to the dynamic aspects of prison environments.
	-Explanations do not focus on the interactions among the subcultural groups involved (administration, COs, inmates).

	Conflict
Conant (1968)	Focus is on the impact of the repressive power
Smith (1973)	structure of prisons:
Cohen (1976)	-Special attention is given to the resulting
	subcultural (value) conflicts and the limited
	options available for their resolution.
	-Little attention is given to interactions between the
	formal and the informal sources of power (control).
	-Total neglect of the positive contributions of
	official power and control.
	Collective Behavior and Social Control
Clemmer (1940)	Focus is on the formal and informal mechanisms of
Hartung and Floch (1957)	social control within the prison environment:
Smelser (1963)	-These mechanisms are examined against the back-
Gould (1974)	drop of changes in the prison environment that
Stotland (1976)	operate to disrupt the balance of institutional
Crouch (1980)	control.
Irwin (1980)	-Special attention is given to the consequences of
DiIulio (1987)	breakdowns in the normal mechanisms of social
Clear and Cole (1990)	control, especially the less formal mechanisms.
	-Little attention is given to the overriding role of
	conflict or to the importance of spontaneous or
	precipitating events.
	Power Vacuum
Desroches (1974)	Focus is specifically on the role of abrupt
Barak-Glantz (1985)	changes in the network of formal control
	mechanisms and consequent shifts in power
	relationships (anomic correctional system):
	-This model contains elements of the conflict
	and the social control approaches to explaining
	collective disturbances.
	-Special attention is given to the role of changing
	goals and/or administrations in disturbing this
	equilibrium.
	-Little attention is given to environmental
	conditions or spontaneous precipitating events.
	Rising Expectations
Conant (1968)	Focus is on the gap between inmates' expectations
Cloward (1969)	about the quality of the institutional environ-
Davies (1972)	ment and the quality of life experienced:
Gurr (1972)	-This model is linked closely to the notions of
Desroches (1974)	relative deprivation and differential opportunity.
Flynn (1980)	-Special attention is given to the role of correc-
	tional administrators and groups external to cor-
	rections (the courts) in creating higher levels of
	inmate expectations.
	-Little attention is given to the mechanics of how
	the group perception develops.

The Environmental Conditions Model

Most analyses of prison riots focus on the conditions that existed prior to the riot, probably because most analyses are conducted by government officials or sometimes by reformist groups. The purpose of such investigations is typically the assignment of responsibility (blame) for the riot and/or the reformation of the environmental conditions that presumably caused the riot. These investigations are one component of the political aftermath of a riot (Fox, 1972; Sykes, 1958), and the findings are often self-serving. Thus, Fox (1972) argues, official investigations and reports tend to produce invalid and unreliable information because they are used so frequently to justify political (and sometimes partisan) positions. The political orientations of official investigations often result in skewed and one-dimensional conceptualizations of factors that are believed to have preconditioned an institution to riot. Even more problematically, causal attributions typically are assigned to these preconditions.

Barak-Glantz (1985) notes that official reports and the other literature on the causes of riots reveal a "relatively consistent melange" of contributing factors, including: poor, insufficient, and/or contaminated food; overcrowding; institution size;[2] public indifference; a lack of professional leadership; substandard personnel; inhumane administration; brutality; inadequate or no treatment programs; idleness and monotony; political interference; and groups of refractory, hard-core inmates. Other lists include additional factors such as: meaningless employment; a lack of communication between staff and inmates; isolated rural locations (Dillingham & Montgomery, 1985); recent change in prison administration (Barak-Glantz, 1985); aggregate of different types of inmates in one facility; and the destruction of the semi-official inmate self-governance (Hartung & Floch, 1957).

The South Carolina Department of Corrections (1973) identified eight conditions or characteristics as conducive to riots. Although these preconditions overlap somewhat with those from other studies, they are interesting in that they are quite specific. These conditions/characteristics are: a maximum-security institution; large planned capacity (300 or more); older prison; little contact between the warden and inmates; more educated inmates and officers; absence of meaningful and productive job assignments; inadequate recreational programs; and the presence of administrative and punitive segregation units.

The American Correctional Association (1981) concluded that the causes of riots and other disturbances could be classified into four categories: institutional environment; characteristics of the inmate population; administrative practices; and noninstitutional causes. Corrections administrators usually cite some combination of these kinds of factors as the causes of riots (Desroches, 1974). Indeed, the dominant explanatory theme of correctional administrators is that riots are produced largely by environmental conditions and other factors over which administrators' control is limited for budgetary, political, or other reasons. At face value, such causal interpretations may seem feasible. These preconditions are present, however, in the great majority of American prisons, and the great majority of those facilities do not experience riots. Thus, these factors may be necessary conditions for prison riots, but they certainly are not sufficient causes (Babbie, 1989). Therefore, the explanatory value of such environmental variables is limited.

As summarized in Table 17.1, the Environmental Conditions model focuses on the distal, not the proximate causes of prison riots. Special attention is paid to pre-existing environmental conditions that, consistent with Sykes's (1958) model of prison riots, almost foreordains the conclusion that these conditions collectively create "a bomb, waiting to explode." While it is clear that riots do not simply occur divorced from any historical context, it is also clear that the presence of conditions ripe for disorder is not sufficient to explain a prison riot. Analyses based on this model are insufficient by themselves because they are, at worst, the product of political blame-laying and, at best, they represent a static and therefore incomplete explanation of why prisoners riot.

The Spontaneity Model

Several theorists (Conant, 1968; Fox, 1971, 1972; Mahan, 1985; Sykes, 1958) argue that riots are largely unplanned, spontaneously initiated events. Fox (1972) distinguishes riots from disturbances, arguing that disturbances are planned and coordinated, and typically culminate as sit-down strikes, hunger strikes, slow-downs, and self-inflicted injury. Riots occur when some incident sets off a chain of events that becomes a collective violent disturbance aimed at taking control of a prison or some portion of a prison. Fox (1971, 1972) postulates a two-dimensional causal process consisting of predisposing and precipitating factors. The predisposing factors are essentially the set of environmental conditions described above. These factors create a "time bomb" waiting to be detonated; the detonator is some spontaneous precipitating event (Dillingham & Montgomery, 1985), such as an altercation between an officer and an inmate or an unannounced lockdown.

According to Fox (1972), prison riots go through a five-stage process: (1) explosion, (2) organization, (3) confrontation, (4) termination and (5) reaction and explanation. Stage 1 is initiated by a spontaneous event, and is characterized by undirected and diffuse violence. The other four stages relate to the dynamics of a riot once it is underway, and are more a description of the process than an explanation of a riot's origins. Fox (1971) recognizes that the precipitating event is seldom the real cause, although he believes that this fact is frequently obscured by the obligatory official investigation (Stage 5). As Conant (1986) points out, however, no matter how spontaneous or directionless they may appear, prison riots are rarely senseless outbursts.

Spontaneity models focus on the unique proximate cause of an individual disturbance (see Table 17.1). A series of dysfunctional, unyielding environmental factors is viewed as preconditioning the institutional milieu, creating a climate that is receptive both for a riot and for the salient spontaneous event (or precipitating cause) that triggers the riot. Like the Environmental Conditions models, Spontaneity models do not focus on the power or the processing structures of institutions, on the constituencies to a riot, or on the problems and choices faced by these groups in the evolution of a riot. Thus, neither the Environmental Conditions models nor the Spontaneity models, alone or together, provide more than the "necessary" components for an explanation.

The remaining four explanatory models in our typology attempt to deal with the sufficiency criterion by focusing on structural and subcultural factors, and on the interactions of those factors, as causes of prison riots.

The Conflict Model

Conflict models are based on the presumption that the pervasive official repression in prisons has two consequences that can contribute to the occurrence of a riot. The first consequence of official repression is that it generates subcultural (value) conflicts; the second is the structural limitations that this orientation imposes on the alternatives available for resolving conflict in prisons. Although the process of subcultural conflict is not inherently destructive, it can become so when behavioral alternatives are constrained.

Cohen (1976), in his sociological explanation of prison violence, asserted that it is a misconception to view violence as necessarily abnormal, perverse, or pathological. Violence may be used as a dramatic way to call attention to one's helplessness and desperation, to grievances, and to injustices. In normal circumstances there are usually other ways to accomplish these ends, but in the "abnormal" environment of prison, the range of behavioral options is drastically restricted. Cohen argued that to understand why violence occurs, violent acts must be understood in the context of the behavioral opportunities and alternatives available to the actors. From the Conflict perspective, the first-order cause of this situation is the official repression that inheres in the structure of the prison environment.

Smith (1973) argues that conflict exists when individuals or groups disagree about the way power is exercised. In prison, when such conflicts occur and go unresolved, a riot may result. To support his contention, Smith points out that an integral part of the etiology of the modern prison riot is "conflict declaration"—that is, a verbal and/or written specification of how one side wants the other side to exercise power. From Smith's perspective, then, it is appropriate that the presentation of demands is included in several of the more contemporary definitions of the concept "prison riot." There are four possible reactions to conflict declarations: bargaining, withdrawal by one participant, physical combat, or third-party mediation. Extending Smith's argument, it seems possible that variants of these reactions might be employed at different points in the sequence of events leading up to and during a riot.

The structural aspects and social dynamics operating in a correctional setting serve to make the third reaction, physical combat (i.e., a riot), a highly viable possibility when conflicts arise. As Cohen (1976) observed, most inmates have little in the way of bargaining power. They also cannot easily employ avoidance (withdrawal) as a means of conflict resolution because of their closed and restrictive environment. A level of irony exists with respect to the third-party mediation alternative; although the courts provide a seemingly appropriate vehicle for such intervention, political and economic realities operate to decrease the likelihood that inmates will experience any real change. Even favorable court decisions usually do not resolve the problems that undergird prison conflicts; judicial intervention is an imprecise tool for securing change, and rarely is accompanied by political and public support. Consequently many inmates perceive physical combat to be their only viable option. As Cohen eloquently described the situation, violence becomes "the one currency of those who have nothing else" (1976).

Another macro-level component of this conflict process is that our legal and social structures provide individuals and groups with considerable opportunity to air their complaints, but in the face of a consistent failure to respond to these grievances, collective disturbances become more likely (Fox, 1972). Both Conant (1968) and Flynn (1980) carried this notion to its extreme, suggesting that conflicts over unsatisfied needs are the ultimate source of collective disturbances in society, and specifically in prisons.

Conant (1968) proposed three universal factors associated with riots: preconditions, riot phases, and social control. He argued that all riots stem from intense value conflicts, and he characterized these conflicts as "preconditions." The "riot phases" represent the dynamics of riots once they are in progress, and are very similar to the riot stages identified by Fox. The third factor, "social control," relates to the inattention of the prison administration to value conflicts and to failures in the repressive control mechanisms that characterize penal institutions.

The elements of the Conflict model are summarized in Table 17.1. This model focuses on the impact of the repressive power structure in prison, the subcultural conflicts generated by that power, and the lack of perceived alternatives to violence. This explanation concentrates on the interactions among and within the major subcultural groups of the prison environment (inmates, line staff, and administration). On the other hand, analyses of prison riots based on the Conflict model give little direct attention to the informal sources of power and control, and to the interactions between these and the formal sources of power in prison. Such models also disregard the positive contribution of official power and control in creating a safer prison environment (Johnson, 1987).

The Collective Behavior/Social Control Model

The primary mechanism of control in a correctional institution is not force but, as Barak-Glantz (1985) states, "an intricate web of informal and symbiotic social relationships" among the inmates, staff, and administration. Anything that disrupts these interrelationships becomes a potential threat to the delicate balance of control. Changes in the prison environment, whether perceived as positive or as negative, can disturb this balance, and an outbreak of collective violence can be a delayed reaction to such changes. This interpretation is similar to that offered by Hartung and Floch (1957) when they identified the destruction of semi-official, informal inmate self-governance as a central factor in riots.

Prisons are controlled with the tacit consent and through the active cooperation of the inmates (Clemmer, 1940; Irwin, 1980). Control in prisons is based on a series of "exchange relationships" (Clear & Cole, 1990) between inmates and staff on mutual accommodations among inmates. These observations make it clear that controlling prisons only through the application of custodial force is not a realistic long-term option. Contemporary corrections administrators, however, are faced with a paradox: Although institutional control cannot rely primarily on custodial force, over time inmates have exhibited a decreased willingness to exert controls over one another (Flynn, 1980). Prisons typically emphasize containment and order, which promote in prisoners an oversimplified approach to reality (Cohen, 1976). The Social Control model suggests that when internal control in a prison is weakened, the associated internal reality is threatened and a variety of tensions and conflicts are produced. When an institutional environment is destabilized in this manner, the potential for individual and collective behavioral problems is compounded greatly. From this perspective, riots are produced when there is a breakdown in informal (Clemmer, 1940; Flynn, 1980; Irwin, 1980) and/or formal control (Crouch, 1980; DiIulio, 1987; Gould, 1974; Mahan, 1985; Stotland, 1976).

The Collective Behavior and Social Control model, summarized in Table 17.1, focuses on the interplay of formal and informal mechanisms of social control within the prison. These mechanisms are examined against the backdrop of environmental conditions and the ways in which those conditions operate to disrupt the balance of institutional control. Explanations based on this model pay special attention to the consequences of breakdowns in the normal mechanisms of social control, but give little attention to the role of conflict or to spontaneous or precipitating events.

The Power Vacuum Model

Discussing the anatomy of a 1981 riot that occurred in the State Prison of Southern Michigan, Barak-Glantz (1985) identified a rift between guards and administration as a central factor. He described the underlying conditions in this institution as constituting an "anomic correctional system." Such a system is characterized as being in a state of powerlessness, or as exhibiting a "power vacuum." It was such a vacuum that the inmates in Southern Michigan rushed to fill. In a broader context, Baro (1988) advanced the premise that the lack of coherent political control over correctional institutions in recent years has created a general leadership vacuum that inhibits effective administration.

This conceptualization contains obvious elements of the Conflict model and implications for Social Control. For example, Barak-Glantz (1982) discusses the problem of mixed goals. When the leadership changes but when no accompanying ideological shifts occur, it is unlikely that the social order of an institution will be threatened. When administrations sequentially pursue different goals, however, problems can arise. Barak-Glantz suggests that such problems are especially likely if staff and inmates are not prepared for a shift in the ideological rationale upon which prison operations are predicated. Fox (1971), describing the consequences of goal-hopping from a custody to a treatment orientation in a prison, argues that in the face of such shifts a tenuous balance develops between controlling and changing behavior, and conflicts (often open in nature) can develop between staff and administration. This situation, Fox maintains, is highly conducive to collective disturbances.

As is the case with many of the other models, the Power Vacuum model is multidimensional. That is, vacuums of power and responses to these vacuums may operate simultaneously at several levels, and the arrangement of these factors may change during the course of a disturbance.

As summarized in Table 17.1, the Power Vacuum model focuses on the role of abrupt and significant changes in the network of formal control mechanisms. These discontinuities in control create fissures in the fabric of official power that inmates perceive to be exploitable. This model contains elements of both the Conflict and the Social Control approaches, with special attention to the role of changing goals and/or administrations in disrupting the existing equilibrium of institutional power. Conversely, this model attributes little importance to environmental conditions or spontaneous precipitating events.

The Rising Expectations/Relative Deprivation Model

Relative deprivation refers to the gap between what people believe they deserve and should have and what they actually receive (Gurr, 1972). This concept is linked very closely to the theory of rising expectations, which holds that collective violence is more likely when progress decelerates after a period of growth or improvement (Davies, 1972). Rising expectations and the perceived discrepancy between what inmates have been led to expect (e.g., improved conditions) and what they actually receive have been cited by several researchers as important contributing factors in riots (Barak-Glantz, 1985; Conant, 1968; Flynn, 1980; Fox, 1972).

A modification of this general notion was presented by Des Roches (1974) when he discussed the problems that arise when officials try to increase control (tighten security) after a period of informal tolerance for officially proscribed activities. Des Roches argued that the accommodation of illicit activities over time creates an illegitimate opportunity structure for inmates. Trying subsequently to eliminate this structure produces a situation in which the forces of rising expectations and relative deprivation operate jointly. A parallel process was identified by Cloward

(1969), who suggested that riots may occur when disenfranchised inmates try unsuccessfully to join inmates who have power and access to illegitimate opportunities.

The Rising Expectations explanation of prison riots (Table 17.1) focuses on the gap between the actual quality of institutional life and inmates' views of what prison life should be. The model is linked closely to the notions of relative deprivation and differential opportunity. It focuses on the role of correctional administrators and groups external to corrections (the courts) in creating higher levels of expectations among inmates, but gives little attention to how these expectations develop or how they can produce a riot.

The various explanations for prison riots have been described briefly, but even from the general treatment offered it should be apparent that these models are by no means independent of one another. As Dillingham and Montgomery (1985) point out, while the models emphasize different variables, they are for the most part compatible; they tend to supplement rather than to supplant one another. It should also be apparent that none of these models alone offers an adequate explanation for the phenomenon of prison riots. Finally, the later models contain some elements that can be tested with information about individual riots, which was gathered through social scientific methods. One such recent crucible for testing components of these models is the 1986 riot at the West Virginia State Penitentiary.

The West Virginia Riot

Our description and analysis of the West Virginia riot are limited because we, like others, have access only to retrospective information. The primary source of data is the analysis of the riot by Useem and Kimball (1989), which included a series of semi-structured interviews with inmates and staff, as well as a content analysis of media representations about the riot. The second source of information is one of the author's experiences and interactions with inmates and staff as an "observer-as-participant" (as described by Babbie, 1989) in the prison before and after the riot. The third information source is the official reports concerning the riot and other official documents (cited in Useem & Kimball, 1989) that pertain to the situation preceding, during, and after the riot.

The Story

The roots of the January 1, 1986 West Virginia Penitentiary (WVP) riot can be traced back at least seven years. Prior to 1979, WVP was considered an "inmates'" prison; official authority was exercised loosely, and the day-to-day operation of the institution was largely under inmate control. However, following a mass escape in 1979 in which an off-duty state trooper was killed, the environment at WVP underwent a series of dramatic changes. The most far-reaching of these changes were the imposition of very tight internal control measures and the elimination of many privileges that inmates had come to expect, such as no restrictions on clothing and hair length, almost unlimited access to personal possessions in their cells, and high levels of mobility within the institution.

These circumstances interacted with the general upsurge in inmate litigation across the country so that by 1981 the civil rights division of the State Attorney General's office was processing two to five cases per week filed by inmates concerning conditions at WVP. Eventually a "totality of conditions" case emerged, and in June 1981 it was consolidated by the State Supreme Court with 35 other petitions. The conditions at WVP were among the worst in the country, according to the testimony of two expert witnesses. Michael Lane, Director of the Illinois Department of Corrections, stated that WVP had the "most dismal" conditions he had ever seen. These sentiments were echoed by Michael Mahoney, a Chicago-based prison reformer, who described WVP as the worst maximum security facility he had ever visited. In 1983 the West Virginia Supreme Court found the penitentiary to be below constitutional standards, and ordered mass reforms (Useem & Kimball, 1989).

There was no significant compliance with the court-ordered reforms, largely because of the dire financial straits that West Virginia faced at that time. This crisis made it very difficult for the state to improve its prison system without cannibalizing other state agencies and programs. By October of 1985 the situation had not improved. In a quarterly report filed by the Special Master appointed by the court to oversee the changes, the state was severely criticized for its lack of compliance, and the Master expressed considerable pessimism about the likelihood of movement toward compliance. In another report filed near the end of 1985, the Special Master observed that not only were the court-mandated goals not being met, but the prison's security system had begun to deteriorate because of a lack of corrections officers. Thus on the eve of the riot, the Special Master concluded that fewer than 10 percent of the court-ordered changes from 1983 had been implemented (Useem & Kimball, 1989).

In addition to the ongoing problems with the physical facility, the West Virginia Penitentiary underwent a series of changes in senior personnel during the mid-1980s. In 1983 the warden who had restored discipline to WVP after the 1979 incident resigned and was replaced by his deputy warden. The new warden was generally respected and liked by the inmates and staff for his honesty and fairness. In September 1985, however, he was moved to a post in the Department of Corrections' central office, and a new warden was appointed. This new warden (the third in three years) was a harsh disciplinarian, and quickly earned the dislike and distrust not only of the inmates but also of many staff members. During the first months of his tenure he imposed stricter visitation rules, prohibited inmates from receiving packages from ex-inmates, tightened security procedures in the segregation unit, and ordered cutbacks in the amount of personal property permitted in the cells. He also ordered major changes in the Christmas visitation policy, but these were overruled by the Commissioner when the inmates initiated a formal appeal (Useem & Kimball, 1989).

From late November to December 1985, the prison grapevine carried the rumor that some type of collective disturbance or mass resistance to the new warden would occur before January 5. According to information reported to Useem and Kimball (1989), one group of four inmates had even plotted a "constructive riot," but according to the subsequent personal accounts of these inmates, the events that ultimately transpired on January 1, 1986, came as a surprise to them. In addition, a correctional officer on the January 1 morning shift filed an "incident report" stating that an inmate had informed him that the Avengers motorcycle gang had plans to take over the facility on that day. The Avengers were a strong and cohesive group within the inmate population, with 20 to 25 core members at the time. The founder of the prison's chapter of the Avengers was a lifer who was a dominant figure in the inmate subculture and who had a history of conflict with the WVP administration.

On New Year's Day 1986, the day of the riot, 16 of the 47 guards on the 3-to-11 shift called in sick. Even though several of the day shift officers agreed to stay over, the evening shift started four guards short of the critical level that had been identified as necessary for the safe operation of the facility (Useem & Kimball, 1989). Standard operating procedure called for a lockdown under these circumstances, but this was not carried out. Instead that shift commander juggled personnel, leaving some positions understaffed and others vacant. Two of the positions left vacant were the shift commander's post in the captain's office and the cage officer's position. The officer in the cage operates the main grills in and out of the prison and provides a vantage point for aiming weapons into the hallway that ultimately became a main thoroughfare for inmate movement during the takeover. Also, rather than serving the evening meal to small groups of inmates, as is standard operating procedure, the guards took two to three tiers of prisoners at a time to the dining hall (Useem & Kimball, 1989).

The rumors of an impending disturbance proved to be true and, during the evening meal, the inmates at WVP began to seize control of the institution. The dining hall was taken quickly because of the severe manpower shortage there. Simultaneously, five inmates subdued a guard in one of the cell blocks in the north wing; it, too, fell into the hands of the prisoners. In minutes the inmates seized control of the prison's entire north wing.

During the takeover, 15 guards and one food service worker were taken hostage. The inmates maintained control of the north wing for three days. They demanded direct negotiations with the Governor, to which he agreed, but only after all the hostages had been released. After direct negotiations with the Governor and the signing, on television, of an agreement to initiate changes in the physical conditions and the operation of the prison, the north wing was surrendered to corrections and law enforcement personnel.

The hostages were well treated for the most part and were protected from serious physical injury. One of the officers whose watch was taken during his capture even had it returned by the inmates. The WVP riot resulted in neither the carnage nor the destruction that characterized other recent prison riots, like those at Attica and Santa Fe. Three inmates, all suspected of being informants, were killed by their fellow prisoners, but no other deaths or serious physical injuries occurred. The destruction of property was minuscule when contrasted with comparable riots in other institutions. Most astonishing of all, the inmates requested time to clean up the facility before returning control to the authorities; a prison spokesperson told the media that the living areas were cleaner after the riot than they had been before (Useem & Kimball, 1989).

The riot seems to have been well organized, although this was not apparent while events were unfolding. It also appears that the uprising was planned in advance; the warnings, the meticulous timing, and the relative restraint enforced by the inmate leaders suggest prior coordination. The most likely locus of planning, organization, and control was the Avengers motorcycle gang: the leader of the Avengers was one of the inmates who stepped to the forefront as a leader and negotiator during the riot. In addition, an Avenger reportedly led the disturbance in the dining hall that started the takeover process, and four of the five inmates who overpowered security in the cell block were Avengers (Useem & Kimball, 1989).

Analysis of the WVP Riot

The Environmental Conditions model postulates that riots occur as a consequence of a series of debilitating physical, social, and personal factors that "precondition" an institution to riot. Collectively, the conditions at WVP in early 1986 constituted "a bomb, waiting to explode." As described above, those conditions were among the worst in the country, making the institution a prototype of prisons that are susceptible to riot. While this finding appears to offer significant support for explanations based on the environmental conditions model, the fact is that there are other prisons with the same problems and of similar magnitudes that have not experienced riots. This again suggests that environmental factors can be necessary but never sufficient causes for prison riots. Although the conditions clearly contributed to the problems at WVP, environmental factors alone cannot explain the events of January 1, 1986.

From the perspective of the Spontaneity model, prison riots occur when some unexpected event escalates, igniting the "bomb" that was created by environmental conditions. There is considerable evidence to suggest that the West Virginia riot was not triggered by a spontaneous event. Two factors are relevant to assessing the level of spontaneity. First, the riot began with simultaneous disturbances in the dining hall and the north wing cell block. The fact that two of the five inmates who led the north wing takeover were from another cell block strengthens the conclusion that these two events had been coordinated beforehand. Without some prior knowledge, it seems improbable that inmates in the cell block and in the dining hall would have simultaneously become aware of the occurrences in each area.

The second factor, in isolation, might appear to constitute a classic spontaneous cause: there was a severe manpower shortage in the custodial staff at the time of the takeover. The question is whether this shortage and the consequent chain of events provided the impetus for some opportunistic inmates to try to seize the moment, or whether the absenteeism could have been anticipated and incorporated into a larger plan. Useem and Kimball (1989) report that the absenteeism was "predictable" because it had occurred every New Year's Day.

There is no way to determine absolutely whether the riot began in response to the opportunity presented by the critical shortage of guards or whether a more comprehensive plan had anticipated this occurrence. Still, it is clear that a takeover had been discussed in some detail before the events of January 1 and that some level of coordination must have been operating. In addition, the first stage of the riot, which Fox (1972) calls the "explosion," did not exhibit the "wild party" atmosphere that characterizes other spontaneous riots described in the literature (Desroches, 1974; Dillingham & Montgomery, 1985). In summary, the available information suggests that the Spontaneity model is not an explanation for the WVP riot.

The Conflict model focuses primarily on the repressive power structure characteristic of prisons and on its impact on the institution and its inhabitants. By many accounts, the level of overt conflict among inmates and between inmates and corrections officers was generally low in WVP prior to the 1986 riot. While the day-to-day operation of the prison was not mired in open physical confrontations, an element of conflict was present before the riot. Much of this conflict was generated by the change in administration that occurred when a new warden was appointed in September 1985. Even though he had held the post for only 2½ months when the riot took place, the inmates believed (many on the basis of previous exposure, when he was a deputy warden under an earlier administration) that the new warden was punishment-oriented. There is also strong evidence that the staff had little respect for the new warden and disliked his style (Useem & Kimball, 1989). In this environment of anticipated and perceived repression, the inmates believed that their options for expressing their concerns were limited and that their chances of "being heard" were virtually nonexistent. Thus, the events at WVP provide strong support for the Conflict model.

The Collective Behavior/Social Control model focuses on breakdowns in the formal and informal mechanisms of control within the prison environment as precipitating riots. In WVP before January 1, 1986, forces were operating that altered both control structures. Change, good or bad, causes problems for people because they are forced to adapt. Change is particularly difficult for those in prison because of the limited options for adaptation (Flynn, 1980; Johnson, 1987), and when changes in a prison administration represent a shift toward more control (heightening the perception of oppression), riots become more likely (Barak-Glantz, 1985).

There was a collective belief on the part of the WVP inmates that under the new warden, there would be a shift toward tighter control and harsher punishment. Consequently they believed that something had to be done, and done soon, before the new policies were in place (Useem & Kimball, 1989). Because the inmates' general impression was that things would change for the worse, it is logical to assume that their cooperation in maintaining order became much more tenuous. In such situations, when the informal control structure deteriorates, the burden of maintaining order and security falls more directly on formal mechanisms. If the official control structure is capable of filling the void, effective control of the institution cannot be maintained (Crouch, 1980; Gould, 1974; Stotland, 1976). This was the case at WVP; the official control structure was incapable of maintaining institutional security as the informal control system faltered. The personnel shortage on January 1, 1986 stretched thin the fabric of official control, and the lapses in security procedures rent it. When personnel shortages reach the critical level, standard operating procedure dictates a lockdown, but this was not done. The control problem was exacerbated by the decision to shuffle the limited custodial personnel to allow larger-than-normal groups of inmates to be fed at the evening meal.

In summary, the West Virginia riot provides considerable evidence to support the salient features of the Collective Behavior/Social Control model. By January 1, 1986 the informal control system was in disarray, and the formal mechanisms of institutional control were strained to the limit. In this climate, the personnel shortages and management errors that occurred on that day made it highly unlikely that any significant incident could be managed.

It is interesting to note that, although the usual level of informal control (which normally "keeps the lid on" a penitentiary) had broken down, relations among the inmates remained relatively civil during the riot. While it is true that three inmates were killed, this is far from the massive levels of violence experienced in other recent riots (Santa Fe, for example). It seems that straightforward considerations of self and collective interests restrained the West Virginia rioters, whereas in many other riots such restraints were absent (Useem & Kimball, 1989).

The Power Vacuum model identifies a lack of consistency in prison administration as a leading causal factor. From this perspective, prison riots tend to occur when abrupt changes occur in the network of formal control mechanisms. The consequent shifts in the power relationships create a situation in which the correctional environment becomes increasingly disorganized and drifts toward anomie. The riot is an attempt to fill the power void.

Serrill and Katel (1980) report that prior to the Santa Fe riot, the New Mexico Department of Corrections had five corrections directors in five years; during the same five-year period, the Santa Fe prison had five wardens. Mahan (1985) concluded that in New York State before the Attica revolt and in New Mexico before the Santa Fe riot, there existed unstable and inconsistent policies, personnel changes, and conflict over security goals and reform goals. Such a state of affairs represents what Barak-Glantz (1982, 1985) calls a "power vacuum." Such a vacuum is created when the staff cannot accommodate shifts in administrative goals and personnel, and when cooperation, respect, and trust between the staff and the administration break down. The resulting power void provides the inmates with an opportunity to seize control and power.

The available evidence indicates that a power vacuum had developed at WVP before the 1986 riot. There were three wardens in West Virginia between 1983 and 1986. More important, the changes in wardens were accompanied by dramatic changes in organizational goals. The inmates believed that the most recent warden in the series was installing an especially repressive regime. While their own hostility toward this warden was growing, they also perceived that he did not have the respect or loyalty of the corrections officers. Interviews with the officers generally support the validity of this perception. One officer stated that the warden had a "very poor relationship" with the corrections officers and that the "majority of them" would like to see him go (Useem & Kimball, 1989). At the time of the riot the cooperation between staff and inmates, upon which informal control is based, had broken down, and the formal power structure had failed. These factors produced a vacuum of power that contributed directly to the planning and the "success" of the riot.

The Rising Expectations model focuses on the gap between inmates' expectations about the quality of the institutional environment and the quality of life they experience. When inmates' expectations are not met, they perceive that they are inappropriately being deprived of things to which they are "entitled." This perceptual set is linked closely to the general theoretical notion of relative deprivation. These factors contributed to the riot in West Virginia, but they had evolved over a long period.

The policy changes that the new warden was trying to institute in 1985 reminded many inmates of the deprivations they had suffered in 1979 as part of the official response to the mass escape. If the prison was moving again in this direction, it would be a giant step backward from the progress promised in the 1983 court rulings. As one inmate observed, in June 1983 "just wait and things will change" was a viable message, but it started to wear thin by June 1984. By June 1985 it was clear that the changes were not coming. During the meeting with the Governor that terminated the riot, one inmate complained, "They keep...taking away from us. Every time it gets calm in here they (the administration) want to initiate...shakedowns, changes in recreation procedures and visitation" (Useem & Kimball, 1989).

This situation has clear implications for the subsequent riot. In light of the court-mandated changes, it is easy to see how inmates came to expect major improvements in the institutional environment. Those improvements did not occur, and a perception of (relative) deprivation was the outcome. The frustration and anger that resulted from the perceived deprivation, and from the expectation that it would continue, were dominant underlying motivational factors for the riot. Thus the events in West Virginia support the salience of the Rising Expectations model as an explanation of prison riots.

The 1986 riot at the West Virginia Penitentiary possessed some elements of most of the models of prison riots described in the literature. The environmental "preconditions," by all accounts, were deplorable. Conflict was present at various levels, collective perceptions were operating, and control problems existed. WVP also housed a great number of aggressive, hostile, and desperate people. However, as discussed above, these factors do not differentiate WVP from most other correctional facilities in this country; furthermore, many of these factors had been present at WVP throughout its history.

Two factors played major roles in the riot: First, the long history of unfulfilled promises of change developed rising expectations and a strong sense of perceived deprivation among the inmates. This situation provided a strong emotional and psychological impetus. The second and final ingredient was a power vacuum, which seems not to have been present until the time of the riot. No major acts of collective violence had occurred during the seven previous years, conceivably because the two prior administrations had commanded (in their own distinctive ways) the respect, trust, and cooperation of the inmates and staff. This interpretation is consistent with that of Wilsnack (1976), who said that if a riot was to erupt, inmates must perceive themselves to be deprived and powerless and must be interacting with an ineffective and unstable administration.

The Spontaneity model was the only explanation of prison riots that clearly was not supported by the West Virginia analysis. The staff took no action that provoked the inmates directly to riot. In fact, it was quite the opposite; inmates were not locked down and were being fed in larger groups in an attempt to accommodate their perceived desire to watch the New Year's Day football games. There was no inmate-to-inmate incident that escalated to a point where control was lost. A "time bomb" indeed had been created by the long-term, systematic inattention to various environmental and structural conditions. The riot was ignited, however, not by some random "spark" but by a planned and orchestrated chain of events, initiated by the inmates in response to the power vacuum that had been created by the change in administration.

The 1986 WVP riot consequently provides some support for all the models of prison riots except the Spontaneity model. This finding reinforces our earlier contention that while the various perspectives underlying the models in our typology offer useful insights, it is unlikely that any single model will be adequate to explain any riot. Conversely, this suggests that multidimensional approaches are needed to understand the causes of riots, and ultimately to prevent their occurrence.

Comparisons: Attica, Santa Fe, and West Virginia

Investigative reports have found striking similarities between the riots at Attica and at Santa Fe. Mahan (1985) identified five primary areas of similarity between those two prisons before the riots: (1) prisoners believed they were not treated as human beings; (2) line officers were unprepared; (3) administrations lacked consistency; (4) legislators were insensitive to the needs of the correctional system; and (5) the public was unconcerned. Our discussion of the WVP riot should make clear that these conditions also were present in varying but significant degrees in West Virginia before January 1, 1986.

The five areas identified by Mahan are directly correlated with most of the models classified in our typology. The second area, the lack of preparedness of line officers, relates to the earlier discussion of factors involved in the Collective Behavior/Social Control model and to their influences in the West Virginia riot. The third area, administrative inconsistency, is a main factor in the Power Vacuum

model, and areas 4 and 5, the insensitivity of legislators and the lack of public concern, are central elements in the Rising Expectations/Relative Deprivation model.
These three areas also had clear implications in West Virginia. In concert, Areas 2
through 5 can be interpreted as creating an environment in which conflict becomes
highly likely. Finally, the first area of similarity identified by Mahan—the prisoners' belief that they were not treated as human beings—may be seen as the product of forces relating to all of the explanatory models, including the environmental
conditions to which the inmates were subjected in Attica, Santa Fe, and West
Virginia.

The Attica, Santa Fe, and West Virginia riots differ in two important areas, in
addition to the dramatic divergences in the level and nature of violence and the
amount of property destruction. These areas are the motivations behind the disturbances and the nature of the inmate leadership prior to and during the riots. The Attica
incident was very instrumental; the rioters were involved in a type of "political
consciousness," and an "overarching" leadership group was in place. The Santa Fe
riot seemed to be much more expressive; unity was based more on similarity of inmates'
backgrounds and experiences than on political ideology, and personal cliques vied
for power. Attica was a riot begun over demands, but grievances did not emerge at
Santa Fe until later (Barak-Glantz, 1985). Inmate negotiators at Attica tried to
accommodate the needs of all prisoners, but at Santa Fe, negotiations were attempts
to enhance the interests of specific groups.

West Virginia seems to fall somewhere between Attica and Santa Fe on these
dimensions. A fairly strong leadership element seemed to have been in place before
insurrection, but political consciousness did not appear to be the overriding motivation. It seems more feasible that one major motivation was a collective desire for
changes in the immediate conditions; the most notable may have been to get rid of
the current warden. There is also reason to believe that a more individualized power
motive was operating among a group of dominant inmates, who apparently wished
to more firmly solidify their position.

Thus it seems that the distal causes of the riots in Attica, Santa Fe, and West
Virginia were fundamentally the same; the environmental conditions as well as the
social, organizational, and political dynamics of these institutions before the riots
were quite similar. Out of these similarities, however, grew very different riots.
The key differences, then, lie not in why the riots took place, but in how. In all
three jurisdictions the tinder for a riot was present, but the fire was lit in different
ways. In Attica and Santa Fe a random spark ignited the tinder, whereas in West Virginia
it was arson. Mahan (1985) claims that rumors persisted at both Attica and Santa
Fe for months prior to the riots, and that precautions taken by officers actually
sparked the riots in both cases. Although there were rumors of trouble in West
Virginia before the riot, it was not the case that provocative actions by the corrections officers in response to these rumors precipitated the riot.

These findings speak directly to the general applicability of the Spontaneity model.
From our analysis it seems that Fox's (1971, 1972) conceptualization of the process

by which riots are generated (i.e., a process involving both predisposing and precipitating factors) is fundamentally correct. Rather than relying exclusively on spontaneous events as precipitators, however, we would argue that any explanation of proximate causes must be broad enough to encompass planned and orchestrated events as well.

The analysis of similarities and differences among these three prison riots again highlights the conclusion that no model included in our typology provides a necessary and sufficient explanation for why prison riots occur. The analysis also reinforces an important point made by Toch (1976): explanations of riots are not explanations of the violence and other behaviors that occur within them. Although structural and sociological factors shed considerable light on the general etiology of prison riots, more individualized approaches may be necessary to explain the specific behaviors and motives of the actors involved.

Summary and Implications

Many explanations of current correctional dysfunctions focus on "structural" problems such as sentencing practices and fiscal constraints. Overcrowding and inadequate facilities are symptomatic of these more basic, fundamentally political impediments (Mahan, 1985). Because it is evident that many of these problems are beyond the control of correctional authorities (e.g., funding, legislation), it is convenient but inappropriate for correctional officers to blame riots solely on these external factors. On the other hand, several social-scientific analytic approaches have been explored that contribute to a better understanding of prison riots. The types of "explanations" that have evolved both from the investigations and from the social science analyses contain discrete themes that we have identified and classified into a typology of causal explanations.

Each model of prison riots in the six-group typology presented here summarizes the perspectives and concepts undergirding a unique explanatory orientation. Although these typological constructs are broader than our underlying individual "explanations," they are still individually incapable of explaining prison riots. These constructs emerged out of different approaches to the analytic process, but they are not necessarily incompatible in the context of explaining the genesis of the individual riot. The fact that none of the current models alone is adequate to the explanatory task strongly suggests the need to develop more integrative models. These "new" models must look beyond the simple, the obvious, and the static conditions that represent necessary causes. To be effective, such models must integrate the fundamental structural, functional, and processual factors operating at all levels in the complex milieus that make up our correctional systems.

The need for such an approach has been suggested both by Barak-Glantz (1985) and by Flynn (1980), who argue for an explanation of the deeper "fabric" of the social milieu of prison. To date the most promising effort at developing a comprehensive model of prison riots is that of Lombardo (1988), who integrates transactional and dynamic interactive processes with the more "objective preconditions" of the prison environment. More efforts of this type are needed to move us into the next generation of explanations. Also, it is clear that Lombardo, as do we, concurs with Cohen's (1976) observation that if we wish to understand human violence (in prison or elsewhere), the full range of human motives must be considered, along with the factors that affect those motives.

While it is important to recognize the value of a more integrative approach to understanding collective violence in prison, we also must recognize that the development of the next generation of explanatory models is limited by the nature of prison riots and by the associated constraints on the quality and quantity of available data. The major implication of our findings for correctional policymakers and administrators is: in light of our current state of knowledge and the resulting inability to predict riots with any certainty, all that can be suggested is that effective management offers the best hope for prevention. In spite of the tremendous difficulties involved in developing truly integrated models, however, the effort seems worthwhile. At worst, we will be left with a residue that will help us to structure our knowledge base to identify more adequate management strategies that have preventive value. At best, such efforts will lead to the development of valid models for predicting, and subsequently for preventing, prison riots.

Notes

[1] There are exceptional cases in which, for one reason or another, researchers had prior information about a prison that subsequently experienced a riot. See, for example, Serrill and Katel's (1980) analysis of the Santa Fe riot.

[2] Farrington and Nuttall (1985) contend that there is no empirical support for absolute institution size as a factor in riots.

References

American Correctional Association (ACA) (1981). *Riots and Disturbances in Correctional Institutions.* College Park, MD: American Correctional Association.

Babbie, E. (1989). *The Practice of Social Research.* Fifth Edition. Belmont, CA: Wadsworth.

Barak-Glantz, I.L. (1982). "A Decade of Disciplinary, Administrative, and Protective Control of Prison Inmates in the Washington State Penitentiary." *Journal of Criminal Justice,* 10, 481-492.

Barak-Glantz, I.L. (1985). "The Anatomy of Another Prison Riot." In M. Braswell, S. Dillingham and R. Montgomery, Jr. (eds.) *Prison Violence in America* (pp. 47-71). Cincinnati, OH: Anderson Publishing Co.

Baro, A. (1988). "The Loss of Local Control Over Prison Administration." *Justice Quarterly,* 5(3), 456-473.

Clear, T.R. and G.F. Cole (1990). *American Corrections.* Second Edition. Pacific Grove, CA: Brooks/Cole.

Clemmer, D. (1940). *The Prison Community.* New York, NY: Holt, Rinehart and Winston.

Cloward, R.A. (1969). "Social Control in Prison." In L. Hazelrigg (ed.) *Prison Within Society* (pp. 78-112). New York, NY: Doubleday.

Cohen, A.K. (1976). "Prison Violence: A Sociological Perspective." In A.K. Cohen, G.F. Cole and R. G. Bailey (eds.) *Prison Violence* (pp. 3-22). Lexington, MA: Lexington Books.

Conant, R. (1968). "Rioting, Insurrectional and Civil Disorderliness." *American Scholar,* 37, 420-433.

Crouch, B. (1980). *Keepers: Prison Guards and Contemporary Corrections.* Springfield, IL: Charles C Thomas.

Davies, J.C. (1972). "Toward a Theory of Revolution." In. I.K. Feierabend, R.L. Feierabend and T.R. Gurr (eds.) *Prison Violence in America* (pp. 67-84). Englewood Cliffs, NJ: Prentice-Hall.

Desroches, R. (1974). "Patterns of Prison Riots." *Canadian Journal of Criminology and Corrections,* 16, 332-351.

Dillingham, S.D. and R.H. Montgomery, Jr. (1985). "Prison Riots: A Corrections Nightmare Since 1774." In M. Braswell, S. Dillingham and R. Montgomery, Jr. (eds.) *Prison Violence in America* (pp. 19-36). Cincinnati, OH: Anderson Publishing Co.

DiIulio, J.J., Jr. (1987). *Governing Prisons.* New York, NY: The Free Press.

Farrington, D.P. and C.P. Nuttall (1985). "Prison Size, Overcrowding, Prison Violence, and Recidivism." In M. Braswell, S. Dillingham and R. Montgomery, Jr. (eds.) *Prison Violence in America* (pp. 113-129). Cincinnati, OH: Anderson Publishing Co.

Flynn, E. (1980). "From Conflict Theory to Conflict Resolution: Controlling Collective Violence in Prisons." *American Behavioral Scientist,* 23, 745-776.

Fox, V. (1971). "Why Prisoners Riot." *Federal Probation,* 35(1), 9-14.

Fox, V. (1972). "Prison Riots in a Democratic Society." *Police,* 26(12), 35-41.

Garson, D. (1972). "Force vs. Restraint in Prison Riots." *Crime and Delinquency,* 18, 411-421.

Gould, R. (1974). "The Officer Inmate Relationship: Its Role in the Attica Rebellion." *Bulletin of the American Academy of Psychiatry and the Law,* 2(1), 34-35.

Gurr, T.R. (1972). "Psychological Factors in Civil Violence." In I.K. Feierabend, R.L. Feierabend and T.R. Gurr (eds.) *Anger, Violence, and Politics* (pp. 31-57). Englewood Cliffs, NJ: Prentice-Hall.

Hartung, F. and M. Floch (1957). "A Social-Psychological Analysis of Prison Riots." In R. Turner and L. Killian (eds.) *Collective Behavior* (pp. 24-28). Englewood Cliffs, NJ: Prentice-Hall.

Irwin, J. (1980). *Prisons in Turmoil.* Boston, MA: Little, Brown.

Johnson, R. (1987). *Hard Times: Understanding and Reforming the Prison.* Monterey, CA: Brooks/Cole.

Lombardo, L.X. (1988). "Stress, Change, and Collective Violence in Prison." In R. Johnson and H. Toch (eds.) *The Pains of Imprisonment* (pp. 77-96). Prospect Heights, IL: Waveland Press.

Mahan, S. (1985). "An 'Orgy of Brutality' at Attica and the 'Killing Ground' at Santa Fe." In M. Braswell, S. Dillingham and R. Montgomery, Jr. (eds.) *Prison Violence in America* (pp. 73-78). Cincinnati, OH: Anderson Publishing Co.

Serrill, M. and P. Katel (1980). "New Mexico: The Anatomy of a Riot." *Corrections Magazine*, 6(2), 6-24.

Smelser, N.J. (1963). *Theory of Collective Behavior*. New York, NY: The Free Press.

Smith, A. (1973). "The Conflict Theory of Riots." In South Carolina Department of Corrections (Collective Violence Research Project), *Collective Violence in Correctional Institutions: A Search for Causes* (pp. 34-36). Columbia, SC: State Printing Company.

South Carolina Department of Corrections (Collective Violence Research Project) (1973). *Collective Violence in Correctional Institutions: A Search for Causes*. Columbia, SC: State Printing Company.

Stotland, E. (1976). "Self-Esteem and Violence by Guards and State Troopers at Attica." *Criminal Justice and Behavior*, 3(1), 85-96.

Sykes, G.M. (1958). *The Society of Captives: A Study of a Maximum Security Prison*. Princeton, NJ: Princeton University Press.

Toch, H. (1976). "A Psychological View of Prison Violence." In A.K. Cohen, G.F. Cole and R.G. Bailey (eds.) *Prison Violence* (pp. 43-51). Lexington, MA: Lexington Books.

Useem, B. and P.A. Kimball (1989). *States of Siege: U.S. Prison Riots 1971-1986*. New York, NY: Oxford University Press.

Wilsnack, R.W. (1976). "Explaining Collective Violence in Prisons: Problems and Possibilities." In A.K. Cohen, G.F. Cole and R.G. Bailey (eds.) *Prison Violence* (pp. 61-78). Lexington, MA: Lexington Books.

Section IV

Doing Something About Prison Violence

Solutions to prison violence are too often reactive rather than proactive. Facilities and lives left in shambles in the aftermath of a riot typically result in blue-ribbon committees and expert consultants making official that which is already obvious. New and improved facilities, more and better paid and trained staff, programs for inmates...the list goes on. Of course there are also a variety of other pervasive forms of physical and psychological violence that exist in most prisons. Fear of physical and sexual assault, psychological intimidation, and emotional stress resulting from severe overcrowding are several examples. As the forms of violence in prison are varied, so must the responses be to whatever conditions cause or contribute to them.

In the last section of this volume, a variety of approaches to addressing and resolving prison violence are examined. Innovative unit management, experiential and crisis training, support systems for victims, as well as better understanding the climate for prison violence offers examples for a progressive approach to more effectively addressing such violence. An alternative, less traditional approach explores the work of Bo and Sita Lozoff through their correspondence with inmates based on a spiritual perspective.

The role of the press in educating as well as informing the public about prison and corrections issues also offers a proactive response to potential violence in prisons.

The final reading in this section looks to the future of criminal justice through a more feminist vision, a vision that focuses on such core values as empathy and compassion and how they need to be affirmed in a public and professional context as well as in more private, personal relationships.

18

A Case Study in Regaining Control of a Violent State Prison[†][††]

J. Forbes Farmer

Prison administrators often have to develop solutions under extreme pressure and need higher political support. What follows is a case study of a problem-directed search for solutions to violence and administrative confusion at Walpole State Prison in Massachusetts. The ultimate adoption of Unit Management was seen as a way to achieve the goals of four prison groups: (1) the inmates wanted to live and live without fear, (2) the correctional officers wanted a say in the classification process, a safe working environment, and control over inmates, (3) the non-custodial staff wanted equity with the custodial staff and more information about and more consistent contact with inmates so that treatment could be imposed, and (4) the administration wanted to regain control.

The maximally secure Walpole State Prison (now called the Massachusetts Correctional Institution: Cedar Junction) began implementing a policy of Unit Management in 1980 in the wake of a 10-year history of violence, cost overruns, and general administrative turmoil. Unit Management is still operational at Cedar Junction and has been implemented at other Massachusetts correctional institutions including Norfolk and Gardner. The policy is well known within the correc-

†Reprinted from *Federal Probation*, March, 1988 by permission.

††The author wishes to thank Superintendent James Bender and Deputy Superintendent of Treatment Mike Walonis at NCCI Gardner, Massachusetts where he observed management for several months. He extends appreciation to all of the following who were interviewed in 1986 because of their knowledge of or involvement with the Massachusetts Correctional Institution at Walpole: Commissioner Michael Fair; Peter Argeropulos, Associate Commissioner of Administration; Norman Carver, Superintendent of MCI Concord; Gail Darnell, Director of Public Affairs; Tom DaSilva, Director of Security at MCI Bridgewater; Charlie Fenton, President of Buckingham Security Ltd.; Tim Hall, Deputy Superintendent at MCI Walpole; The Honorable William Hogan, Judge of Dedham District Court; and Joseph Ponte, Superintendent of Old Colony Correctional Center.

tions profession and is (and was before its appearance at Walpole) also operational at many other prisons around the country. The decision-making process and the circumstances surrounding it are reconstructed here through written record and recent interviews with nine people who worked for the Massachusetts Department of Corrections at the time Unit Management was being considered. The two key individuals in the Unit Management decision at Walpole were the 1979-80 Commissioner and an NIC consultant. The latter was first a member of the National Institute of Corrections (NIC) team that was invited by the Commissioner to study Walpole and then was subsequently brought in by the Commissioner as a consultant. Participating were several other players such as a Deputy Commissioner in charge of a region that included Walpole, the Superintendent of Walpole, and his two Deputies: Deputy of Operations and Deputy of Programs.

Cooperation between administrators, politicians, and National Institute of Corrections (NIC) consultants cut through reigning chaos and reigning status quo at Walpole to facilitate positive changes. Although the tool was a multidisciplinary management approach (Unit Management) which is partly a control measure, the key was the personnel involved in the decision to adopt Unit Management and their identification of the major issues.

Walpole's Violent History

The history of events at Walpole loomed in the minds of the decisionmakers. Discipline ruled in the mid 1960s.

> It wasn't harsh discipline. Inmates weren't beaten or chained to the wall. When the inmates screwed up, they were transferred to Cellblock Ten or to the segregation unit at Bridgewater for up to six months or longer. There were no exceptions to this rule, and the inmates knew it. Violence was not tolerated. It was discouraged through discipline. And discipline was enforced at all levels.[1]

The past Deputy of Operations reminisced that staff walked down the middle of the corridor and inmates walked down the sides. Inmates had their names on the back of their shirts and shirttails were tucked in. Not doing these things was a major infraction of the rules.

Several factors weakened this prevailing disciplinary posture. Beginning in the late 1960s inmates became restless over injustices they saw in the system. They began pressing themselves as a solid oppositional front and they had prison reform groups as an outside audience. At the same time, drugs flowed into the prison at a much greater rate than before. Inmate Remick wrote "The drug users and drug pushers have caused more of the turmoil within Walpole than any other single factor."[2] But the inmates were also changing; they reflected the anti-authoritarianism and rebelliousness of the times. Also transforming was the public and administrative attitude towards prisons.

An era of permissiveness, under the rubric of prison reform, eased into Walpole in the early 1970s. Walpole was in turmoil. Action taken by guards against disruptive inmates seemed futile as guards perceived no support from their superiors. Policies that had previously been exercised to maintain control and discipline were revoked as either concessions to the National Prisoners' Rights Association (NPRA) or as steps towards reform. Murders and riots were countered by shakedowns and lock-ups. Walpole was an unsafe place for inmates to live and for correctional officers to work.

> The chief complaint of the staff was that conditions at Walpole made it dangerous for them to perform their duties. This created a breakdown in the organization; and within a short period, all control over inmates was completely lost.... Any attempt to enforce regulations ceased.[3]

Many attempts were made to tighten security at Walpole after the warden resigned. But a situation where "there had been a violent death at Walpole on the average of once every thirty-nine days"[4] was very formidable to reverse. A series of interim Commissioners, well liked by the correctional officers, were ineffective in giving Walpole a safe and harmonious environment.

Politics and the NIC Report

In November 1979, Edward King had just defeated incumbent Governor Michael Dukakis after running a law and order campaign. The press and politicians were pushing for things to get done. When Edward King took over as Governor of the Commonwealth of Massachusetts in January 1980, he inherited Walpole State Prison.

Change made its debut at Walpole when Governor King asked a colleague to take over as Commissioner. Prior to being appointed on September 15, the colleague contacted another friend, the Director of the Federal Bureau of Prisons. The soon-to-be Commissioner also gained permission to have a task force from the National Institute of Corrections (NIC) sent to Massachusetts to study the Department of Corrections' organizational structure, the classification system, and, more specifically, Walpole. The NIC technical assistance report concluded that Walpole had many serious problems, mostly relating to the management of inmates. The principal cause was seen as the permissiveness forced into the system in the early 1970s.

The environment at Walpole remained hostile throughout the 1970s, and Unit Management was to commence there in 1980. Persons working at Walpole or elsewhere within the Department of Corrections during this time agreed that the two major problems at Walpole were (1) a lack of control over staff and inmates and (2) the polarization between custodial and noncustodial staff.

None of the nine people interviewed for this study laid blame on the previous Superintendent. He was seen as having sufficient knowledge of the system but no support from it. The top administration at the Department of Corrections was content provided he maintained the status quo. But there loomed a general lack of accountability that could mostly be attributed to a lack of organizational structure and clear policy. The resulting lack of safety and poor working conditions drove the officers to fear for their lives and to be reluctant to enter dangerous sections of the prison.

The Guards' Union and Working Conditions

Another problem recalled by both the Director of Public Affairs and the past Deputy of Operations was that the relations between the policymakers, management, and the Walpole correctional officers union between 1976 and 1979 were horrendous. According to the Director of Public Affairs and the Deputy, the guard union leadership was viewed as radical and not representative of the rank and file. The union, however, signaled strength. Efforts by the administration and the union to join forces and clean up the safety issues were unsuccessful. Work stoppages and strikes continued and were doubtlessly at least partially responsible for the continued violence.

The violence involved both inmates and staff. Staff was continuing to be assaulted by inmates and inmates were still killing, stabbing, and assaulting each other. Five murders, eight assaults, at least three stabbings, and numerous beatings occurred in the 9 to 10 months just before Unit Management was implemented. This level of violence was an almost continuous feature of Walpole life during the late 1970s.

Schism Between Custody and Treatment

Prisons have historically served several different functions, such as custody, treatment, and classification, and the emphasis placed on any one of these has been a matter of public sentiment and state and national political climate. Methods of reaching these varied goals have usually been delegated to a specialized administrative branch within the prison where autonomy and territoriality have been the norm. In Massachusetts, for example, prisons have traditionally had two Deputy Superintendents: one for Operations (custody) and one for Programs (treatment or noncustody). The goals of these two departments had been separate and usually conflicting with no internal consensus.

Teamwork and sharing of information at Walpole had been rare. Social workers, teachers, and other noncustody personnel had a reputation of being gullible, over-educated, under-trained "do-gooders." They had more decision-making authority than custodial people and more promotional opportunities, which spawned resentment. Unit Management was later perceived by both custodial and noncustodial personnel as a way to obtain that to which they both aspired.

In prisons, however, coordination depends upon standard policies and procedures that should be formulated at the top and directed downward. But Commissioners changed so often at Walpole State Prison that staff was confused. Policies of leniency were followed by strictness, liberalism by conservatism, and vice-versa. The NIC report stated that "there has never been a master plan, and, consequently, the Department has been like a rudderless ship.[5] The report also stated that

> Management has been in a defensive role, putting out brush fires and pursuing a policy of containment. Frequent and lengthy lockdowns in cellblocks were used as a partial means of control but inmates responded with verbal abuse to officers, threw urine upon some and generally hurled all manner of foods, debris, and fecal matter in unbelievable quantities in some cellblocks.[6]

Troubled Organizational Communication

An affinitive problem with communication generating much inmate and staff dissatisfaction and low morale centered on decisions affecting inmates being produced at the bottom of the organizational chart by the guards or treatment staff. The decisions were eventually reviewed by the Deputy Superintendents who did not know the circumstances surrounding them and who, in turn, were often reversing them. The custody and treatment arms were still clashing but with the additional factor of a chain of command that was too long. Unit Management would eventually allow for decisions to be made at the lower levels but the policies guiding them would be sent down from the top.

The Unit Management Decision-Making Process

Unit Management commenced at Walpole State Prison between September and November 1980, when the new Commissioner called his friend, the Director of the Federal Bureau of Prisons, to ask about some technical assistance. A future Superintendent of Walpole, who was working for the Department of Corrections in Boston at the time of the swearing in, remembered puzzling over why they needed the report when everyone knew Walpole was in turmoil. The past Commissioner explained that he thought they needed experts from the outside with backgrounds in corrections to give credibility to what they already thought needed doing. The current (1988) Commissioner recalled that the strategy was to import people without a vested interest or history in the department—people who could not be accused of trying to protect anyone or soften the blow.

The NIC team of consultants made their preliminary visit on September 25, 1979, just 10 days after the Commissioner was sworn in. They concluded their overview noting that a return visit would include (1) the development of an effective classification system, (2) a review of the operations of Walpole and recommendations for improvements in security classification, inmate programs, food service, and other areas of concern, and (3) a review of the Central Office administrative structure.[7] One of the individuals on the review team was then the Warden of the Federal Penitentiary in Lewisburg, Pennsylvania. Arrangements were completed for the team to return for their focused visit between October 15 and 19, 1979.

The NIC report was in the Commissioner's possession by November 1979. The majority of the 167 specific recommendations were directed at Walpole with the prominent recommendation being the adoption of Unit Management. The two key parties involved in the decision-making process that eventually led to implementation were the 1979-80 Commissioner and the NIC technical assistance team, which included the Lewisburg warden as the administrative specialist. After receiving the study, the Commissioner held a press conference at Walpole and released it entirely except for that part that would have compromised security. The major conclusions of the study were just what the Commissioner had requested, reflecting most of the historical and contemporary issues already of concern to he and the Lewisburg warden.

Although the Commissioner now had his expert's call for action, he needed additional help. Rather than looking within the Department of Corrections, he decided to get someone from outside of the Massachusetts system altogether. He called the National Institute of Corrections for a consultant. The Lewisburg warden, who had just retired and who the Commissioner had known prior to being sworn in, was sent.

Management Team

The next important step in the decision-making process centered on weighing the value of replacing the incumbent Superintendent of Walpole while the consultant was starting his work. This Superintendent had been "a good man" whose problems were not his fault. Political officials only dealt with him in crisis situations and then it was critical rather than supportive. Desiring to make a clean break with the past, the Commissioner and the consultant, along with the Deputy Commissioner, chose a man with limited experience but deemed to have great potential. The assembled team consisted of the Commissioner, Deputy Commissioner, newly appointed Superintendent, and the consultant.

According to the consultant, this management team was only an administrative device through which his plans could be disseminated. He was stationed at Walpole to assist the new Superintendent, and the team convened every Friday and made weekly, monthly, and long-range plans. Generally, they endeavored to carry out the recommendations of the task force. The Superintendent was publicly in charge of Walpole and the consultant anchored to give advice.

Crisis Goals

Despite having the NIC report in hand, they had little time to consider it in light of the pressing and immediate problems that confronted them. By dint of circumstance, their major goals at this time were (1) to wrench Walpole away from the inmates and correctional officers and place control back in the hands of the administration and (2) to depolarize the friction that demoralized the custodial and the noncustodial staff. According to the consultant, the question was not how they would regain control, but whether they would. Regaining control and depolarizing the friction were two goals that could only be achieved by chipping away at the numerous issues one at a time. Unit Management was ineffectual if the institution was unsafe or if the inmates and staff lived and worked in fear. It could not even be instituted if there was no accountability of staff or no firm authority at the top. Unit Management could be used to maintain control once control had been regained, but it was not the solution to the regaining process.

Quick, Decisive, and Intimidating Intervention

Several things were done at Walpole between September when the Commissioner was appointed and November, when the NIC task force report was sent to him. He clearly assumed the position that Walpole was not going to operate as it had. The costs in terms of continued violence, budget overruns, and poor morale were not in the public or inmates' interest. He initiated regular meetings with union officials and then proceeded to clean up the institution. The litter and feces were remembered as a significant enigma because resistance erupted from the correctional officers who believed the inmates should clean up their own mess. The commissioner had only been on the job for a week when an inmate at Walpole went on a hunger strike. The Commissioner recalled a staff meeting when a doctor said he could not guarantee that the inmate would live. "He said the vermin would cause the inmate to die of infection in a filthy cell. I said, 'No, he's not. That Block Ten is going to be cleaned out.' And it was."

On two occasions inmates almost took over the prison. The past commissioner recalled that the first threat menaced soon after the management team had been established. Officials discovered that a riot was to take place within 24 to 48 hours, that the inmates had over 200 weapons and a hit list with seven names on it. The Superintendent observed a practice of making himself and other key staff available at the noon lunch hour in front of the chow hall. The inmate leaders hoped to hand out free drugs to the inmates at noontime and then kill every block officer and the seven administrators standing out front.

The Commissioner remembered that his staff identified about 20 ring leaders and decided that the easiest way to relieve the threat was to bus the leaders out of Walpole. He called his Deputy of Operations and arrangements were made to remove 10 inmates at about 3 a.m. Walpole was as still as a mill pond on Monday. This was a major turning point. The administration was beginning to take control of the prison. The Federal Prison System had given them an option they had not had before: the option to move inmates out of Walpole to another prison. The threat of shipping an inmate to the isolation of Oxford, Wisconsin was key to increasing inmate order and compliance.

Increasing Certainty

It is easy to understand why Unit Management took so long to come to the forefront. A reversal of the long history of administrative confusion, inmate control, and violence was prerequisite to the implementation of long-term order, safety, and maintenance strategies. This signal of authority showed the inmates that their disruptive behavior would definitely get them shipped in the federal bus to the Oxford, Wisconsin prison. The administration was posturing so that it could guarantee the certainty of its policies going relatively unchallenged. By demonstrating to the correctional officers that the administration would support them on some of their concerns, the administration was increasing the certainty that the guards would be backed up; the critical certainty of no back up was the norm prior to this. Management was also making it more certain that the staff would be held accountable for its behavior; gaps in rules and policies were being filled and training was being provided. These changes were calculated decisions aimed at increasing the chances of success in the mind of at least three of the management team members: the consultant, the Commissioner, and the Deputy Commissioner.

Unit Management

The issue at this point was how to maintain the regained control. The consultant pressed Unit Management as the answer. Unit Management, which had been brought to violence-marked Lewisburg, would have a little different appearance of Walpole due to the different facilities and staffing.

Unit Management has been described by Levinson and Gerard as "a Functional Unit [that] can be conceptualized as one of a number of small, self-contained 'institutions' operating in semi-autonomous fashion within the confines of a larger facility."[8] The concept is operationalized by housing between 50 to 100 inmates together in one physical area (preferably) and keeping them together for as long as possible. The composition of these groups usually only varies as inmates' sentences and release dates vary. The inmate group (units) are supervised by a preferably group-specific, multidisciplinary management team normally composed of at least a (1) unit manager, (2) caseworker, (3) secretary, (4) correctional counselor, (5) correctional officer, (6) educator, and (7) psychologist or other mental health worker. The Unit Management teams have discipline, classification, and programmatic authority and are guided by sets of common policies and procedures.[9]

A few irksome problems complicated bringing Unit Management to Walpole. Sergeants would lose much of their traditional everyday influence over the inmates on their block. Staffing the unit manager positions lingered as a potential issue. Plenty of sergeants were available but they would have to work longer hours and they might have to take action against their peers. It was believed that the unit managers should be in management positions. The right people had to be attracted. There was also the dilemma of physical space. Walpole was an overcrowded cell block type facility and there was no room for a unit manager officer.

While the consultant began explaining and pushing Unit Management, he was also contriving with the Superintendent and the other members of the management team to create other features at Walpole. They developed orientation and training programs for new and seasoned staff and instituted new prison procedures. These included the reinstatement of stand-up counts, removal of blankets from the cell bars, creation of Internal Perimeter Security (IPS) teams trained in criminal investigation methods, and restriction of inmate movement within the prison. Nonetheless, serious problems still remained.

What Else Unit Management Could Do

Unit Management had the potential of solving the remaining problems of staff and inmate morale, polarization, and equity of treatment. The consultant believed that, from his experiences with it, Unit Management would not only eliminate these problems but would also serve as a future deterrent to issues of the same kind.

The major dilemma faced by the management team was the demoralizing rift, or depolarization, that still existed between the treatment (program or noncustodial) staff and the guards (correctional officers or custodial staff). The demoralization could be solved with the communication and cooperation between these two groups, which was inherent in the Unit Management process.

Unit Management also offered a way of bringing fairness to the inmates. The units would be much smaller than before, and the unit staff would get to know the inmates much better. Policies could be enforced more consistently and since a unit manager was given authority, accountability was added. This would decrease overtime since permission for that would now be the responsibility of the unit manager and he would be told to keep that within the budget.

Separating the Population

One final barrier to regaining control of Walpole remained. Unit Management could never succeed without the prison administration having the ability and authority to separate the population. The staff at Walpole had been using its own unofficial and crude brand of classification. According to the Superintendent, they had been simply assigning inmates to cell blocks based upon general staff agreement as to the degree of aggressiveness. They were dividing the inmates into four groups at Walpole: (1) Suffolk, (2) Bristol, (3) Essex, and (4) Orientation unit. But inmates were becoming increasingly litigious and the administration had to protect itself from lawsuits. Prison personnel are quite familiar with the Quay system. Quay was a new, scientific system of classification that came into Walpole simultaneously with Unit Management. It legitimated the separation of inmates by personality and their degree of aggressiveness.

Those interviewed for this study disagreed as to whether Unit Management might have worked without Quay, but Quay was a legal necessity and it was only marginally and scientifically different from past procedure. What is important here is that without the combination of Quay *and* Unit Management, which is the method the consultant used in Lewisburg to turn a good treatment tool on its head to get control, all the goals for Walpole would not have been reachable. Quay, the legitimate method of replacing fear with safety, was a necessary outside input.

Weighing the Benefits

The problem-oriented search for solutions at Walpole was quite clearly focused on the avoidance of a return to the prison turmoil and violence that had characterized the place in the past. The consultant assured the Commissioner and the Superintendent that Unit Management would: (1) allow inmates to live without fear, (2) give correctional officers involvement in classification, a safer work environment, and inmate control, (3) increase the parity between custodial and noncustodial staff and provide the latter more inmate contact, and (4) give the administration a control mechanism. The Commissioner, Superintendent, and the Deputy of Programs weighed these benefits against the problems associated with adopting Unit Management.

As they were perceived, the reservations regarding physical space, staffing, overcrowding, and sergeants' loss of influence over the inmates did not outweigh the positive consequences. The alternative to Unit Management was the continuance of status quo, administrative chaos, violence, and the demoralization that accompanied it. Unit Management was new and different for Walpole. Doing something different made sense and Unit Management had a successful federal model that could be followed. It was not very likely that Walpole would be hurt by the adoption of a similar model and it might just work as another step towards the regaining and maintaining of control.

Conclusion

The Massachusetts Correctional Institute (MCI) at Walpole has had a very violent history coupled with an administrative record that, between 1972 and 1979, has best been characterized as "rudderless." In 1980, the prison administration began to implement Unit Management after a decision-making process that began with a newly appointed Commissioner in September 1979.

The hostile conditions at Walpole have been all but eliminated, and it is a much improved facility in which to live and work. Although Walpole (MCI: Cedar Junction) is still overcrowded, there is much less violence and fear. Correctional officers and noncustodial personnel share control over the inmates. Treatment activity is facilitated by noncustodial personnel having access to the prison population. The top administration in the Department of Corrections maintains amiable relations with the supportive Dukakis gubernatorial administration, and prison policy is specific, written down, and issued from the top.

The use of Unit Management since 1980 has made these conditions possible. This management policy encourages and depends upon continuous communication between administration, correctional officers, noncustodial personnel, and inmates. Misunderstandings and polarization between these groups are greatly reduced due to the sharing of information and responsibilities. The emphasis on teamwork and resultant feelings of unit ownership of problems and successes facilitates cohesion in crises. The constant assessment of the prison behavioral and attitudinal climate prevents complacency and the infiltration of cancerous tradition that obscured the call for change in the past.

Change is prepared for in Walpole's Unit Management system, which mandates clear, written, and decisive policy. Each Unit team works cooperatively in a participatory management style that has resulted in higher morale and commitment to purpose. Decisions are made more openly in the flatter organizational structure. Under the old traditional system the prison officials spent most of their time reacting to crises. With Unit Management, the seeds of discontent are identified early and problems are prevented.

As can be seen from this case study, however, prisons cannot be converted to Unit Management overnight. Several factors facilitated the adoption of Unit Management at Walpole. First, there was the pressing urgency, political pressure, and support for immediate action. Secondly, the Governor and Commissioner were committed to change and succeeded, through their determination, in fostering cooperation towards this end. Thirdly, outside experts in corrections (the NIC team and the consultant) brought strength and credibility to these convictions. And finally, visible change came quickly and decisively in the form of (1) certainty of safety for inmates and staff, (2) clear, equitable, and enforced policy from the top administration, and (3) administrative support for staff.

The Department of Corrections clearly succeeded in reversing Walpole's historic brutality and lack of direction and simultaneously met the goals of inmates, correctional officers, noncustodial staff, and administration.

Notes

1 Peter Remick. "In Constant Fear." New York, NY: *Reader's Digest Press,* 1975, p. 175.

2 Remick, p. 3.

3 Walter Waitkevich, "An Interview on a May 18th, 1973, Riot at Walpole" in Remick's "In Constant Fear," p. 122.

4 Remick, p. 172.

5 Olin Minton, "National Institute of Corrections Technical Assistance Report of Massachusetts Department of Corrections." Washington, DC: National Institute of Corrections, 1979, p. 8.

6 Ibid., p. 3.

7 Ibid., p. 7.

8 Robert B. Levinson and Roy E. Gerard, "Functional Units: A Different Correctional Approach," *Federal Probation,* December, 1973, Vol. 37, No. 4, pp. 8-17.

9 The goals of Unit Management are really prison-specific, but the following article provides valuable insight on the topic: W. Alan Smith and Charles E. Fenton, "Unit Management in a Penitentiary: A Practical Experience," *Federal Probation,* September, 1978, Vol. 42, No. 3, pp. 40-46.

19   Social Climate and
Prison Violence†

Hans Toch

There are two favored perspectives relating to prison violence. One—which appeals to would-be prognosticators—centers on violent inmates. This view has it that some inmates are consistently violent persons, who happen to be explosive in prison, but are likely to act out in almost any setting. A second portraiture conceives of inmate violence as at least partly a prison product. The most extreme version of this view is that of abolitionist critics who see prison aggression as a natural—and presumably, legitimate—reaction to the frustration of being locked up. Other critics argue that prison incidents denote lax security, and thus suggest negligence. This view is to some extent shared by prison administrators, who think of controlling violence through perimeter architecture, ingenious hardware, and deployment of custodial personnel. This context-centered view is a negative one, because it seeks to prevent violence by reducing the opportunities for aggression, rather than by trying to affect the motives and dispositions of violent participants.

In this chapter, I shall argue for a different context-centered view of prison violence that may offer more positive programming options than those that are conventionally envisaged. The view is also one that may have implications for research and policy.

The Advent of the Contextual View

In the mid 1960s, the inmate-centered tradition was at its peak, and researchers attended to offender background characteristics, such as MMPI profiles and prior criminality, with an eye toward locating high-risk offender groups.

---

†Reprinted from *Federal Probation*, December, 1988 by permission.

Among exceptions to this trend was a subgroup of The California Task Force to Study Violence in Prisons. In describing inmate aggression, this group focused on the victimization incident, highlighting immediate motives of inmate participants that went into producing each incident (Mueller, Toch & Molof, 1965). This sort of analysis illuminated, among other things, the contribution of predation and extortion, homosexual relationships and pressures, debts, stealing, and routine prison disputes to the genesis of violent prison encounters in the mid 1960s.

This focus made possible a new approach to the motivational patterns of chronic, recurrent aggressors, especially trends in the way violent incidents arose for the same individual (Toch, 1969). This approach involved seeing violence-precipitation as an intersection between personal dispositions and the situational stimuli that invoked these dispositions. In this view, a prison incident could result, for instance, given a perceived affront to an inmate who is oversensitive to such affronts, or from the availability of a tempting target to an inmate who is a habitual bully.

There are probably several ways of defining violence-relevant contextual stimuli. One way of thinking about settings that is helpful is the concept of "social climate" (Moos, 1974; Toch, 1977), which includes the inmate himself. In prison, the concern would be with each inmate's immediate world, including prison staff, other inmates, and the physical milieu, as the inmate experiences it and reacts to it. The presumption is that any prison setting in which inmates spend a significant portion of time, such as tiers, shops, and classrooms has behavior-relevant attributes that stand out for individual inmates. A shop, for instance, may feature a paternalistic or stern foreman, relaxed or firm supervision, a group of street-raised youths or lifers, high or low levels of noise, a playful or businesslike regime. Such factors may be more salient for most inmates than the fact that the shop teaches the plumbing trade, though this learning opportunity is another climate attribute that will be significant to inmates. Three fairly obvious points are of theoretical and practical concern: (1) any social climate feature may be critical in the life of one inmate and irrelevant to another; (2) the same feature may be welcomed by some and noxious to others, and (3) positive and negative reactions to features of climate help to spark inmate behavior, including participation in violent incidents.

How do climate features enter into the genesis of violence? Consider the following examples, some of which are more complex than others:

1. A farm setting in a youth prison is an informal haven for "problem" inmates because of its low level of supervision, which reduces resentment and rebellious behavior; inmates who have been aggressors before arriving on this farm become relatively well-behaved; however, (a) an inexperienced rural inmate is assigned to the farm; he promptly becomes the target of homosexual pressure; (b) the victim evokes a panic reaction to the setting and the other inmates; in an effort at self-protection he assaults one of his tormentors.

2. A recreation room is popular on a tier because it offers opportunities for playful socializing; (a) recreational preferences develop into conflicts between two inmates, which produces a fight, (b) the incident-participants are members of ethnic cliques, which become polarized and divide the recreation room into turfs; incidents arise as a result of jurisdictional disputes, and in retaliation for prior incidents.

3. A prison is tightly supervised, except for certain areas in which an acknowledged need for privacy, or constant comings and goings, produce custodial lacunae; the places-and-times of low supervision acquire standard connotations; for instance: (a) the yard shower is avoided by many inmates because it is frequented by sexual aggressors; a new inmate may wander into such an area unaware, and become an incident-victim; (b) a stairway used for movement from a tier to breakfast is comparatively unsupervised; it becomes a "gladiating arena" in which aggrieved inmates—some armed with knives—challenge their enemies; (c) in a tier with a tradition of informality, officers open gallery doors on request; the practice is abused by inmates wishing to invade the cells of fellow inmates to victimize them; (d) the inmate picnic becomes a drug-trafficking bazaar, with resulting jurisdictional disputes.

I have included examples in which traditional variables—particularly, the extent of supervision—play a role, but my implication is not that we must have prisons in which monitoring is omnipresent. We know that custody is less effective in governing persons than programming. Moreover, officers cannot be stationed where they are not otherwise needed, on the off-chance that incidents may occur. Deployment of security measures of necessity must be uneven, leaving times and places of lower-density supervision. My point, in fact, is that neither custody deficits nor other formal arrangements of the environment produce violence. Incidents arise, as they do in the free world, because the relationships that spring up among people in a subsetting misfire or become sequentially more destructive. There are chains of these motives, some of which get imported from outside the prison, such as the toughness-proving needs of our prison farm youths and the ethnic tensions in the recreational room. Such personal motives get mobilized by other people in the environment who press the relevant motivational button. Once a violence-related motive exists, meanings assigned to features of the environment—such as sex to the shower or gladiating to the stairway—then determine where and when incidents may occur.

Social Climate and Aggressors

I have implied that to understand incident-motives and violence-proneness means more than to locate prior behavior patterns or consistencies; it also means that we must know the stimuli that invoke the person's motives, the contexts that facilitate or invite them, the group that encourages or applauds them, and the milieu that makes them fashionable or susceptible to rationalization.

We must start with the incident; we ask ourselves how the victimizer arrived at his resolve. Was his goal profit? Retribution? Loyalty to his group? Wounded self-esteem? Search for reputation? Escape from danger? The temptation of another's vulnerability? Ethnic prejudice? Resentment of authority? Adherence to a "code?"

It is true that we can often guess at the inmate's motives from his folder where the information we have about his prior behavior may point to patterns; and the folder helps us to differentiate chronic victimizers—whose personal behavior patterns must be addressed—from occasional victimizers, whose conduct is more of a product of specific situational forces.

But situational context is always of relevance—even with chronicity. A bully merits rehabilitative attention, but what such a person immediately needs is to be deprived of access to inmates with victim-attributes. In a setting that is exclusively composed of self-styled "toughs" the predatory inmate's pattern is less likely to be elicited. Similar impact may be achieved by promoting solidarity among victim-prone inmates, because bullies pick on isolates, or by promoting anti-bully norms among the bully's peers.

Violence-Promotion by Climate Features

Our point about situational context is not that the context produces the incident but that it increases or reduces the probability of incident occurrence. If our view holds, it follows that incident prevalence can be increased or decreased through contextual interventions, even though incident motives are personal and may be manifestations of personality traits. Contextual facilitation of violence in prison occurs in several ways, some of the more obvious being:

1. **By providing "pay offs."** We can reinforce the motives of aggressors by conferring status or other types of rewards for violent behavior. In some cases the rewards are obvious, as when the aggressor secures peer-admiration. Elsewhere there are more "hidden" reward systems, as when "punishment" consists of sending a predator to a status-conferring segregation setting.

2. **By providing immunity or protection.** Violence in prison benefits from the same "code of silence" that is highlighted by

Westley (1970) for police violence; however, the significance of the protective code in prison is compounded by inmate-staff social distance, by taboos against "ratting," by fear of retaliation, and so forth. Legalistic solutions to the victimization problem are encumbered by difficulties in securing reliable information from witnesses and victim-complainants. Prisons share this difficulty with other "subcultural" settings, such as those of organized crime.

3. **By providing opportunities.** The prison world features predictability and routine in physical movement, custodial supervision patterns, and types of staff reactions. The inmate aggressor is in the same position as the residential burglar who knows homeowner vacation patterns, and can plan the time and locus of his predatory forays.

Predictability, paradoxically, cuts both ways; by studying incident concentrations, we can re-adjust supervision patterns; staff re-adjustments can produce short-term amelioration, followed by new incident clusters over time if the staff responses are predictable.

4. **By providing temptations, challenges, and provocations.** Climate features may unwittingly or unavoidably spark victimization, as does the "red flag" that mobilizes the bull. Prison juxtaposes "strong" and "weak" inmates, members of rival gangs, dealers and consumers of contraband, homosexual rivals, debtors and creditors, racketeers and "marks." Such stimuli are often "built into" population mixes, or into personal characteristics of inmates; others are "taken up" as optional roles. For instance, there are gangs that spring up in prison, in reaction to other indigenous inmate groupings—as among Mexican-American inmates in California. Prison gangs may engage in mutual retaliatory exercises in which each serves as the occasion for the other's violence.

5. **By providing justificatory premises.** Most inmates have more-or-less serious reservations about other inmates (Toch, 1977a). Fellow inmates may be: (1) viewed as natural enemies or as personally contemptible; or (2) "dehumanized" to make them "fair game" for predation or exploitation. To the extent to which this is the case, controlling population mixes separates or combines potential aggressors, victims, and violent contenders.

Research and Program Implications

Prison outsiders have a penchant for outlandish recommendations. Worse still, they often ship coal to Newcastle. Some of my points will be familiar to prison staff; some suggest formalizing what is done, and affirming its value:

> 1. **Understanding violence "hot spots" and low-violence subenvironments.** Measures such as disciplining aggressors require little information about the causation of violence because the issue is culpability. Furthermore, incident participants are reticent in such inquiries, except for arguments-in-mitigation of their involvement. A corollary is that control and prevention of institutional violence cannot depend on information secured through fact-finding that occurs in disciplinary contexts.

I am not suggesting that formal research must be routinely deployed, but that inquiries into the reasons for "cold" violent incidents—those no longer being processed—be undertaken. One form of such inquiry that strikes me as useful relates to settings in which violent incidents are generated, or where violence is scarce. Parallel investigation can trace the institutional careers of violent inmates for "high points" and "low points" in their incident profiles. Staff and inmates in violent subsettings—including incident participants—should be interviewed for clues about the high or low level of violence in their settings. Given everyone's stake in minimizing trouble, there is incentive for problem-centered information sharing that has no disciplinary consequence.

Available statistics about unique subsettings—their types of inmates, schedule of activities, levels of interaction, population movements, patterns of supervision—can be collated, and compared to: (1) details about statistics relating to other subsettings, and (2) information about incident participants. Such data are merely clues to violence motives, but they serve to check or validate data from interviews. Moreover, statistics "fed" to inmates and staff can help them understand their violence problem.[1] This use is related to:

> 2. **Helping inmates and staff in high-violence settings to address their own violence problem.** This gambit presumes that solutions that originated with those affected by their implementation are least likely to mobilize resistances. It also assumes that subsettings can become communities that have a stake in reducing localized danger and disruption. The point holds even for groups of violent individuals. Such persons have elsewhere become successfully engaged in "solving the violence problem" in their settings (Toch, Grant & Galvin, 1975). Staff and inmate groups can be run separately or together, charged with docu-

menting the reasons for violence patterns, and asked to recommend policy changes to neutralize violence patterns. This must obviously be done with the understanding that documented and practical suggestions will be implemented.

3. **Creating support systems for victims and potential victims.** The most common measures used to deal with violence address aggressors; by segregating them, prison enclaves can be formed, such as segregation wings, in which levels of violence become disproportionately high. Obvious victim-centered strategies also entail problems. They stigmatize inmates, such as in "sissie companies," or may secrete prisoners in program voids, such as protective segregation areas. Less drastic options are made available through the creation of new settings in which victim prone inmates are mixed with others to receive mental health services or for clear programmatic purposes. Activity-centered inmate groups can also provide victims with peer support and with respectable staff links.

4. **Crisis intervention teams.** Such teams are an example of support measures designed to be invoked where the violence problem is still "hot." One use of this strategy was the California deployment of inmate Social Catalysts (Summer, 1976) who acted as liaison and calming influences in gang wars, racial conflict and other group disturbances. Teams can be made up of persons who are trained to mediate or defuse violent conflicts and who refer participants, if necessary, for professional assistance. Such teams can range in composition from chaplains to custodial officers or inmates. A less drastic option is to "debrief" violence participants to prevent lingering disputes from flaring up after the protagonists leave segregation settings and return to the yard.

5. **Using violence-related data in staff training and inmate indoctrination.** This approach requires no technology beyond collation of relevant information. My suggestion is that such data should be as setting-specific as possible. In other words, the training content would not consist of general "human relations" lectures for staff, or of rule-centered, legalistic lectures to inmates, but of statistics and illustrations that sensitize staff and inmates to situations they are likely to encounter on the tier in which they live or work. This means that "canned" curricula could be enriched or supplemented by updated information

about prevailing interpersonal problems, group tensions, etc., and about solutions that have been tried and that have worked. Inmates and staff could also be specifically informed during their induction about the parameters of their assignments, such as informal routines or population attributes, so as to avoid dependence on scuttlebutt or trial-and-error learning.

None of these strategies will "solve" emerging problems. No matter what any of us do, low-visibility disputes can arise and dedicated predators can find room for predation. The goal is the reduction of violence through the creation of a climate that faces occasions for violence and begins to defuse them. If we accomplish this goal, residual violence will be "person centered," and can be addressed as such.

Notes

[1] One use of data feedback relates to fear of violence (secondary victimization), a topic I have not touched upon because it deserves detailed rumination. Fear relates imperfectly to violence, and this means that we may be afraid without cause, or unafraid where apprehension might well be functional. Information about violence that does occur in a setting can be a corrective to irrational apprehension. Similarly, fear can be separately mapped, and such data can be discussed as one makes a direct effort at fear-reduction/or fear alignment.

References

Moos, R.H. (1974). *Evaluating Treatment Environments: A Social Ecological Approach.* New York, NY: Wiley.

Mueller, R.F.C., H. Toch and M.F. Molof (1965). *Report to the Task Force to Study Violence in Prisoners.* Sacramento, CA: California Department of Corrections (August).

Summer, G.W. (1976). "Dealings with Prison Violence." In A.K. Cohen, G.F. Cole and R.G. Bailey (eds.) *Prison Violence.* Lexington, MA: Lexington Books.

Toch, H. (1969). *Violent Men: An Inquiry into the Psychology of Violence.* Chicago, IL: Aldine.

Toch, H. (1977). *Living in Prison: The Ecology of Survival.* New York, NY: The Free Press.

Toch, J., J.D. Grant and R.T. Galvin (1975). *Agents of Change: A Study in Police Reform.* Cambridge, MA: Schenkman (Halsted/Wiley).

Westley, W.A. (1970). *Violence and the Police: A Sociological Study of Law, Custom and Morality.* Boston, MA: MIT Press.

20   The Faces of Corrections: Selected Case Studies[†]

Michael C. Braswell, Tyler Fletcher & Larry Miller

An important problem area for most people regarding corrections, including those of us who work with or relate to offenders, is our built-in attitude or mind-set of "us against them." Our images of unshaven, diabolical movie criminals, headlines touting rising, out-of-control crime rates, and special articles and media programs on the most gruesome crimes and offenders, make it easy for us to become convinced that most if not all criminals are dangerous and should be severely punished—no matter what the costs. Even with criminal justice professionals, such as correctional counselors who should be better informed, there is often a strong sense of "us against them." After all, criminals are sent to prison or placed on probation or parole; they do wear uniforms, and their world (particularly in prison) is much different than the world in which the rest of us live. With our frustrations and fears over crime rates and the justice process itself, increases in the costs of living, and difficulties law-abiding citizens have in finding good jobs, we are inclined to feel that offenders should be sent to prison *for* punishment rather than *as* punishment. In fact, even if the offender serves his or her time and does everything possible to learn from past mistakes, we often think they should still feel guilty and burdened with their offense after their release. In other words, we want them to get well—become corrected, but not feel good about it. Of course, while such retributive notions may make us feel better emotionally, they may often add to, rather than diminish, the probability that the released offender will return to crime. We might ask ourselves: Are we willing to want offenders to become happy people? Are offenders who continue to be ridden with guilt after their release from the criminal justice system more or

---

[†]Reprinted from *The Faces of Corrections: Selected Case Studies*, Third Edition, 1990. Reprinted by permission of Waveland Press, Inc.

less likely to return to crime? We believe that offenders should feel bad about their crimes, but feeling bad about themselves to the point of having no hope for a better life may not be such a good idea. We do want to help them "correct" their ways of thinking and behaving in order that they can begin to feel better about themselves and the society to which they usually return.

Before we can help offenders change their attitudes about their criminal behavior, we may need to first work on our own attitudes about offenders. We need to better understand what they need in order to correct themselves. Part of this understanding includes our gaining more insight into the other players who participate in the correctional process—including judges, probation and parole officers, family members, counselors, guards, administrators, and of course, the offenders themselves. The keepers and the kept and the offenders and their victims are bound by the common destiny of their experiences together. Whether on the right or wrong side of the law, we each have our full measure of pain to bear and our hopes to hold onto no matter how distant or unreachable they might seem. To the extent we see each other as enemies, as us against them, the insight and understanding necessary for a lasting, positive change to occur is not possible. Henry Wadsworth Longfellow once wrote, "If we could read the secret history of our enemies, we should find in each man's life sorrow and suffering enough to disarm all hostility."[1] In order to read the "secret histories" of our enemies and our own hearts, we have to learn more about the lessons of compassion and empathy. Compassion and empathy allow us to see the world we have in common with our enemies and friends through their uncommon eyes. And it is not only seeing their world, but feeling their world as well. Frederick Buechner wrote, "Compassion is the sometimes fatal capacity for feeling what it's like to live inside somebody else's skin."[2] Compassion and empathy allow us the opportunity to make the most of what time and space we have left between us. The time may be short and the space limited as with the relationship between a chaplain and an inmate on death row, or it may seem full of possibilities as a counselor works through burnout and moves on with his or her life, clear-minded and full of purpose. Whatever the situation, whatever the time, better understanding of ourselves and those we work with moves us along our spiritual journey as well as helps us encourage others on theirs.

Case studies can provide us with one way to gain such insight and understanding. Such an approach can be useful in helping us to better understand and deal with the ambiguities and frustrations which are so much a part of the criminal justice and correctional process.[3] Broadening our attitudes, opening our minds and hearts to the various aspects and possibilities of corrections will not make us "soft" on crime and criminals, but can help us to make clearer, more workable correctional choices even when they have to be tough choices. Remember, a solution to a problem that is not clearly understood is often no solution at all. Instead, such solutions simply become problems themselves, making the original problem more confusing than ever.

The following five case problems will offer you an opportunity to gain a sense of what it feels like to experience corrections from the viewpoint of the different players in the correctional process. Judge and probation or parole officer, inmate and guard, and counselor all have their own problems and priorities. Yet, each is a living, breathing human being connected by circumstances; a part of the same human family. As you will notice, in corrections as in life there are often no easy or clear solutions to problem situations in which we may find ourselves. Each choice we make carries with it both obvious and hidden consequences. Commentary and discussion questions that follow each case problem are designed to help encourage you to think clearly and compassionately about what you would do and to share those thoughts with your classmates and teacher. After looking at corrections through the eyes of each of these participants, it is our hope that you will be able to have a better understanding of the nature of the correctional process and that you will have more empathy and compassion— even when the choices have to be tough ones—for those who live and work in correctional environments.

Case 1
The Minister and the Ex-Offender

As one of your community's leading ministers, you have always spoken out for progressive correctional reform. Your congregation has usually backed you, and on the few occasions when they did not, they still remained tolerant of your views. Now, however, things are different. Sally, a former member of your church, was once active in working with the church youth. She has since been convicted of embezzlement from the local bank where she worked and has been sentenced to one year in prison.

As her minister, you kept in contact with her from the beginning of her imprisonment. No one ever really believed she would have to serve time; since the money was returned, no one expected that her boss would even bring charges against her. Everyone has financial burdens at one time or another, and Sally had experienced a succession of problems over a long period of time. The clincher was her husband's permanent disability as a result of an accident. The bills began to pile up faster than she could get them paid. They had mortgaged their house and sold one of their two cars. Finally, in desperation, Sally "borrowed" several thousand dollars from the bank where she had worked as a teller for years. When her crime was discovered, her world crumbled around her.

She has not returned to the community after serving a prison term for embezzlement. When you talked to her the day after she returned, you realized that she was a broken woman. Her daughter had dropped out of school to care for the father, and his disability check was their primary source of income. You counseled her and encouraged her to try and regain her place in the community. You also helped her find work and even suggested that she return to your church where she had previously been very active. She was reluctant to rejoin the church, fearing rejection by the congregation. You tried to reassure her that everyone was behind her and wanted her to return to the church. In fact, a substantial number of the members had told you as much. When you learned that there would soon be an opening in the Sunday School for a youth director, you asked Sally to consider taking the position. After several days of thinking about it, she agreed.

You have now brought her name before the Sunday School Committee and they have, to a person, refused to allow her to be the youth leader. Their bitterness has taken you totally by surprise; their words remain all too clear in your mind: "How would it look to the rest of the community to have an ex-convict directing our youth?" Should you fight for what you believe is right and risk dissension or even possibly splitting the church, or should you tell her that her fears are more valid than you had thought, that her former fellow church members have not been able to forgive and forget?

Case 1: Commentary and Questions for Discussion

You must make a difficult decision. If you insist on Sally being allowed to become a youth leader and the dissenting members relent, what kind of emotional pressure would this put on Sally, and how would she handle it? On the other hand, if you "give in" to the disagreeable committee members and inform Sally of their decision, what impact will your action have on Sally's and your own self-concept, as well as your leadership ability in the church? Perhaps you are not fully aware of the church's true attitude concerning Sally as an ex-offender. How could you have possibly made yourself more aware of their feelings? This is a painful and embarrassing experience for you. Yet, how can this experience teach you something for your own personal and spiritual journey?

Case 2
Six Months to Go

Six months ago, the biggest concern in your life was finishing college. Now your biggest concern is your own personal safety. Never in a million years did you dream that you would be spending the twentieth year of your life in a state prison. As a sociology major in college, you studied about crime, criminals and prisons, but it was nothing compared to the real thing. The constant noise of steel and concrete; the smell of bodies, cigarettes, and old buildings; the inability to go where you want to go, eat what you want to eat—all this is foreign and confusing to you.

Sure, you smoked some grass and sometimes used pills to stay up and study for exams when you were in college; a lot of other students did the same. You had never expected to get "busted" with just three joints. But you did. Since it was your first offense, your lawyer said probation was a sure thing. Unfortunately for you, however, you got a judge who was fed up with drug abuse. He decided that it was time to crack down, and he used you for an example. As a result, he sentenced you to three years in the state prison. When he pronounced sentence, the sky fell for you and your family.

Your experiences in prison have left you confused and frustrated. During those first few months of incarceration, you felt hopeless and alone. Your family, although upset and embarrassed, has stuck by you. It was the efforts of a young prison counselor and the support of your family that have kept you going. Only six months remain on your sentence before you come up for parole. You have "kept your nose clean" with the prison staff and other inmates.

Last night a terrible incident occurred: your 18-year-old cell mate, Sam, was brutally raped and beaten by four older inmates, who informed you that the same fate would be yours if you reported them. You remember only too well the whistles and the threats directed toward you during the first several days you were in the cellblock. You realize that your size and former athletic conditioning allowed you to establish a relative amount of independence in the prison; your cellmate, being smaller and weaker, had no such natural defense qualities. You also realize that if you report what they did to your friend, the four inmates are likely to make good their threat. Still, you cannot rid yourself of the rage and sickness you feel because of your friend's humiliation and helplessness. You know that he might be attacked again. Yet, you are also confronted with your own needs of survival and well-being.

The only employee you trust in the prison is a young counselor. Not having been at the prison very long, he has only limited influence with the prison administration. Nevertheless, he is enthusiastic and well-intentioned. You cannot forget what happened to your cellmate, yet with only six months before parole you are also thinking of your own welfare.

Case 2: Commentary and Questions for Discussion

This is a nightmare experience to have to go through. The fear, anger, and frustration are almost too much. Still, you have to try to hang on. Why couldn't the administration have protected Sam from such abuse? You are not even sure that keeping quiet will protect you. Survival, blaming the administration, even blaming Sam all run through your mind. The guilt of keeping quiet, the fear of reporting it—what will you do?

Case 3
The Judge and the Juvenile Delinquent

You are a juvenile judge. The job is not so easy as some people think. The judicial process in any court is somewhat ambiguous, but the process in a juvenile court is even less defined. With so many options available in the rehabilitation or institutionalization of juveniles, the juvenile judge needs to be particularly careful concerning his or her final decision.

As a juvenile judge, your job is not simply to determine guilt or innocence. Most of the time you have to determine the degree of the juvenile's involvement in a criminal act. Cases come to you informally through complaints and formally through juvenile petitions. You have to interpret and apply not only state criminal laws, but also laws called "Unruly Acts" that apply only to juveniles. The philosophy of the juvenile court is to treat and rehabilitate the juvenile offender if at all possible. This philosophy of rehabilitation sometimes results in the same juvenile coming before your court for a second or third appearance. Still, you are reluctant to institutionalize a juvenile except as a last resort.

Today's case presents a difficult problem to you as a juvenile judge. The juvenile is a 15-year-old male with whom you are very familiar. He has been in your court several times since he was 10 years old. His first encounter with the law was for habitual truancy from school. The problem centered around a lack of parental supervision and concern. The boy began to associate with a "bad" crowd and his delinquent behavior began to increase. His next encounter with the juvenile justice system was for shoplifting. He was placed on six months' probation. During his probation, he was suspected in several breaking and entering offenses, and it was eventually proved in court that he did participate in one burglary. At age 14, he was incarcerated in a juvenile corrections center. After seven months, the boy was released on parole. During the next year, he was involved in various liquor violations which, of course, violated his conditions of parole. He spent another four months in the juvenile corrections center.

In the present case, this juvenile is accused of the vandalism of a public school. Loss of property resulting from this offense has been estimated at $15,000. The state has requested that the juvenile be tried as an adult. This is one of your toughest decisions as a juvenile judge. Under the law, the court must place the child under legal restraints if it decides that to do so is in the best interest of the community. If the juvenile court feels that this is warranted, the criminal court must accept the case after a hearing. The case will then go to the grand jury for indictment.

Once the child is released from the juvenile court, he is subject to adult punishment and can be incarcerated in the state prison. You feel sure that if he is convicted on the $15,000 vandalism charge, he will be sentenced to prison. You wonder if this particular juvenile will ever be able to recover from the stigma of an "adult" prison and become a productive citizen. On the other hand, you do have a duty to protect the community from incorrigible juveniles. You must decide whether the severity of this case warrants that the child be tried as an adult. Should the community be protected by the legal restraint of this juvenile, or should the boy be protected under the juvenile court in an effort to rehabilitate him?

Case 3: Commentary and Questions for Discussion
In this case, you must decide whether to try the juvenile as an adult. Certainly the youth seems to be incorrigible, even though his offenses to date have not been

of a distinctly serious nature. Prison cannot help him, yet he is a nuisance to the community. Should "one" more effort be made to salvage this juvenile or should you be realistic and "throw in the towel?" Using your heart and mind, what makes the most sense from where you sit as judge?

Case 4
An End, or a Beginning?

You have been a correctional officer at the state prison for three years. You have had your ups and downs, but the job has always been interesting. For the last year, you have been in charge of Cellhouse B., which is home to 100 male inmates.

Fifteen minutes ago, you made your hourly check around the cellhouse, and since everything appeared to be quiet, you returned to your desk which was located near the main entrance gate. You had just begun making headway with some overdue paperwork when several inmates at the far end of the cellblock began yelling for you to come quickly.

Upon arriving at the scene of the disturbance, you found a 26-year-old inmate (who had been incarcerated about six months) semiconscious, with a sheet tied around his neck and looped around an overhead steam pipe. With the help of a nearby inmate, you untied the sheet from the young man's neck and laid him on his bed. After calling on the intercom to the medical section for assistance, you returned to the young inmate, who had by then regained consciousness.

While waiting for him to be transported to the prison hospital, you attempt to carry on a conversation in an effort to help him relax. The results of your efforts are surprising. Although depressed, the young inmate begins to openly discuss his problems with you. It is apparent that he trusts you, but you are becoming increasingly unsure as to how you should handle the situation. You are not a professional counselor, and perhaps you are venturing too far out of your area of expertise.

Should this young inmate be a problem just for the prison counselor or psychologist, or should you allow yourself to become involved with him, with his problems and his feelings? One part of your instincts tells you to keep your distance, while another part tells you to help him if you can. What should you do?

Case 4: Commentary and Questions for Discussion

You wish you had more training for this kind of problem. Where's a counselor when you need one? You are unsure, but this person really needs you right here and now. Can you make a difference and still keep your distance? Your heart says to do what you can; your head isn't so sure.

Case 5
Dealing with Anger

You have been a counselor for 10 years, but this is one part of your job that has never gotten any easier.

Doug, an inmate at the institution where you work, has just been turned down for parole for the second time in six years. The two of you are sitting at the hearing room table silently staring out the barred window. You can see the tears silently streaming down Doug's face. You can sense the anger and humiliation he is feeling and the explosion within himself that he is fighting to contain.

Doug has a good prison record with respect to both his conduct and his commitment to rehabilitation programs. The problem is apparently a political one. The local judge simply does not want Doug released in his county. As the institutional counselor, you know several other inmates who have been granted parole to that particular county. They were paroled despite having committed more serious offenses than Doug and having been much less receptive to the various institutional rehabilitation programs. Doug also knows of these paroles. To make matters worse, the parole board did not even give him a reason for rejecting his application, nor did they tell him what he could do to increase his chances for parole.

Doug spent weeks in preparation for his parole hearing. The letters of recommendation, the acquisition of his high school diploma, and other related material had in the end meant nothing. The board had convened less than 10 minutes to make a parole decision based on six years of Doug's life. The chairman simply told you that Doug's parole had been denied and for you to pass the decision along to Doug. You had reluctantly done so, knowing that Doug could see the decision in your eyes before you even spoke. So here the two of you sit, bitter and disillusioned.

Case 5: Commentary and Questions for Discussion

Even though the parole denial in this particular case may have been politically motivated, how could the "hearing" have been better handled? You feel sick-at-heart about Doug's denial. The politics stink! As hopeless as Doug's situation seems, you want to keep yourself and Doug as calm and centered as possible. You need all the creative energy you can muster to think of other possibilities. Surely there is another way. But is there?

Notes

1 "Sunbeams," *The Sun*, 1987, Issue 134.

2 Buechner, Frederick. *Wishful Thinking*. New York, NY: Harper & Row, 1976.

3 Braswell, Michael, Tyler Fletcher and Larry Miller. *Cases in Corrections*. Prospect Heights, IL: Waveland Press, 1985.

21

Letters of Violence†

Bo Lozoff & Michael C. Braswell

Introduction

This chapter is composed of correspondence between Bo Lozoff and inmates, including family members and friends. The letters are organized around the themes of violence, victims, confusion, and hope. As you read and reflect upon these letters, you may find that they offer valuable lessons for your own personal journey. We encourage you to put yourself in the place of these letter writers and imagine how you would feel and what you would try to do.

Why do we act violently toward ourselves and others? It is often hard to understand how we can become so filled with anger, hate, confusion, and even indifference, that we can take someone else's life. Too frequently, alcohol, drugs, and unhappy childhoods combine with misplaced values and volatile situations can result in tragic consequences for both the offender and the victim.

These letters of correspondence express a variety of violent acts and responses ranging from murder to a nonviolent response. As you read each of these letters and Bo's responses, try to imagine yourself in the worlds of the letter writers. How could life have been different for them? For some it may seem to be too late, but is it? For others, the odds may be in their favor for another chance. What would have to happen to you to become a part of the violent world of these inmates?

As you reflect on this section let yourself come to see more clearly how the path of violence is more a process feeding on itself than simply isolated acts. Use your imagination not only to see what brings human beings to such violence, but also to

---

†Reprinted from *Inner Corrections: Finding Peace and Peace Making*, 1989, Anderson Publishing Co.

look at the bigger picture for ways society can encourage persons not to follow violent paths.

> *Violence*
> *In this place, touching hurts so much.*
> *Love, hate, lust and violence, all hurt so much;*
> *they overlap, they merge,*
> *then separate again.*
>
> *What Nightmare is this?*
> *My God, when will I awaken?*

Tommy

Dear Friends,

I'm searching for my spiritual awakening that so far I've not been able to find, but my life has come to a point where I need to find myself before I'm lost in the terrible maze of unknowing.

Let me take a few minutes to tell you a little about myself and my present situation. Hopefully it will help you to know what it is I'm trying to find. I'm 27 years old, born Sept. 9, 1950. I'm presently in the Idaho State Prison for first-degree murder, two counts. I was sentenced to death in March 1976, but the Idaho Supreme Court vacated my death penalty. (Tommy's death penalty has been reinstated, and at this time [1985] he's back on death row). These two charges in Idaho aren't the only ones I have. There are seven more in other states. Please let me explain why I did these cold-blooded, without any mercy, killings.

In April of 1974, eleven men entered my home in Portland, Oregon, raped my 17-year-old wife, who was three months pregnant at the time, then threw her four stories out our apartment window.

You see, I had been running drugs and guns for some people out of Nevada. My wife had asked me to stop so I tried to get out but they said no. On my next run I kept the goods I was to deliver and told them I'd turn it over to the feds if they tried causing me any trouble. I never would have, but they thought I was serious. Well, they set me up on a phony bust to get me out of the way thinking I had told my wife where I had stashed the stuff. I never did!

So, when they went to our house, after beating her and realizing she really didn't know where I put the stuff, they gang-raped her and threw her out the window. By some freak accident she lived for several months after that, long enough to tell me who most of the eleven were. She committed suicide while in a state mental institution, as her body was so crippled up from the fall, she had lost all hope and just wanted to die. In August of 1974, I went after the eleven guys who did it and caught nine of them in several different states. I was unable to complete my death mission and get the last two because I got caught here in Idaho.

Since all of this happened, I've had no inner peace at all. All I can think of is my wife, the only person who ever loved me and all I had in this world. I can see the men I killed and the look of pure fear and disbelief that I'd found them, as I took their lives. I'm not saying I was right for what I did, and I can't really say I'm sorry. I only know that I have no peace, happiness, or love, but at times I feel that I can have, but I just don't know where to look. I need help but I have nobody to turn to. My family has turned from me and I have nobody to write to or to visit me. I can't carry my burden alone anymore, so I ask you from the deepest of my heart, please send me any material that you think might help me. I am in maximum-security solitary confinement and have been for almost four years.

Really, all I want to do is find that something that I know for a fact exists that will free me from all my burdens. I would appreciate any correspondence that can help me find my way to a new and better life. Thank you for your time. Please reply!

Sincerely yours, Tommy/Idaho

Dear Tommy,

Your letter has touched me and Sita deeply. We're happy to know you. In one sense, you've got an unusual story; yet in another sense, you're in exactly the same place we all are: Simply a person who's waking up to the journey, and wondering what you can do to get on with it. As heavy and fierce as your own life has been, it's not the details so much that matter once we start this process of awakening.

It's true that every thought, word and deed counts. But it's also true that the journey is a much bigger one than most people imagine. And in the course of all that time, it's possible that each one of us has to pass through the very gates of hell and madness like you, your wife, and her attackers did during the past few years.

I don't mean to imply that you should look back and feel good about it, but just to try to understand that no accidents happen in this universe. Even the most horrible experiences can still be steps along the way. And the pain which may still lie before you as a consequence of killing nine people—just more of the same: difficult, necessary steps on your path.

This understanding is the beginning of true faith. My faith first woke up when I was eighteen and I drove head on into a tractor-trailer at close to 100 mph. I was a bodybuilder at the time. My whole life was based on body-stuff, and suddenly I'd never be able to do any of that again. I had permanent injuries; I could bitch about them, but they were what they were regardless.

The same thing happened to me as is happening to you: I knew there had to be something, some way of looking at my life, that could open the door back up to the possibility of happiness. In your case, the "permanent injuries" are the fact that you'll probably never see the streets again in this lifetime. That's a fact you need to face in order to plan a strategy for your life.

A good first step is to begin quieting the mind, and this is what all our meditation materials are about. All the answers, all the guidance you ever need, is already within you, but the noisy mind can't figure out how to tune into it. What I mean by noise is stuff like desire, fear, guilt, self-pity, anger, hatred, pride, pettiness and so forth. The way most of us grow up, our lives are pretty much a confusing combination of such noise from the time we get up in the morning until we fall asleep exhausted each night. No wonder we're so tired!

But meditation practices, especially with the kind of time you're doing, can be your gateway into the deeper realities of life, the deeper parts of yourself which can help you go *through* your pain rather than trying in vain to go around it.

It's not going to be fun or easy. Meditation is always pretty hard, and when you may be opening into intense guilt or grief, it's harder still. The only thing harder would be to try to ignore it all, and live an empty life feeling alone and isolated. It's more a matter of facing whatever experiences your life brings you and using them to become free.

Of course, all of this is much easier said than done, I know. I know you've been through terrible pain. I'm just trying to help, and I figure if I throw about a million words at you, maybe three or four will hit home. At least you can count on having a family again. Much Light for your day,

Love, Bo

Dear Bo,

I just received your most beautiful and encouraging letter and I was so happy to hear from you. Thank you so very much!

I'm not always an emotional person as far as letting my feelings show, as my past lifestyle required that I never let nobody get close or at no time let anyone know what I was feeling at any time. But in these past few weeks since I first read INSIDE-OUT, I've been becoming aware of myself and of other people more each day, and I've been experiencing feelings that I had all but forgotten. Then today when I got your letter and the books, something happened to me that I never would have dreamed possible.

Since that first day I picked up a half-torn copy of INSIDE-OUT and began to read it, I felt that at last I had found what it was I had been looking for all my life. And something told me to write and find out more of what this had to offer me in my search for spiritual awakening. At first I was pretty skeptical because I had been through so many other trips, and had been let down so many times. But something kept telling me not to just read this to help pass the hours away but to read it and keep it in my heart and mind.

LETTERS OF VIOLENCE **365**

So, each day I've been applying some of the things that I've read to my daily life, and I've been like a new person.

When I got your letter today, I noticed my hands were shaking as I was taking it out of the envelope. Well, as I started to read I felt a warmth come over me as I have never felt before, and a voice within stilled my fears and seemed to say that at last you're coming home and you have no need to fear ever again. As I read on I noticed that I kept having trouble seeing and my face felt like it was on fire. So I reached up and started to rub my eyes and it was only then that I realized that I had tears in my eyes and running down my face. Then they came freely as I knelt to thank God for that little book and for you and all the others that are trying to bring the world together to live in harmony with each other and with God.

It has been a long time since I was able to let my heart open up and let myself really be free and feel again. What can I say except, I thank you and you have my undying gratitude and friendship. Not only because you have come into my life and touched me, for the many others that I know you have touched and helped to find that wonderful road to a new and better life, the only life! Thanks, Bo, for the letter and for sharing part of your life with me. May God give me the strength, faith and courage to continue on this journey that I have been fortunate enough to find. Now I'm happy again and it's been a long time, but it sure feels good...

I enclose a couple of poems for you and hope you enjoy them. Please feel free to use my letters or poems in any way you feel might help others. I'm not ashamed to tell the whole world that I have found a new life. I see a lot of changes in my life already from my daily meditation practice; it's working wonders, and I seem to be getting closer to people already.

With Love and respect, your friend and brother, Tommy

Lloyd

Dear Bo,

I hope this letter finds you exceptionally fine. A lot has happened in my life since I last wrote you. I decided to cut my own foot to get into the hospital. When I cut it I went in at the bottom of my foot in which now I'll never be able to run again.

Also I got hooked up on a "battery on another inmate" charge. This dude who was involved in the death of my partner came here, and I couldn't back off from trying to take him out after I heard him bragging about it. I took an iron leg of a chair and walked up behind him while he was playing cards and tried to knock his brains out, but it only knocked him out and put him in a coma. I was locked up and now am on maximum-security lockdown.

I don't have any regrets at trying to kill him and even if he died and I received a life sentence, I still would not regret it. I know you feel I'm wrong, but I respected my partner and I's friendship to the extent that I felt what I did had to be done. I'm old-fashioned when *it comes to values and morals and living by the convict code, but that's me, and I've never claimed to be anyone but.*

In eternal friendship, Lloyd/La.

Dear Lloyd,

I hope you meant it about "eternal friendship," because I'm going to be straight with you. Sounds like you're snowing yourself, my friend. You're picking an argument with me over what you did, when I haven't judged you in the first place. I think you're arguing with yourself, and laying it off on me.

I'll play along; I'll answer as that part of yourself that wants to argue about what you did. You talk about the convict code, but that's bullshit. There's a higher code that we all answer to, and it says that when we purposely bring more suffering into the world, our own lives will suffer as well. The guy you offed brought suffering to your partner. Now you've brought suffering to him. Next maybe a friend of his will hear about it and come looking for you. And then a friend of yours.... You know, with good "old-fashioned" convicts like you around, the state hardly needs the death penalty!

You knew what this letter would be like before I wrote it, because it's coming from the part of you that has been hip to the stuff we've been sending you through the years. I appreciate how much it hurts to feel the death of a friend, and especially to hear someone bragging about it. And I'm not even saying you shouldn't have done what you did. All I'm saying is cut the shit, and face up to exactly what it was: A self-destructive, spiritually uncool act that came out of attachment and anger. It had nothing to do with living up to codes or moral values.

In view of what you did to your own foot, too, it's got to be getting obvious that you're way out of tune with your own happiness right now. So stop making excuses and inventing philosophies, and start thinking about whatever you need to do to come back into the center of the picture. Since you're in the hole now, maybe you can use some of this time to pray for help, and get back into meditation and that sort of thing.

You can't undo anything you've done; none of us can. But you can start taking honest control of your life again and open yourself up to the deeper, higher realities which can help you get your head straight. Life is really much bigger than you've been allowing yourself to experience. Did you think all this spiritual stuff is just a bunch of poetic words and high-sounding nonsense? It's a lot more real and powerful than the convict code!

Come on back, brother, Bo

છ   છ   છ   છ   છ

A young Samurai warrior stood respectfully before the aged Zen master and said, "Master, teach me about Heaven and Hell." The master snapped his head up in disgust and said, "Teach *you* about Heaven and Hell?! Why, I doubt that you could even learn to keep your own sword from rusting! You ignorant fool! How dare you suppose that you could understand anything *I* might have to say?"

The old man went on and on, becoming even more insulting, while the young swordsman's surprise turned first to confusion and then to hot anger, rising by the moment. Master or no master, who can insult a Samurai and live?

At last, with teeth clenched and blood nearly boiling in fury, the warrior blindly drew his sword and prepared to end the old man's sharp tongue and life all in one furious stroke. But at that very moment the master looked straight into his eyes and said gently, "That's Hell."

Even at the peak of his rage, the Samurai realized that the master had indeed given him the teaching he had asked for. He had hounded him into a living Hell, driven by uncontrolled anger and ego.

The young man, deeply humbled, sheathed his sword and bowed low in awe to this great spiritual teacher. Looking up into the master's ancient, smiling face, he felt more love and compassion than he had ever felt in all his life—and at that point the master raised his index finger and said kindly, "And that's Heaven."

– an old story

છ   છ   છ   છ   છ

Arthur

Dear Bo,

I got out of prison a little over a year ago. I went to Tucson and attended the 3HO drug program. But it didn't work out for me. My father had a stroke and I returned to Michigan. I was in Michigan for only three months when I was arrested and sent to prison again, this time for 20 years with a 10 year minimum sentence. If I don't win my appeal, I'll be here until I'm 39 years old.

I hurt someone I really cared for, that's what put me here. I can't forgive myself, let alone expect anyone else to forgive me. I can't understand why my life keeps going in a direction contrary to my wishes. I try and I pray, but my ego takes control for just five minutes, and I do something I regret for the rest of my life. Is it really my karmic destiny to be nothing in this life that I want to be?

I appreciate all the help I got from you before. I guess It's time to start all over again. I guess with ten years of lockup to look forward to, I may finally be able to get a grasp on myself. I hope so, I never want to hurt anyone again. I never wanted to this time, but I just cracked and before I knew what I was doing, it was over. I've suffered a lot in this life and I guess I'll suffer a lot more before it's over. It's all because I can't control myself; never have been able to. Any insights you may have would be appreciated.

Love, Arthur/Michigan

Dear Arthur,

I remember you from the last time you were inside. Sorry it didn't work out for you. But I think your image of "starting all over again" is part of what keeps throwing you off. The spiritual journey takes us through a lot of ups and downs. You seem to see it more as a straight climb, and if you're not getting to the top, you must be at the bottom. But that's not the way it goes.

Like it or not, everything that's happened has been part of your journey. Your violence shows you're still stumbling over the same stuff as before. You didn't mention whether you still have a drinking or drug problem, but I'll make a wild guess you do, and that you were tanked up when you blew it this last time, Right?

Changing old behavior patterns requires a lot of work, Arthur. The great spiritual truths you've read don't lessen that work for you; you've still got to do it for yourself just like anyone else. Now that you're back inside, you could slide right back into the spiritual books and philosophies and fool yourself once again about how much you've changed. But then you're a sucker next time you get out and you head for the nearest bar.

It's not your "destiny" to go on like this; it's just an old pattern. Patterns can be broken, and people do it all the time, with enough self-honesty and effort. Part of the self-honesty is to take full responsibility for your life - no talk of destiny or karma or lack of control. If booze gets you crazy, then just never, ever, take another drink again. That's taking responsibility. Take course and let me know if I can help.

Love, Bo

Dear Bo,

My last letter was written in a very freaked-out state. But from my earliest memories, I've always been a disturbed person. Things that have carried over into my adult life. I was born with these things and they have gotten worse. I was born with (as my father says) a mean streak: the need to dominate, if not physically, then psychologically. As I grew older I attempted to repress this anger I was born with. I started drug use early but drinking was my downfall. Drinking brought out all my anger and still does.

I'm a lonely person and need to have a woman around me. I fall in love easy but it has never worked out for me. My nature seems to thwart me in everything I do. I try to be a good husband (married twice) or boyfriend but it just never works out.

I had a nice girlfriend this time, but she caught me in the sack with her best friend. Two days later she wanted me to come over and help her fix her car. But actually, it was only to tell me to get my stuff out of her house. We had a big argument and I forced her to have sex with me. After I left, she called the police and told them I had raped her (I didn't hit her, just used psychological force). She lied to them about our relationship and made them think I was just someone she had met in a bar who came over and raped her. There was a very nasty trial and I was found guilty. My case is being appealed and I will probably get a new trial.

The facts are, I did love this woman and I just cracked up for awhile. I have never done this before to a woman. Usually I just get pissed, and I have hit them or slapped them before. What I did was wrong and I know it. I'm sick about the whole thing. What I want to know is why? Why has my life been surmounted with problems since I was a child? Why is it only getting worse? I've thought about killing myself, but damn it, I believe in reincarnation, and my next life will only be worse.

I may be in here until I'm 39. What can I do when I get out with all this hate I'm now growing? I love God very much. I accept what I've done and where I'm at, but I don't see any reason for it. The things I've done in this life haven't been bad enough to account for everything that's gone wrong in my life. I've always been a very emotional person, but now I'm becoming hard and callous. I'm in a rut and I'm burying myself further. I have some awful thoughts going through my head that I can't get rid of even though I try. I'm frightened of what I'm capable of doing. I'm really frightened by what I might do whenever I get out.

I don't want to be mean or hateful. I don't want this girl to hate me though she does. I want to be good and know God. I want His Love. He used to talk to me sometimes through drugs and meditation. But now though I pray every day and try to meditate, it just doesn't happen. All my mind does is run wild on horrible thoughts. There's a reason, I know there is, and God knows what it is, but I don't. I need a helping hand before I sink in my own shit. Thank you for listening to me. I'm sorry this letter is so negative, but I have to get it out. I really have no one else I can tell this to.

Love, Arthur

Dear Arthur,

Definitely sounds like sink-or-swim time for you; congratulations. Really. When we feel the very lowest, that's when we're ripest for some *real* change, the kind that sinks in instead of just staying in the head. So try to have faith in the whole process, even the suffering. I know that doesn't make it hurt any less, but it does help to endure it. Just like it's easier to put up with a terrible toothache if you know the dentist is on his way.

You still need to be more honest with yourself. You say things like "I accept what I've done and where I'm at;" but really Arthur, you don't at all. You just know that you're *supposed* to feel that way. If you really accepted it all, you wouldn't say "But I don't see any reason for it." What does that mean? What accounting system are you using when you say "The things I've done in this life haven't been bad enough to account for everything that has gone wrong in my life?" What accounts for a sweet little baby getting cancer or nice old people getting mugged and beaten, or a farmer losing all his crops? Was your life "supposed to" be problem-free? Look around, Arthur. Happiness isn't a measure of bad things not happening to you; it's a measure of how you deal with everything that comes down the pike.

If you're really serious this time about unloading your suffering and making some deep inner changes, you've got to let go of all the cop-outs and self-deceptions that you've created about how you were born at a disadvantage and you have no control over your destiny. You're wasting the present by being trapped in the past.

You have all the "right" ideas about God and the spiritual journey, but you're still back in the joint. It's time to stop assuming that you have a harder time than anyone else in *applying* those ideas; it's time to join the rest of us and do the day by day, moment by moment work of getting free: Be simple, be truthful, be kind. Don't run away from yourself by bitching about the past. Meditate without expecting psychedelic talks with God every time you sit down; just develop your own one-pointedness so you don't feel so weak. Pray for patience and courage and openness, not for God to wave a magic wand and take away all your spiritual work.

The work is hard for all of us, really it is. Sometimes we feel like we're just hanging on to the barest shred of faith and we're slipping fast. Nothing wrong is going on in your life; this is the journey to God. Take more responsibility and go for it.

Love, Bo

Dear Bo,

Whenever I receive a letter from you I always have to read it quite a few times. The first time my fragile ego freaks out. "What's he saying?," I ask. "Surely he must have mixed up my letter with somebody else." So I set it down and think for a few hours. When I read it again the truth always rings through. With each successive reading, my ego barriers are splintered and finally my heart opens to what is really being communicated. Thank you!

In 1976 I paid $125 for a mantra from TM (Transcendental Meditation). It was the best money I ever spent. The problem now is I'm kinda hung up on mantra meditation, *though now I usually use "Shree Ram" since Ram Dass mentioned it in a lecture in 1980. I've attempted to try Vipassana meditation, but I couldn't get my mind to follow my breath. I just can't seem to get in a calm state. My mind is often filled with thoughts that aren't good.*

I still smoke cigarettes. I'm trying to quit but my will power hasn't been up to it. Occasionally I smoke pot or hash in here. I really haven't been getting enough exercise. I need to work on some yoga postures but I don't know very many. Could you perhaps advise me on a few postures and techniques that I should stick with for awhile?

Whatever you think would help me would be appreciated. I often let other people read your material or the letters you send me. Right now, though, I know I need to calm down. I need to relax my mind before I can even begin to worry about where I'm headed. I have always loved God, but I've never loved myself, so I guess that's not really loving God, only fooling myself. I really need to feel better about myself. I do want to be a useful person in society, I really do. I pray that your continued support will help my lotus to unfold, no matter how long it takes or what kind of obstacles I need to overcome.

Love, Arthur

Dear Arthur,

Well, it sounds like things are lightening up a little for you, anyway. But don't slack off on watching for all the old patterns of thinking to come up; keep the self-honesty fresh in your mind.

For example, the problem about being "hung up on mantra meditation" is a smoke-screen. Any form of meditation is as good as any other; just pick one and use it without wondering whether it's the right one, etc. It's not so technical; all you're trying to do is focus your mind on one point in order to strengthen your concentration.

Of course, drugs, cigarettes, and various foods like sugar, caffeine, and so forth, may be making it harder for you to sit still. I know it's tough to have self-discipline about that stuff while you're in prison, but someday you're going to have to realize that what you want—spiritual freedom and peace—is a tough goal, and you'll have to get a lot tougher to attain it.

You asked me for some yoga postures, but I think you know enough already. Just *do* some of what you've learned from all these different groups and books; don't keep collecting more.

Jesus said, "In your patience possess ye your souls." Try to patiently apply one form of meditation, a few yoga postures, some breathing techniques, and plenty of self-honesty, to your daily life. That's all you need to do. If the water is 100 feet below the ground, you can't get to it by digging ten ten-foot wells. You have to go all the way without starting over at every interesting new spot. Learning new things is always easier than taking the old ones deep inside your guts. Don't fall blindly into that pattern as you have for so many years.

Let's really get down to it this time, no shit.

Love, Bo

Dear Bo,

Your letters inspire me a lot. This time I want to take it slow and one step at a time. I really want to be a useful member of society, and I want to be prepared for whatever God has in store for me.

I'm now taking 19 credit hours in college and am involved in creative writing. I read a lot, mostly science fiction. I hope to become good enough in writing sci-fi stories to sell some while I'm still in here. I'm working on my spelling and grammar, because as it now stands, someone must proofread my work and then I have to get out the dictionary. Prison life may not be all fun and games, but for a struggling writer it's not that bad. Plus I'm getting a well-rounded education.

I meditate every night but I don't want to burn myself out so I'm taking it slow and easy one day at a time. I will progress at whatever level I find comfortable. No rush this time, I will have a lot of time to work on myself.

Thanks for all your help; I hope the holidays bring cheer for you and yours.

Love, Arthur

(and a few months later)

Dear Bo,

This term in college was the first perfect "4.0" average I've ever had (for 18 credits!). I'll be receiving my AA in liberal arts pretty soon, and then I enter the BS program in Interdisciplinary Studies. So mentally, I'm planning on a full productive life. I'm still writing, and my writing teacher is trying to get Tate Wilhelm, the 1976 Hugo Award winner for best sci-fi novel, to look over my work.

I get along real well in the college program, and fairly well in population. I'm managing all right and have a lot of outside support I never expected.

I often ask God to guide my path, and ask advice on if I'm doing things right. I'm just acting on feelings anymore; but I must be doing something right, because things are not the way I expected them to be. And I feel like if I keep working on all facets of myself, something good will come out of all this.

Love, Arthur

Maury

Maury Logue, #89201 at the Oklahoma State Penitentiary, is a very bright guy and a gifted artist. He is also considered one of the most dangerous convicts in the country. He has stabbed so many other inmates that now he is on 24-hour lockup and is handcuffed even to be led to shower three times a week. He has been on lockup longer than any other convict in Oklahoma, with no end in sight.

We first heard from Maury around 1975. He wrote intelligent, gentle letters and sent us some of his artwork. At some point over the next four years, a terrible bitterness ate into Maury's heart like sulfuric acid, burning a deep, smoking hole that was more painful than he could bear. Now, because of his violence in the past few years, Maury has so much time piled on top of his original sentence that he does not expect to ever see the streets again—unless he escapes.

Writing letters of encouragement to Maury, I've had to keep in mind that he spends every day of his life in a cell smaller than my bathroom, surrounded by people who fear and hate him. I've had to remember that the only human touch he ever experiences are the hands which cuff his own.

I have no interest in helping Maury to "cope" or play mind games with himself in order to survive. I see myself as his second in a duel; just holding his cloak, reminding him of his truest weapons, and wondering, with a good deal of awe, just how well I would fare on the same field of battle.

Here is a taste of some of our correspondence, along with a few of my favorites of Maury's artwork. This chapter begins in 1979, with Maury's first written description of his vicious transformation.

Dear Bo,

Since as far as I know...you and your family are the only people on Earth who sincerely care for the people, the poor people who are confined in teeny tiny cages like animals; it is to you, I wish to pour out "some" of my pent-up feelings concerning society in general.

I stole $25 in an unarmed robbery, I was later apprehended, and sentenced to 25 years in a rusted-out cage...simply to "rehabilitate" me (according to the prison authorities). Society supports these cages which house only indigent people! Society is a malevolent mass of morons as far as I'm concerned! I have a friend in here who got drunk one night, thrown in a jail cage, and ended up kicking the toilet off the wall. The courts sentenced him to 12 years in a cage...to "rehabilitate" him! At $10,000 per year, per prisoner, that toilet will cost $120,000 to get revenge on a drunk for destroyin' a stinkin' toilet! You see in Oklahoma a toilet is held in higher esteem than 12 years of a man's life! In a materialistic country like America it's considered a terrible thing to steal money, but it's okay to put poor people in cages and leave them there until they go mad, and then release them on society.

I was a robber when I entered prison, and now after only four years of being "rehabilitated," in a cage, I am contemplating becoming a sniper when released. Society has gotten its revenge on me...they've shown me revenge is the righteous, holy way...that the only way to "rehabilitate" people is to punish, punish, punish! So after completing a four year course in "rehabilitation" I want to spread this "divine rehabilitation" to our wonderful society! Yes...just as the authorities have attempted to ameliorate me by punishment...so in like manner, I do wish to ameliorate society by punishment! I have reached the inevitable conclusion that society is insane! They MUST BE EXTERMINATED, beginning with the "leaders."

Now, I can't afford to purchase cages to put society in like they do the poor...instead, I can only afford a high-powered rifle with a scope. I will simply blow the tops of their skulls off...it will be quick and efficient, and it will have an auspicious deterrent effect on all aspiring lawyers, judges, d.a.'s, and politicians.

Perhaps you might even think I'm just "talking," I can assure I intend to do everything I've said I would, and then some!

I love speaking to you, Bo, for you listen, and you don't go for the lie that society does, that they're too pure, too innocent to associate with us "bad ones." The only thing that separates convicts from society is the fact that the convicts got caught! Society...there's not a single one of those pompous assholes that haven't broken a law or two. Not a one of them are innocent!

Hey, the authorities only "blew" 40,000 tax dollars to convert a small-time robber into a big-time sniper! (me). I'm soooo very grateful for all the "rehabilitation" they've given me to make this possible! Will the joys of incarceration never cease?

Luv, Maury

Dear Maury:

Sounds like heavy times for you. I really hope you're feeling better than when you wrote. Getting out and killing people is quite a bit different from the kinds of things we seem to have had in common so far. I mean, what is it about my family that you love so much? Whatever you admire and respect in us also exists in you. If you love it in us, then you'd like to be that way too.

Your anger and bitterness are excess baggage that you can no longer afford to lug around with you. I really do understand your pain and anger, and wanting revenge on those people who have made your life so miserable. But if you go kill a few people, then those people will simply check out of this life and take birth again too. The world will go on much the same as before, with a little *more* suffering, rather than any less. And then you're born into that world of greater suffering, which means you may have it even tougher than you did this time; and maybe you go to prison again, and get out again, and kill some more people, and get killed again, and take another birth, and suffer more...Maury, aren't you tired of it yet?

There's really no such thing as "society." There's a bunch of scared, lonely people who *seem* like an organized society, but we're not. And you and I are as much a part of it all as anyone else. So if you're going to start shooting, you may as well shoot me, Sita and Laxmana first.

We're friends, and to me that means we don't have to pull any punches with each other. Take the luxury of being absolutely straight with me, and know that nothing you say or do will change my love for you. You're my brother, even if I think you're full of shit.

Love, Bo

Dear Bo,

Thank you, dear friend, for taking the time to write me. As for my aspirations of becoming a proficient sniper: You seem to have misunderstood my motive...you seem to think I'm "vindictive." On the contrary, I want to repay society for the "kindness," "compassion," and "obvious concern" they've shown me. I want to "help" them; do you see?

You're wrong in your assumption that the world will go on much the same as before; after I pick off a myriad of "leaders." For it will start a "fad." America will be like Italy...there are many anarchists in America waiting for someone to kick it all off. I shall be that one.

You're wrong again in your assumption I might be slain and have to reincarnate in this miserable terrestrial realm. By your philosophy I can tell you're familiar with the Bhagavad Gita...Well, in it there is such a thing as akarma—action without fruitive reaction! It's when you are in KRSNA consciousness, which is exactly what I'm in!

Bo, why don't you "help me," to "help society?" Take a gun, pick out your "friendly" neighborhood district attorney, or judge, and simply exterminate the ugly body that confines his wretched, unclean soul? DO YOU WISH TO HELP?? REALLY HELP?? THEN DO IT!!!

Luv, the "rehabilitated one," Maury

P.S. Definition of a politician—that's a person who's got what it takes, to take what you got!

Dear Maury,

Sorry, but I just can't buy your trip about wanting to kill people. First of all, you and I are very far from being in the state of "Krishna Consciousness." That's the same as being in Christ consciousness; it's a state of pure Love, a love so profound and intense that you see beauty in everyone and everything. Maury, you're angry and bitter and hurt, and your own hatred is driving you up the wall. You could kill everyone in the world, and you'd still be sitting there the biggest loser of all, because you have no peace.

You don't have to keep explaining to me how unjust and unfair society is; I know all about that, I assure you. Meanwhile, when you really come to understand karma you'll see that no one ever gets away with anything. Everyone pays for their unkindness and unfairness, and *you* don't have to be the fool who delivers their punishment. That's just more karma for you.

I know they've done awful things to you, Maury; I really do. And if you just want to strike back in some way, of course there's nothing I can do to stop you. But let's cut out the bullshit about it being spiritual or holy, all right? Bitterness and revenge are not going to get you closer to God. It just makes you more like the people you hate.

When are you going to let it sink in that what I tell you is for *your* sake, not for the sake of the people you hate? I'm not defending anyone's actions or misdeeds; I'm just trying to help out a brother who's in an incredible amount of pain. All this stuff about love and peace are *not* just head-trips for goody-goodies. It's the heaviest, most revolutionary message in town, only for super-strong dudes who *see* that they can't let other people's trips drive them crazy. So far, you're just not as strong as you want to be. And you know it.

I love you, Bo

Dear Bo,

If you think I'm one of those "phonies" who just talk big—all you need do is examine my prison records and mental asylum records. Since the last time I wrote you, I've stabbed three reprobates, beaten a myriad of others, and put several on protective custody. I don't like fools, I have no patience or sympathy for them. I haven't actually killed anyone yet, but it's only been because I was drug off before I finished the job. All my life fools have provoked me. I'm quiet, introverted, and a curiosity to them. Thus, they seek to "test" me. They only need test my mettle ONE time and they will immediately realize they made a fatal mistake!

I meet their arrogant, bold, stupid, otiose threats with a smile cold as ice. And when the doors open to the cages I'll still be smiling as I stroll into their cage with a nice long razor-sharp knife. I grin all the way through the stabbing...their screams are music to my ears! The horror on their faces is testimony to their newfound respect for me. I experience no remorse in eliminating human pests.

It's a law of the jungle! Only the craftiest, toughest, most dangerous of men is treated with the deference he rightly deserves. Not only did my dad beat me as a child, but so did groups of older boys. Since I've been in here, eight big guards (goon squad), armed with clubs the size of baseball bats, attacked me in my cage. I hurt three of them, and knocked two completely out of my cage. One was knocked out and quit his job. I eventually was "subdued" ...and naturally beaten and scarred for life. After my arms were cuffed behind my back and legs shackled, I was beaten and kicked again. I was bruised from head to toe. Do you think that will change my mind about exterminating as many advocates of prison that I possibly can!?!

No mercy offered, and none shall be given. And my record speaks for itself.

"Love," Maury

Maury obviously wasn't asking for (nor taking) my advice on how to get his head straight. And yet, it's always been clear that he wanted to keep our connection going. I didn't especially feel like reading letter after letter of his violent hatreds, so I tried to slant our correspondence more toward his artwork and the family stuff he related to like building our house.

He began sending a lot more of his artwork, too. On one envelope, he sketched this sensitive "self-portrait" of Maury/E.T., which we used for the cover of one of our newsletters.

But still, in every letter Maury wrote was at least a passing mention of stabbing or killing people, and a lot of racist jokes. And in my every response, I let him know that I thought he was a few quarts low. We've stayed straight with each other right down the line.

Once after reading one of his super-angry letters, I wrote out a short fairy tale that I asked him to illustrate for me. I called it "The Convict and the Kittycat," and it must have hit him just right, because he opened up quite a bit. This was his response; the illustrated story follows.

Dear Bo,

I'm very impressed by the concise, heart-rending short story you wrote about the kitty cat. That story really "touched home..." It's very prison oriented, for many prisons have cats for mascots. We had a legend here named "canteen Tom," one tough ol' perverted tom cat (he raped skunks—true!).

Bo, you impressed me with your sensitivity. Never since I read Kahlil Gibran have I encountered a male who is "evolved enough" to express such sensitive feelings! I really HATE "men;" they're crude, fatuous, bellicose, vulgar—I regard men as dirty filthy brute beasts which are incapable of rational behavior.

You, Bo, really surprise me. You're an exception to my opinion of men. You're more highly evolved; you function upon a superior level of consciousness than the majority of men do.

Hey Bo, I felt my ego was dead—but when I got that issue of the Prison-Ashram Project newsletter and saw my envelope art on the cover ("E.T.")—gosh, what a LIFT! It copied so well it looks better than my original!

I love you folks like you're kin of mine—and that's 'cause violent as I am, I identify with your level of consciousness. Just remember, I'm a reflection of everyone I meet. Those who come to me with sensitivity and compassion, intelligence, receive back the same from me. Those who come to me in ignorance and violence get back the same —10 times worse. Y' all take care,

Love, Maury

ONCE upon a time, there was a convict --- a very mean, tough, nasty bitter convict who hated everyone & everything.

WELL, actually there was **one** thing in the world he didn't hate: A small, black & white funny-looking kittycat who lived all around the prison.

BUT of course, the mean, tough, nasty bitter dude had an image to live up to, so he had to hide his feelings for the little kittycat, which he managed to do very easily. He was *excellent* at hiding his feelings.

THE kittycat didn't know anything about images or hiding feelings, though. In fact, she didn't even know the place was a prison, so she walked around every day feeling purrfectly free and comfortable. friendly and trusting to everyone except for a very few sicko-types who tried to mistreat her or do wierd things to her.

AND SO, one day this funny-looking black & white kittycat strolled over to the bench on the yard where our mean, tough, nasty bitter man sat every day thinking all his terrible thoughts, and she began rubbing against his shoes and purring very loudly.

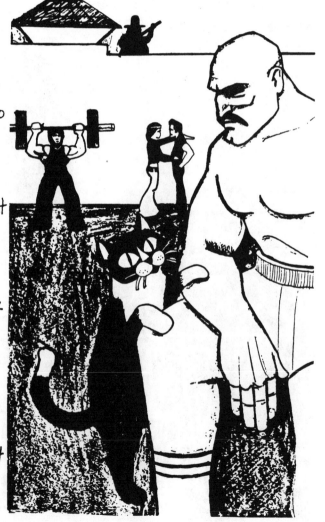

SHE looked up into the convict's face with her light green eyes, which were more innocent than anything he had ever seen. She had two white cheeks and a black raccoon-mask around her eyes, and a ridiculous little tuft of black fur under her mouth, like a tiny goatee on her white neck.

NOW, it's pretty hard to feel mean, tough, nasty & bitter when you're looking at a trusting little face like that. He might have done it, though (because he was **so** good at it), if it hadn't been for the little black goatee. That was just too ridiculous, and his face broke into a wide grin before he could stop himself.

THE mean, tough, nasty bitter convict reached down and picked up the kittycat and put her on his lap, stroking the top of her furry little head while she kept adjusting herself on his lap, as cats will do, purring all the time.

AND all the other convicts, secretly watching from the shadows, smiled & felt new hope for themselves, though none would dare admit it.

THE END
(of our tail)

Maury went on to talk about his growing friendship and respect for two women psychologists, Charlotte and Brenda. He refused to speak to any men. However, much to his dismay, Charlotte and Brenda had both resigned by the time I got his letter. He was still in touch with Brenda via mail, but now she was no more directly available to him than I was.

He also sent me a newspaper article from the *Tulsa Tribune* (June 14th, '83) that featured him and another lock-up inmate under the title "Hate-Filled Convicts Become Like Animals." Maury was clearly proud that the article described him as one of the most dangerous convicts in the state. But what struck me more, was the remarkable likeness between the newspaper photo of him and the character he drew for "The Convict and The Kittycat."

As we kept writing, every now and then he seemed to be softening:

Dear Bo,

Mahatma Gandhi said prison is a place for robbers, "but for me it's a temple." I admire Gandhi—he's intrepid! The authorities tried to hire an assassin to waste Gandhi in prison. Gandhi heard about it—and confronted his would-be assassin—and said, "I hear you're looking to kill me; so I delivered myself to you." And the killer turned away shamefacedly from this little 90-lb., toothless, brave little man. Gandhi's spirit gots BIG HEART.

Bo, I confess you're right about my needle being stuck on violence. I need to get my mind off this hold for awhile! Violence is becoming the total content of my thoughts! Bo, I'm really starting to "lose it." I have a permanent anxious/panicky feeling I've been experiencing lately. I used to get it about twice each year but it would leave after a couple of days. But this time it's lasted three weeks and is intensifying. It's the same kind of panic one feels after awakening in a coffin underground. I'm not exaggerating; that's how intense it is. I'm introverting more each day—once my introversion is complete, I shall mentally ostracize myself from this entire world and its worthless inhabitants—I shall never speak nor write to another person as long as I live. My request for correspondence is the cry of a drowning man reaching out for a little assistance—before the final descent into ...madness.

Later, Maury

Dear Maury,

I feel bad that you're in such low spirits. You're my friend and I love you. I just wish you could see that your own hatred-and-violence trip is killing you; it's not just being in the hole, I swear! I do believe you're going to succeed in driving yourself crazy if you keep trying so hard. Do you think it's just a coincidence that you're losing your mind, and your mind is filled with hatred? When are you going to cop to what's happening?

You've definitely succeeded in making the point that you're a big, dangerous man. So now what? You're going to be awfully embarrassed when you die and look around the astral planes and see that the size of your arms and color of your skin meant nothing at all. You say you respect Gandhi so much, but then you live exactly the opposite of everything he stood for. (By the way, his biceps were skinny and his skin was brown!)

Listen Maury, you and I have been friends for a lot of years now and you have to admit I've never tried to forcibly change you. And even now, I'm not doing that, so don't get me wrong. The only reason I'm harping on this stuff is that *you're* the one who keeps writing me that you're coming apart at the seams. I hurt when you hurt; that's how it is with friends. It's like I'm watching you butt your head up against the wall, and you keep crying that your head hurts. You and you alone— not the prison, not the hole, not your past —are responsible for the state of your own mind. Nobody, including me or Brenda, will be able to save your sanity if you keep up this super-macho, super-bitter routine which you've perfected. You'll just shut me and Brenda out eventually, claiming that we've become "ignorant" or something.

There's an old saying: The only way out is through. You've got so much pain to unlock and let go of; it's going to be tough and scary, but you can do it right where you are. The inner journey is more real than *anything* else you're experiencing, and there *is* relief from everything that hurts so badly.

We're praying for you, pal.

I love you, Bo

Maury replied with some great sketches and a note saying he felt a little better, having found a new (woman) pen pal and therefore some "escapism" from the hole. He closed with:

I'm trying to re-adjust to the conduct espoused by you and Brenda—I'm making an honest attempt. I shared your letters with Brenda; she cheers everything you say (especially where you said I was a few quarts low when it came to violence and racism). It's like listening to an echo, both of you are giving me the same advice. Between her and you, I'm succumbing to your peer pressure. For I know both of you love me and know what's best for me. I haven't taken advice from anyone in years. But I know you and Brenda are right. Trying to clean up my act. heh heh.

Love, "too cool fool," Maury

[In early April, 1985, Maury was stabbed to death by two other inmates while taking a shower. This note has been included so that we may all take Maury into our hearts and wish him well on his journey.]

Victims of Violence

We all know what it feels like to be a victim at some point in our lives. Feelings of frustration, helplessness, and anger flood our hearts and minds during such times. As you read this section of correspondence, you may be able to taste the rage, hopelessness, and fear of the writers. The parents of a kidnapped and raped child and the victim of repeated brutal sexual assaults are situations that seem completely overwhelming. We may find ourselves asking how any good could come from such experiences. There are other victims as well; the anxiety of those waiting for their loved ones to return from the world of prison, a world much different from their own; and prison workers, confused and burned-out, living the reality that the "keeper" and the "kept" are bound by a common environment—one that is often more hopeless than hopeful.

Let yourself feel the range of emotions generated through these letters. Let yourself begin to become more familiar with the world as seen through the victims' eyes. Try to imagine how you could open your heart and mind to such victims to help them through their experiences.

Tom

Dear Bo,

I just re-read your newsletter for March, 1982, and once again your philosophy has touched me.

In 1968, I was beaten, tortured, and gang-raped in a county jail. This took place over a 24-hour period during which, besides the "usual" brutality of such incidents, I was also wrapped up in a sheet and set on fire. My attackers urinated on me to put it out. Although I was released two weeks later, I never really left it emotionally. Emotionally, the clock stopped for me on October 15, 1968. Few days have gone by since, that I haven't experienced at least a few moments of shame and self-disgust and the wish for death.

For the first few years, I numbed myself with marijuana. But after I stopped using drugs in '72, I slipped into a depression that lasted until 1980 when I finally began therapy. After two years of therapy, my rage is greater than ever. And now my rage may be a factor in the break-up of my 12-year marriage. A therapist has warned me that I may have become obsessed with being heard about my assault because of so long a silence.

For the two years before my rape, I had been a full-time political activist living in the barrios of San Antonio. I published and edited a tiny liberal community paper in Spanish and English. I often marched and demonstrated alone against poverty, against the Vietnam War, against discrimination and injustice of any kind. I was in jail for smashing two closed-circuit tv cameras in a restroom of a factory, to help workers publicize their grievances and win their strike. It was my first offense.

You said "our greatest acts of violence are how we constantly judge others." I understand these words but I feel so powerless to rid my heart of the desire for revenge.

I know how overloaded you are with pleas of help from prisons all over the country, but in your prayers, could you please remember me? I do the same for you and all the brothers and sisters in the Prison-Ashram Project.

On my forth-sixth birthday, February 14, I began fasting from solid food. On Feb. 22nd I cloistered myself inside my leaky, uninsulated camper. I am also not speaking. I communicate only in writing. I am withdrawing from society and—if necessary—from life, unless I am blessed with justice and/or enlightenment.

God bless you for your wonderful work.

Tom

Dear Tom,

You're certainly in our prayers, and in the prayers of thousands of people who may read this. I really don't know whether anything I put into words will help you at all, but I'll try. Maybe between the lines we can communicate as if I were sitting next to you in your camper. I wish I could be.

You know that I've been involved for a long time now with people who have gone through the same sort of nightmare as you. I've never met anyone who had an easy time of it, or who looked back and said "boy, I sure am glad that happened!" So I won't try to snow you with any spiritual fairy tales. There are some terribly painful things that can happen to us in life, and you've been through one of the worst imaginable. That's the way things are.

But it's possible to come out of it with both your sanity and humanity intact, and even stronger than ever. Jesus's response to humiliation and torture has endured as an inspiration to the human spirit for thousands of years. Since you describe yourself as an activist, standing up for truth and justice, maybe now you're being given the opportunity to *really* be an activist, like Jesus was. Maybe this is the excruciating degree of compassion, pain, and forgiveness required to bring about truly effective social change; change which lasts.

I know it's tempting for you to say that no one could understand what you've been through. In one sense that's surely true, and it would be arrogant of me to say how I would handle your situation if it happened to me. But in another sense—a deeper one—all of us really do understand the pain, fear, loneliness, shame, and despair that you've described. It just comes in different forms, that's all.

When I was eighteen I had a 100-mph head-on crash with a tractor trailer. I've gone through a lot of operations and intense pain during the past 20 years, and I can remember times when the pain just wore me down so much that I didn't know if I could keep going through it. Many times I squeaked by on the thinnest shred of faith or Grace; who knows which? I became addicted to painkillers, went through periods of denial, over-exertion, depression and oceans of self-pity. And like you, I also heard about things like meditation and yoga and the whole spiritual trip.

I noticed that when I was able to *open* around the pain rather than trying to push it away, every now and then I experienced the "transcendence" that all the spiritual teachers talk about. Pain still hurts like hell during those times (like the Buddha said,

"Pain will always be inherently unpleasant; that's just its nature"), but you can get so *big* that you're able to allow it to be just what it is. It no longer takes you over so fully; it no longer plunges you into despair. And the pain brings so much wisdom, humility, patience and other good lessons, eventually we come to appreciate its divine purpose in our lives.

You can say that my pain is different from yours, and yours is different from the young mother whose child was raped and murdered, and from my Canadian friend who fell off a mountain and is permanently paralyzed, and from all the other people in the world who meet an endless variety of suffering during their lives. But pain is pain is pain, if we're willing to open up rather than shut ourselves down. If you look perhaps more openly than you have, you can find in your wife, your therapist, your neighbors and everyone else, a place which understands your suffering more than you've been willing to appreciate.

But what more can I say to you while it's hurting so much? These may sound like meaningless words as you sit in your camper wishing that half your life hadn't happened like it did. I send this letter more as a token of my love and friendship rather than an eloquent argument for or against any point of view. If you do decide to come through this instead of ending your life, just imagine the depth of compassion and understanding you can offer to others who suffer in their own forms of hell. I hope for you, me, and for the world, that you can emerge from this struggle as a true spiritual activist, with a loving heart which has been forged in the hottest fire of pain.

Love, Bo

Dear Bo,

Just received your wonderful letter. It really has brightened my day. What you had to pass on to me is really good and clear medicine.

I have been sweating out a lot of demons in my "cloister." This is the thirteenth day in my truck and the 22nd of my fast. I think I will be leaving the truck and breaking my fast in a few days. For one thing, my family is taking it very hard. They think I want to die, but they are only partially right.

Anyway, I'm feeling much better and clearer, and your letter has really helped. I'll treasure the letter in my spiritual diary and I'm sure that I will often refer to it in the future whenever I'm wrestling with my demons.

I would like to rest now, so I'll close. Thank you and may the light continue shining on you.

Tom

To One Who Has Been Done Dirt

Cry or curse or call it unfair, but be grateful 'til the grave That in this hurt you're the one who received, and not the one gave.

-Carol Lynn Pearson

Donny the Punk

(Donny, aka Robert Martin, is a published writer who experienced nearly unimaginable horrors being raped more than 50 times in a 24-hour period after being thrown in the D.C. jail due to a political protest. Some years afterward, while in federal prison, he wrote me asking for help in setting up a network of pen pals especially for prison punks. Here is an edited version of that correspondence.)

Dear Bo,

My impression after reading your stuff was that sexuality was noticeable for its absence, and that your readers were living lives of enforced (if not voluntary) celibacy. But this is not in accord with my own experiences and extensive knowledge of prison and jail life, which is drenched with sexuality, both consensual and coerced.

Jail punks are more oppressed than any other group within the walls, living lives of abject slavery, sold and traded among the powerful, forced into prostitution, tossed about as footballs and prizes in racial and other power structures, tormented by conflicts over their sexual identity and role, isolated, humiliated, ashamed, and often suicidal. There's a crying need for someone to reach out to punks, someone who understands oppression.

I am suggesting primarily a network of pen-pals. I believe these should in the first instance be heterosexual or bisexual women, ideally young women, both because women are more likely to be able to deal with rape victims and help them to understand the nature of their oppression, and because it is vital that the punks' need for feminine contact be supported.

I'm 95 days into my solitary retreat now, with no end in sight. The period in solitary has been a real blessing so far, but signs of stress are beginning to manifest. More grist for the mindful mill.

May all be happy! Donny the Punk/Ct.

Dear Donny,

Certainly the problems of punks are terrible, and need to be dealt with far better than anything that's currently going on. But your idea for a network of pen-pals doesn't strike me as workable.

It seems to me that this planet can hardly survive one more special interest group. A feeling of group identity may feel great and be very valuable at first, but it needs to be quickly expanded to an identity with the whole human race. Instead, what's starting to happen is that in addition to the separateness many of us unfortunately feel due to race, religion, color, or sex, we're now adding whole *new* labels by which we can feel disconnected from the person next door. From where I sit, humanity as a whole is not necessarily being brought closer together by this tidal wave of "you can't understand me unless you're like me" support groups.

The bottom line is, everyone suffers. Everyone truly knows loneliness, pain, humiliation and defeat. I agree with you that we need to open our eyes more to the suffering of punks, but I don't think reinforcing their identity as punks is the solution.

I really do feel your compassion and your desire to serve others. My own instincts are that it would be more useful to remind punks that their "punkhood" is not the center of their lives. If they feel that it is, then *that's* the problem to work on; see what I mean? Let's keep in touch and see whether we can figure something out together.

Love, Bo

Dear Bo,

I am sensitive to the matter of proliferating narrow-issue groups. One important distinction you should keep in mind is that most punks would give their left testicle to escape from that identity. As I envisioned it, the support would facilitate that rather than strengthen the identity. In concrete terms, everyone in his environment treats the punk as a punk. To those on the street who communicate with him, he cannot ever be open about the most important aspects of his life experiences, for fear that knowledge of his "loss of manhood" will spread in his home community. Our hypothetical pen-pal would be precisely someone with whom he can discuss everything, yet know that the person outside sees him as a person and relates to him as a person.

Bo, my writing and working on the rape question and the enslavement of punks (and gays) poses a major dilemma for my own spiritual work, though I am hardput to articulate it. It is work in the plane of duality, of concepts, and everything I do in it reinforces my own identity as a punk, since I am speaking out of experience. It would be a lot easier to just work on my own invisibility and blur my identities rather than sharpen one of them. But compassion must operate on that level, so in a sense it is the old Bodhisattva dilemma of trying to help beings while not losing track of the reality that there are no beings to help.

Perhaps one reason why I work to help other punks in transcending their punk identity is that the destructive results of assuming that identity are all too manifest in my own life—where the identity has become so firmly attached as to be part of my own name, "Donny the Punk." Oh physician how to heal thyself?

May all be happy, Donny the Punk

Dear Donny,

I really value your insights and I'm learning a lot from you, though I still don't agree with your proposal. In fact, the last paragraph of your letter pushed me further away from agreement than ever.

You mentioned "blurring your identities," but your spiritual work isn't a matter of "blurring" anything; if that's all it were, you could do it with booze or drugs.

The spiritual path is to not *cling* to any identities, but let them come and go as necessary. As Ram Dass puts it, "Grab tightly, let go lightly." It sounds like you've grabbed tightly to your punk identity but forgotten how to let go at all. And this has been my concern about your proposal all along.

The other thing is, Bodhisattvas don't *have* an "old dilemma." Bodhisattvas are enlightened people who stick around to help others become enlightened. You and I are simply not in that league. We're not free enough to "sacrifice" our own development for the sake of others. Anything you do which hurts yourself is not going to be for the good of others. The best thing you can do for others is to get free of all your identities, confusion, and conflicts.

You said that punks need to be able to write about "the most important aspects of their life experiences," meaning their "punkhood." But that's where you and I fundamentally disagree. I don't see victimization, violence, or sexuality being "the most important aspect" of anyone's life. It may be the most painful, the most challenging, the most demanding, but not the most important. The most important aspect of any of our lives is to get free. And I hear you yearning to be free, yet then imprisoning yourself once again by signing "Donny the Punk."

I honestly think the best service you could perform for punks is to struggle free of the stranglehold this identity has on your life. Calling yourself "Donny the Punk" is like somebody calling herself "Susie the rape victim," or "Sammy who always gets mugged." If other cons cruelly call you that, that's one thing; but for *you* to wear it like a badge is quite a different matter.

I really feel for your suffering and send you all my blessings for your work. Your mind is sharp and your will is strong, and I have faith that someday you'll be able to cross this ocean of pain, and then be able to help many other people across as well.

Love, Bo the Human

Donna

Dear Prison-Ashram folks,

For years we have witnessed the fine work done through you all. We thank you. Now I find myself coming to you for something directly connected to my own life and family.

Our daughter, who's four, was kidnapped last summer by a two-time rapist. The police found them in 4¹/₂ hours and she was remarkably all right though much darkness went her way.

Those hours were an incredible test of our work of these past years. Between the streams of terror and panic and tears, we did all we could to surround the two of them with love, to pray, to meditate. And we found, then and afterwards, that many many people hearing of the kidnapping were stopping doing what they were doing, and doing as we were.

Police, hospital, strangers, all were surrounding us and our daughter with love. And when we got her back, she was still whole and filled with innocence, in spite of the violence and sexuality she was subjected to. She had spent most of the time talking to him, of right and wrong, of her understandings of the order around her. "I loved him a little and hated him a little" was one of the first things she told us.

Then came months of assimilating and sorting the great pain. And all that still continues, though quieter now. And during that time, the legal issues were being drawn into it. We could not find any peace in the "Catch-22"-ness of it all: Having our 4-year-old testify and be torn apart by defense lawyers; dropping the case, which was threatened if she didn't testify; sending this man back to jail which had not done him any good before, etc., etc. We were all victims.

Finally, we fasted and prayed for three days and came to a peaceful relationship to it all with this understanding. The proper responsibility in the guilt was in his hands and demanded a public confession. He did plead guilty and it was settled out of court. He was sentenced on the violated probation and on the new sentences. He stood up in court and said, facing my husband, that though he has no memory of the incident (supposedly he has blocked out the whole thing) he was sorry for all the pain he caused to our family.

So now, the children ask what he does in prison, how long he'll be there, how old they'll be when he gets out, and on and on. We wonder if our relationship to him is done. Do we have any more responsibility now than to hold him in our hearts and prayers, and do our own work to come to a full forgiveness? I still wonder if I should personally go to him or write him, to tell him all the specifics of what went on so he can come to some peace with what he did instead of spending all those years in jail for an offense he has no memory of.

All I've come up with so far is to pass his name on to you. From what I understand, he has a very mild and inward nature unless he's drinking. Maybe meditation would be a door for him. Would you send him whatever you have, and just know that he's there in case you go to his prison?

Thank you from the bottom of our hearts for all the fine work you've been doing.

In Love, Donna/New Mexico

Dear Donna,

Sita and I thank you deeply for sharing your ordeal with us. Your letter is awe-inspiring for the compassion and consciousness you've brought to such a nightmarish experience.

I'm sure your process of "assimilating and sorting the great pain" will go on for awhile, but it sounds like your faith and vision are remarkably unclouded. It's through such pain that many of us discover what the spiritual life is really all about. The opening, deepening, pain, and wisdom all go hand in hand. Sometimes God's blessings are excruciating, but blessings all the same. It seems that you and your whole family have been given one of those.

You asked for my advice about your relationship to Oscar. I can't think of any "shoulds" or "shouldn'ts" that wouldn't sound stupid after all you've been through. Oscar has already been greatly blessed just by the fact of you being his victims. Your forgiveness and concern are profound contributions to his spiritual journey, like Jesus forgiving those who nailed Him to the cross.

My only advise is to try to be as self-honest as possible, and make sure that whatever you do is what you're *able* to do from the heart—not what your mind thinks you should do in order to be "good." If you're ever able to truly open to Oscar and offer him your kinship, I think that act could do more for world peace than a hundred summit conferences, because this is really the nitty-gritty of bringing God-consciousness into our worldly lives.

Our love to you all, Bo

But I say that even as the holy and the righteous cannot rise beyond the highest which is in each one of you, So the wicked and the weak cannot fall lower than the lowest which is in you also.

Kahlil Gibran

22   Reporting from Behind the Walls: Do it Before the Sirens Wail[†]

Frederick Talbott

On November 23, 1987, an Atlanta police source called veteran police reporter Orville Gaines of the *Journal and Constitution* with a blockbuster: The Atlanta Federal Penitentiary was under siege. "He said the [Cuban] detainees had taken over part of the prison," Gaines recalls. "And he said they might have hostages."

Gaines passed the tip to Herbert Steely, the day city editor. Within minutes, amid the normal pressure of an early deadline, the newsroom kicked into high gear. During the 11-day crisis, Assistant Managing Editor Wendell Rawls, Jr. would assign more than 100 staffers to the story.

"We had constant updates for all seven editions," Rawls says. The staff produced nine to 12 new stories daily. "In 48 hours we did mini-profiles on 65 of the hostages plus nine others who had been released. And a 5,000-word history of the Marielitos...and a 2,500-word piece about what life is like inside the prison."

Four extra open pages provided prison news each day. Photographers were stationed in helicopters, in cherry pickers, in trees and on rooftops around the clock. Reporters worked shifts at the prison, and each shift included one person who was fluent in Spanish.

A Spanish-speaking copy editor was sent with a news team to Oakdale, Louisiana, to cover events at the federal detention center there, where rioting had begun two days before the Atlanta uprising. A Hispanic copy clerk monitored radio transmissions in the newsroom. Suburban reporters maintained a 24-hour vigil at Dobbins Air Force Base near Atlanta to alert editors if federal troops arrived. (They didn't.) The Washington bureau covered angles at the Immigration and Naturalization Service and the Justice Department.

[†]The article was originally published in *The Quill*, February, 1988. Reprinted by permission of the author.

Meanwhile, investigative reporter Dale Russell of Atlanta's WAGA-TV was involved in several projects when the rioting began. "I was sitting in our office," says Russell, "when the boss came in and said, 'Can you make some calls, we hear there's something going on in the prison.'"

Russell called an Atlanta police source, who said, "Fire trucks were on the way. Shots had been fired. Possibly a small riot." A reporter and camera crew were dispatched, and reporter Ken Chambers was on the scene for the noon news.

"Everett Bevelle, one of our photographers, was the first on the scene," Russell recalls. Bevelle climbed to the steeply slanting roof of an auto parts store directly across from the prison and set up a coverage command post. WAGA-TV would pay $100 a day for exclusive use of the roof and maintain an around-the-clock news watch.

The station expanded its evening newscast to two hours, its late news to one hour, and simulcast its 6 p.m. show in Spanish on WRFG-AM and FM radio. Reporter Iliana Bravo of Miami CBS-affiliate WTRJ-TV would help with translations in the field. Weekend anchor Cynthia Good would report from Cuba.

"In my 10 years in the media, it was the best coverage effect I've seen. Every cylinder clicked," Russell says. "It was a competitive madhouse. When things happened, they happened within minutes."

Coverage by the *Journal and Constitution* and by television stations WAGA, WXIA and WSB was remarkable—which was not too surprising. News organizations often do great work when presented with a crisis, such as a prison riot.

But after the flames have been extinguished, the sirens stilled, and the lights and cameras packed away, news organizations generally switch back to their business-as-usual mode. And insofar as prisons are concerned, that means ignoring what goes on behind the walls. Few news organizations regard day-by-day prison coverage as worth their time.

Earlier in 1987—before the Atlanta and Louisiana revolts—I surveyed 68 newspapers to pinpoint prison coverage practices, attitudes, and problems. I selected newspapers that were close to prisons. They ranged from major dailies in Atlanta, Philadelphia, and San Francisco to small prison community weeklies in La Grange, Kentucky, and Buena Vista, Colorado. Editors or reporters from 29 newspapers in 24 states responded. They cited major prison-coverage weaknesses, while calling for more scrutiny of prisons by the news media.

Should prisons be covered more thoroughly? Consider: In 1986, there were 547,000 inmates in America's 1,019 state and federal prisons. Another 273,000 were in local jails. According to a Justice Department report, one of every 55 adult Americans—3.2 million—was on probation, parole, or incarcerated at the end of 1986.

Also in 1986, 35 states reported prison overcrowding, and 21 states had enacted early release programs to ease the pressure. Prison operating budgets topped $8.83 *billion*, with another $1.59 billion for capital expenditures. Prisons employed more than 217,000 people, including 111,175 guards.

Prisons have a direct impact on society, ranging from public spending to human rights, from public safety to the spread of AIDS. Yet, according to journalists,

prison officials, and criminal justice experts, few newspapers—and fewer TV stations—provide regular prison beat coverage.

My survey suggested that prison coverage is generally hit-or-miss. Time, tight
news budgets, uncooperative prison officials and—particularly—a lack of news
interest were given as the chief reasons for that. A majority of those polled termed the
media's coverage of federal and state prisons and overall prison issues inadequate.

This lack of coverage creates a blind spot for readers and viewers. How can the
public and its elected officials make adequate choices about a system they don't know
or understand?

And, finally, consider a fact so obvious that it may be overlooked: "The reason you need to understand prisons is that well over 90 percent of those people who
go in are going to come out," says David Altheide of Arizona State University's School
of Justice Studies. "And what we do to them in there is ultimately going to have some
impact on what's going to happen with they come out. And we're going to have to
face them."

Amy Wallace, who was assigned to the *Atlanta Journal and Constitution*'s new
prison beat two months before the November riots, says the news media used to cover
prisons more extensively than today. "Yet the problems are certainly as important,
or more important, today," she adds.

Nineteen of the 29 journalists who responded to my survey said newspapers should
develop full-time prison beats. Too often, prison coverage is combined with other
beats and takes up residence on a back burner. Or thinly staffed state capital bureaus
combine prisons with overall state government coverage.

And, too, prisons are often located in remote areas—too far from the metropoli-
tan areas to be of much interest, and they are so large that they overwhelm the
resources of small local dailies or weeklies. "Our staff is too small to provide adequate coverage of five prisons in our community," says Kit Millay, editor of *The Oldham
Era* in La Grange, Kentucky.

Time, the eternal newsroom nemesis, bites heavily into attempts to cover prisons well. "Reviewing police blotters [for crime news] is economical," says Hans Toch
of the Department of Criminal Justice at the State University of New York in
Albany. "But there's no such economical way to view what goes on in prisons. In
prison coverage, news 'pegs' require knowledge."

There is also a thick layer of bureaucracy between a reporter and potential
stories. Prison rules and regulations, designed to protect public safety, inmate privacy, and to manage hard-to-manage people, often stand between a reporter and the
"inside."

While one can readily launch a request for a prison visit or interview on the bureaucratic sea, one may also have to wait a substantial amount of time before the interview can take place. Days, perhaps; weeks, maybe. (When the interview finally takes
place, notes Roger W. Stuart, II, assignments editor of *The Pittsburgh Press*, it will
not be conducted in private, for security reasons.)

Prison reporters may also face the geographical challenge of a system spread over thousands of square miles. Texas has 28 units; Virginia's prisons extend from Chesapeake, near the coast, to Bland, in the Blue Ridge mountains 300 miles west.

Walls—stone, brick, and psychological—keep people in prisons and out of prisons.

"Prisons tend to get ignored in the press mostly because the challenge of getting good, solid information is very difficult," says Lucien Lombardo, of Old Dominion University's Sociology and Criminal Justice Department. "Prison administrators have been traditionally closed-mouthed. For years the courts didn't even deal with prisons. So anything from the outside was seen as an interference, be it the court or the press."

Nevertheless, says Lombardo, prison wardens and press officers are beginning to see the need for more press coverage. He advises the press to concentrate on in-depth reporting, "to really tell the public what's going on."

In the past, adds Lombardo, the press concentrated on sermonizing, reporting about individuals, and criticizing prison administrations. "But the experiences of confinement and working in that atmosphere and all the experiences surrounding it, and what it means to society, are much more complex," he says.

Part of the complexity for reporters stems from the simple ambiguity of not knowing precisely how to judge the reliability of sources. Convicts are notorious for their ability to con outsiders. And prison officials and prison-reform activists have their own axes to hone.

Getting the facts on a prison story may be an exceedingly long and frustrating process, a fact that does not enchant managing editors and news directors.

"The barrier is commitment," says David Ashenfelter, an investigative reporter for the *Detroit Free Press* who won a Sigma Delta Chi Distinguished Service Award for his 1984 series about Michigan's troubled penal system.

"Prison issues are complicated and time consuming. Most reporters are too busy to master these issues," says Ashenfelter.

That reporters often lack the time to master a story—on any beat—is not an uncommon complaint in newsrooms or journalism reviews.

But perhaps it is particularly unnerving to corrections officials, who, unlike many of their colleagues in other kinds of governmental jobs, seldom see reporters.

"We find that reporters are often very, very uninformed," says Kathy Morse, public information officer for the U.S. Bureau of Prisons. Morse tells of a network reporter who "did a piece on our prison in Marion, Illinois, and she came in totally biased. She was very, very naive. Another reporter, trying to get a name for herself...reported a story based only on statements from an inmate. And then she called the [public information officer] the next day for comments, and he said, 'Why didn't you call me the day before?'"

Covering prisons properly need not be an intractable problem. Journalists, prison officials, and academic experts I've surveyed or talked to have offered a host of insights, which can lead to better coverage.

- Reporters and editors must overcome stereotypes, prejudices and assumptions in reporting from behind the walls.

"Often, all the press knows is what they've seen in Jimmy Cagney movies," says Morse. Adds Arizona State University's Altheide: "There is no such thing as a 'typical inmate.' You have a great variety of people in prisons. The media should recognize this.

"The core images of prisons comes from movies, and they are greatly sensationalized," adds Altheide. He urges the news media to "make sure the general public knows what goes on in prisons. We get many comments like, 'It's a country club atmosphere,' and these people have no idea what the conditions and the routine are like."

- Class bias may also affect prison coverage and must be done away with. In recent decades, journalists increasingly have been drawn from middle- and upper-income sectors. How many reporters, editors and producers have had a relative, a neighbor or family friend in prison? How many have had any direct knowledge of prisons? Prisons and prisoners remain unnoticed and poorly covered.

- Sensitivity is crucial on the prison beat. During the November riots, WAGA-TV's Russell quickly learned that news reports can immediately affect what goes on "inside." Knowing that the Cuban detainees were watching the news made each news decision critical.

"It was frightening knowing how closely they were watching us," says Russell. "We had to keep that in mind, because we realized anything we said could potentially cause problems."

Old Dominion's Lombardo, who taught at New York's Auburn Prison between 1969 and 1977, says, "When I worked inside Auburn you could see the relationships between guards and inmates change after a story. It was that direct." In prison coverage, every event, proposal or conflict may affect inmates. Their world is small, contained, controlled, and everything is important.

- Journalists should be aware that prison news may also have an exaggerated impact on the outside. Even *good* news says SUNY-Albany's Toch, can have a negative impact. "If what happens is humane, and a fair number of people [outside] are bloodthirsty and vengeful in the way they view prisons, it risks" such programs. But, he adds, "if a prison does things that are indefensible," strong news coverage is essential.

- Thoroughness is fundamental. View events strategically. Strive to understand issues. Consider, for example, the matter of over-crowding. Politicians might say, "'These prisoners don't deserve more space,'" explains Altheide. "That reflects the strong law-and-order and punitive mentality. But a problem with over-crowding, or double-bunking—putting two inmates in a cell that might be 7' by 10'—is, if violence erupts, a guard is going to have to go into that. And chances are he's going to get hurt."

- Regular beat coverage is also basic. Stay in touch, and don't avoid the complexities. Prison officials complain that the news media often focus on crises, overlooking deeper issues.

Says John Woestendiek, a Philadelphia Inquirer reporter who in 1987 won a Pulitzer Prize for his stories about prisons: "A real common complaint from prison administrators is, 'The only time we hear from you guys is when there's an escape or a riot.' Then we follow with the hastily done post-mortem story about what went wrong, when we could be writing all along that this is brewing and what the ingredients are."

Adds Kenneth G. Robinson, press secretary for the Pennsylvania Department of Corrections: "Prisons are not something people pay a lot of attention to unless a problem develops. And when the problem develops, the question that comes from administrators is, 'Where were you when we were running these programs that had a great deal of positive impact?' They sometimes feel you ignore it when we do things right, and the media's attitude is often, 'Well, you are there to do things right, and if something goes wrong, that's a news story.' That's difficult to explain to someone who is proud of their institution and efforts."

- "Know your key players," says WAGA-TV's Russell. "Know the people fighting for prisoners' rights, the religious groups, your law enforcement people." Develop a rapport with academic experts, prison officials, guards, inmates, inmates' families and prison teachers and pastors. And don't forget legislators.

- Visit the prisons before a crisis erupts, advises the *Atlanta Journal and Constitution*'s Wallace. Prisons vary like individual cities. "I've tried to set up a prison-a-week club," says Wallace.

- Read. state law; federal law; prison regulations; academic jour-nals; prison newspapers; prison administration newsletters; newsletters from prisoners' rights groups. Set up a story exchange with prison reporters in other states. Become an expert. "News pegs require knowledge," says Toch. Prison officials say knowl-edge and professional concern are the best ways to establish trust.

Toch urges wardens to establish more press contacts and prepare press releases. "Put guards and staff on notice," he urges, "to look for interesting stories in the prisons."

- Follow the dollars. View conditions. Learn about the "politics" of the inmates, the leaders, the gangs, the systems. Drugs and contraband. Medical care. Rates of recidivism. Patterns of inmate discipline and protection. The constant stress faced by guards. Does the "system"—from intake to parole—work?

- Know your state's prison policies. The Pennsylvania and Texas systems show a contrast in management styles. Pennsylvania has a trained spokesman at each of its 12 prisons. Three people handle all media inquiries for the massive 38,000-inmate Texas system.

- Remember to cover the "indirect" prison beat areas, including your state legislature. Be aware of proposed state laws that may affect inmates or prison operations.

If your news organization can't afford to assign a reporter to the prison beat full time, advises the Philadelphia Inquirer's Woestendiek, "find someone on the staff who is interested and ask them to do what they can. A few trips to local prisons can establish some valuable contacts that might lead to getting some stories that might otherwise be missed."

If your news team accepts the "throw away the key" mindset, you may be taking the prison system for granted. Shallow, Johnny-come-lately reporting misses the mark.

"There are many opportunities for award-winning stories on the prison beat," Arizona State University's Altheide says. "Even the everyday life is fascinating, and sometimes incredible."

The beat's greatest challenge focuses on the people—inside and out—affected by prisons...inmates; guards; families; crime victims; and the pressures and dangers of confinement.

"The media have a duty to educate the public about prisons," says Old Dominion's Lombardo. "If they do quick flash stories, they simply perpetuate myths and symbols."

In Atlanta, Rawls created a full-time prison beat at the Atlanta newspapers before the November riots, "because I think it's very important. It's a mark of the level of civilization how we treat incarcerated people.

"I do think it is something that is an important part of society," says Rawls, a former Southern bureau chief and corrections reporter for *The New York Times*. "The public has a right to know how their money is being spent...and whether we are involved in rehabilitation or just retribution. That's the central question."

Does the public care? Maybe. Maybe not. Perhaps, because of the media's poor performance, the public doesn't know enough to care.

"With so many people who don't know and don't care about people in prisons," advises the *Inquirer*'s Woestendiek, "and with bureaucrats who realize that and whose bottom line is saving money, somebody needs to be watching."

23

Moving Into the New New Millennium: Toward a Feminist Vision of Justice†

M. Kay Harris

Conventional Approaches to Criminal Justice Reform

Most proposals for change in policies directed at crime and criminal justice concerns fall within one of two types. Many proposals are developed from a systems improvement orientation. This orientation takes for granted existing political, economic, and social institutional structure, and the values that undergird them, assuming that they are proper, or at least, unlikely to be changed within the foreseeable future. Reform proposals generated from a systems improvement perspective characteristically are framed as if crime were primarily an individual problem best addressed through more effective or more rigorous enforcement of the law. Thus, they focus on trying to find better means of identifying and intervening with individual offenders and of strengthening and increasing the efficiency of existing criminal justice institutions and agencies.

The other familiar way of framing reform proposals involves a broader crime prevention/social reform orientation. Reformers with this orientation emphasize the social and economic underpinnings of crime and the need to address them through policies and programs focused on families, neighborhoods, schools, and other institutions. In recent years, advocates of a prevention/social reform approach have moved considerably beyond the ameliorative strategies of the 1960s toward proposals for more sweeping social and economic reconstruction, stressing that policies aimed at strengthening families and communities need to be coupled with efforts to promote economic development and full employment.[1] Although they do not excuse

---

†This article was originally published in the *Prison Journal* and is reprinted here by permission of the Prison Society.

individual offenders or ignore possible advances to be made by improving criminal justice practices, these reformers tend to view interventions with identified offenders more as last lines of defense than as promising avenues for reducing crime.

There are significant problems associated with trying to formulate recommendations for the future on the basis of either of these two conventional ways of framing the issues. The systems improvement approach has the apparent advantage of offering advances in the identification, classification, control, or treatment of offenders and in the operation, efficiency, effectiveness, or accountability of criminal justice agencies. However, this approach ignores the political, economic, and social aspects of crime and has little or nothing to contribute to the overall, long-term development of social life. Furthermore, it offers, at best, only limited, short-term utility in dealing with crime.

Many systems improvement advocates promise dramatic increases in crime control if only sanctions can be made more frightening, severe, certain, restrictive, or corrective. But such promises lack both theoretical and scientific support. Current knowledge provides little basis for expecting significant reductions in crime through reshaping policies in hopes of achieving greater deterrent, incapacitative, or rehabilitative effects. Other systems improvement supporters concede that notable increases in domestic tranquility are unlikely to be secured at the hands of crime control agents, but argue that until more fundamental changes have been made in social relations and policies, there is no alternative but to continue working toward whatever marginal increases in efficiency, effectiveness, or even-handedness might be achievable.

To date, prevention/social reform advocates have made scant progress in overcoming the notion that their proposals already have been tried in the "War on Poverty"/"Great Society" era and found ineffective. Many who agree that the measures championed by these advocates are prerequisites for dramatic shifts in crime and social relations doubt that the massive changes envisioned are economically or politically feasible. Furthermore, prevention/social reform advocates have had little influence in ongoing criminal justice policy debates because their recommendations concerning interim criminal justice policies have been meager and uncompelling. They have offered little more than echoes of system improvement reform proposals, accompanied by warnings of the risk of simply reinforcing the underclass and increasing the social divisions in society if repressive measures targeted on offenders are pursued too zealously.

Thus, despite widespread dissatisfaction with the results of current policies and their burgeoning costs, it is difficult to find grounds for believing that the future toward which we are heading holds much promise of anything beyond more of the same. If current trends hold the key to seeing what the criminal justice system will look like in the next few decades, we face the prospect of maintaining a punishment system of awesome proportions without being able to expect much relief from the problems it supposedly exists to address.

Current Trends: Iron Bars and Velvet Ankle Bracelets

Over the last decade, approximately 200,000 beds have been added to state and federal prisons across the United States, increasing their confinement capacity by more than two-thirds (*Bureau of Justice Statistics Bulletin*, June 1986 and May 1987). In a recent random sample survey of local jails, officials in 44 percent reported that facility construction or renovation was underway (*Corrections Compendium*, Nov./Dec. 1986). And despite the fact that at least 22 states had to make spending cuts in their fiscal 1987 budgets and 23 passed or considered increases in gasoline, cigarette, or sales taxes, a review of spending proposals by governors across the country suggests that substantial additional increases in institutional networks are being planned (Pierce, February 9, 1987).

If the average annual growth during the 1980s in the number of federal and state prisoners continues through 1987, the nation's prison population will have tripled over the last 15 years.[2] But the recent expansion of the punishment sector of the system has not been limited to prisons and jails. At the most drastic extreme, there are now more than 1,800 persons awaiting state execution across the United States (*Lifelines*, Jan./Feb. 1987). At the other end of the penal spectrum, the adult probation population has been increasing even more rapidly in the 1980s than the incarcerated population.

As of the end of 1985, the total population under the control or supervision of the penal system has risen to 2.9 million persons, representing fully 3 percent of the adult males in the country.[3] An estimated one in every 10 black adult men was on probation or parole or in prison or jail.[4] The proportion of Hispanics under penal control is not fully reported, but the number of Hispanics in the nation's prisons reportedly has doubled since 1980, a rate of growth that could result in Hispanics constituting one-fourth of the incarcerated population by the year 2000[5] (Woestendiek, February 2, 1987).

Not only have the numbers and mix of persons under penal control been changing, but the nature of that experience has been changing as well. For those incarcerated, such forces as overcrowding, de-emphasis on programs and services, mandatory sentences, and other reflections of an increasingly harsh orientation toward offenders have worked to offset gains made through litigation and other efforts to improve the situation of those confined. Idleness, demoralization, isolation, danger, and despair permeate the prison and the jail.

For those subject to non-incarcerative penalties, levels of intervention and control, demands for obedience, and the sheer weight of conditions never have been heavier. As of the spring of 1986, intensive supervision programs were operating in at least 29 states, and an additional eight states reportedly were planning to implement such programs in the near future (Byrne, 1986). Typical requirements in such programs include not only increased contact and surveillance, but also mandatory restitution and community service obligations; payment of supervision fees, court and attorney costs, and fines; curfews and periods of "house arrest";

urinalyses, blood tests and other warrantless searches; and even periods of incarceration. The latest popular addition to these and other non-incarcerative sanctions is electronic surveillance. There are now more than 45 programs in 20 states using electronic devices to monitor the whereabouts of convicted offenders or defendants awaiting trial (Yost, 1987).

Just as the velvet glove only thinly cushions and screens the iron fist, it is important to recognize that "the velvet ankle bracelet" and its ostensibly more benign community penalties brethren are facilitating the diffusion and expansion of social control through the penal system and augmenting the iron bars rather than replacing them. With little fanfare or protest, we have come to accept levels of state intrusiveness into individual lives remarkable in a society that professes to value liberty. The nature and direction of the bulk of changes undertaken in the criminal justice system in recent years are such that the most pressing tasks in the coming years necessarily will involve damage control. Massive efforts will need to be devoted to coping with, undoing, and trying to ameliorate the effects of the present blind, determined push for greater punishment and control. Pursuing a more hopeful future requires exploration of alternative visions of justice.

The Need for New Approaches

Many common citizens, scientists, futurists, and leaders are predicting that the next 25 years portend a series of collisions, conflicts, and catastrophes. Recent world experience with increasing interpersonal violence, terrorism, social injustice, and inequality—along with such growing problems as overpopulation, ecological damage, resource shortages, the continuing arms build-up, and the specter of nuclear holocaust—has generated heightened awareness of the need to think globally and much more creatively about the future. To begin to adequately envision what criminal justice should look like in the year 2012, we need to step outside of the traditional ways of framing the issues and consider approaches that transcend not only conventional criminological and political lines, but also national and cultural boundaries and other limiting habits of the mind. At the same time, "...focusing on the principles and tools of punishment" can help us "understand the most prevalent way we have chosen to relate to each other in the twentieth century" (Sullivan, 1980:14).

A number of movements, models, and philosophies in various stages of development have arisen in response to the critical problems of the day, ranging from those focused on world order or global transformation, to pacificism or peace studies, reconciliation, humanism, feminism, and a wide range of other visions of a better world and a better future. While few have been focused on criminal justice problems, they offer a rich resource for a fundamental rethinking of our approach to crime and justice.

In seeking to escape the fetters on my own thinking and aspirations for the future, I have found much of value in a number of orientations. Indeed, I have been struck by the common themes that emerge across a variety of perspectives with a wide range of labels. This suggests the possibility of articulating a new direction for the future by drawing from many orientations and avoiding attaching any label to the values and concepts discussed. Such an approach would help prevent burdening the ideas with unnecessary baggage or losing the attention of people put off by the images any particular school of thought raises in their minds. For me, however, the most significant breakthroughs in thought and hope came when I began to apply myself to considering what the values and principles of one particular orientation—feminism would mean in rethinking crime and justice issues. Thus, the rest of this chapter shares ideas that emerged from this path of exploration, a path that continues to hold increasing meaning and inspiration for me and one that I hope will attract interest from a variety of people who otherwise might not devote attention to these issues. At the same time, it is my hope that people who find themselves more attuned to other orientations, or who see feminism differently, may find it useful to consider how the values described fit with theirs and what a future based on these values might look like, no matter what terms are used to describe it.

Values Central to a Feminist Future

Feminism offers and is a set of values, beliefs, and experiences, a consciousness, a way of looking at the world. Feminism should be seen not merely as a prescription for granting rights to women, but as a far broader vision. There are a number of varying strands within feminist thought, but there are some core values that transcend the differences. Among the key tenets of feminism are three simple beliefs—that all people have equal value as human beings, that harmony and felicity are more important than power and possession, and that the personal is the political.

Feminist insistence on equality in sexual, racial, economic, and all other types of relations stems from recognition that all humans are equally tied to the human condition, equally deserving of respect for their personhood, and equally worthy of survival and of access to those things that make life worth living. This is not to argue that all people are identical. Indeed, feminism places great emphasis on the value of difference and diversity, holding that different people should receive not identical treatment, but identical consideration. Feminists are concerned not simply with equal opportunities or equal entitlements within existing social structures, but with creating a different set of structures and relations that are not only nonsexist, but also are nonracist and economically just.

In the feminist view, felicity and harmony are regarded as the highest values. Viewing all people as part of a network on whose continuation we all depend, feminists stress the themes of caring, sharing, nurturing, and loving. This contrasts sharply with an orientation that values power and control above all else. Where the central goal is power, power conceived as power-over or control, people and things are not viewed as ends in themselves, but as instruments for the furtherance of power. Hierarchical institutions and structures are established both to clarify power rankings and to maintain them. The resulting stratifications create levels of superiority and inferiority, which carry differential status, legitimacy, and access to resources and other benefits. Such divisions and exclusions engender resentment and revolt in various forms, which then are used to justify greater control.

Feminists believe that it is impossible to realize humane goals and create humane structures in a society that values power above all else. A major part of feminist effort involves better identifying and confronting characteristics and values— the political, social, economic, and cultural structures and ideologies—that are not conducive to the full realization of the human potential in individuals or society, the negative values that underlie stereotypes, rationalize discrimination and oppression, and serve only to support the groups in power.

Feminist belief that the personal is the political means that core values must be lived and acted upon in both public and private arenas. Thus, feminists reject the tendency to offer one set of values to guide interactions in the private and personal realms and another set of values to govern interactions in the public worlds of politics and power. Empathy, compassion, and the loving, healing, person-oriented values must be valued and affirmed not only in the family and the home but also in the halls where public policymaking, diplomacy, and politics are practiced.

Modes of Moral Reasoning

Research on moral development and on how people construe moral choices has identified two orientations that reflect significant differences (see Gilligan, 1982a; Gilligan, 1982b). In a "rights/justice" orientation, morality is conceived as being tied to respect for rules. It is a mode of reasoning that reflects the imagery of hierarchy, a hierarchy of values and a hierarchy of power. It assumes a world comprised of separate individuals whose claims and interests fundamentally conflict and in which infringements on an individual's rights can be controlled or redressed through rational and objective means deducible from logic and rules.

In a "care/response" orientation, morality is conceived contextually and in terms of a network of interpersonal relationships and connection. This mode of reasoning reflects the imagery of a web, a nonhierarchal network of affiliation and mutuality. It assumes a world of interdependence and care among people, a world in which conflicts and injuries can best be responded to by a process of ongoing communication and involvement that considers the needs, interests, and motivations of all involved.

At present, the "care/response" mode, with its emphasis on contextuality, relationship, and the human consequences of choices and actions, tends to be viewed as representing a lesser stage of moral development and as less broadly applicable than the "rights/justice" orientation, with its emphasis on standards, rights, and duties (see Scharf et al., 1981:413). This tendency to contrast and rank the differing modes of reasoning has limited the moral and conceptual repertoires with which problems are approached in the worlds of government, science, and world power. Devotion to peacekeeping and nonviolent conflict resolution often are dismissed as irrelevant or less important than devotion to the "rules of the game" or abstract notions of rights and responsibilities. Thus, the potential contributions of a "care/response" orientation to dealing constructively with the major global crises of security, justice, and equity have hardly begun to be tapped (see Reardon, 1985:89-90).

There is a need for a massive infusion of the values associated with the "care/response" mode of reasoning into a wide range of contexts from which they have been excluded almost entirely. It would be a mistake, however, to try to simply substitute a "care/response" orientation for one focused on justice and rights. Especially at present, when there are such vast differences in power among people, we are not in a position to trust that the interests of the less powerful will be protected in the absence of rules designed to insure that protection.

Studies by Carol Gilligan suggest that although most people can and do understand and use both modes of reasoning, they tend to focus more on one or the other in confronting moral issues. In her research, the mode of reasoning around which people tended to center was associated with gender. Men were more likely to employ a "rights/justice" orientation and women were more likely to reflect a "care/response" orientation, although responses from women were more mixed than those for men. Given the capacities of both men and women to use both modes of moral reasoning, and because there is no reason to believe that differing emphases or priorities in moral reasoning are innate or biological (see Bleier, 1984), we have an opportunity to explore more fully the contributions each can make to resolving moral dilemmas of all kinds.

Thus, the challenge involves searching for a more complete vision of justice and morality, a vision that encompasses concern for process and outcomes, as well as principles and rules, and for feelings and relationships, as well as logic and rationality. We need to labor to find ways of more fully integrating abstract notions of justice and rights with contextual notions of caring and relationships in both public (political) and private (personal) realms.

The Criminal Justice Context:
The Dilemmas of Defense and Protection

The criminal justice system provides a clear picture of the challenges ahead. In the criminal justice arena, there is no attempt to disguise the fact that the goal and purpose of the system is power/control. The stated goal is control of crime and criminals, but it is widely recognized that the criminal justice system serves to achieve social control functions more generally. Law is an embodiment of power arrangements; it specifies a set of norms to be followed—an order—and also provides the basis for securing that order: coercive force. Coercive force is seen as the ultimate and the most effective mechanism for social defense. And once the order to be protected and preserved is in place, little attention is given to whether the social system to be defended is just or serves humane goals.

It is important to bear in mind that penal sanctions, like crimes, are intended harms. "The violent, punishing acts of the state...are of the same genre as the violent acts of individuals. In each instance these acts reflect an attempt to monopolize human interaction, to control another person as if he or she were a commodity" (Sullivan, 1980). Those who set themselves up as beyond reproach define "the criminal" as less than fully human. Without such objectification, the routine practice of subjecting human beings to calculated pain infliction, degradation, domination, banishment, and execution clearly would be regarded as intolerable.

Feminist analysis of the war system can be applied to the criminal justice system; the civil war in which we are engaged—the war on crime—is the domestic equivalent of the international war system. One has only to attend any budget hearing at which increased appropriations are being sought for war efforts, whether labeled as in defense of criminals, communists, or other enemies, to realize that the rationales and the rhetoric are the same. The ideologies of deterrence and retaliation; the hierarchal, militaristic structures and institutions; the incessant demand for more and greater weaponry, technology, and fighting forces; the sense of urgency and willingness to sacrifice other important interests to the cause; the tendency to dehumanize and objectify those defined as foes; and the belief in coercive force as the most effective means of obtaining security—all of these and other features characteristic of both domestic and international "defense" systems suggest not just similarity, but identity. People concerned with international peace need to recognize that supporting "the war on crime" is supporting the very establishment, ideology, structures, and morality against which they have been struggling.

We are caught in a truly vicious cycle. Existing structures, institutions, relations, and values create the problems that we then turn around and ask them to solve, or rather control, using the very same structures, forms, and values, which in turn leads to more problems and greater demand for control. We all want to be protected from those who would violate our houses, our persons, and our general welfare and safety, but the protections we are offered tend to reinforce the divisions and distorted relations in society and exacerbate the conditions that create much of the need for such protections. The complicated issues surrounding self-defense, whether in an immediate personal sense (as when confronted by a would-be rapist or other attacker), in a penal policy sense (as when deciding how to deal with known assaulters), or in even broader terms (as when confronted by powers and structures that seem bound to destroy us), vividly illuminate the dilemma.

Sally Miller Gearhart vividly describes the dilemma surrounding trying to work toward the future we dream of while living in the present world by citing a science fiction work, *Rule Golden*, in which Damon Knight wipes violence from the face of the earth by having every agent feel in his/her own body any physical action he/she delivers. "Kick a dog and feel the boot in your own rib; commit murder and die yourself. Similarly, stroking another in love results in the physical feeling of being lovingly stroked" (Gearhart, 1982:266). Such imagery highlights:

> the necessary connection between *empathy* and *nonviolence*, [the fact that] *objectification* is the necessary, if not sufficient, component of any violent act. Thinking of myself as separate from another entity makes it possible for me to "do to" that entity things I would not "do to" myself. But if I see all things as myself, or empathize with all other things, then to hurt them is to do damage to me....

> But empaths don't live long if the Rule Golden is not in effect. Our world belongs to those who can objectify... and if I want to protect myself from them I learn to objectify and fight back in self-defense. I seem bound to choose between being violent and being victimized. Or I live a schizophrenic existence in which my values are at war with my actions because I must keep a constant shield of protectiveness (objectification) intact over my real self, over my empathy or my identification with others; the longer I keep up the shield the thicker it gets and the less empathic I am with those around me. So every second of protecting myself from violence makes me objectify more and ensures that I am more and more capable of doing violence myself. I am caught always in the violence-victim trap (Gearhart, 1982:266).

Clearly, the standard approach in recent years has been to seek more control—more prisons, more time in confinement for more people, more surveillance and restriction of those not confined. Our willingness to cede greater and greater power to the institutions of social control is a reflection of a desperate society. But "no amount of police, laws, courts, judges, prisons, mental hospitals, psychiatrists, and social workers can create a society with relative harmony. The most institutions can do is to impose the appearance of relative harmony..." (French, 1985). To the extent that we acquiesce to continuing escalation of social controls, especially those delivered by the crime control agents of the state, we reduce correspondingly the prospects for the kind of safety that cannot be achieved through force.

It will not be easy to escape from the cycle in which we find ourselves swirling. Legitimate concerns for safety and protection pose difficult dilemmas for feminists. How can we meet the serious and all-too-real need for protection against violence without violating our peaceful values and aspirations? How can we respond effectively to people who inflict injury and hardship on others without employing the same script and the same means that they do? How can we satisfy immediate needs for safety without elevating those needs over the need to recreate the morality, relations, and conception of justice in our society?

As Marilyn French has put it, "The major problem facing feminists can be easily summed up: there is no clear right way to move" (French, 1985). However, we can expand the conceptual and practical possibilities for change in criminal justice by reexamining our assumptions and expectations.

> ...[W]e need to begin picturing the new order in our minds, fantasying it, playing with possibilities.... An exercise in first stepping into a desired future in imagination, then consciously elaborating the structures needed to maintain it, and finally imagining the future history that would get us there, is a very liberating experience for people who feel trapped in an unyielding present....[S]ocieties move toward what they image. If we remain frozen in the present as we have done since World War II, society stagnates. Imaging the future gives us action ideas for the present (Boulding, 1987).

Emerging Guides for the Future

Identifying values central to feminist beliefs does not automatically yield a specific formula for better responding to crime and other conflicts, or for resolving the dilemmas with which we are confronted. Indeed, feminists do not see the best way of moving toward a more positive future as involving primarily analytic and abstract efforts to describe specific structures and processes. Such approaches almost never encompass any explicit element of human relations or affective, emotional content, and few display any cultural dimension (Reardon, 1985). "We need theory and feeling as rough guides on which to build a next step and only a next step; flexible, responsive emotional theory capable of adjusting to human needs and desires when these create contradictions" (Reardon, 1985:89-90).

Feminist values do offer, however, some beginning guides for approaching the future. A key standard to help in making choices is to ask: What kinds of behavior and responses will achieve the goal of the greatest possible harmony? Thus, the task is not to discover how to eradicate crime, but to discover how to behave as befits our values and desire for harmony.

Acceptance of human equality and recognition of the interdependence of all people requires rejection of several current common tendencies. We need to struggle against the tendency toward objectification, of talking and thinking about "crime" and "criminals" as if they were distinct entities in themselves. We also need to reject the idea that those who cause injury or harm to others should suffer severance of the common bonds of respect and concern that bind members of a community.

We should relinquish the notion that it is acceptable to try to "get rid of" another person, whether through execution, banishment, or caging away with other people about whom we do not care. We should no longer pretend that conflicts can be resolved by the pounding of a gavel or the locking of a cell door.

A feminist orientation leads to greater awareness of the role and responsibility of society, not just the individual, in development of conflict. This suggests that individuals, groups, and societies need to accept greater responsibility for preventing and reducing those conditions, values, and structures that produce and support violence and strife. Removing the idea of power from its central position is key here, and requires continually challenging actions, practices, and assumptions that glorify power, control, and domination, as well as developing more felicitous alternatives.

Commitment to the principle of equality means striving for interactions that are participatory, democratic, cooperative, and inclusive, characteristics that are incompatible with hierarchy, stratification, and centralized decisionmaking. Thus, rules, which often are substituted for sensitive, respectful engagement of persons in cooperative problem solving, should not be regarded as sacrosanct. And because people learn from the nature of the processes in which they participate, as well as from the objectives of those processes, we should give greater attention to what the process teaches and how it is experienced.

It may be difficult to imagine how some conflicts could be resolved amicably. Especially while we are in the process of transition, we have to contend with all of the effects that our present structures, values, and stratifications have had on people. Thus, we are unlikely to soon reach a stage in which we can expect never to feel the need to resort to exercising control over another person. But we can greatly reduce our current reliance on repressive measures, and we should aim to move continually in the direction of imposing fewer coercive restraints on other people.

Indeed, we need to question and rethink the entire basis of the punishment system. Virtually all discussion of change begins and ends with the premise that punishment must take place. All of the existing institutions and structures—the criminal law, the criminal processing system, the prisons—are assumed. We allow ourselves only to entertain debates about rearrangements and reallocations within those powerfully constraining givens. We swing among the traditional, tired philosophies of punishment as the weight of the inadequacies of one propels us to turn to another. We swing between attempting to do something with lawbreakers—changing, controlling, or making an example of them—and simply striving to dole out "a just measure of pain." The sterility of the debates and the disturbing ways they are played out in practice underscore the need to explore alternative visions. We need to step back to reconsider whether we should punish, rather than just arguing about how to punish.

We may remain convinced that something is needed to serve the declaratory function of the criminal law, something that tells us what is not to be done. We may conclude that there is a need for some sort of process that holds people accountable for their wrongful actions. We may not be able to think of ways to completely eliminate restraints on people who have done harmful things. But we should not simply *assume* that we cannot develop better ways to satisfy these and other important interests as we try to create our desired future.

While we are in the transition process, and where we continue to feel that it is necessary to exercise power over other people, we should honor more completely certain familiar principles that are often stated but seldom fully realized. Resort to restriction of liberty, whether of movement, of association, or of other personal choices, should be clearly recognized as an evil. Whenever it is argued that it is a necessary evil, there should be a strong, non-routine burden of establishing such necessity. And where it is accepted that some restriction is demonstrably necessary, every effort should be made to utilize the least drastic means that will satisfy the need established. Thus, we should approach restriction and control of others with trepidation, restraint, caution, and care.

In addition, we should recognize that the more we restrict an individual's chances and choices, the greater is the responsibility we assume for protecting that person and preserving his or her personhood. We should no longer accept the routine deprivations of privacy, healthful surroundings, contacts, and opportunities to exercise choice and preference that we have come to treat as standard concomitants of restriction of liberty. Such deprivations are not only unnecessary but also offensive to our values and destructive to all involved.

These principles make it apparent that we should abandon imprisonment, at least in anything like the way we have come to accept the meaning of that word. There is no excuse for not only continuing to utilize the dungeons of the past, but also replicating the assumptions, ideology, and values that created them in their newer, shinier, more "modern" brethren now being constructed on astonishing scale. While tiers of human cages stacked one upon another are the most apparently repugnant form, all institutions erected for the purpose of congregate confinement need to be acknowledged as anachronisms of a less felicitous time.

How should we deal with people who demonstrate that, at least for a time, they cannot live peacefully among us unrestrained? Although the answers to that question are not entirely clear, feminist values suggest that we should move toward conceiving restriction of liberty as having less to do with buildings, structures, and walls and more to do with human contacts and relations. Few if any creatures are dangerous to all other creatures at all times, especially to those with whom they are directly and closely connected on an ongoing basis. Perhaps we can fashion some variant of jury duty and of citizens standing up for one another in the tradition of John Augustus, in which a small group of citizens would be asked to assume responsibility for maintaining one person safely for a period of time. A range of compassionate, constructive, and caring arrangements need to be created. And we should not allow the most difficult cases to stand in the way of more rapidly evolving better approaches for the rest.

At the same time, we need to stop thinking about issues related to how best to respond to those who caused harm as if they were totally separate from, or in competition with, issues related to how best to respond to those who have been harmed. There is not a fixed quantity of compassion and care, or even of rights, that will be diminished for those who have been victimized as they are extended to those who victimized them.

Many of these ideas may seem foreign, naive, or beyond our abilities. If they seem foreign, that may be because the ideas of care, community, and mutuality seem foreign. If these dreams for the future seem naive or out of reach, that may be because we have lost confidence in our capacity to choose, to create relations, and to realign priorities. It may be tempting to conclude that no efforts in the directions suggested here will be worthwhile, that nothing can be done until everything can be done, that no one can confront crime humanely until everyone is willing to do so. And it is true that we will never approach making such a vision reality if we focus only on issues of criminal justice. Our energies must be focused on the full panoply of global peace and social justice issues. But when we turn our attentions to criminal justice, we should choose and act according to the values and aims we seek more generally, not to increase division, alienation, bitterness, and despair. And every day, we should try to act as we believe would be the best way to act—not just in the future, but in the present.

What is advocated here is radical, but hardly novel. It simply echoes themes that have been heard through the ages, if rarely lived fully. We should refuse to return evil with evil. Although we have enemies, we should seek to forgive, reconcile, and heal. We should strive to find within ourselves outrageous love, the kind of love that extends even to those it is easiest to fear and hate. Love frequently is seen as having little relevance outside the personal realm. Yet the power ethic has failed to serve human happiness. To have a harmonious society, we must act in ways designed to increase harmony, not to further fragment, repress, and control. There is no other way. The means and the end are the same.

Notes

[1] A collection of articles that well exemplifies this approach is assembled in a book designed to provide an update of the report of the National Commission on the Causes and Prevention of Violence, commonly referred to as the Eisenhower Commission, after its chair, Milton S. Eisenhower. (See, Lynn A. Curtis, ed., *American Violence and Public Policy: An Update of the National Commission on the Causes and Prevention of Violence*, New Haven, CT: Yale University Press, 1985.)

[2] In 1972, there were 196,813 state and federal prisoners (Mullen, et al., *American Prisons and Jails*, Vol. 1: *Summary and Policy Implications of a National Survey*. Washington, DC: U.S. Department of Justice, 1980). At year-end 1986, there were 546,659 state and federal prisoners (Bureau of Justice Statistics Bulletin, "Prisoners in 1986," May 1987). If the average annual growth rate of the 1980s of 8.8 percent continues through 1987, the total will exceed 590,000 state and federal prisoners.

[3] These numbers are reported only for males, presumably because men make up most of the correctional population. (See "Criminal Justice Newsletter," January 16, 1987, p. 5.) It should be noted, however, that the number of women in state prisons has more than doubled since 1981 (up to 26,610 from 11,212 in 1981), and the rate of growth in the population of female prisoners has been faster in each of those years than that of male prisoners (Peter Applebome, "Women in U.S. Prisons: Fast-Rising Population." *New York Times,* 15 June 1981).

[4] Given that nearly 87 percent of the adult correctional population was male and 34 percent was black, an estimated 850,000 adult black men were under correctional control at year-end 1985 (Bureau of Justice Statistics Bulletin, "Probation and Parole 1985," January 1987). The Census Bureau estimates that there were 8,820,000 black adult male residents in the U.S. at midyear 1985 (U.S. Department of Commerce, Bureau of the Census, "Estimates of the Population of the United States, by Age, Sex and Race: 1980 to 1986," Current Population Reports, Population Estimates and Projections, Series P-25, No. 1000, p. 24). At year-end 1985, there were approximately 1,617,492 white adult males under some form of correctional control, out of approximately 72,780,000 white adult male residents in the U.S., representing a correction control rate for white adult males of about 1 in 45. (Neither these BJS or Census Bureau data report separate figures for Hispanics or other specific ethnic or racial groups.)

[5] This discussion is based on an oral presentation by Carol Gilligan at the Community College of Philadelphia in April 1984. See also other Gilligan works cited in this article.

References

Bleier, R. (1984). *Science and Gender: A Critique of Biology and Its Theories on Women.* New York, NY: Pergamon Press.

Boulding, E. (1987). *Warriors and Saints: Dilemmas in the History of Men, Women, and War.* Paper presented at the International Symposium on Women and the Military System, Siuntio Baths, Finland, January.

Bryne, J.M. (1986). "The Control Controversy: A Preliminary Examination of Intensive Probation Supervision Programs in the United States." *Federal Probation,* 50, 9.

Bureau of Justice Statistics Bulletin (1986). "Prisoners in 1985," June.

Bureau of Justice Statistics Bulletin (1987). "Prisoners in 1986," May.

Corrections Compendium (1986). November/December.

French, M. (1985). *Beyond Power: On Women, Men and Morals.* New York, NY: Summit Books.

Gearhart, S.M. (1982). "The Future—If There is One—Is Female." In O. McAllister (ed.) *Reweaving the Web of Life: Feminism and Nonviolence.* Philadelphia, PA: New Society Pub.

Gilligan, C. (1982a). *In a Different Voice: Psychological Theory and Women's Development.* Cambridge, MA: Harvard University Press.

Gilligan, C. (1982b). New Maps of Development: New Visions of Maturity. *American Journal of Orthopsychiatry,* April.

Lifelines (1987). Newsletter of the National Coalition Against the Death Penalty. January/February, 8.

Pierce, N. (1987). "Prisons Are Proving Costly to the States." *The Philadelphia Inquirer,* 9, 11A.

Reardon, B.A. (1985). *Sexism and the War System*. New York, NY: Teachers College Press, Columbia University.

Scharf, P., L. Kohlberg and J. Hickey (1981). "Ideology and Correctional Intervention: The Creation of a Just Prison Community." In P.C. Kratcoski (ed.) *Correctional Counseling and Treatment*. Monterey, CA: Duxbury.

Sullivan, D. (1980). *The Mask of Love: Corrections in America (Toward a Mutual Aid Alternative)*. Port Washington, NY: Kennikat Press.

Woestendiek, J. (1987). "An Influx of Hispanics is Challenging the Prisons." *The Philadelphia Inquirer*, 2, 1A, February.

Yost, P. (1987). "Electronic Alternative to Prison is in 20 States." *The Philadelphia Inquirer*, 2, 5A, February.

Index

Contributors

Agnes L. Baro, School of Criminal Justice, Grand Valley State University, Grand Rapids, MI

James Bonta, Ottawa-Carleton Detention Centre, Ontario, CN

Michael C. Braswell, Department of Criminal Justice & Criminology, East Tennessee State University, Johnson City, TN

Therese Coupez, Prisoners Rights Union, San Francisco, CA

Ben M. Crouch, Department of Sociology, Texas A & M University, College Station, TX

Rolando V. del Carmen, School of Criminal Justice, Sam Houston State University, Huntsville, TX

Helen M. Eigenberg, Department of Sociology, Old Dominion University, Norfolk, VA

J. Forbes Farmer, Department of Sociology, Franklin Pierce College, Rindge, NH

Mark Fleisher, Department of Criminal Justice, Illinois State University, Normal, IL

Tyler Fletcher, Department of Criminal Justice, University of Southern Mississippi, Hattiesburg, MS

Frances E. Hoze, Prisoners Rights Union, San Francisco, CA

Paul Gendreau, Division of Social Sciences, University of New Brunswick in Saint John, New Brunswick, CN

Mark S. Hamm, Department of Criminology, Indiana State University, Terre Haute, IN

M. Kay Harris, Department of Criminal Justice, Temple University, Philadelphia, PA

George Jackson, deceased

Stephen C. Light, Department of Sociology, State University of New York, Plattsburgh, NY

Daniel Lockwood, Department of Criminal Justice, Temple University, Philadelphia, PA

Lucien X. Lombardo, Department of Sociology & Criminal Justice, Old Dominion University, Norfolk, VA

Bo Lozoff, Human Kindness Foundation, Durham, NC

Randy Martin, Department of Criminology, Indiana University of Pennsylvania, Indiana, PA

James W. Marquart, Criminal Justice Center, Sam Houston State University, Huntsville, TX

Sue Mahan, Department of Criminal Justice, University of Central Florida, Orlando, FL

Larry S. Miller, Department of Criminal Justice & Criminology, East Tennessee State University, Johnson City, TN

Reid H. Montgomery, Jr., College of Criminal Justice, University of South Carolina, Columbia, SC

Peter Scharf, Department of Sociology, Seattle University, Seattle, WA

Frederick Talbott, Journalism Program, Old Dominion University, Norfolk, VA

Hans Toch, School of Criminal Justice, State University of New York, Albany, NY

Corey Weinstein, Prisoners Rights Union, San Francisco, CA

Kevin N. Wright, Criminal Justice Center, School of Education and Human Development, State University of New York at Binghamton, Binghamton, NY

Sherwood Zimmerman, Department of Criminology, Indiana University of Pennsylvania, Indiana, PA